SAT

Vocabulary Classified 词汇（上）

词以类记

■ 张红岩 编著

群言出版社
Qunyan Press

图书在版编目(CIP)数据

词以类记：SAT词汇 / 张红岩编著 .—北京 ：群言出版社，2011（2013.9重印）
ISBN 978-7-80256-272-1

Ⅰ．①词… Ⅱ．①张… Ⅲ．①英语—词汇—高等学校—入学考试—美国—自学参考资料 Ⅳ．①H313

中国版本图书馆CIP数据核字（2011）第206614号

出版人　范　芳
责任编辑　张　茜
封面设计　大愚设计
出版发行　群言出版社(Qunyan Press)

地　　址　北京东城区东厂胡同北巷1号 （100006）
网　　站　www.qypublish.com
电子信箱　bj62605588@163.com　qunyancbs@126.com
总 编 办　010-65265404　65138815
发 行 部　010-62605019　62263345　65220236
经　　销　全国新华书店
读者服务　010-62418641　65265404　65263345
法律顾问　北京市国联律师事务所

印　　刷　北京海石通印刷有限公司
版　　次　2012年5月第1版　2013年9月第2次印刷
开　　本　880×1230　1/32
印　　张　21.75
字　　数　641千字
书　　号　ISBN 978-7-80256-272-1
定　　价　58.00元

新东方图书策划委员会

主任　俞敏洪

委员　（按姓氏笔画为序）

王　强　　包凡一

仲晓红　　沙云龙

陈向东　　张洪伟

邱政政　　汪海涛

周成刚　　徐小平

谢　琴　　窦中川

作者自介

余自幼随知青父母拓荒于大兴安岭，长于辽西古镇兴城，求学乃率性而为，先后修习英语、计算机和工商管理，奉行"Live and learn"，现于北京大学教育学院就读教育经济与管理博士课程。曾于新东方早期挥汗于三尺讲坛，五年间学生超二十万众。受益于新东方讲坛对讲师心智与技能多方面的磨炼，后于留学法国期间以五分钟英语演讲在学生会竞选中获得来自全球四十二国的、两百多名中高层经理人同学百分之七十的支持，当选法国高商（HEC）MBA学生会主席。乃有机会深入了解所谓欧洲精英阶层，深悟外语在国际交流中的重要，反思我国留学教育中的积弊，现主张将应试教育与应用能力二者尽可能和谐推进。本书以备考SAT和实际应用为双重目的，方法上沿用"词以类记"这一已证实的有效途径，选词上遍寻最新资料提炼出最全词集，期冀读者多听勤记，尽早超越词汇瓶颈，并应用于考场、课堂和未来管理工作当中。

自 序

过去的二十年，承载了本书大部分读者的出生和成长历程，而这二十年也是我们国家稳步发展为世界强国的关键时期，加入 WTO 更使我国各行业直接面对来自全球的挑战和机遇，有史以来中国再也没有比今天更需要精通外语的人才了。事实上，放眼今日中国各行业的领军人物，均能看到众多留学归国人员的身影，在一些国际竞争较强的行业中，拥有国外学习的经历仅仅是个起点。各位读者，国家实力的提升和社会的发展已经为你未来成为一个具有国际视野的人提供了机遇：人均家庭财富上升使更多家庭有可能转向欧美寻找教育机会，人民币升值降低留学成本将近20%，信息化社会和成熟的中学教育共同使青少年的思想成熟度加快，西方频发的经济危机使得他们对留学生更加友好。这一切直接把我们推向国际平台寻找最合适的本科教育，这其中美国的一流院校成为很多留学生的首选，而参加美国大学入学考试 SAT 考试就成为了精英高中生的必经之路。

过去十五年，我一直在近距离观察中国的留学生群体，由于受国内应试教育模式或深或浅的影响，他们在实际学习中表现出的外语水平严重低于考试水平，因而，几乎每个留学生在留学生涯初期的强烈愿望均是要尽快克服外语难关，尽快听懂授课、参与讨论问题以及应付各类演示。克服这个困难的最佳时机不是在到达留学目的地之后，而是在此之前，即备考时就要有意识地提高实力；而解决问题的关键在于掌握足够多的积极词汇（active vocabulary，指能够熟练掌握运用的词汇，相对于消极词汇 passive vocabulary 而言）。

积极词汇量的多寡直接影响学术表现。记得我留学期间参加的第一次期末考试考的是市场案例分析（Marketing Case Analysis），试卷有 40 多页 A4 纸，考试时间为 4 小时。我当时注意观察了一下同学们完成阅读开始提笔写作的时间：中国大陆的同学多数要两个多小时读完这个案例，剩下写作的时间并不充分，读得比较慢的一个同学感慨案例太长读完就剩半个小时了，而美国和英国的同学说他们都是在一小时内读完动笔的。这差距太大了！也许现在你就能从这个例子中看到未来读书时你与母语者在英语语言上的巨大差距，将来也就不会因为考出比美国同学还高的 SAT 分数而骄傲了。母语者语言中大量的积极词汇是用其生命经历来积淀的，我们记住的很多词汇还有待于转化为积极词汇。

背单词常常被误解为消极词汇量产生的原因，而我要强调的是：背单词不是问题的源头，有问题的是背单词的方法。是否该背单词是不需要讨论的问题，因为除了科幻中的"记忆芯片移植"外，现实中没有任何其他方法能够帮助你在较短时间内完成近万词汇量的积累，关键的问题是如何在背单词的过程中找到合适的方法，最大限度地提高消极词汇到积极词汇的转化率。

词汇量与 SAT 考试各部分的关系

背单词首要解决的是听力和阅读的词汇量问题，而不是解决口语和写作中应用的问题，那需要其他的努力才行。但仅这个意义就足够重大了，因为听力是最难过的一关。本书的分学科词汇目的就在于，让你在开始听力前预先熟悉可能接触到的词汇再去答题，这是对你信心培养的必要手段(如果一个人的信心在备考初期就被打碎是很难拾起的)；阅读，绝对需要较大的词汇量来支撑，阅读速度和解题效率均取决于词汇量。

口语和写作需要有相当扎实的积极词汇储备，词不在多，而在于精。这里必须提到一点，仅通过背诵词汇了解单词的意思离写作中的应用还很遥远，需要有目的地将一些写作中常用的词汇做辨析后再考虑应用，同时在阅读篇章中也要认真揣摩其用法，并在实战中不断自我挑战和查证，这样才能真正懂得"proper word at proper place"(合适的词用在合适的位置上)。口语的词汇量更是少而精，例如美国国家庭主妇的词汇量约在 3000 左右，足够一生使用。我们的口语词汇是要在学习正确的范例并不断实践中掌握的。

为何要"词以类记"?

在我们的脑海中，单词的存储是有规律的，这个规律显然不是按照字母顺序，很明显我们不是电脑，我们储存的单词是成串分类的，这样我们在调用的时候就会很方便。比如我们要表达"奇怪、怪异"这个概念，现在问自己一下，有几个你能想到的呢，strange, bizarre, odd, eccentric, erratic，如果没有，你要警醒了，因为这是最有用的存储方式，这样记忆的单词才能使你在未来写 ESSAY、公众演示、课堂讨论、小组辩论时调用其中最合适的单词。可见，按学科和意群分类是实现这种关联记忆的最佳方法。

在早期新东方课堂上，我发现同学们最专注、觉得自己最有收获的一个环节就是我借着考题中的某一个词汇来发散讲解，提到可能在考试中出现的与这个词相关的一组词。当时主要用的思路就是将同学科或同意群词汇总结到一起，这种联想很有效，但由于课上时间有限不能做到全面。2004 年我留学回国后用一年时间将这一系统工程完成，首先应用在《词以类记：TOEFL iBT 词汇》中，之后有关 IELTS、GRE、GMAT 的词汇书陆续出炉，如今大家看到的是专为 SAT 考试预备、通过计算机程序词频统计并辅以人工筛选的方式得到的最新最全的词表，主要以学科、意群为分类线索，并以词根词缀法为微观记忆辅助，此外还设置适当的练习。

使用本书记忆单词的方法：

记诵词汇的方法多种多样，下面我用功夫的"五式"来做类比，提供几条建议，大家可以根据实际情况选用。

一、囫囵吞枣式

背本书的第一遍，一定要求效率，可以牺牲质量（实际上你再努力也不可能背一遍记住 50% 以上）。务必要在一个月内完成背第一遍单词的任务。这样做具有双重意义：1. 初步建立基本印象和信心 2. 培养心理成就感：知道不过如此，再有两遍就搞定了。

二、螺旋式上升

昨天背过的单词今天一定要复习一遍，记不住的要打记号，明天还要看，这样螺旋式地上升，有效且容易操作。当然如果你不嫌麻烦，也有人根据艾森豪宾遗忘曲线设计过背单词各个 LIST 的顺序，提醒你哪天背哪个 LIST，大家可以网络搜索查证。

三、练中求精式

背单词和大家做书后练习以及真题模考题是并行的，在没有背完第二遍之前，不要因为不认识的单词而自责，而是应该在做题中强化已经认识的那部分词汇，并将有问题的词汇标注，重点记忆。这样记住的词汇印象极其深刻。

四、听力主导式

这是扩大积极词汇量的一个关键，无论是为了解决目前的听力问题，还是满足留学中的学习和生活需要，你都需要一听到背过的词汇马上就能反应出来是什么意思，这样听教授讲课时问题就会少很多。绝大多数学生根本不结合音频记忆单词，这样记的单词听到后反应不过来。听配套 MP3 内的音频来学习每天应掌握的词汇非常重要，并且使用听音方式来复习单词也最有效，听时必须要求自己在听过英文录音后一秒内记起该单词含义，这样才算过关，否则须继续练习。

五、有问必究式

很多学生有这样的经历，在阅读或做题中偶尔碰到似曾相识的单词，或者偶尔想到要用某个背过的词，但却一时想不起来，这时一定不要放弃，要花时间尽量找寻，可以在本书附录中查寻按音序排列的单词索引，也可以使用在线词典以英汉或汉英方式查证，这样的词汇如果不花时间征服，它们恐怕会在考试中为难你。

本书内容安排：

本书在选词方面本着全面、最新、高效三个原则，通过词频统计软件对 1995 年至今可获得的全部 SAT 真题、官方指南、巴朗词表等资料进行统计，并根据高效原则进行人工筛选，剔除过易过难词汇，共获得核心词汇 6002 条。另外，为各专项考试词汇预备了数学词汇 272 条、物理词汇 728 条、化学词汇 427 条、生物词汇 578 条。全书共收录 8007 个词条，可以完全满足参加 SAT 考试所需词汇量。本书根据词汇在历年考试中出现的频率将所收录词条分为三个级别，并加以标注，一星★为出现一次，二星★★为出现两次，三星★★★为出现三次及以上。

本书主要内容有三部分：

第一部分为按学科分类词汇，有 15 个 WORD LIST，覆盖 26 个学科。

第二部分为按意群分类词汇，有 41 个 WORD LIST，包含 253 个意群。

第三部分为专业词汇，有数学、物理、化学、生物四个专项考试的专业词汇表。

建议同学们以每天两个 WORD LIST 为基本任务量，学科词汇可以根据你当前要看的阅读文章或要听的听力短文的学科属性来判定，这样可以做到学习后马上应用。如果没有结合真题学习，就可以按顺序背诵。

认真学习这些词汇的经历是非常宝贵的，这些词汇将超越考试本身，伴随你终生，在你未来的留学生活和事业舞台上是非常好用的工具。对一些人来说，目前的吃苦是最终把你带向全球顶尖院校的必经之路；对另外一些人来说，哪怕只是历练，你的英语能力也会因曾付出的努力而提升。

最后，我祝福每一个读者在学习本书的过程中都能充满信心、盼望和智慧，在锻造词汇砖瓦的过程中始终看到未来辉煌的大厦！

非常感谢梁翠、周倩和新东方的编辑在本书编辑中所做的工作，她们的协助使本书的出版得以圆满完成。

张红岩

目 录

按学科分类（Word List 1–15）

按意群分类（Word List 16–56）

正向评价

负向评价

行 为

语 言

心 理

人物及其相关动作

专业词汇（Word List 57-60）

SAT
按学科分类
Subjects

Word List 1

数学·物理·化学

数 学

binary [ˈbaɪnəri] *adj.* 成双的（of or involving a pair or pairs）；二进位的 *n.* 二进制数字

***divisible** [dɪˈvɪzəbl] *adj.* 可除尽的
【例】8 is *divisible* by 2 and 4, but not by 3.

facet [ˈfæsɪt] *n.* 平面
【例】The stonecutter decided to improve the rough diamond by providing it with several *facets*.

***sequence** [ˈsiːkwəns] *n.* 序列
【记】sequ(跟随)+ ence → 一个跟着一个 → 序列

****circulate** [ˈsɜːrkjəleɪt] *v.* (使)循环
【例】Open a window to allow the air to *circulate*.

compute [kəmˈpjuːt] *v.* 用计算机计算(to calculate sth with a computer)
【例】Scientists have *computed* the probable course of the rocket.

***calculate** [ˈkælkjuleɪt] *v.* 计算，估计(to count)；计划
【例】Mary *calculated* her monthly expenses.

***enumerate** [ɪˈnuːməreɪt] *vt.* 列举，枚举；计数(to count; numerate)
【记】e(出)+ numer(数字)+ ate → 按数列出 → 列举
【例】Sam can *enumerate* all the presidents of the United States.

***evaluate** [ɪˈvæljueɪt] *vt.* 评价，估计(to estimate; assess)
【记】e + valu(价值)+ ate → 评价
【例】The assessor *evaluated* the plot of land before Anne sold it.

****fraction** [ˈfrækʃn] *n.* 分数
【记】fract(碎裂)+ ion → 碎裂的整数 → 分数

arithmetic [əˈrɪθmətɪk] *n.* 算术
【记】arithm(数学)+ etic → 数学的分支 → 算术
【例】*Arithmetic* is a basic school subject.

decimal [ˈdesɪml] *adj.* 十进制的；小数的 *n.* 小数
【记】decim(十分之一) + al → 十进制的
【例】The metric system is a *decimal* system.

multiplication [ˌmʌltɪplɪˈkeɪʃn] *n.* 乘法
【例】*multiplication* table

beeline [ˈbiːlaɪn] *n.* 直线，最短路线(direct quick route)

indices [ˈɪndɪsiːz] *n.* 指数(signs; indications)
【记】index的复数

exponentially [ˌekspəˈnenʃəli] *adv.* 指数地；迅速增长地
【记】exponent(指数) + ially → 指数地

***diametrical** [ˌdaɪəˈmetrɪkl] *adj.* 直径的；正好相反的

***semicircular** [ˌsemiˈsɜːrkjələr] *adj.* 半圆的
【例】The hotel, freshly built by decree of the progressive, tourism-minded king, was *semicircular* in shape.

***tangential** [tænˈdʒenʃl] *adj.* 切线的；离题的(divergent; digressive)
【反】*tangential* point(非要点) → gist(*n.* 要点)

***elliptical** [ɪˈlɪptɪkl] *adj.* 椭圆的；晦涩的(ambiguous)；省略的
【反】palpable(*adj.* 明显的)

***circuitous** [sərˈkjuːɪtəs] *adj.* 迂回的(indirect; roundabout)
【记】circuit(绕圈) + ous → 迂回的
【例】You could tell Mary that she was evading our question when she gave a *circuitous* response.

***curvature** [ˈkɜːrvətʃər] *n.* 弯曲形状，弯曲(curved form; curving)
【例】the *curvature* of the earth's surface

***tangency** [ˈtændʒənsi] *n.* 相切，(在一点上)接触
【例】Based on the analysis, determine the unicity of point of *tangency* and point of intersection.

***halve** [hæv] *vt.* 把…对半分(to divide sth into two equal parts)
【例】The latest planes have *halved* the time needed for crossing the Atlantic.

****vertex** [ˈvɜːrteks] *n.* (三角形、多边形等的)角的顶点；顶点，最高点(highest point; summit)
【例】The origin in a polar coordinate system; the *vertex* of a polar angle.

***symmetry** [ˈsɪmətri] *n.* 对称(性)，匀称(balance; harmony)
【记】sym(共同) + metry(测量) → 两边测量结果一样 → 对称

plumb [plʌm] *adj.* 垂直的(straight; vertical)

*perpendicular [ˌpɜːrpən'dɪkjələr] *adj.* 垂直的(exactly upright; vertical)

【记】per(每) + pend(挂) + icular → 全部挂的 → 垂直的

*cylindrical [sə'lɪndrɪkl] *adj.* 圆柱形的, 圆柱体的

【例】His car had *cylindrical* glass holders attached to either door and a white leathery interior.

*parameter [pə'ræmɪtər] *n.* 参量, 变量(any of the established limits within which sth must operate)

【记】para(辅助) + meter(测量) → 辅助测量 → 参量

*axiom ['æksiəm] *n.* 公理(maxim); 定理

【记】ax(斧子) + iom → 斧子之下出公理 → 公理

*aggregate ['ægrɪgət] *n.* 合计, 总计; 集合体

**deduction [dɪ'dʌkʃn] *n.* 扣除, 扣除之量; 推论, 演绎法

**scatterplot *n.* 散点图

**pictogram ['pɪktəgræm] *n.* 象形图

*vector ['vektər] *n.* 矢量 (quantity that has both magnitude and direction, e.g. velocity)

*imponderable [ɪm'pɑːndərəbl] *adj.* (重量等)无法衡量的

【记】im(不) + ponder(衡量) + able → 无法衡量的

*discrete [dɪ'skriːt] *adj.* 不相关的; 不连续的; 离散的(separate)

【例】A computer can perform millions of *discrete* functions per second.

*determinant [dɪ'tɜːrmɪnənt] *n.* 决定因素 *adj.* 决定性的(decisive)

【记】来自determine(*v.* 决定, 下决心)

*chart [tʃɑːrt] *n.* 航海图

【例】a naval *chart*

物　理

*opaque [oʊ'peɪk] *n.* 不透明物 *adj.* 不透明的; 不传导的

**echo ['ekoʊ] *n.* 回声, 回波

*resound [rɪ'zaʊnd] *vi.* 回响 (to be filled with sound); 鸣响 (to be loudly and clearly heard)

*leverage ['levərɪdʒ] *n.* 杠杆作用

**forcemeter ['fɔːrsmiːtər] *n.* 测力计

centigrade ['sentɪɡreɪd] *adj.* 百分度的; 摄氏的

【记】centi(百) + grade(级, 度) → 百分度的

【例】*Centigrade* scale is used in most countries except the United States.

*celsius	[ˈselsiəs] *adj.* 摄氏的 *n.* 摄氏度
	【例】Boiling point is 100 *Celsius*.
*filament	[ˈfɪləmənt] *n.* 灯丝；细丝
	【记】fila(丝) + ment → 灯丝；细丝
**circuitry	[ˈsɜːrkɪtri] *n.* 电路，电路系统
galvanize	[ˈgælvənaɪz] *vt.* 电镀；给…通电；激励(to stimulate)
	【记】来自galvanic(*adj.* 电流的)
	【反】lull(*vt.* 使麻痹，使平静)
electromagnetic	[ɪˌlektroʊmæɡˈnetɪk] *adj.* 电磁的
magnetic	[mæɡˈnetɪk] *adj.* 有磁性的(with the properties of a magnet)
	【例】The block becomes *magnetic* when the current is switched on.
refraction	[rɪˈfrækʃn] *n.* 折射(bending of a ray of light)
lumen	[ˈluːmen] *n.*(*pl.* lumens, -mina) 流明(光通量单位)
	【例】A former luminance unit was equal to one *lumen* per square foot.
*diffuse	[dɪˈfjuːs] *v.*(使)传播，(使)扩散(to scatter; spread)
	【记】di(分开) + f + fuse(流) → 分流 → 扩散
	【例】The winds *diffused* the smoke throughout the neighborhood.
**emit	[iˈmɪt] *vt.* 发出，放射(to discharge; give off)
	【例】All the cars that *emit* poisonous gas have been called back.
*density	[ˈdensəti] *n.* 密度
	【例】The population *density* is very high in Hong Kong.
*foam	[foʊm] *n.* 泡沫(bubble; froth)
*clutter	[ˈklʌtər] *n.*(雷达显示器上的)杂乱回波；混乱，杂乱 *vt.* 使混乱(to litter; disarray)
	【例】My office is filled with useless *clutter*.
*thaw	[θɔː] *v.*(使)溶化，(使)融解(to melt; defrost)
	【例】Last week it was so warm that the frozen pond *thawed*.
fusion	[ˈfjuːʒn] *n.* 熔合
*constituent	[kənˈstɪtʃuənt] *n.* 成分(component)
**incompatible	[ˌɪnkəmˈpætəbl] *adj.* 不兼容的(inconsistent; incongruous)
	【记】in(不) + compatible(融合的，兼容的) → 不兼容的
**compatible	[kəmˈpætəbl] *adj.* 融合的，兼容的(harmonious; congruous)
	【例】Is this software *compatible* with my computer?
dissolution	[ˌdɪsəˈluːʃn] *n.* 分解，溶解；崩溃，瓦解 (disintegration; looseness in morals)

【例】 Experiments were carried out at 100℃ and pressures sufficiently low to prevent *dissolution*. // The profligacy and *dissolution* of life in Caligula's Rome appall some historians.

*dynamic [daɪˈnæmɪk] *adj.* 动态的（opposed to static）；有活力的（energetic; vigorous）

【记】 dynam(力量)＋ic → 有活力的

***mechanics [məˈkænɪks] *n.* 力学；机械学

*cohesion [koʊˈhiːʒn] *n.* 内聚力；附着，结合；凝聚力

【例】 *Cohesion* is the force causing molecules of the same substance to stick together.

*impetus [ˈɪmpɪtəs] *n.* 推动力（urge; momentum）

【记】 im(进入)＋pet(追求)＋us → 追求力 → 推动力

【例】 The physical object in motion needs *impetus*. // His longing for another kind of life is a major *impetus* for his hard working.

decelerate [ˌdiːˈseləreɪt] *v.* （使）减速（to decrease the speed of）

【例】 A parachute is used to *decelerate* a fast-moving object. // Many countries are seeking measures to *decelerate* the arms buildup.

【反】 accelerate（*v.* 加速）

accelerate [əkˈseləreɪt] *v.* （使）加速（to expedite; speed）

【记】 ac＋celer(速度)＋ate → 加速

【例】 The car *accelerated* as it went downhill.

*expedite [ˈekspədaɪt] *vt.* 使加速（to speed up; hasten）

【记】 ex(出)＋ped(脚)＋ite → 脚跨出去 → 加速

【例】 Use of a rotary vacuum evaporator will *expedite* the concentration steps in the procedure. // The person I talked to on the phone promised to *expedite* the shipment of the book I ordered.

*radiate [ˈreɪdieɪt] *v.* （使）散发，发射（to emit; give off）

【例】 Heat *radiated* from the stove.

quiver [ˈkwɪvər] *v.* （使）振动，（使）颤抖（to shiver; tremble）

【例】 The dog *quivered* in the rain.

centrifugal [ˌsentrɪˈfjuːɡl] *adj.* 离心的（moving or tending to move away from a center）

【记】 centri(中心)＋fug(逃跑)＋al → 逃离中心的 → 离心的

centripetal [senˈtrɪpɪtl] *adj.* 向心的（moving or tending to move toward a center）

【记】 centri(中心)＋pet(追求)＋al → 追求中心 → 向心的

circuit [ˈsɜːrkɪt] *n.* 电路 (complete path along which an electric current flows); 环行；环行道；线路 (a curving path that forms a complete circle round an area)

declivity [dɪˈklɪvəti] *n.* 下倾的斜面
【记】de(下) + cliv(斜面) + ity → 下倾的斜面

***indexer** [ɪnˈdeksər] *n.* 分度器

gravitational [ˌɡrævɪˈteɪʃnl] *adj.* 万有引力的，重力的
【记】来自 gravitation(*n.* 万有引力，重力)

projectile [prəˈdʒektl] *n.* 抛射物，发射体 (a body projected by external force)
【记】pro(向前) + ject(扔) + ile → 扔向前的东西 → 抛射物

tensile [ˈtensl] *adj.* 张力的，可伸展的 (capable of being stretched)

***elastic** [ɪˈlæstɪk] *adj.* 有弹性的，能伸展的 (easily resuming original shape after being stretched)
【记】e + last(持久) + ic → 能伸展的
【反】inelastic (*adj.* 无弹性的)

***cohesive** [koʊˈhiːsɪv] *adj.* 有凝聚力的

****aerodynamics** [ˌeroʊdaɪˈnæmɪks] *n.* 空气动力学

aerodynamical [ˌeroʊdaɪˈnæmɪkl] *adj.* 空气动力学的

＊＊disperse [dɪˈspɜːrs] *v.* 消散，驱散
【记】di(分开) + sperse(散开) → 分散开 → 驱散
【反】focus(*v.* 聚集); aggregate(*v.* 聚集)

chafe [tʃeɪf] *vt.* 擦热 (to rub; scrape)
【例】Coarse fabric will *chafe* your skin.

dehydrate [diːˈhaɪdreɪt] *v.* (使)脱水 (to dry)
【记】de(去除) + hydrate(水合物) → 使脱水
【例】Her body had *dehydrated* dangerously with the heat.

****fathom** [ˈfæðəm] *n.* 英寻 (水深测量单位，等于1.83米) *v.* 彻底明白，领悟 (to understand thoroughly)
【记】fathom 原意为"伸展手臂测量"，引申为"伸展手臂后的长度"

***candlepower** [ˈkændlˌpaʊər] *n.* 烛光

***interatomic** [ˌɪntɜːrəˈtɑːmɪk] *adj.* 原子间的
【例】*Interatomic* forces were considered as a function of the separation of atoms.

***edgewise** [ˈedʒwaɪz] *adv.* 刀口朝向外边，沿边

carat [ˈkærət] *n.* (钻石等的重量单位)克拉；(金子的纯度单位)开

*brink [brɪŋk] *n.* 边缘(margin; edge; rim)

【例】A fence was built along the *brink* of the cliff to prevent accidents.

化 学

indissoluble [ˌɪndɪˈsɑːljəbl] *adj.* 不可溶解的，不可分解的；牢固持久的(firm and lasting)

【例】an *indissoluble* compound // The Roman Catholic Church regards marriage as *indissoluble*.

*soluble [ˈsɑːljəbl] *adj.* 可溶的（capable of being dissolved）；可以解决的（capable of being solved）

【记】solu(松开) + ble → 可溶的

*detergent [dɪˈtɜːrdʒənt] *adj.* 净化的(cleansing) *n.* 清洁剂

【记】de(除去) + terg(擦) + ent → 擦掉 → 净化的；清洁剂

hermetic [hɜːrˈmetɪk] *adj.* 密封的(completely sealed by fusion; airtight)；深奥的

【记】her(她) + met(遇到) + ic(看做ice，冰) → 她遇到冰进不去了 → 密封的

【反】easily comprehended(易被理解的)

*impurity [ɪmˈpjʊrəti] *n.* 杂质；不纯

**composite [kəmˈpɑːzɪt] *adj.* 混合的 *n.* 混合物(made up of different parts or materials)

【例】a *composite* substance // The play is a *composite* of reality and fiction.

*liquefy [ˈlɪkwɪfaɪ] *v.* (使)液化，(使)溶解(to make or become liquid; melt)

【记】liqu(液体) + efy → 变成液体 → (使)液化

*dissolve [dɪˈzɑːlv] *v.* (使)溶解，(使)融化

【例】Water *dissolves* salt as heat *dissolves* ice.

*corrosive [kəˈroʊsɪv] *adj.* 腐蚀性的，腐蚀的（tending or having the power to corrode）

corrode [kəˈroʊd] *v.* 腐蚀，侵蚀(to erode; eat away)；受腐蚀

【例】Battery acid *corroded* the inside of the camera.

*additive [ˈædətɪv] *n.* 添加剂

evaporate [ɪˈvæpəreɪt] *v.* (使)蒸发(to vaporize)

【记】e + vapor(蒸汽) + ate → (使)蒸发

【例】The rubbing alcohol *evaporated* as soon as the nurse dabbed it on the patient's arm.

*tentative ［ˈtentətɪv］ *adj.* 试验性的（trial）

【记】tent(=test 测试) + ative → 试验性的

【例】*Tentative* measures have been taken to settle these refugees.

miscellany ［ˈmɪsəleɪni］ *n.* 混合物（a collection of various items or parts）

【记】misc(混合) + ellany → 混合物

【派】miscellaneous(*adj.* 混杂的，各种各样的)

*flammable ［ˈflæməbl］ *adj.* 易燃的（easily set on fire）

【记】flamm(=flam 火) + able → 易燃的

combustible ［kəmˈbʌstəbl］ *adj.* 易燃的（flammable）；易激动的（easily aroused）

【记】com + bust(燃烧) + ible → 易燃的

propellant ［prəˈpelənt］ *n.* 推进物，推进燃料，发射火药

*explode ［ɪkˈsploʊd］ *v.* (使)爆炸（to blast）

【例】The red balloon *exploded* when I popped it with a pin.

molten ［ˈmoʊltən］ *adj.* 熔化的（melted）

*rust ［rʌst］ *v.* (使)生锈；(使)成铁锈色 *n.* 铁锈

【例】An iron plow would get *rusted* under wet weather. // If you leave your metal tools outside in the rain, they will *rust*.

*smolder ［ˈsmoʊldər］ *vi.* (无火焰)缓慢燃烧

kindle ［ˈkɪndl］ *vt.* 点燃，燃起（to ignite; inflame）；激起(情绪等)

【记】和candle(*n.* 蜡烛)一起记

【例】The sparks *kindled* the dry grass. // Her cruelty *kindled* hatred in my heart.

**sear ［sɪr］ *vt.* 灼烧，烧焦

【例】The hot iron *seared* the trousers.

*ignite ［ɪgˈnaɪt］ *vt.* 点燃，使燃烧（to inflame; kindle）

【例】A smoldering cigarette *ignited* the newspapers.

distill ［dɪˈstɪl］ *v.* 蒸馏，提炼（to turn a liquid into vapor by heating）

【记】di(分开) + still(滴下) → 蒸馏

leaven ［ˈlevn］ *n.* 发酵剂，酵母（a substance used to produce fermentation in dough or a liquid）；影响力 *vt.* 使发酵（to raise with a leaven）；影响

【记】leave(离开) + n → 离开旧的状态 → 使发酵；和heaven(*n.* 天堂)一起记

carbon ［ˈkɑːrbən］ *n.* 碳

*scorch ［skɔːrtʃ］ *vt.* 烤焦，烫得褪色（to discolor）

【例】Do not leave the iron on that delicate fabric or the heat will *scorch* it.

*chlorinate ［ˈklɔːrɪneɪt］ *vt.* 使氯化

erode [ɪˈroʊd] vt. 侵蚀，腐蚀(to corrode; wear away)

【例】A constant stream of water *eroded* the rock mountain.

blend [blend] v./n. 混和(to combine; mix)

【例】The room's decoration was a good *blend* of traditional and modern pieces. // The artist *blended* painting with etching.

ferment [fərˈment] v./n. (使)发酵(to cause fermentation in)；(使)骚动(to excite; agitate)

【记】ferm(=ferv 煮沸) + ent → 发酵

【反】tranquility(n.宁静)

assay [əˈseɪ] v./n. 试验，测定(to test for quality)

【记】as(正如) + say(说) → 正如试验数据所说 → 试验

synthesize [ˈsɪnθəsaɪz] vt. 合成，综合

blanch [blæntʃ] v. (使)变白，漂白(to make or become white)；(使脸色)变苍白(to turn pale)

【记】和blank(adj. 空白的)一起记

coagulate [koʊˈægjuleɪt] v. (使)凝结(to curdle; clot)

【记】co(一起) + ag(做) + ulate → 使到一起 → (使)凝结

rarefy [ˈrerɪfaɪ] v. (使)变稀薄(to make thin, less compact or less dense)；提炼(思想等)，使纯化

【记】来自rare(adj. 稀薄的)

【例】Everyone ought to *rarefy* his spiritual life.

【反】concentrate(v.集中，浓缩)；condense(v.压缩，浓缩)；make denser(使浓缩)

ossify [ˈɑːsɪfaɪ] v. (使)硬化，(使)骨化；(使)(传统)僵化

【记】oss(骨) + ify(…化) → (使)骨化

【反】transcend conventions(超越传统)

concentrate [ˈkɑːnsntreɪt] v. (使)聚集，(使)浓缩(to bring into one main body)

【记】con + centr(中心) + ate → 聚集

【反】deploy(v. 展开)；dilute(v. 稀释)；rarefy(v. (使)变稀薄)

acetic [əˈsiːtɪk] adj. 醋的；酸的

brass [bræs] n. 黄铜

bronze [brɑːnz] n. 青铜

bicarbonate [ˌbaɪˈkɑːrbənət] n. 碳酸氢盐，重碳酸盐

millilitre [ˈmɪliliːtər] n. 毫升

blast [blæst] n. 爆破，爆炸；(一阵)疾风

【例】Several passers-by were killed by the *blast*. // The leaves were lifted into the air by a sudden *blast* of wind.

**ingredient	[ɪnˈgriːdiənt] *n.* 成分（element） 【记】in（进入）+ gredi（走）+ ent → 走进去成为一部分 → 成分
*amalgam	[əˈmælgəm] *n.* 混合物（a combination or mixture） 【记】am + alg + am → 前后两个am，中间alg → 混合物
alchemy	[ˈælkəmi] *n.* 炼金术
**filter	[ˈfɪltər] *n.* 滤纸，多孔过滤材料（a porous article（as of paper）through which a gas or liquid is passed to separate out matter in suspension） *vt.* 过滤（to remove by means of a filter）
*aluminium	[ˌæljəˈmɪniəm] *n.* 铝
effervescence	[ˌefərˈvesns] *n.* 冒泡，沸腾
*crystal	[ˈkrɪstl] *n.* 水晶；结晶体 【例】Salt *crystals* can be found in every home.
*inhalation	[ˌɪnhəˈleɪʃn] *n.* 吸入；吸入药剂
emollient	[iˈmɑːliənt] *n.* 润肤剂（a medicine applied to surface tissues of the body） 【记】e + molli（=soft 软）+ ent → 使（皮肤）变软 → 润肤剂
mote	[moʊt] *n.* 微粒，微尘（a speck of dust）
nitrogen	[ˈnaɪtrədʒən] *n.* 氮
synthetic	[sɪnˈθetɪk] *adj.* 综合的；合成的（artificial; man-made）

Patience is better than pride.
存心忍耐的，胜过居心骄傲的。

——《圣经·旧·传》7:8

练 习 题

填空题

compatible	composite	corrosive	detergent	diffuse
circulate	disperse	dissolve	emit	erode
enumerate	incompatible	liquefy	resound	rust
sear	smolder	soluble	synthesize	tentative

1. The hours of the job are _____ with family life.
2. Unemployment is having a _____ effect on our economy.
3. The new system will be _____ with existing equipment.
4. Most synthetic _____ are in the form of powder or liquid.
5. Problems are not readily _____.
6. He reached some _____ conclusions about the possible cause of the accident.
7. The play is a _____ of reality and fiction.
8. Blood _____ through the body.
9. The minimum pressure required to _____ a gas at its critical temperature is its critical pressure.
10. Laughter _____ through the house.
11. Salt _____ in water.
12. The underneath of the car was badly _____.
13. Police _____ the protesters with tear gas.
14. She _____ the items we had to buy, sugar, tea, soap, etc.
15. The bonfire was still _____ the next day.
16. DDT is a pesticide that was first _____ in 1874.
17. The problem is how to _____ power without creating anarchy.
18. The metal container began to _____ a clicking sound.
19. The heat of the sun _____ their faces.
20. Her confidence has been slowly _____ by repeated failures.

配对题

1. celsius	回声	11. clutter	空气动力学
2. flammable	电路	12. mechanics	杠杆作用
3. bronze	灯丝	13. filter	杂质
4. bicarbonate	成分	14. density	英寻
5. opaque	测力计	15. foam	添加剂
6. forcemeter	不透明物	16. additive	泡沫
7. ingredient	碳酸氢盐	17. fathom	密度
8. filament	青铜	18. impurity	滤纸
9. circuitry	易燃的	19. leverage	力学
10. echo	摄氏度	20. aerodynamics	杂乱回波

练习题答案

填空题答案

1. The hours of the job are <u>incompatible</u> with family life.
2. Unemployment is having a <u>corrosive</u> effect on our economy.
3. The new system will be <u>compatible</u> with existing equipment.
4. Most synthetic <u>detergents</u> are in the form of powder or liquid.
5. Problems are not readily <u>soluble</u>.
6. He reached some <u>tentative</u> conclusions about the possible cause of the accident.
7. The play is a <u>composite</u> of reality and fiction.
8. Blood <u>circulates</u> through the body.
9. The minimum pressure required to <u>liquefy</u> a gas at its critical temperature is its critical pressure.
10. Laughter <u>resounded</u> through the house.
11. Salt <u>dissolves</u> in water.
12. The underneath of the car was badly <u>rusted</u>.
13. Police <u>dispersed</u> the protesters with tear gas.
14. She <u>enumerated</u> the items we had to buy, sugar, tea, soap, etc.
15. The bonfire was still <u>smoldering</u> the next day.
16. DDT is a pesticide that was first <u>synthesized</u> in 1874.
17. The problem is how to <u>diffuse</u> power without creating anarchy.
18. The metal container began to <u>emit</u> a clicking sound.
19. The heat of the sun <u>seared</u> their faces.
20. Her confidence has been slowly <u>eroded</u> by repeated failures.

配对题答案

1. celsius	摄氏度	11. clutter	杂乱回波
2. flammable	易燃的	12. mechanics	力学
3. bronze	青铜	13. filter	滤纸
4. bicarbonate	碳酸氢盐	14. density	密度
5. opaque	不透明物	15. foam	泡沫
6. forcemeter	测力计	16. additive	添加剂
7. ingredient	成分	17. fathom	英寻
8. filament	灯丝	18. impurity	杂质
9. circuitry	电路	19. leverage	杠杆作用
10. echo	回声	20. aerodynamics	空气动力学

Word List 2
地理·地质·气象·天文

地 理

*geographic [ˌdʒiːə'græfɪk] *adj.* 地理的，地理学的
【例】Each nation also got a figure for rural agricultural production, which was assigned a *geographic* location.

*continental [ˌkɑːntɪ'nentl] *adj.* 大陆的，大陆性的；［C-］欧洲大陆的（of or pertaining to or typical of Europe）
【例】This strategy ultimately led to the creation of an inter-colony organization, the *Continental* Congress.

*temperate ['tempərət] *adj.* (气候)温和的
【例】*temperate* latitudes

maritime ['mærɪtaɪm] *adj.* 海的(marine; oceanic)；海上的，海事的；近海的
【记】mari(海) + time → 海的

*oceanographic [ˌoʊʃə'nɑːgrəfɪk] *adj.* 海洋学的，有关海洋学的(oceanographical)
【例】The Year should be used to enhance co-operation between the *oceanographic* community and their land-based counterparts.

*caribbean [ˌkærɪ'biːən] *adj.* 加勒比人的，加勒比海的，加勒比语的 *n.* ［the C-］加勒比海
【例】In the *Caribbean* and Mexico, you can find a lot of resorts there.

*underwater [ˌʌndər'wɔːtər] *adj.* 水面下的，水下使用的，水下行动的(situated or used or done below the surface of the water)
【例】*underwater* caves

*groundwater ['graʊndwɔːtər] *n.* 地下水

*watershed ['wɔːtərʃed] *n.* 分水岭

*shoreline ['ʃɔːrlaɪn] *n.* 海岸线，海岸线地带

*coastline ['koʊstlaɪn] *n.* 海岸线
【例】Besides being physically close to Italy, Libya also has a long, relatively unpopulated and unpatrolled *coastline*.

*seafloor [ˈsiːflɔːr] n. 海底

*ledge [ledʒ] n. (近海岸的)暗礁
【记】l(形状似突起的物体) + edge(边) → 海边水里突起的物体 → (近海岸的)暗礁

*reef [riːf] n. 礁，礁脉（ridge of rock, shingle, sand, etc at or near the surface of the sea）
【例】The ship was wrecked on a coral *reef*.

**navigation [ˌnævɪˈɡeɪʃn] n. 航海

*waterway [ˈwɔːtərweɪ] n. 水路，航道

promontory [ˈprɑːməntɔːri] n. (伸入海中或湖中的)悬崖，岬，海角（area of high land jutting out into the sea or a lake; headland）

*archipelago [ˌɑːrkɪˈpeləɡoʊ] n. 群岛；群岛周围的海（sea surrounding a group of many islands）

ebb [eb] vi. 退潮
【例】The water washed up on the shore, then slowly *ebbed* away.

*endemic [ɪnˈdemɪk] adj. 地方性的(native)
【例】This disease is *endemic* to the southerners, and will not spread in the cold north.

*terrestrial [təˈrestriəl] adj. 地球的，陆地的
【例】*terrestrial* heat // *terrestrial* magnetism

*cosmopolitan [ˌkɑːzməˈpɑːlɪtən] adj. 全世界的(global)
【记】cosmo(世界) + politan(人民) → 所有人民组成了世界 → 全世界的
【例】The farmer was unused to the *cosmopolitan* ways of life in a large city.

***extraterrestrial [ˌekstrətəˈrestriəl] adj. 地球和大气层外的，来自天外的（of or from outside the earth and its atmosphere）
【例】*extraterrestrial* life

*transcontinental [ˌtrænskɑːntɪˈnentl] adj. 横贯大陆的(crossing a continent)
【例】a *transcontinental* highway, flight, journey

*overland [ˈoʊvərlænd] adj./adv. 横越陆地的（地），经由陆路的(地)(across the land; by land)
【例】an *overland* route, journey, etc

*subterranean [ˌsʌbtəˈreɪniən] adj. 地下的

*abyssal [ə'bɪsl] *adj.* 深渊的；深海的；深不可测的

【例】Ancient seas, for example, could explain why the planet's northern lowlands hold extensive sedimentary deposits that resemble those seen in the *abyssal* plains of Earth's ocean floors.

*cavernous ['kævərnəs] *adj.* 似巨穴的，洞穴状的，凹状的

【例】It is known for its *cavernous*, white-columned baths in the style of Ancient Rome.

cleft [kleft] *n.* 裂缝（crevice）

*flaw [flɔ:] *n.* 裂隙；缺点，瑕疵

【例】The *flaw* in your theory is that you didn't account for gravity.

**abyss [ə'bɪs] *n.* 深渊；深不可测的事物

【例】He threw the brightness of his nature over every *abyss* and cavern through which he strayed. // an *abyss* of ignorance, despair, loneliness, etc

chasm ['kæzəm] *n.* 深渊，大沟（abyss; gorge）；大差别（a pronounced difference）

hinterland ['hɪntərlænd] *n.* 内陆地区（an inland region）；穷乡僻壤（back country）

【记】hinter(=hinder 后面的) + land(土地) → 海岸后面的土地 → 内陆地区

ambience ['æmbɪəns] *n.* 环境，气氛（environment; atmosphere）

【派】ambient(*adj.* 周围的，四面八方的)

*savanna [sə'vænə] *n.* 热带或亚热带之大草原

*sierra [si'erə] *n.* 锯齿状山脉（尤指在西班牙及西班牙语系的美洲国家的）

tundra ['tʌndrə] *n.* 冻原，苔原（vast flat treeless Arctic regions of Europe, Asia and North America where the subsoil is permanently frozen）

【例】*tundra* vegetation

*lune [lju:n] *n.* 半月形，弓形

*cavern ['kævərn] *n.* 大山洞，大洞穴

【记】cavern是large(大的)cave(洞)

【例】Inside the *cavern* were the remnants of an ancient fire.

*insularity [ˌɪnsjə'lærəti] *n.* 岛国状态，岛屿生活状况，与外界隔绝的生活状况；（思想、观点等的）偏狭与僵化

【反】cosmopolitanism(*n.* 世界大同主义)

**terrain [tə'reɪn] *n.* 地形

*geologist [dʒi'ɑ:lədʒɪst] *n.* 地质学者

*elevation [ˌelɪ'veɪʃn] n. 高地；海拔

*volcano [vɑːl'keɪnoʊ] n. 火山

*midseason ['mɪdˌsiːzən] n. 季节中期(指仲春、仲夏、仲秋、仲冬)

*chan [tʃæn] (=channel) n. 海峡；水道，航道；槽，沟渠

outskirts ['aʊtskɜːrts] n. 外围地区；郊外，郊区 (outlying districts, especially of a city or large town; outer areas)

latitude ['lætɪtuːd] n. 纬度
【记】lati(开阔) + tude → 纬度

*Atlantis [æt'læntɪs] n. 亚特兰蒂斯(传说沉没于大西洋的岛屿)

subsidiary [səb'sɪdieri] adj. 附属的，从属的 (connected to but smaller, of less importance, etc than sth else; subordinate)
【记】sub(下面) + sidi(坐) + ary → 坐在下面辅助的 → 附属的，从属的
【例】He followed the subsidiary stream to trace its origin.

metropolis [mə'trɑːpəlɪs] n. 大城市，首都，首府 (chief city of a region or country; capital)
【例】a great metropolis like Tokyo

clime [klaɪm] n. (尤指气候宜人的)地区，气候区；气候

atlas ['ætləs] n. 地图集，地图册

topography [tə'pɑːgrəfi] n. 地形，地志，地形学

*leeway ['liːweɪ] n. (船或飞行器因风而致的)偏航，漂移(sideways drift of a ship or aircraft, due to the wind)；回旋余地 (amount of freedom to move, change)
【例】This itinerary leaves us plenty of leeway.

**charcoal ['tʃɑːrkoʊl] n. 木炭
【例】a stick/piece/lump of charcoal

*mound [maʊnd] n. 小丘，土墩，小土岗

abut [ə'bʌt] v. 接界，毗连(to border upon)
【记】about去掉o；注意不要和abet(vt. 教唆)相混

*intersect [ˌɪntər'sekt] v. 相交(to cross; meet)；横穿
【记】inter(中间) + sect(切，割) → 从中间相切 → 相交
【例】These two fences intersect at the creek.

地 质

**cataclysmic [ˌkætə'klɪzmɪk] adj. 大变动的；洪水的
【例】Few had expected that change to be as cataclysmic as it turned out to be.

*outburst	[ˈaʊtbɜːrst] n. (火山、感情等)爆发，喷出 (surge; explosion)
*lava	[ˈlɑːvə] n. 熔岩，火山岩
*erupt	[ɪˈrʌpt] vi. 爆发 (to explode; burst out)

【例】We feared that the volcano would *erupt* again.

stratum	[ˈstreɪtəm] n. 地层
*magma	[ˈmægmə] n. (有机物或矿物的)稀糊状混合物，岩浆
*sediment	[ˈsedɪmənt] n. 沉淀物，沉积
protuberance	[proʊˈtuːbərəns] n. 凸出，隆起 (a swelling; bulge)

【记】pro(向前) + tuber(块茎) + ance → 向前的部分像块茎一样 → 凸出，隆起

*marble	[ˈmɑːrbl] n. 大理石
**granite	[ˈɡrænɪt] n. 花岗岩
*fissure	[ˈfɪʃər] n. 裂缝，裂隙 (a long, narrow and deep cleft or crack)

【记】fiss(裂) + ure(名词后缀) → 裂缝，裂隙

*limestone	[ˈlaɪmstoʊn] n. 石灰石
tremor	[ˈtremər] n. 震动；地震

【记】trem(抖动) + or → 震动

seismic	[ˈsaɪzmɪk] adj. 地震的

【例】*seismic* wave

*magnitude	[ˈmæɡnɪtjuːd] n. 震级
*glacial	[ˈɡleɪʃl] adj. 冰的，冰状的；冰河的，冰河时代的

【例】*glacial* drift // *glacial* epoch

*permafrost	[ˈpɜːrməfrɔːst] n. 永冻土，永冻层
petrify	[ˈpetrɪfaɪ] v. 变为化石；使石化

【记】petr(石头) + ify(使) → 使石化

【例】Folklore has it, as reinforced in classrooms and national parks, that *petrified* wood takes "millions and millions" of years to form.

气 象

meteorology	[ˌmiːtiəˈrɑːlədʒi] n. 气象学 (the scientific study of weather conditions)

【记】meteor(陨石；天气) + ology(学科) → 气象学

*torrid	[ˈtɔːrɪd] adj. 酷热的 (hot)

【记】torr(热) + id → 酷热的

muggy ['mʌgi] *adj.* 闷热的

arid ['ærɪd] *adj.* 干旱的(dry); 枯燥的(dull; uninteresting)
【反】damp(*adj.* 潮湿的)
【派】aridness(*n.* 干燥)

drought [draʊt] *n.* 干旱; 干旱时期(period of continuous dry weather)
【记】dr(看做dry, 干燥) + ought(可能) → 干
燥可能会演变为干旱 → 干旱

gusty ['gʌsti] *adj.* 刮风的, 阵风的(windy)
【例】The *gusty* weather made sailing precarious.

bluster ['blʌstər] *vi.* (指风)猛刮
【例】The wind *blustered* around the house.

gust [gʌst] *n.* 一阵强风(a sudden, strong rush of wind); 一阵(情绪)爆发
(an outburst)

stuffy ['stʌfi] *adj.* 通风不良的, 闷气的(oppressive to the breathing)
【记】stuff(填满) + y(形容词后缀) → 填满不流通的空气 → 通风不
良的, 闷气的

leeward ['liːwərd] *adj.* 顺风的, 向下风的 (in the direction toward which the
wind blows)
【记】lee(下风) + ward → 向下风走 → 顺风的

humid ['hjuːmɪd] *adj.* 湿润的(damp)

dank [dæŋk] *adj.* 阴湿的(damp; clammy)
【例】Our cellar is *dank* and dark.

precipitation [prɪˌsɪpɪ'teɪʃn] *n.* 降水

cloudburst ['klaʊdbɜːrst] *n.* 大暴雨, 倾盆大雨(a sudden, very heavy rain)
【记】cloud(云) + burst(爆裂) → 乌云爆裂, 要下暴雨 → 大暴雨

cumulus ['kjuːmjələs] *n.* 积云(a cloud formed of, rounded, massed, heaped on a
flat base); 堆积

downpour ['daʊnpɔːr] *n.* 暴雨(a heavy fall of rain)

drizzle ['drɪzl] *v.* 下毛毛雨(to rain or let fall in fine, mistlike drops) *n.* 毛毛雨
(a fine, mistlike rain)
【例】A cold *drizzle* was falling.
【反】deluge(*n.* 暴雨 *vt.* 使淹没)

monsoon [ˌmɑːn'suːn] *n.* (印度的)季雨, 季风(the season wind or rain of the
Indian Ocean)
【记】来自阿拉伯语, 意为"季节"

tempest [ˈtempɪst] *n.* 暴风雨，暴风雪（a violent storm）；骚动（tumult; uproar）
【记】temp（看做temper，脾气）+ est → 老天爷发脾气 → 暴风雨，暴风雪

inclement [ɪnˈklemənt] *adj.* （天气）严酷的（severe; stormy）；严厉的（rough; severe）
【记】in(不) + clement(仁慈的) → 不仁慈的 → 严厉的
【反】balmy(*adj.* 温和的)

blizzard [ˈblɪzərd] *n.* 暴风雪（a severe snowstorm）

frigid [ˈfrɪdʒɪd] *adj.* 寒冷的(very cold)；冷淡的，死板的(lacking in warmth and life)

hail [heɪl] *n.* 冰雹(frozen rain drop) *vi.* 下冰雹

gloaming [ˈgloʊmɪŋ] *n.* 黄昏，薄暮(evening dust; twilight)

vernal [ˈvɜːrnl] *adj.* 春季的，春季似的(fresh or new like the spring)
【例】The linnet chirps her *vernal* song.

aureole [ˈɔːrioʊl] *n.* 日冕，光轮(sun's corona; halo)
【记】来自拉丁文aureolus(*adj.* 金黄色的)

***landslide** [ˈlændslaɪd] *n.* 山崩；压倒性胜利(overwhelming victory)
【记】land(地) + slide(滑行) → 地向下滑 → 山崩

天　文

****galaxy** [ˈgæləksi] *n.* 星系；银河系

***lunar** [ˈluːnər] *adj.* 月的，月亮的

***Mars** [mɑːrz] *n.* 火星；战神

***Venus** [ˈviːnəs] *n.* 金星

***Jupiter** [ˈdʒuːpɪtər] *n.* 木星

***dwarf** [dwɔːrf] *n.* 矮星

****cluster** [ˈklʌstər] *n.* 星团

****asteroid** [ˈæstərɔɪd] *n.* 小游星，小行星

***satellite** [ˈsætəlaɪt] *n.* 卫星(a natural body in space orbiting round a larger body, especially a planet)
【例】The moon is the Earth's *satellite*.

sidereal [saɪˈdɪriəl] *adj.* 星的；恒星的(of stars or constellations; astral)
【记】sider(星) + eal → 星的

***telescope** [ˈtelɪskoʊp] *n.* 望远镜

spatial [ˈspeɪʃl] *adj.* 有关空间的，在空间的（of or connected with space）

aloft [əˈlɔːft] *adv.* 在空中，在上面，在头顶上（in the air）
【记】a + loft（阁楼，鸽房）→ 在阁楼上 → 在上面
【反】grounded（*adj.* 接地的）

*apogee [ˈæpədʒiː] *n.* 远地点（卫星距离地球最远的点）（the point in the orbit of an object, as a satellite, orbiting the earth that is at the greatest distance from the center of the earth）
【记】apo（远）+ gee（=geo 地球）→ 远地点
【反】perigee（*n.* 近地点）

eclipse [ɪˈklɪps] *n.* （日、月）蚀；黯然失色
【记】ec + lipse（看做 leave，离开）→ 太阳射向地球的全部或部分光线离开 →（日、月）蚀；和 lapse（*vi.* 时间流逝）一起记
【例】a total / partial *eclipse* of the sun // She used to be a famous actress, but she's now in *eclipse*.

*calendar [ˈkælɪndər] *n.* 日历（chart showing the days, weeks and months of a particular year）
【例】Do you have next year's *calendar*?

universal [ˌjuːnɪˈvɜːrsl] *adj.* 宇宙的

cosmic [ˈkɑːzmɪk] *adj.* 宇宙的
【例】*cosmic* radiation // *cosmic* rays

celestial [səˈlestʃl] *adj.* 天上的，天体的；神圣的（astronomical; heavenly）
【记】cel（天）+ est + ial → 天上的
【例】The book showed a map of the *celestial* realms.

*astronomical [ˌæstrəˈnɑːmɪkl] *adj.* 天文的，天文学的；（数量）庞大的
【例】*astronomical* observatory

zodiac [ˈzoʊdiæk] *n.* 黄道带

aerial [ˈeriəl] *adj.* 空中的，空气中的（of, relating to, or occurring in the air or atmosphere）

constellation [ˌkɑːnstəˈleɪʃn] *n.* 星座；星群（an arbitrary configuration of stars）
【记】con（一起）+ stell（星星）+ ation → 星星在一起 → 星群

meteoric [ˌmiːtiˈɔːrɪk] *adj.* 流星的（relating to a meteor）；流星似的，昙花一现的（transient; swift）
【记】来自 meteor（*n.* 流星，陨石）
【反】gradual（*adj.* 逐渐的）；plodding（*adj.* 缓慢进行的）

aeronautics [ˌerəˈnɔːtɪks] *n.* 航空学
【记】aero（空气）+ naut（航行）+ ics → 航空学

| nova | ['noʊvə] *n.* 新星（a star that suddenly becomes much brighter and then returns to its original brightness）|

*supernovae | [ˌsuːpər'noʊvə] *n.* 超新星

【例】*Supernovae* are the extremely bright explosions that mark the end of the life of some stars.

**stellar | ['stelər] *adj.* 恒星的

*nebulous | ['nebjələs] *adj.* 星云的，云状的（cloudlike）；模糊不清的（hazy; vague; indistinct）

【记】来自 nebula（*n.* 星云）

【反】distinct（*adj.* 明显的）；clear-cut（*adj.* 清晰的）

horoscope | ['hɔːrəskoʊp] *n.* 占星术（an astrological forecast）；算命天宫图（diagram of the positions of stars at a given moment used by astrologers）

Not only so, but we also rejoice in our sufferings, because we know that suffering produces perseverance; perseverance, character; and character, hope. And hope does not disappoint us...

不但如此，就是在患难中也是欢欢喜喜的。因为知道患难生忍耐，忍耐生老练，老练生盼望，盼望不至于羞耻……

——《圣经·新约·罗》5:3

练习题

填空题

ledge	terrain	watershed	charcoal	marble
gust	sediment	drought	landslide	stuffy
temperate	continental	endemic	arid	torrid
muggy	underwater	outburst	bluster	erupt

1. The country's entire grain harvest has been hit by _____.
2. The house was buried beneath a _____.
3. It gets very hot and _____ here in summer.
4. Britain has a _____ climate.
5. Prices are often higher in Hawaii than in the _____ United States.
6. Malaria is _____ in many hot countries.
7. The pioneers hoped to transform the _____ outback into a workable landscape.
8. She almost can tolerate any kind of _____ days.
9. She was alarmed by his violent _____.
10. Outside the wind was _____.
11. The volcano could _____ at any time.
12. They walked for miles across steep and inhospitable _____.
13. The middle decades of the 19th century marked a _____ in Russia's history.
14. The artist sketched the pattern in _____ on the cloth.
15. A _____ of wind blew his hat off.
16. The climbers rested on a sheltered _____ jutting out from the cliff.
17. At the center of the square stands a monument in black _____.
18. She scooped out the yeasty _____.
19. Yesterday was a _____ August day.
20. Take a deep breath and see how long you can stay _____.

配对题

1. galaxy	花岗岩	11. lava	加勒比人的
2. shoreline	群岛	12. limestone	海洋学的
3. coastline	礁，礁脉	13. magma	刮风的
4. seafloor	水路，航道	14. meteorology	地理的
5. navigation	星系；银河系	15. cataclysmic	气象学
6. waterway	海岸线地带	16. geographic	大变动的
7. reef	海岸线	17. gusty	岩浆
8. archipelago	海底	18. oceanographic	石灰石
9. granite	航海	19. caribbean	熔岩
10. fissure	地球和大气层外的	20. extraterrestrial	裂缝

填空题答案

1. The country's entire grain harvest has been hit by <u>drought</u> .
2. The house was buried beneath a <u>landslide</u> .
3. It gets very hot and <u>stuffy</u> here in summer.
4. Britain has a <u>temperate</u> climate.
5. Prices are often higher in Hawaii than in the <u>continental</u> United States.
6. Malaria is <u>endemic</u> in many hot countries.
7. The pioneers hoped to transform the <u>arid</u> outback into a workable landscape.
8. She almost can tolerate any kind of <u>torrid</u> days.
9. She was alarmed by his violent <u>outburst</u> .
10. Outside the wind was <u>blustering</u>.
11. The volcano could <u>erupt</u> at any time.
12. They walked for miles across steep and inhospitable <u>terrain</u> .
13. The middle decades of the 19th century marked a <u>watershed</u> in Russia's history.
14. The artist sketched the pattern in <u>charcoal</u>on the cloth.
15. A <u>gust</u> of wind blew his hat off.
16. The climbers rested on a sheltered <u>ledge</u> jutting out from the cliff.
17. At the center of the square stands a monument in black <u>marble</u> .
18. She scooped out the yeasty <u>sediments</u> .
19. Yesterday was a <u>muggy</u> August day.
20. Take a deep breath and see how long you can stay <u>underwater</u> .

配对题答案

1. galaxy	星系；银河系	11. lava	熔岩
2. shoreline	海岸线地带	12. limestone	石灰石
3. coastline	海岸线	13. magma	岩浆
4. seafloor	海底	14. meteorology	气象学
5. navigation	航海	15. cataclysmic	大变动的
6. waterway	水路，航道	16. geographic	地理的
7. reef	礁，礁脉	17. gusty	刮风的
8. archipelago	群岛	18. oceanographic	海洋学的
9. granite	花岗岩	19. caribbean	加勒比人的
10. fissure	裂缝	20. extraterrestrial	地球和大气层外的

Word List 3
动物学(一)

动物学(一)

**carnivore ['kɑːrnɪvɔːr] *n.* 食肉动物

**amphibian [æm'fɪbiən] *adj.* 两栖类的；水陆两用的

*gregarious [grɪ'geriəs] *adj.* 群居的；合群的，爱社交的
【记】greg(群体)＋ari＋ous(⋯的) → 群居的
【例】*gregarious* bird species // My *gregarious* sister makes friends wherever she goes.

*carnivorous [kɑːr'nɪvərəs] *adj.* 食肉动物的(flesh-eating)
【记】carn(肉)＋i＋vor(吃)＋ous(⋯的) → 食肉动物的

**herbivorous [hɜːr'bɪvərəs] *adj.* 食草的

**aquatic [ə'kwætɪk] *adj.* 水的，水上的；水生的，水栖的

*cannibalistic [ˌkænɪbə'lɪstɪk] *adj.* 同类相食的，自相残杀的
【例】He has to carry that Bible through a landscape populated by murderous, illiterate, *cannibalistic* roughnecks to a safe place he saw in a dream.

**spineless ['spaɪnləs] *adj.* 无脊椎的

anthropoid ['ænθrəpɔɪd] *adj.* 像人类的(resembling a human) *n.* 类人猿
【记】anthrop(人类)＋oid(像⋯一样) → 像人类的

omnivorous [ɑːm'nɪvərəs] *adj.* 杂食的；兴趣广泛的

*primate ['praɪmeɪt] *n.* 灵长类动物(member of the most highly developed order of mammals that includes human beings, apes, monkeys and lemurs)
【记】prim (最初的)＋ate → 灵长类动物是人类最初的形态 → 灵长类动物

**predator ['predətər] *n.* 掠夺者，食肉动物

*herd [hɜːrd] *n.* 兽群，牧群

entomology [ˌentə'mɑːlədʒi] *n.* 昆虫学(the study of insects)
【记】entomo(n)(希腊语，昆虫)＋logy(⋯学) → 昆虫学

**scavenger [ˈskævɪndʒər] *n.* 清道夫，食腐动物

*furry [ˈfɜːri] *adj.* 毛皮的

*canine [ˈkeɪnaɪn] *adj.* 犬的，似犬的(of or like a dog)

【记】can(犬)＋ine → 犬的

*feathery [ˈfeðəri] *adj.* 有羽毛的；柔软如羽毛的

*dormant [ˈdɔːrmənt] *adj.* 休眠的(inactive)

【记】dorm(睡觉)＋ant → 休眠的

【例】The *dormant* volcano has not erupted for two hundred years.

*feathered [ˈfeðərd] *adj.* 有羽毛的；移动迅速的

*hind [haɪnd] *adj.* (指成对的事物之一位于)后面的，在后部的(of things in pairs situated at the back)

【例】a dog's *hind* legs

swarm [swɔːrm] *n.* (蜜蜂、蚂蚁等)群(throng; crowd; horde)

*tusk [tʌsk] *n.* (大象、野猪等的)长牙(an elongated, greatly enlarged tooth)

【记】和task(*n.* 任务)一起记

chameleon [kəˈmiːliən] *n.* 变色龙，蜥蜴；善变之人 (someone who is very changeable)

*wing [wɪŋ] *n.* 翅膀，翼

*grease [griːs] *n.* 动物油脂

phoenix [ˈfiːnɪks] *n.* 凤凰，永生或再生的象征 (an imaginary bird believed to live for 500 years and then burn itself and be born again from the ashes)

**beaver [ˈbiːvər] *n.* 海狸(毛皮)

*sponge [spʌndʒ] *n.* 海绵，海绵体，海绵状物

badger [ˈbædʒər] *n.* 獾 *v.* 一再烦扰，一再要求(to torment; nag)

*dinosaur [ˈdaɪnəsɔːr] *n.* 恐龙

**cheetah [ˈtʃiːtə] *n.* 猎豹 (产于非洲和西南亚)(a long-legged, swift-running wild cat of Africa and southwest Asia)

【记】和cheese(*n.* 奶酪)一起记，A cheetah doesn't like to eat cheese.

*caterpillar [ˈkætərpɪlər] *n.* 毛虫

*oyster [ˈɔɪstər] *n.* 牡蛎，蚝

**dragonfly [ˈdrægənflaɪ] *n.* 蜻蜓

*appetite [ˈæpɪtaɪt] *n.* 食欲

*jellyfish [ˈdʒelifɪʃ] *n.* 水母

【记】jelly(果冻)＋fish(鱼) → 像果冻一样透明的鱼 → 水母

*hawk [hɔːk] *n.* 隼，鹰(a kind of eagle)

*bloodsucking	[ˈblʌdsʌkɪŋ] n. 吸血动物；吸血鬼	
*shrimp	[ʃrɪmp] n. 小虾	
incrustation	[ˌɪnkrʌˈsteɪʃn] n. 硬壳，外层（hard coating or crust）	

【记】in（里面）+ crust（壳）+ ation → 硬壳

*spawn	[spɔːn] n. 卵 v. 产（卵）（to generate; produce）
*zebra	[ˈziːbrə] n. 斑马
**leopard	[ˈlepərd] n. 豹（a large African and Southern Asian flesh-eating animal of the cat family with a yellowish coat and dark spots）
**giraffe	[dʒəˈræf] n. 长颈鹿
**alligator	[ˈælɪɡeɪtər] n. 短吻鳄
*crocodile	[ˈkrɑːkədaɪl] n. 鳄鱼（a large river reptile with a hard skin, a long body and tail, and very big tapering jaws, that lives in hot parts of the world）
**pigeon	[ˈpɪdʒɪn] n. 鸽子（any of several types of wild or tame bird of the dove family）
*seabird	[ˈsiːbɜːrd] n. 海鸟
*beetle	[ˈbiːtl] n. 甲虫
slough	[slaʊ] v.（蛇等）蜕（皮）（to cast off one's skin）n.（蛇等蜕下的）皮

【记】蛇蜕皮（slough）是一个缓慢的（slow）过程。

*synaptic	[saɪˈnæptɪk] adj. 突触的，（染色体）联合的
*tactor	[ˈtæktər] n. 触器 → 神经电缆
*vermin	[ˈvɜːrmɪn] n. 害虫，寄生虫（small common harmful or objectionable animals）

【记】verm（害虫）+ in → 害虫

*pest	[pest] n. 有害的动植物
*ram	[ræm] n. 公羊；撞击，猛撞；填塞
*beluga	[bəˈluːɡə] n. 白鲸
*termite	[ˈtɜːrmaɪt] n. 白蚁

【记】ter + mite（小虫）→ 白蚁

*salmon	[ˈsæmən] n. 大麻哈鱼；鲜肉色（yellowish-pink）
*chimpanzee	[ˌtʃɪmpænˈziː] n. 黑猩猩
**menhaden	[menˈheɪdn] n. 鲱鱼
*walrus	[ˈwɔːlrəs] n. 海象（a large gregarious marine mammal）
**porcupine	[ˈpɔːrkjupaɪn] n. 豪猪，箭猪

【记】porcu（猪）+ pine（=spine 刺）→ 有刺的猪 → 豪猪，箭猪

*canary	[kəˈneri] n. 金丝雀；淡黄色

| quarry | ['kwɔːri] n. 猎物（one that is sought or pursued; prey）|
| | 【记】和quarrel(v. 争吵)一起记 |

*falcon	['fælkən] n. 猎鹰；隼
scale	[skeɪl] n. 鳞片
gadfly	['gædflaɪ] n. 虻，牛虻（a kind of fly that swarms around cattle）；讨厌的人（an annoying person）
	【记】gad(尖头棒)+fly(蝇)→像尖头棒一样蜇牲畜的、体形类似苍蝇的昆虫→牛虻
*gigas	['dʒaɪgəs] n. 牡蛎
*birdseed	['bɜːrdsiːd] n. 鸟饵，鸟食
*plumage	['pluːmɪdʒ] n. 鸟类的全身羽毛
	【例】They threw off their soft white plumage.
*beak	[biːk] n. 鸟嘴，喙
*crab	[kræb] n. 蟹；蟹肉
**copepod	['koʊpɪˌpɑːd] n./adj. 桡脚类动物(的)
**muskrat	['mʌskræt] n. 麝鼠
*vulture	['vʌltʃər] n. 秃鹫
	【记】和culture(n. 文化，文明)一起记
**humpback	['hʌmpbæk] n. 驼背；座头鲸
*fawn	[fɔːn] n. 未满周岁的小鹿（a young deer less than one year old）
*murrelet	['mɜːrlɪt] n. 小海鸦
*codfish	['kɑːdˌfɪʃ] n. 鳕，鳕鱼
*lair	[ler] n. 野兽的巢穴（a resting place of a wild animal）；躲藏处
*plume	[pluːm] n. 羽毛（a feather of a bird）v. 整理羽毛（to preen and arrange the feathers of）；搔首弄姿（to indulge in pride with an obvious or vain display of self-satisfaction）
	【记】和preen(v. 整理羽毛)一起记
*mustang	['mʌstæŋ] n. (北美平原产的)小野马
*hart	[hɑːrt] n. 雄鹿（尤指五岁以上的雄红鹿）（adult male of deer; stag）
wallow	['wɑːloʊ] vi. （猪等在泥水中）打滚；沉溺于 n. 打滚；堕落
	【记】wal(看做wall, 墙)+low(低的)→在墙底下打滚→打滚
*hamster	['hæmstər] n. 仓鼠
**vervet	['vɜːrvɪt] n. 长尾黑颚猴
*bumblebee	['bʌmblbiː] n. 大黄蜂

*ermine	[ˈɜːrmɪn] *n.* 貂
*thrush	[θrʌʃ] *n.* 画眉；鸫科
*raccoon	[ræˈkuːn] *n.* 浣熊；浣熊皮毛
*coyote	[kaɪˈoʊti] *n.* 郊狼（北美洲西部平原上的小狼）(a small wolf of the plains of western North America)
*blubber	[ˈblʌbər] *n.* 鲸脂（fat of whales and other sea animals from which oil is obtained)
**python	[ˈpaɪθən] *n.* 巨蛇，蟒蛇（a large snake that crushes and kills its prey by twisting itself round it)
*peafowl	[ˈpiːfaʊl] *n.* 孔雀

【例】More recently, a thriving exotic-wildlife trade sent a ragged parade of escapees into the wild: parakeets, *peafowl*, swamp eels, and squirrel monkeys.

*cere	[sɪə] *n.* (鸟喙底部的)蜡膜
**mastodon	[ˈmæstədən] *n.* 乳齿象（似象之巨兽，现已绝种）(a large animal like an elephant, now extinct)
**pesticide	[ˈpestɪsaɪd] *n.* 杀虫剂
*koala	[koʊˈɑːlə] *n.* 考拉，树袋熊
*aquarium	[əˈkweriəm] *n.* 水族馆，水族箱，养鱼缸(a building containing an artificial pond or glass tank where live fish and other water creatures and plants are kept)

练 习 题

填空题

amphibian	aquatic	canine	cannibalistic	carnivore
carnivorous	dormant	feathered	feathery	furry
gregarious	herbivorous	hind	leopard	pesticide
predator	primate	scavenger	spineless	sponge

1. His mind was like a _____, ready to absorb anything.
2. Chimps are among the most intelligent _____.
3. Foxes and other _____ go through the dustbins.
4. You didn't really expect her to be on time, did you? A _____ can't change its spots.
5. Frogs and newts are _____.
6. It has a thick, _____, brown or black coat.
7. Do wolves belong to the _____ species?
8. All human beings have a _____ instinct.
9. It is snowing with _____ snowflakes.
10. Bears are large _____ mammals.
11. The camel is a _____ animal.
12. Many forms of _____ life inhabit ponds.
13. Game birds are very _____ under any circumstances.
14. At a time of crisis, why are Britain's politicians so _____?
15. During the winter the seeds lie _____ in the soil.
16. The little bird will grow feathers or become _____ soon.
17. The horse reared up on its _____ legs.
18. Young birds are very vulnerable to _____.
19. Tyrannosaurus rex was a large _____.
20. The flea-infested room had to be sprayed with a strong _____.

配对题

1. tusk	短吻鳄	11. copepod	驼背；座头鲸
2. wing	海狸(毛皮)	12. muskrat	乳齿象
3. grease	毛虫	13. herd	鲱鱼
4. menhaden	猎豹	14. humpback	麝鼠
5. beaver	桡脚类动物	15. giraffe	鸽子
6. porcupine	恐龙	16. vervet	豪猪，箭猪
7. dinosaur	蜻蜓	17. alligator	巨蛇，蟒蛇
8. cheetah	长颈鹿	18. pigeon	(大象、野猪等的)长牙
9. caterpillar	动物油脂	19. python	长尾黑颚猴
10. dragonfly	兽群，牧群	20. mastodon	翅膀，翼

练习题答案

填空题答案

1. His mind was like a <u>sponge</u>, ready to absorb anything.
2. Chimps are among the most intelligent <u>primate</u>.
3. Foxes and other <u>scavengers</u> go through the dustbins.
4. You didn't really expect her to be on time, did you? A <u>leopard</u> can't change its spots.
5. Frogs and newts are <u>amphibians</u>.
6. It has a thick, <u>furry</u>, brown or black coat.
7. Do wolves belong to the <u>canine</u> species?
8. All human beings have a <u>gregarious</u> instinct.
9. It is snowing with <u>feathery</u> snowflakes.
10. Bears are large <u>carnivorous</u> mammals.
11. The camel is a <u>herbivorous</u> animal.
12. Many forms of <u>aquatic</u> life inhabit ponds.
13. Game birds are very <u>cannibalistic</u> under any circumstances.
14. At a time of crisis, why are Britain's politicians so <u>spineless</u>?
15. During the winter the seeds lie <u>dormant</u> in the soil.
16. The little bird will grow feathers or become <u>feathered</u> soon.
17. The horse reared up on its <u>hind</u> legs.
18. Young birds are very vulnerable to <u>predators</u>.
19. Tyrannosaurus rex was a large <u>carnivore</u>.
20. The flea-infested room had to be sprayed with a strong <u>pesticide</u>.

配对题答案

1. tusk	(大象、野猪等的)长牙	11. copepod	桡脚类动物
2. wing	翅膀，翼	12. muskrat	麝鼠
3. grease	动物油脂	13. herd	兽群，牧群
4. menhaden	鲱鱼	14. humpback	驼背；座头鲸
5. beaver	海狸(毛皮)	15. giraffe	长颈鹿
6. porcupine	豪猪，箭猪	16. vervet	长尾黑颚猴
7. dinosaur	恐龙	17. alligator	短吻鳄
8. cheetah	猎豹	18. pigeon	鸽子
9. caterpillar	毛虫	19. python	巨蛇，蟒蛇
10. dragonfly	蜻蜓	20. mastodon	乳齿象

Word List 4

动物学(二)·生物学

动物学(二)

hibernate [ˈhaɪbərneɪt] *vi.* 冬眠
【例】Polar bear can *hibernate* for a long time.

*incubate [ˈɪŋkjubeɪt] *vt.* 孵化(to keep eggs warm until they hatch)
【记】in(里面) + cub(睡) + ate → 睡在里面 → 孵化

**camouflage [ˈkæməflɑːʒ] *v./n.* 伪装,掩饰
【例】use the branches of trees as *camouflage* // They *camouflaged* their hatred with professions of friendship.

**trot [trɑːt] *vi./n.* (马等)小跑,慢跑(jog)
【例】The horses *trotted* along the road.

*domesticate [dəˈmestɪkeɪt] *vt.* 驯养,教化(to tame)
【例】No one has ever been able to *domesticate* the African elephant.

aerie [ˈɪri] *n.* 猛禽的窝(nest of a large bird of prey);高处的房子或城堡

aviary [ˈeɪvieri] *n.* 大鸟笼,鸟舍(a large cage to keep many birds)
【记】avi(鸟) + ary(场所) → 大鸟笼,鸟舍

grasshopper [ˈɡræshɑːpər] *n.* 蝗虫,蚂蚱(a jumping insect that makes a shrill chirping noise)

lobster [ˈlɑːbstər] *n.* 龙虾

mammal [ˈmæml] *n.* 哺乳动物
【记】mamma(乳) + l → 哺乳动物

prey [preɪ] *n.* 被掠食者,牺牲者

scavenge [ˈskævɪndʒ] *n.* 清道夫,食腐动物

zoophagous [zoʊˈɑːfəɡəs] *adj.* 食肉的

cohabit [koʊˈhæbɪt] *vi.* 共栖,同居(to live together)
【记】co(共同) + habit(居住) → 共栖,同居

dormancy [ˈdɔːrmənsi] *n.* 休眠状态(state of being temporarily inactive)
【记】dorm(睡觉) + ancy → 休眠状态
【反】activity(*n.* 活动)

	drove	[droʊv] *n.* 畜群(flock; herd)；人群(a moving crowd of people)
		【记】和drive的过去式drove拼写一样
	firefly	[ˈfaɪərflaɪ] *n.* 萤火虫
		【记】fire(火) + fly(蝇) → 火蝇 → 萤火虫
	gorilla	[gəˈrɪlə] *n.* 大猩猩(very large powerful African ape)
	ivory	[ˈaɪvəri] *n.* 象牙，长牙(the tusks of elephants, walruses, etc)
	ostrich	[ˈɑːstrɪtʃ] *n.* 鸵鸟；不接受现实的人(one who refuses to face the unpleasant realities)
		【记】ost+rich(富有的) → 富有的人才能穿得起鸵鸟羽毛的衣服 → 鸵鸟
	parasite	[ˈpærəsaɪt] *n.* 食客(a person who lives off others and gives nothing in return)；寄生物(an animal or a plant that lives on or in another and gets its food from it)
		【记】para(旁边) + site(食物) → 在旁边白拿食物 → 食客；寄生物
		【派】parasitic(*adj.* 寄生的)
	reptile	[ˈreptaɪl] *n.* 爬行动物(any of the class of cold-blooded, egg-laying animals)；卑鄙的人(a groveling or despised person)
		【记】rept(爬行) + ile → 爬行动物
	ruminant	[ˈruːmɪnənt] *adj.* (动物)反刍的；沉思的(meditative; thoughtful)
		【记】rumin(=rumen 反刍动物的第一胃"瘤胃") + ant → 反刍的
	swine	[swaɪn] *n.* 猪(pig)
		【记】s + wine(酒) → 喝酒喝多了，像猪一样邋遢 → 猪
	hedgehog	[ˈhedʒhɔːg] *n.* 刺猬；[美]豪猪
		【记】hedge(树篱) + hog(猪) → 在树篱间活动的猪 → 豪猪
	hippopotamus	[ˌhɪpəˈpɑːtəməs] *n.* 河马
		【记】hippo(马) + potam(河流) + us → 河马
	rodent	[ˈroʊdnt] *n.* 啮齿类动物(如鼠等)
		【例】That winged *rodent* has been our only obstacle.
	blare	[bler] *v.* 刺耳地高声鸣响(to sound or utter raucously)
		【记】和bleat(*v.* 小牛/小羊叫)一起记
		【例】Before Steven could answer him, the trumpets *blared*.
	molt	[moʊlt] *v.* 换(羽)，脱(毛) *n.* 换羽(期)，脱毛(期)
		【反】fledge(*v.* 长羽毛)
	warble	[ˈwɔːrbl] *v.* (尤指鸟)发出柔和的颤音，啭叫(especially of a bird sing in a continuous gentle trilling way)
		【例】larks *warbling* in the sky

apiary ['eɪpɪerɪ] *n.* 养蜂场，蜂房（a place where bees are kept）

【记】api(蜂)＋ary(表场所) → 养蜂场，蜂房

aquiline ['ækwɪlaɪn] *adj.* 鹰的，似鹰的（of, relating to, or resembling an eagle）

【记】aquil(鹰)＋ine → 鹰的

behemoth [bɪ'hiːmɔːθ] *n.* 巨兽，庞然大物（huge creature; something of monstrous size or power）

equine ['iːkwaɪn] *adj.* 马的，似马的（characteristic of a horse）

【派】equitation(*n.* 骑马术)

ewe [juː] *n.* 母羊（female sheep）

grouse [graʊs] *n.* 松鸡 *vi.* 发牢骚，诉苦（to complain; grumble）

【记】g(看做GRE)＋rouse(唤起) → GRE太难唤起考生的牢骚满腹 → 发牢骚

【反】rejoice(*v.* 喜悦)

ichthyology [ˌɪkθi'ɑːlədʒi] *n.* 鱼类学（study of fish）

【例】Jacques Cousteau's programs about sea life have advanced the cause of *ichthyology*.

marsupial [mɑːr'suːpiəl] *n.* 有袋动物 *adj.* 有袋的

【记】"马修皮" → 马多修了一张皮，动物多了一张皮做口袋 → 有袋动物

mite [maɪt] *n.* 小虫；极小量（a very little）

【记】mite原意为"螨虫"

ornithologist [ˌɔːrnɪ'θɑːlədʒɪst] *n.* 鸟类学家，鸟类学者（expert in ornithology）

【记】ornitho(鸟)＋logist(…学家) → 鸟类学家

ornithology [ˌɔːrnɪ'θɑːlədʒi] *n.* 鸟类学（the branch of zoology dealing with birds）

pterodactyl [ˌterə'dæktɪl] *n.* 翼龙（extinct flying reptile）

【例】The remains of *pterodactyls* indicate that these flying reptiles had a wingspan of as much as twenty feet.

quadruped ['kwɑːdruped] *n.* 四足兽（four-footed animal）

【记】quadr(四)＋u＋ped(足) → 四足兽

simian ['sɪmiən] *adj.* 猿的，猴的（resembling apes）*n.* 猴，类人猿（monkey, ape）

【记】simi(＝simil 相似的)＋an → 和人类相似的动物 → 猴，类人猿

talon ['tælən] *n.* 猛禽的锐爪（claw of a bird of prey）

【记】tal（看做tall, 高）＋on（在…上） → 在高空中的猛禽的锐爪 → 猛禽的锐爪

tarantula [tə'ræntʃələ] *n.* (*pl.* tarantulas, tarantulae)（产于欧洲等地的）狼蛛，多毛毒蜘蛛

whelp [welp] n. 犬科的幼兽（a young offspring of a mammal, such as a wolf or dog）

antenna [æn'tenə] n.（pl. antennae）触角（a sensitive feeler）；天线（a device that collects or receives electromagnetic signals）
【记】ante(前面) + nna(表名词) → 前面的东西 → 触角

carapace ['kærəpeɪs] n.（蟹或龟等的）甲壳
【记】car(汽车) + a + pace(步伐) → 汽车一步一停，慢得像乌龟 → 龟的甲壳

cocoon [kə'kuːn] n. 茧（silky covering made by an insect larva）
【记】coco(椰子树) + on → 椰子和茧的形状相近 → 茧

cougar ['kuːgər] n. 美洲豹，美洲狮
【记】"酷哥" → "美洲豹"很漂亮，像酷哥一样；注意cougar也被叫做 puma，panther

cub [kʌb] n. 幼兽（one of the young of certain animals）；年轻无经验的人（an inexperienced and awkward youth）
【记】和cube(n. 立方体)一起记；cub作为词根是"睡觉"之意，如：incubation(n. 孵卵，孵化)

fledge [fledʒ] v. 长羽毛（to acquire the feathers necessary for flight or independent activity）；给(箭)装上羽毛；喂养小鸟
【记】fl(看做fly) + edge(边缘) → 鸟在飞翔的边缘 → 幼鸟刚学会飞 → 长羽毛
【反】molt(v. 脱毛)

invertebrate [ɪn'vɜːrtɪbrət] adj./n. 无脊椎的（动物）(any type of animal lacking a spinal column）
【记】来自vertebrate(adj./n. 有脊椎的(动物))

kennel ['kenl] n. 狗舍，狗窝(a doghouse)
【记】ken(=can 犬) + nel → 狗窝；注意不要和kernel(n. 核心)相混

larva ['lɑːrvə] n.（昆虫的）幼虫

panther ['pænθər] n. 美洲狮，美洲豹；黑豹(a black leopard)
【记】美国汽车品牌Panther"美洲豹"

ecdysis ['ekdɪsɪs] n.（动物）蜕皮，脱壳，换羽(the shedding of an outer layer of skin or integument）
【记】和ecdysiast(n. 脱衣舞舞女)一起记

*crustacean [krʌ'steɪʃn] n. 甲壳类动物

**robin ['rɑːbɪn] n. 欧鸲；知更鸟

生物学

**microscope ['maɪkrəskoʊp] *n.* 显微镜

**protein ['proʊtiːn] *n.* 蛋白质 *adj.* 蛋白质的

**mosquito [mə'skiːtoʊ] *n.* 蚊子

【记】"貌似黑头" → 像鼻子上的黑头 → 蚊子

**bacteria [bæk'tɪriə] *n.* 细菌

*digestion [daɪ'dʒestʃən] *n.* 消化，吸收

【记】来自digest(*v.* 消化)，di(下去) + gest(带) → 带下去 → 消化

*immature [ˌɪmə'tʃʊr] *adj.* 发育未全的，不成熟的

【记】im(不) + mature(成熟) → 不成熟的

【例】She said I was too *immature* to get married.

*vital ['vaɪtl] *adj.* 活的，有生命的；维持生命必需的

*biotic [baɪ'ɑːtɪk] *adj.* 生物的；有关生命的(biological)

【例】The digestive system, cholesterol level and immune system are all claimed to benefit from these *biotic* drinks.

*nostril ['nɑːstrəl] *n.* 鼻孔

*ripeness ['raɪpnəs] *n.* 成熟，老练(maturity)

【例】Roasting fruit perfectly depends on its *ripeness*, so baste the pears and check on them often.

*squid [skwɪd] *n.* 枪乌贼，鱿鱼

【例】Would you like some *squid*?

*flea [fliː] *n.* 跳蚤 (a small jumping insect without wings that feeds on the blood of animals and humans)

【例】I must have been bitten by a *flea*; my arms are itchy.

*exhalation [ˌekshə'leɪʃn] *n.* 呼气；蒸发，散发(evaporation; vaporization)；散发物

【例】She shook her head again, this time with a horsey, nasal *exhalation* of disgust.

*immune [ɪ'mjuːn] *adj.* 免疫的(unaffected; unsusceptible)；免除的

【记】im(没有) + mune(责任) → 没有责任 → 免除的

【例】I had the mumps when I was six, so now I am *immune*.

*biosphere ['baɪoʊsfɪr] *n.* 生命层，生物圈

【记】bio(生命) + sphere(球，圈) → 生物圈

**microorganism [ˌmaɪkroʊ'ɔːrɡnɪzəm] *n.* 微生物，细菌(bacterium)

【记】micro(微小) + organism(生物) → 微生物

biodiversity [ˌbaɪoʊdaɪ'vɜːrsəti] *n.* 生物多样性(biological diversity)

【例】The judges also found that the poster demonstrated a clear understanding of the challenges to *biodiversity*.

homogeneity [ˌhɑːmədʒə'niːəti] *n.* 同质，同种(homogeneousness)

【例】Some bloggers said Poland's ethnic *homogeneity* may have played a role in changing the photo.

*antibiotic** [ˌæntibaɪ'ɑːtɪk] *n.* 抗菌素，抗生素(如青霉素) *adj.* 抗菌的，抗生的

*proliferate** [prə'lɪfəreɪt] *v.* （使）繁衍，（使）增殖；（使）增加（to multiply; increase）

【记】pro(前)+ lifer(后代)+ ate → 繁衍，增殖

【例】Autumn is the best season for crab to *proliferate*.

*specimen** ['spesɪmən] *n.* 标本，样品(sample; instance)

*subsist** [səb'sɪst] *vi.* 生存(to live; survive)

【例】The poor farmer's family *subsisted* on potatoes.

*propagate** ['prɑːpəgeɪt] *v.* 繁殖(to multiply; proliferate)；传播

【例】Plants won't *propagate* in these conditions. // Missionaries went far afield to *propagate* their faith.

*assimilate** [ə'sɪməleɪt] *vt.* 同化，吸收(to absorb; integrate; incorporate)

【记】as + simil(相同)+ ate → 使相同 → 同化，吸收

【例】I have not quite *assimilated* the new rules so I sometimes violate them by mistake.

differentiation [ˌdɪfəˌrenʃi'eɪʃn] *n.* 变异，分化(variation)；区别(distinction)

【例】Globalisation is leading to new forms of social *differentiation* at the international and national levels.

extinct [ɪk'stɪŋkt] *adj.* 灭绝的

【记】ex + tinct(刺)→ 动物被刺杀 → 灭绝的

instinctual [ɪn'stɪŋktʃuəl] *adj.* 本能的

physiological [ˌfɪziə'lɑːdʒɪkl] *adj.* 生理的（of or concerning the bodily functions）；生理学上的(of or concerning physiology)

【记】来自physiology(*n.* 生理学)

*mutant** ['mjuːtənt] *n.* 突变体，突变型（living thing that differs basically from its parents as a result of genetic change; mutation）

stodgy ['stɑːdʒi] *adj.* 难消化的

symbiosis [ˌsɪmbaɪ'oʊsɪs] *n.* 共生(现象)；合作(互利、互依)关系

*cellular** ['seljələr] *adj.* 细胞的，由细胞组成的(of or consisting of cells)

【例】*cellular* tissue 细胞组织

biomass ['baɪoʊmæs] *n.* (单位面积或体积内的)生物量

metamorphosis [ˌmetə'mɔːrfəsɪs] *n.* 变形，变态，蜕变

【例】Butterflies and moths undergo complete *metamorphosis*.

membrane ['membreɪn] *n.* (动植物体内的)薄膜

【记】mem(看做membrane) + brane(看做brain，头脑) → 人的头脑有保护膜 → 薄膜

fecundity [fɪ'kʌndəti] *n.* 多产，富饶；繁殖力，生殖力

【记】来自fecund(*adj.* 生殖力旺盛的；多产丰饶的)

【反】deprivation(*n.* 剥夺，缺乏)

【派】infecund(*adj.* 不结果的，不孕的)

paleontology [ˌpeɪliɑːn'tɑːlədʒi] *n.* 古生物学

【记】paleo(古，旧) + (o)n(生物) + t + ology(…学) → 古生物学

yeast [jiːst] *n.* 酵母；发酵物；泡沫

【记】y + east（东方）→ 太阳从东方冉冉升起，像美丽的泡沫一样 → 泡沫

mimicry ['mɪmɪkri] *n.* 模仿；拟态(camouflage)

【记】来自mimic(*vt.* 模仿)

【例】The stick caterpillar's vivid *mimicry* enlarged its chances of survival.

bioluminescence [ˌbaɪoʊluːmɪ'nesns] *n.* 生物体之发光

bacillus [bə'sɪləs] *n.* 杆菌；细菌，病菌

biorhythm ['baɪoʊrɪðəm] *n.* 生物节律；生物周期

atavism ['ætəvɪzəm] *n.* 隔代遗传，返祖现象(resemblance to remote ancestors rather than to parents; reversion to an earlier type; throwback)

【派】atavistic(*adj.* 隔代遗传的)

symbiotic [ˌsɪmbaɪ'ɑːtɪk] *adj.* 共生的

练 习 题

填空题

antibiotic	assimilate	biodiversity	biotic	camouflage
cellular	cohabit	domesticate	dormancy	hibernate
immature	immune	incubate	mammal	proliferate
propagate	subsist	trot	vital	zoophagous

1. The whiteness of polar bears and arctic foxes provides _____.
2. Our horses slowed to a _____.
3. The samples were _____ at 80°C for three minutes.
4. Some men are very hard to _____.
5. Bears wake for spring, summer, and fall and _____ for the winter.
6. A whale is no less a _____ than a horse is.
7. With the analysis from the tooth structure, they very possibly have both the _____ and the herbivorous characteristic.
8. They were _____ for three years before their marriage.
9. The volcano erupted after years of _____.
10. The mining project threatens one of the world's richest areas of _____.
11. Some people can only _____ change gradually.
12. Television advertising _____ a false image of the ideal family.
13. Old people often _____ on very small incomes.
14. Books and articles on the subject have _____ over the last year.
15. _____ can be used against infection.
16. The classification of organisms based on _____ structure and function, especially on the structure and number of chromosomes.
17. From our study, we verified that plants did not response to _____ and abiotic stress independently.
18. Adults are often _____ to German measles.
19. He was wounded in a _____ part of his anatomy, e.g. the lungs, brain.
20. He's very _____ for his age.

配对题

1. robin	猛禽的窝；高处的房子或城堡	11. gorilla	蝗虫，蚂蚱
2. crustacean	大鸟笼，鸟舍	12. bacteria	龙虾
3. aerie	杆菌；细菌，病菌	13. protein	微生物，细菌
4. aviary	细菌	14. microscope	显微镜
5. grasshopper	生物体之发光	15. mosquito	蚊子
6. lobster	(单位面积或体积内的)生物量	16. bioluminescence	被掠食者，牺牲者
7. prey	甲壳类动物	17. bacillus	蛋白质
8. scavenge	畜群；人群	18. microorganism	欧鸲；知更鸟
9. drove	萤火虫	19. biomass	清道夫，食腐动物
10. firefly	大猩猩	20. yeast	酵母；发酵物；泡沫

练习题答案

填空题答案

1. The whiteness of polar bears and arctic foxes provides <u>camouflage</u>.
2. Our horses slowed to a <u>trot</u>.
3. The samples were <u>incubated</u> at 80° C for three minutes.
4. Some men are very hard to <u>domesticate</u>.
5. Bears wake for spring, summer, and fall and <u>hibernate</u> for the winter.
6. A whale is no less a <u>mammal</u> than a horse is.
7. With the analysis from the tooth structure, they very possibly have both the <u>zoophagous</u> and the herbivorous characteristic.
8. They were <u>cohabiting</u> for three years before their marriage.
9. The volcano erupted after years of <u>dormancy</u>.
10. The mining project threatens one of the world's richest areas of <u>biodiversity</u>.
11. Some people can only <u>assimilate</u> change gradually.
12. Television advertising <u>propagates</u> a false image of the ideal family.
13. Old people often <u>subsist</u> on very small incomes.
14. Books and articles on the subject have <u>proliferated</u> over the last year.
15. <u>Antibiotic</u> can be used against infection.
16. The classification of organisms based on <u>cellular</u> structure and function, especially on the structure and number of chromosomes.
17. From our study, we verified that plants did not response to <u>biotic</u> and abiotic stress independently.
18. Adults are often <u>immune</u> to German measles.
19. He was wounded in a <u>vital</u> part of his anatomy, e.g. the lungs, brain.
20. He's very <u>immature</u> for his age.

配对题答案

1. robin	欧鸲；知更鸟	11. gorilla	大猩猩
2. crustacean	甲壳类动物	12. bacteria	细菌
3. aerie	猛禽的窝；高处的房	13. protein	蛋白质
	子或城堡	14. microscope	显微镜
4. aviary	大鸟笼，鸟舍	15. mosquito	蚊子
5. grasshopper	蝗虫，蚂蚱	16. bioluminescence	生物体之发光
6. lobster	龙虾	17. bacillus	杆菌；细菌，病菌
7. prey	被掠食者，牺牲者	18. microorganism	微生物，细菌
8. scavenge	清道夫，食腐动物	19. biomass	（单位面积或体积内的）
9. drove	畜群；人群		生物量
10. firefly	萤火虫	20. yeast	酵母；发酵物；泡沫

Word List 5

植物学·自然·环境

植物学

balmy ['bɑːmi] *adj.* 芳香的
【记】来自balm(*n.* 香气)

*orchid ['ɔːrkɪd] *n.* 兰科，兰花；淡紫色

*violet ['vaɪələt] *adj.* 紫罗兰色的 *n.* 紫罗兰

*posy ['pouzi] *n.* (小的)花束(bouquet)

bouquet [buˈkeɪ] *n.* 花束(a bunch of cut flowers)；芳香(fragrance)

bulb [bʌlb] *n.* 植物的球茎(an underground bud as in a lily, onion)；灯泡
【记】light bulb(灯泡)，bulb含有"圆形"的意思，如：bulbous(*adj.* 又胖又圆的；球根的，球根状的)

chrysanthemum [krɪˈsænθəməm] *n.* 菊，菊花
【记】chrys(金黄色) + anthe(花) + mum(名词后缀) → 金黄色的花 → 菊花

gardenia [gɑːrˈdiːniə] *n.* 栀子花
【记】garden(花园) + ia → 花园之花 → 栀子花

petal ['petl] *n.* 花瓣(leaf-like divisions of a flower)

florescence [ˌflɔːˈresns] *n.* 繁花时期(condition or period of flowering)
【记】flor(花) + escence(时期) → 繁花时期

windfall ['wɪndfɔːl] *n.* 风吹落的果实(fallen fruit)；意外的好运(unexpected lucky event)

*fig [fɪg] *n.* 无花果；一点儿(a trifling amount; a little bit)

*luxuriant [lʌɡˈʒʊriənt] *adj.* 繁茂的，多产的
【记】luxur(丰富) + iant → 多产的

**kernel ['kɜːrnl] *n.* 果仁；核心(the central; most important part; essence)
【记】kern(=corn 种子) + el → 核心

**chestnut ['tʃesnʌt] *n.* 栗树；栗子

*reed [riːd] *n.* 芦苇(a grasslike plant); 簧片(a thin piece of wood or metal in a musical instrument)

【派】reedy(*adj.* 芦苇状的，细长的；芦苇做的；似笛声的)

mushroom ['mʌʃrʊm] *n.* 蘑菇 *vi.* 迅速成长(或发展)(to grow or expand rapidly)

cone [koʊn] *n.* 松果；圆锥体 (a solid body that narrows to a point from a circular flat base)

【记】和conifer(*n.* 针叶树)一起记

foliage ['foʊliɪdʒ] *n.* [总称]植物的叶子

biennial [baɪ'eniəl] *adj.* 两年一次的(every two years)

【记】bi(两个，双) + enn(年) + ial → 两年一次的

embryonic [ˌembri'ɑːnɪk] *adj.* 胚胎的；萌芽期的(incipient; rudimentary)

【记】来自embryo(*n.* 胚胎), em(=in) + bryo(变大) → 在里面变大 → 胚胎

**germinal ['dʒɜːrmɪnl] *adj.* 幼芽的，胚种的；原始，根源的 (pertaining to a germ; creative)

【例】The middle *germinal* layer of an early embryo consists of undifferentiated cells destined to become the mesoderm. // Such an idea is *germinal*; I am certain that it will influence thinkers and philosophers for many generations.

**starch [stɑːrtʃ] *n.* 淀粉

**stem [stem] *n.* 茎，干

*fern [fɜːrn] *n.* 蕨类植物

**truffle ['trʌfl] *n.* 块菌 (一种食用菌)(a type of edible fungus that grows underground and is enjoyed for its rich flavour)

*germ [dʒɜːrm] *n.* 种子；胚芽，芽孢 (the embryo with the scutellum of a cereal grain); 微生物，细菌

*crossbreed ['krɔːsbriːd] *n.* 杂种 *v.* (使)异种交配，培育杂种

germinate ['dʒɜːrmɪneɪt] *v.* (使)发芽(to sprout)

【记】来自germ(*n.* 胚芽)

【例】After the seeds *germinated*, I transplanted them to a larger pot.

burgeon ['bɜːrdʒən] *v.* 萌芽；迅速成长，发展(to grow rapidly; proliferate)

【记】burg (=bud 花蕾) + eon → 萌芽之后长出花蕾 → 萌芽；burg本身是单词，意为"城，镇" → 成长的地方 → 迅速成长

【反】subside(*vi.* 下沉；平息；减退); wither(*v.* 衰弱，枯萎); subdue(*vt.* 征服；缓和)

*pollen ［ˈpɑːlən］ *n.* 花粉 *vt.* 传授花粉给⋯

*pollinate ［ˈpɑːləneɪt］ *vt.* 对⋯授粉

【例】Many crops require bees to *pollinate* them.

horticultural ［ˌhɔːrtɪˈkʌltʃərəl］ *adj.* 园艺的

【例】They learn basic *horticultural* skills and how to plan and market the small business.

*cypress ［ˈsaɪprəs］ *n.* 柏树（a coniferous tree）

【记】发音似"杉柏立世" → 像杉树柏树一样挺立在世界上 → 柏树

chaff ［tʃæf］ *n.* 谷物的皮壳，米糠（the husks separated in threshing or winnowing）

【记】发音似"擦麸" → 擦下来的麸糠 → 米糠

*redwood ［ˈredwʊd］ *n.* 红木树

sap ［sæp］ *n.*（树等的）汁液；活力，精力（vigor; vitality）*vt.* 削弱，耗尽（to weaken; exhaust）

【反】bolster（*vt.* 支持）；fortify（*vt.* 支持）

*twig ［twɪg］ *n.* 小树枝（small branch）

【记】和wig（*n.* 假发）一起记

【例】Some insects will mime a *twig* when in danger.

*flax ［flæks］ *n.* 亚麻

【记】和flex（*v.* 弯曲）一起记；亚麻做成的布叫linen（亚麻布）

*transplantation ［ˌtrænsplænˈteɪʃn］ *n.* 移植

【记】来自transplant（*v.* 移植）；trans（转移）+ plant（种）+ ation → 转移种过去 → 移植

*elm ［elm］ *n.* 榆树（a kind of deciduous tree）

*flora ［ˈflɔːrə］ *n.*（某一地区或某一时期的）植物群落

【记】flor（花草）+ a → 植物群落

**botanist ［ˈbɑːtənɪst］ *n.* 植物学家

*grapefruit ［ˈgreɪpfruːt］ *n.* 葡萄柚（large round yellow citrus fruit with acid juicy flesh）

【例】*grapefruit* juice

*cedar ［ˈsiːdər］ *n.* 雪松（a tall evergreen coniferous tree）；雪松木材（用以制造箱子、家具、铅笔等）（its hard red sweet-smelling wood, used for making boxes, furniture, pencils, etc）

【例】a *cedar* chest

pine ［paɪn］ *n.* 松树 *v.*（因疾病等）憔悴（to lose vigor; anguish）；渴望（to desire）

【反】become invigorated（变得有活力）

arboretum [ˌɑːrbəˈriːtəm] *n.* 植物园（a place where trees, shrubs and herbaceous plants are cultivated for scientific and educational purposes）

【记】arbor(树) + et + um(地点) → 植物园

frond [frɑːnd] *n.* (羊齿、棕榈等的)叶子(the leaf of a fern)

【记】和front(*n.* 前面)一起记

arboreal [ɑːrˈbɔːriəl] *adj.* 树木的(of or like a tree)

【记】arbor(树) + eal → 树木的

botany [ˈbɑːtəni] *n.* 植物学 （a branch of biology dealing with plant life）

【记】bot(看做about) + any(任何) → 关于任何(植物) → 植物学

【派】botanical(*adj.* 植物学的)

genus [ˈdʒiːnəs] *n.* (动植物的) 属（division of animals or plants, below a family and above a species）

herbaceous [hɜːrˈbeɪʃəs] *adj.* 草本植物的 （of, relating to, or having the characteristics of an herb）

【记】来自herb(*n.* 草本植物)

needle [ˈniːdl] *n.* 针；针叶(a narrow stiff leaf of conifers)

scion [ˈsaɪən] *n.* (接木用的)嫩芽，幼枝(a detached living portion of a plant joined to a stock in grafting)；子孙(descendant; child)

shrub [ʃrʌb] *n.* 灌木(a low bush with several woody stems)

【记】和scrub(*n.* 灌木丛)一起记

sod [sɑːd] *n.* 草地，草皮(a piece of earth with grass and roots growing in it)

【记】上天(god)入地(sod)

sprig [sprɪɡ] *n.* 嫩枝，小枝(a small shoot; twig)

【记】春天(spring)出现嫩枝(sprig)

sprout [spraʊt] *v.* (使)萌芽，(使)生长(to grow; spring up) *n.* 嫩芽(a young shoot)

【记】spr(看做spring) + out(出) → 春天到了，"嫩芽"长出来了 → 萌芽

tare [ter] *n.* 莠草，杂草

【记】stare(*v.* 盯着看)去掉s成为tare

thicket [ˈθɪkɪt] *n.* 树丛，灌木丛(a dense growth of shrubbery or small trees)

【记】thick(密集) + et → 灌木密集地长在一起 → 灌木丛

timber [ˈtɪmbər] *n.* 木材(wood suitable for carpentry)；(人的)品质，才干(personal qualification)

tuber ['tuːbər] *n.* 块茎，球根（a short fleshy underground stem）

【例】Potatoes are the *tubers* of the potato plant.

xerophyte ['zɪroʊfaɪt] *n.* 旱生植物（a plant structurally adapted for life and growth with a limited water supply）

【记】xero（干燥）+ phyte（植物）→ 旱生植物

heliotrope ['hiːliətroʊp] *n.* 向阳植物；天芥菜属植物

【记】helio（太阳）+ trope（转）→ 转向太阳的植物 → 向阳植物

sapling ['sæplɪŋ] *n.* 树苗（a young tree）；年轻人（a young person）

【记】sap（树等的汁液）+ ling（小）→ 树苗

cactus ['kæktəs] *n.* (*pl.* cacti) 仙人掌

【记】复数为cacti

自 然

*spectacle ['spektəkl] *n.* 奇观，景象（sight; scene）

diversity [daɪ'vɜːrsəti] *n.* 多样性，千变万化（the condition of being diverse）

【反】uniformity（*n.* 一致）

*limpid ['lɪmpɪd] *adj.* 清澈的（transparent; clear）

arroyo [ə'rɔɪoʊ] *n.* 干涸的河道（a dry gully）；小河（a creek）

*crest [krest] *n.* 山顶，浪尖（top of a hill or wave）；羽冠（showy feathers on the head of a bird）

gorge [gɔːrdʒ] *n.* 峡谷（ravine; canyon）

【例】I stood on the edge of the cliff and threw a rock into the *gorge*.

cascade [kæ'skeɪd] *n.* 小瀑布（a small, steep waterfall）

【记】cas（落下）+ cad（落下）+ e → 不断落下 → 小瀑布

**torrent ['tɔːrənt] *n.* （水、熔岩等的）急流，湍流；爆发，迸发（violent outburst）

【例】mountain *torrents*; a *torrent* of abuse

*snowstorm ['snoʊstɔːrm] *n.* 暴风雪，雪暴（blizzard）

【例】Chicago, where a blizzard watch already has been issued, is expecting a *snowstorm* of historic proportions.

**rivulet ['rɪvjələt] *n.* 小溪，细流（small stream）

【例】*rivulets* running down the mountainside

*trickle ['trɪkl] *vi.* 滴，淌 *n.* 滴；细流(dribble; drip)

【例】The water *trickled* over the edge of the basin.

fluvial ['fluːviəl] *adj.* 河流的，生长在河中的 (of or living in a stream or river)

【记】fluv(=flu 流) + ial → 河流的

ravine [rə'viːn] *n.* 深谷，峡谷 (a small narrow steep-sided valley that is larger than a gully and smaller than a canyon)

shoal [ʃoʊl] *n.* 浅滩，浅水处 (a sandbank where the water is shallow)；一群(鱼等) *adj.* 水浅的

【记】形似拼音shao(少) → 水少的地方 → 浅滩，浅水处

【反】deep(*adj.* 深的)

estuary ['estʃueri] *n.* 河口，三角湾(an inlet or arm of the sea)

【记】est(看做east, 东) + uary(看做February, 二月) → 二月春水向东流，流到河口不回头 → 河口

quagmire ['kwæɡmaɪər] *n.* 沼泽地(soft miry land)；困境(predicament)

【记】quag(沼泽) + mire(泥潭) → 沼泽地

marsh [mɑːrʃ] *n.* 沼泽地，湿地(a tract of low, wet, soft land; swamp)

【记】红军长征(march)过沼泽地(marsh)

*lush [lʌʃ] *adj.* 繁茂的，茂盛的

【反】sere(*adj.* 干枯的)

gnarled [nɑːrld] *adj.* (树木)多节的 (knotty and twisted)；粗糙的(roughened; hardened)

【记】来自gnarl(*n.* 木节)

【例】*gnarled* branches // The *gnarled* hand gives it to Martin.

*verdant ['vɜːrdnt] *adj.* 青葱的，翠绿的

【记】verd(绿色) + ant → 翠绿的

【反】sere(*adj.* 干枯的)；sterile(*adj.* 贫瘠的)

*spate [speɪt] *n.* 大批，大量(a large number or amount)；(水)泛滥(flood)

【反】trickling flow(细流)；dearth(*n.* 缺乏)

eddy ['edi] *n.* 漩涡，涡流(little whirlpool or whirlwind)

whirlpool ['wɜːrlpuːl] *n.* 漩涡(a place with circular currents of water in a sea)

sultry ['sʌltri] *adj.* 闷热的(very hot and humid; sweltering)；(人)风骚的 (capable of exciting strong sexual desires)

【例】It's very close and *sultry* today.

zephyr ['zefər] *n.* 和风(a gentle breeze)；西风(a breeze from the west)

【记】由希腊神话中西风之神Zephyr而来

summit [ˈsʌmɪt] *n.* 山顶(peak; top; apex)
【例】The climbers placed their country's flag at the mountain's *summit*.

precipice [ˈpresəpɪs] *n.* 悬崖(a very steep or overhanging place)
【记】pre(前面) + cip(落下) + ice → 前面(突然)落下 → 悬崖

*snowdrift [ˈsnoʊdrɪft] *n.* (被风吹在一起的)雪堆(a bank of drifted snow)
【记】snow(雪) + drift(漂流物) → 雪堆

*skyline [ˈskaɪlaɪn] *n.* 地平线(horizon lines)
【例】The sun is falling, silhouetting the forested *skyline* and covering our sails in its yellowy glow.

defoliate [ˌdiːˈfoʊlieɪt] *v.* (使)落叶(to deprive of leaves, especially prematurely)
【记】de(去掉) + foli(叶) + ate → (使)落叶

*etch [etʃ] *v.* 蚀刻(to make a drawing on metal or glass by the action of an acid)
【反】efface(*vt.* 擦掉)

*acclimate [ˈækləmeɪt] *vt.* 使服水土(to adjust to climate); 使适应(to adapt)
【记】ac + climate(气候, 水土) → 使服水土

*overblow [ˌoʊvərˈbloʊ] *vt.* 吹散, 吹落

knoll [noʊl] *n.* 小山, 小圆丘(hillock; mound)
【记】与knot(*n.* 结)有关, 可能是knot的变体

pinnacle [ˈpɪnəkl] *n.* 尖塔(spire); 山峰, 顶峰(a lofty peak; summit)
【记】pin(针) + nacle → 像针一样尖的东西 → 尖塔; 山峰

geyser [ˈɡaɪzər] *n.* 天然热喷泉(a spring from which columns of boiling water and steam gush into the air at intervals)
【记】来自冰岛一个温泉名Geysir

grotto [ˈɡrɑːtoʊ] *n.* 洞穴(a small cavern)
【记】gr(看做great) + otto(看做otter, 水獭) → 大水獭住在洞穴中 → 洞穴

isthmus [ˈɪsməs] *n.* 地峡(a narrow strip of land)
【记】希腊语, 原意为"脖子"

scarp [skɑːrp] *n.* 悬崖, 陡坡(steep slope; escarpment)
【记】scar(看做scare, 惊恐) + p(看做place, 地方) → 让人惊恐的地方 → 悬崖

环 境

*ecological [ˌiːkəˈlɑːdʒɪkl] *adj.* 生态的，生态学的

**ecology [iˈkɑːlədʒi] *n.* 生态学

**ecosystem [ˈiːkoʊsɪstəm] *n.* 生态系统

noxious [ˈnɑːkʃəs] *adj.* 有害的；有毒的（poisonous; toxic）

【记】nox(毒) + ious → 有毒的

imbalance [ɪmˈbæləns] *n.* 不平衡，失衡，失调（inequality）

【例】The current trade deficit indicates a serious *imbalance* between our import and export trade.

*counterbalance [ˌkaʊntərˈbæləns] *vt.* 对…起平衡作用，抵消（to act as a balance to sb/sth）

【记】counter(反对，相反) + balance(平衡) → 相反的两边保持平衡 → 抵消

**contaminate [kənˈtæmɪneɪt] *vt.* 污染（to defile; pollute）

【例】The Department of Resources notified the town council that the water supply was *contaminated*.

*collectible [kəˈlektəbl] *adj.* 可收集的，可回收的

【例】Still, the resale market for high-end *collectible* books remains somewhat murky and difficult to track.

navigable [ˈnævɪɡəbl] *adj.* (指海洋、江河等)适于行船的，可通航的（of seas, rivers, etc suitable for ships, boats, etc to sail on）

【例】The Rhine is *navigable* from Strasbourg to the sea.

*fauna [ˈfɔːnə] *n.* (某一地区或某一时期的)动物群落

**sewage [ˈsuːɪdʒ] *n.* 下水道；污水，垃圾

grove [groʊv] *n.* 小树林，树丛（a small wood or group of trees）

【记】gro(看做grow) + ve(看做five) → five trees grow → 五棵树长在一起 → 小树林；可以和grovel(*vi.* 奴颜婢膝)一起记

*circumstance [ˈsɜːrkəmstæns] *n.* 环境，情形，情况（condition or fact connected with an event or action）

【例】She was found dead in suspicious *circumstances*.

*boulevard [ˈbʊləvɑːrd] *n.* 林荫大道（a wide city street, often with trees on each side）

*submarine [ˌsʌbməˈriːn] n. 潜水艇

【例】a *submarine* officer

*canal [kəˈnæl] n. 运河

【例】The Suez *Canal* joins the Mediterranean and the Red Sea.

*campus [ˈkæmpəs] n. (大学或学院的)校园(grounds and buildings of a university or college)

【例】He lives on the *campus*.

*fume [fjuːm] n. (浓烈或难闻的)烟,气体

*mutualism [ˈmjuːtʃuəlɪzəm] n. 共栖,互利共生 (the relation between two different species of organisms that are interdependent; each gains benefits from the other)

【例】The exchange exemplifies a perfect *mutualism*.

*decibel [ˈdesɪbel] n. 分贝

swelter [ˈsweltər] v. (使)热得难受,(使)热得出汗(to be uncomfortably hot; suffer from the heat)

【例】We were *sweltering* in our winter clothes.

Pride goes before destruction, a haughty spirit before a fall.
骄傲在败坏以先,狂心在跌倒之前。

——《圣经·旧·箴》16:18

练 习 题

填空题

acclimate	crest	etch	flora	limpid
lush	luxuriant	overblow	pollinate	skyline
spate	spectacle	starch	ecosystem	torrent
trickle	truffle	counterbalance	verdant	violet

1. The carnival parade was a magnificent _____.
2. After the winter rains, the stream becomes a raging _____.
3. She gave him a look of _____ honesty.
4. The male is recognizable by its yellow _____.
5. Tears were _____ down her cheeks.
6. The fields were _____ with grass and flowers.
7. The _____ mountain forest turns red gradually in the autumn wind.
8. The bombing was the latest in a _____ of terrorist attacks.
9. Ugly tower blocks dominate the _____.
10. A security number had been _____ on the car window as a protection against theft.
11. May you _____ to the new environment soon.
12. The autumn leaves are _____, leaves to become like gold to shine.
13. There's too much _____ in your diet.
14. _____ mushrooms are plentiful in the southwest Algeria desert.
15. Water is the core of a healthy _____.
16. The _____ is a dainty spring flower.
17. There is _____ tropical vegetation in our country.
18. Bees and butterflies _____ the trees in the orchard.
19. The accused's right to silence was a vital _____ to the powers of the police.
20. Tourism is damaging the _____ and fauna (plants and animals) of the island.

配对题

1. chestnut	植物学家	11. pollen	果仁；核心
2. kernel	栗树；栗子	12. redwood	兰科，兰花；淡紫色
3. botanist	(使)异种交配，培育杂种	13. flax	花粉；传授花粉给…
4. orchid	柏树	14. transplantation	(小的)花束
5. posy	榆树	15. elm	红木树
6. fig	蕨类植物	16. grapefruit	芦苇
7. reed	无花果	17. rivulet	小溪，细流
8. fern	亚麻	18. snowstorm	雪堆
9. germ	胚芽；微生物	19. snowdrift	暴风雪，雪暴
10. crossbreed	葡萄柚	20. cypress	移植

填空题答案

1. The carnival parade was a magnificent <u>spectacle</u>.
2. After the winter rains, the stream becomes a raging <u>torrent</u>.
3. She gave him a look of <u>limpid</u> honesty.
4. The male is recognizable by its yellow <u>crest</u>.
5. Tears were <u>trickling</u> down her cheeks.
6. The fields were <u>lush</u> with grass and flowers.
7. The <u>verdant</u> mountain forest turns red gradually in the autumn wind.
8. The bombing was the latest in a <u>spate</u> of terrorist attacks.
9. Ugly tower blocks dominate the <u>skyline</u>.
10. A security number had been <u>etched</u> on the car window as a protection against theft.
11. May you <u>acclimate</u> to the new environment soon.
12. The autumn leaves are <u>overblown</u>, leaves to become like gold to shine.
13. There's too much <u>starch</u> in your diet.
14. <u>Truffle</u> mushrooms are plentiful in the southwest Algeria desert.
15. Water is the core of a healthy <u>ecosystem</u>.
16. The <u>violet</u> is a dainty spring flower.
17. There is <u>luxuriant</u> tropical vegetation in our country.
18. Bees and butterflies <u>pollinate</u> the trees in the orchard.
19. The accused's right to silence was a vital <u>counterbalance</u> to the powers of the police.
20. Tourism is damaging the <u>flora</u> and fauna（plants and animals）of the island.

配对题答案

1. chestnut	栗树；栗子	11. pollen	花粉；传授花粉给…
2. kernel	果仁；核心	12. redwood	红木树
3. botanist	植物学家	13. flax	亚麻
4. orchid	兰科，兰花；淡紫色	14. transplantation	移植
5. posy	（小的）花束	15. elm	榆树
6. fig	无花果	16. grapefruit	葡萄柚
7. reed	芦苇	17. rivulet	小溪，细流
8. fern	蕨类植物	18. snowstorm	暴风雪，雪暴
9. germ	胚芽；微生物	19. snowdrift	雪堆
10. crossbreed	（使）异种交配，培育杂种	20. cypress	柏树

Word List 6
医学（一）

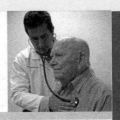

医学（一）

saliva [sə'laɪvə] *n.* 唾液，口水

HICH *abbr.* 高血压脑出血（Hypertensive Intracerebral Hemorrhage）

morbid ['mɔːrbɪd] *adj.* 疾病的（sick; diseased）；病态的，不健康的
【记】morb(病)+id → 疾病的
【例】The patient has a *morbid* imagination that made his illness worse.

epidemic [ˌepɪ'demɪk] *adj.* 传染性的，流行性的（prevalent and spreading rapidly in a community）*n.* 传染病；(传染病的)流行；迅速的传播
【记】epi(在···中)+dem(人民)+ic → 在人群中 → 流行性的

wholesome ['hoʊlsəm] *adj.* 促进健康的（good for the body or likely to produce health）
【记】whole(完整，齐全)+some → 使身体齐全 → 促进健康的
【反】tainted（*adj.* 被污染的）；deleterious（*adj.* 有害的）；insalubrious（*adj.* 有害的）；morbid（*adj.* 病态的）；noxious（*adj.* 有害的）

fragile ['frædʒl] *adj.* 体质弱的；易碎的
【记】frag(碎)+ile → 易碎的
【例】He's feeling a bit *fragile* after last night's party.

sterile ['sterəl] *adj.* 消过毒的（sanitary）

vascular ['væskjələr] *adj.* 血管的，脉管的
【记】vascul(血管)+ar → 血管的

susceptible [sə'septəbl] *adj.* 易受感染的（vulnerable; exposed）
【记】sus(下面)+cept(接受)+ible → 接受的 → 易受感染的
【例】Infants and the elderly are more *susceptible* to illness than other people.

precocious [prɪ'koʊʃəs] *adj.* 早熟的，较早具备某种能力的（premature）
【记】pre(预先)+coc(=cook煮)+ious → 提前煮好 → 早熟的

incision [ɪn'sɪʒn] *n.* 切口(a cut; gash)；切割
【反】suture(*n./vt.* 缝合)

**kinship ['kɪnʃɪp] *n.* 亲属关系，家属关系

【例】He pledged support for "*kinship* care", where youngsters were looked after by close relatives, not parents.

**neuroscience ['njʊroʊsaɪəns] *n.* 神经科学

**smallpox ['smɔːlpɑːks] *n.* 天花

【例】*Smallpox* can vary in its severity, with some strains killing many sufferers and others relatively few.

**vas [væs] *n.* 血管

**diagnosis [ˌdaɪəɡ'noʊsɪs] *n.* 诊断

【记】dia(穿过)＋gnos(知道)＋is → 穿过(身体)知道 → 诊断

**remedy ['remədi] *n.* 治疗法；药物 *vt.* 治疗(to cure; rectify)

【例】The doctor tried all means to *remedy* the wounded man.

**stupefaction [stuːpɪ'fækʃn] *n.* 麻醉，昏迷，麻木状态；惊慌失措

【例】This botched thriller is an old strain of corn that does best in a climate of *stupefaction*.

**scalpel ['skælpəl] *n.* 外科手术刀，解剖刀

【记】scalp(头皮)＋el → 割头皮的手术刀 → 解剖刀

**lineage ['lɪniːdʒ] *n.* 宗系，血统(ancestry)

【记】line(线)＋age(年龄) → 各年龄的人像线一样经络分明 → 宗系，血统

*dislocate ['dɪsloʊkeɪt] *vt.* 使脱臼(to displace a bone from its proper position at a joint)；把…弄乱(to disarrange; disrupt)

【记】dis(不)＋locate(定位，安置) → 不安置 → 弄乱

*salutary ['sæljəteri] *adj.* 有利的(remedial)；有益健康的 (promoting or conducive to health)

【记】salut(健康)＋ary → 有益健康的

【反】unhealthy(*adj.* 不利健康的)；deleterious(*adj.* 有害健康的)

*pathological [ˌpæθə'lɑːdʒɪkl] *adj.* 病态的(unreasonable; irrational)；病理的(of or relating to pathology)

*psychological [ˌsaɪkə'lɑːdʒɪkl] *adj.* 心理学的；心理的，精神的

*anesthesia [ˌænəs'θiːʒə] *n.* 麻醉，麻木 (insensibility to pain)

*disinfectant [ˌdɪsɪn'fektənt] *n.* 消毒剂

*sustenance ['sʌstənəns] *n.* 营养物

【例】For *sustenance*, the vegetarian ate fruits, nuts, and vegetables.

*contagious [kən'teɪdʒəs] *adj.* 传染的(catching; infectious)

【记】con + tag(接触) + ious → 接触病人会被传染 → 传染的

【例】Cancer is not *contagious*, so you shouldn't be afraid to touch someone with cancer.

*hypnotic [hɪp'nɑːtɪk] *adj.* 催眠的(tending to produce sleep) *n.* 催眠药，安眠药

【反】conscious(*adj.* 有意识的); stimulant(*n.* 刺激剂 *adj.* 刺激的)

*multivitamin [ˌmʌltɪ'vaɪtəmɪn] *adj.* 多种维生素的

【例】He also took a *multivitamin* pill and drank a protein shake daily.

*recurrent [rɪ'kɜːrənt] *adj.* 复发的，周期性的; 反复出现的

【例】What's important, say experts, is that patients have multiple strategies to help prevent *recurrent* attacks.

rabid ['ræbɪd] *adj.* 患狂犬病的(affected with rabies); 失去理性的(going to extreme lengths in expressing or pursuing a feeling, interest, or opinion)

【记】来自rabies(*n.* 狂犬病)

【反】logical(*adj.* 有逻辑的)

*acute [ə'kjuːt] *adj.* 急性的

【例】Severe *Acute* Respiratory Syndrome (SARS) was taking its toll on China's tour industry.

*myopic [maɪ'oʊpɪk] *adj.* 近视的; 缺乏远见的 (lacking of foresight or discernment)

【反】discerning(*adj.* 有识别力的)

*clinical ['klɪnɪkl] *adj.* 临床的; 分析的，客观的 (extremely objective and realistic; dispassionately analytic)

【记】clinic(医疗诊所) + al → 临床的

【例】a *clinical* diagnosis

*visceral ['vɪsərəl] *adj.* 内脏的(splanchnic); 内心深处的(felt in or as if in the viscera)

【记】来自viscera(内脏viscus的复数形式)

*neurological [ˌnjʊrə'lɑːdʒɪkl] *adj.* 神经病学的，神经学上的

【例】We need to make clear that these are *neurological* injuries that may have long-term effects.

*kindred ['kɪndrəd] *adj.* 同类的，同种族的(of similar or related origin)

*gular ['gjuːlər] *adj.* 咽喉的，喉部的

*efficacious [ˌefɪ'keɪʃəs] *adj.* 有效的(producing the desired result)

【例】an *efficacious* treatment

*symptomatic [ˌsɪmptə'mætɪk] *adj.* 症状的，症候的

【例】The uprising in Madison is *symptomatic* of a simmering rage among the nation's teachers.

*pharmaceutical [ˌfɑːrmə'suːtɪkl] *adj.* 制药的

【记】来自pharmacy(*n.* 药房；药剂学)

*therapeutic [ˌθerə'pjuːtɪk] *adj.* 治疗的(of the treatment of diseases)

【记】therap(照看，治疗) + eutic → 治疗的

*articular [ɑːr'tikjʊlər] *adj.* 关节的

*antifungal [ˌæntɪ'fʌŋɡəl] *adj.* 抗真菌的，抗霉菌的

*undernourished [ˌʌndər'nɜːrɪʃt] *adj.* 营养不良的 (not provided with sufficient food of the right kind for good health and normal growth)

【例】seriously *undernourished*

*curative ['kjʊrətɪv] *adj.* 有助于治疗的，有疗效的 (helping to, able to or intended to cure illness)

【例】the *curative* properties of a herb

*ailment ['eɪlmənt] *n.* (不严重的)疾病，小病(a mild, chronic disease)

【记】ail(病痛) + ment → 小病

*trauma ['traʊmə] *n.* (身体)外伤，创伤

【例】abdominal *trauma*

*acuity [ə'kuːəti] *n.* (尤指思想或感官)敏锐(sharpness; acuteness)

【记】acu(尖，酸，锐利) + ity(表性质) → 敏锐

virus ['vaɪrəs] *n.* 病毒

【记】发音似"娃弱死" → 小孩身体弱，被病毒感染不幸死了 → 病毒

*engorgement [ɪn'ɡɔːrdʒmənt] *n.* 充血

*artery ['ɑːrtəri] *n.* 动脉，命脉

【记】arter(管道) + y → (体内的)管道 → 动脉

*quarantine ['kwɔːrəntiːn] *n.* 隔离；隔离检疫期 (enforced isolation to prevent the spread of disease)

【记】quarant(40) + ine, 原意指隔离40天 → 隔离

*skeleton ['skelɪtn] *n.* 骨架，骨骼

*allergy ['ælərdʒi] *n.* 过敏症；厌恶(a strong aversion)

【记】all(其他的，奇怪的) + erg(起作用) + y → 起奇怪的作用 → 过敏症

*palliative ['pæliətɪv] *n.* 缓释剂 *adj.* 减轻的，缓和的(serving to palliate)

*plaster	[ˈplæstər] n. 灰泥；热石膏 vt. 抹灰泥；用热石膏处理	

*plaster [ˈplæstər] n. 灰泥；热石膏 vt. 抹灰泥；用热石膏处理
【记】plast(塑造)+ er → 用来塑墙的东西 → 灰泥

*malady [ˈmælədi] n. 疾病
【记】mal(坏)+ ady → 坏的东西 → 疾病

**polio [ˈpouliou] n. 脊髓灰质炎，小儿麻痹症(infectious disease caused by a virus in which the spinal cord becomes inflamed, often resulting in paralysis)

amnesia [æmˈniːʒə] n. 健忘症
【记】a(无)+ mnes(记忆)+ ia(病) → 使没有记忆的病 → 健忘症

— ***inoculation** [ɪˌnɑːkjuˈleɪʃn] n. 预防接种；灌输(思想)，感染
【例】susceptible to a disease transmitted by *inoculation* // The Clintons' 20 Minutes' appearance on Super Bowl Sunday 1992 was the ultimate *inoculation* strategy.

*antidote [ˈæntidout] n. 解毒药
【记】anti(反)+ dote(药剂) → 反毒的药 → 解毒药；注意：dote=dose (药剂)，如overdose(v./n. 用药过量)

dissection [dɪˈsekʃn] n. 解剖，剖析(the act or process of dissecting)

*spirituality [ˌspɪrɪtʃuˈæləti] n. 灵性，精神性

*anatomy [əˈnætəmi] n. 解剖学
【记】ana(分开)+ tomy(切) → 切开 → 解剖学

— **dismember** [dɪsˈmembər] vt. 肢解，分割(to cut a body apart limb from limb)

*neurology [njuˈrɑːlədʒi] n. 神经学
【记】neur(神经)+ ology(学科) → 神经学

— ***kidney** [ˈkɪdni] n. 肾

*corpse [kɔːrps] n. 尸体
【例】The mortician dressed and made up the *corpse*.

*microsurgery [ˈmaɪkrousɜːrdʒəri] n. 显微外科，显微手术

*empathy [ˈempəθi] n. 移情作用，心意相通，(感情等)融为一体
【记】em(进入)+ pathy(感情) → 进入他人的感情 → 心意相通

vertigo [ˈvɜːrtɪɡou] n. 眩晕(a dizzy, confused state of mind)
【记】verti(转)+ go(走) → 转着走 → 眩晕

— ***malnutrition** [ˌmælnuːˈtrɪʃn] n. 营养不良 (a condition resulting from a lack of the right type of food)
【例】children suffering from severe *malnutrition*

*fracture [ˈfræktʃər] n./v. 骨折((to) crack)
【记】fract(碎裂)+ ure → 骨折

*virology	[vaɪ'rɑːlədʒi] n. 病毒学(scientific study of viruses and virus diseases)	
potion	['poʊʃn] n. 一服，一剂(liquid dose)	

— **soporific** [ˌsɑːpə'rɪfɪk] adj. 催眠的(tending to cause sleep) n. 安眠药

【记】sopor(昏睡) + ific → 催眠的

【反】invigorating(adj. 精力充沛的); stimulant(n. 刺激剂 adj. 刺激的); provocative(adj. 刺激的)

— **demented** [dɪ'mentɪd] adj. 疯狂的(insane)

【记】de(去掉) + ment(神智) + ed → 没有理智的 → 疯狂的

— **comatose** ['koʊmətoʊs] adj. 昏迷的(unconscious; torpid)

【例】a state of comatose torpor

aseptic [ˌeɪ'septɪk] adj. 洁净的(not contaminated); 无菌的(not septic)

【记】a(无) + sept(菌) + ic → 无菌的

【反】contaminated(adj. 被污染的)

— **flaccid** ['flæsɪd] adj. 松弛的(soft and limply flabby); 软弱的(weak; feeble)

【记】flac(=flab松弛) + cid → 松弛的

【派】flaccidity(n. 软弱) → firmness(n. 坚定)

*asthmatic [æz'mætɪk] adj. 哮喘的，气喘的

knotty ['nɑːti] adj. 有结的，有节疤的(having or full of knots); 困难的(hard to solve or explain; puzzling)

【记】knot(结，节疤) + ty → 有结的，有节疤的

【反】easy(adj. 容易的); simple(adj. 简单的)

astringent [ə'strɪndʒənt] adj. 止血的(styptic); 收缩的(puckery) n. 止血剂，收缩剂(an astringent substance)

【记】a + string(绑紧) + ent → 绑紧的 → 收缩的

— **hydrophobia** [ˌhaɪdrə'foʊbiə] n. 恐水症；狂犬病

【例】A dog that bites a human being must be observed for symptoms of hydrophobia.

anesthetic [ˌænɪs'θetɪk] n. 麻醉剂 adj. 麻醉的 (relating to or resembling anesthesia; insensitive)

【记】an(无) + esthet(感觉) + ic → 无感觉的 → 麻醉的

— **pore** [pɔːr] n. 毛孔；气孔(a very small opening)

【例】He was sweating through every pore.

anemia [ə'niːmiə] n. 贫血，贫血症(a lack of red blood cells)

【记】a(无) + nem(血) + ia(病) → 贫血症

【派】anemic(adj. 贫血的)

antiseptic	[ˌæntɪˈseptɪk] *n.*杀菌剂 *adj.*防腐的
	【记】anti(反) + sept(菌) + ic → 杀菌剂
insomnia	[ɪnˈsɑːmnɪə] *n.*失眠症
	【记】in(不) + somn(睡眠) + ia → 不能睡着 → 失眠症
aphasia	[əˈfeɪʒɪə] *n.*失语症
	【记】a + phas(语言) + ia → 无语言的病 → 失语症
*manus	[ˈmeɪnəs] *n.*手；前肢
analgesic	[ˌænəlˈdʒiːzɪk] *n.*镇痛剂 (a drug that takes pain away) *adj.*止痛的 (capable of relieving pain)
	【反】sensitivity to pain(对痛敏感)
stupor	[ˈstuːpər] *n.*昏迷，不省人事 (no sensibility; lethargy)
	【记】stup(呆) + or → 昏迷
contusion	[kənˈtuːʒn] *n.*擦伤，撞伤，挫伤 (bruise)
psyche	[ˈsaɪki] *n.*心智，精神 (mind; soul)
	【例】Clearly, something gnaws at her *psyche*.
**bubonic	[bjuːˈbɑːnɪk] *adj.*腹股沟淋巴结炎的
*cholesterol	[kəˈlestərɔːl] *n.*胆固醇 (fatty substance found in animal fluids and tissue, thought to cause hardening of the arteries)
	【例】A high *cholesterol* level in the blood can cause heart disease.
*vaccine	[vækˈsiːn] *n.*牛痘苗，疫苗
	【记】vacc(牛) + ine → 牛痘苗
cadaver	[kəˈdævər] *n.*尸体 (a dead body; corpse)
	【记】cad(=fall倒下) + aver(看做over) → 生命结束倒下的人 → 尸体

填空题

acute	clinical	contagious	diagnosis	epidemic
fragile	kindred	kinship	morbid	pathological
precocious	psychological	recurrent	salutary	sterile
stupefaction	susceptible	vascular	visceral	wholesome

1. From an early age she displayed a _____ talent for music.
2. He had a _____ fascination with blood.
3. Effectively, tobacco companies will be exporting an _____ of smoking-related diseases, the campaign suggests.
4. An accurate _____ was made after a series of tests.
5. Swimming is a _____ pleasure to babies.
6. In her job she was used to dealing with actors' _____ egos.
7. An operating theatre should be completely _____.
8. The mechanism of this anomalous _____ response is unknown.
9. Salt intake may lead to raised blood pressure in _____ adults.
10. Even after meeting only once, they felt a _____.
11. She did nothing but walk up and down the garden path in a state bordering on _____.
12. The accident was a _____ reminder of the dangers of climbing.
13. Stephen was almost _____ jealous of his brother.
14. The patient is still highly _____.
15. Political revolution is a _____ theme in Riley's books.
16. The patient is suffering from a kind of _____ disease.
17. He watched her suffering with _____ detachment.
18. English and Dutch are _____ languages.
19. Abuse can lead to both _____ and emotional problems.
20. She had a _____ dislike of all things foreign.

配对题

1. vas	麻木	11. lineage	近视的
2. remedy	腹股沟淋巴结炎的	12. dislocate	神经病学的
3. polio	消毒剂	13. anesthesia	神经科学
4. vaccine	使脱臼	14. disinfectant	脊髓灰质炎
5. saliva	咽喉的	15. sustenance	治疗法
6. HICH	高血压脑出血	16. hypnotic	唾液
7. neuroscience	催眠的	17. multivitamin	外科手术刀
8. bubonic	切口	18. myopic	牛痘苗，疫苗
9. incision	宗系	19. neurological	营养物
10. scalpel	多种维生素的	20. gular	血管

练习题答案

填空题答案

1. From an early age she displayed a <u>precocious</u> talent for music.
2. He had a <u>morbid</u> fascination with blood.
3. Effectively, tobacco companies will be exporting an <u>epidemic</u> of smoking-related diseases, the campaign suggests.
4. An accurate <u>diagnosis</u> was made after a series of tests.
5. Swimming is a <u>wholesome</u> pleasure to babies.
6. In her job she was used to dealing with actors' <u>fragile</u> egos.
7. An operating theatre should be completely <u>sterile</u>.
8. The mechanism of this anomalous <u>vascular</u> response is unknown.
9. Salt intake may lead to raised blood pressure in <u>susceptible</u> adults.
10. Even after meeting only once, they felt a <u>kinship</u>.
11. She did nothing but walk up and down the garden path in a state bordering on <u>stupefaction</u>.
12. The accident was a <u>salutary</u> reminder of the dangers of climbing.
13. Stephen was almost <u>pathologically</u> jealous of his brother.
14. The patient is still highly <u>contagious</u>.
15. Political revolution is a <u>recurrent</u> theme in Riley's books.
16. The patient is suffering from a kind of <u>acute</u> disease.
17. He watched her suffering with <u>clinical</u> detachment.
18. English and Dutch are <u>kindred</u> languages.
19. Abuse can lead to both <u>psychological</u> and emotional problems.
20. She had a <u>visceral</u> dislike of all things foreign.

配对题答案

1. vas	血管		11. lineage	宗系	
2. remedy	治疗法		12. dislocate	使脱臼	
3. polio	脊髓灰质炎		13. anesthesia	麻木	
4. vaccine	牛痘苗，疫苗		14. disinfectant	消毒剂	
5. saliva	唾液		15. sustenance	营养物	
6. HICH	高血压脑出血		16. hypnotic	催眠的	
7. neuroscience	神经科学		17. multivitamin	多种维生素的	
8. bubonic	腹股沟淋巴结炎的		18. myopic	近视的	
9. incision	切口		19. neurological	神经病学的	
10. scalpel	外科手术刀		20. gular	咽喉的	

Word List 7
医学（二）

医学（二）

**paralysis [pə'ræləsɪs] *n.* 麻痹，瘫痪（loss of feeling in or control of a part of the body）

【例】The *paralysis* affects his right leg and he can only walk with difficulty.

**malaria [mə'leriə] *n.* 疟疾

【例】a bad attack of *malaria*

**amputate ['æmpjuteɪt] *vt.* 截（肢），锯掉

【记】am（看做arm）+ put（切除）+ ate → 切除胳膊 → 截（肢）

【例】The climber was forced to *amputate* his arm in order to save his own life.

**bruise [bruːz] *vt.* 使青肿 *n.* 瘀伤

【例】Mary got a *bruise* after bumping against the table.

painkiller ['peɪnkɪlər] *n.* 止痛药（a medicine that relieves pain）

【记】pain（痛）+ killer（致命之物）→ 止痛药

paranoid ['pærənɔɪd] *adj.* 偏执狂的，过分怀疑的（associated with paranoia）

【记】来自paranoia（*n.* 偏执狂）

*psychiatry [saɪ'kaɪətri] *n.* 精神病学，精神病治疗（study and treatment of mental illness）

【派】psychiatric（*adj.* 精神病学的），例如 a psychiatric clinic

*psychotherapy [ˌsaɪkoʊ'θerəpi] *n.* 精神疗法，心理疗法（treatment of mental disorders by psychological methods）

*caffeine ['kæfiːn] *n.* 咖啡碱，咖啡因（a bitter white alkaloid, often derived from tea leaves and coffee beans）

*anticoagulant [ˌæntikoʊ'ægjələnt] *n.* 抗凝血剂

*immunology [ˌɪmju'nɑːlədʒi] *n.* 免疫学

| paranoia | [ˌpærəˈnɔɪə] n. 偏执狂，妄想狂（mental illness in which a person is obsessed by mistaken beliefs） |

paranoia [ˌpærəˈnɔɪə] *n.* 偏执狂，妄想狂（mental illness in which a person is obsessed by mistaken beliefs）

*physiology [ˌfɪziˈɑːlədʒi] *n.* 生理学（scientific study of the normal functions of living things）
【例】reproductive *physiology*

*pestilence [ˈpestɪləns] *n.* 瘟疫（deadly infectious disease that spreads quickly through large numbers of people）

*cathartic [kəˈθɑːrtɪk] *n.* 泻药（purgative）
【记】cathar(清洁) + tic → 清洁(肠子) → 泻药

*bloodstream [ˈblʌdstriːm] *n.* (体内循环的)血流，血液
【例】Bacteria soon saturate the *bloodstream*, destroying muscles and organs and sending the body into shock.

*munity [ˈmjunɪtɪ] *n.* 易感性（affectability）

*infusion [ɪnˈfjuːʒn] *n.* 注入，灌输（infusing a quality or being infused into）
【例】an *infusion* of medicinal herbs // This company needs an *infusion* of new blood.

*contuse [kənˈtjuːz] *vt.* 挫伤；使产生青肿（to injure; bruise）

*sprain [spreɪn] *vt.* 扭伤（to injure by a sudden twist）
【记】sp + rain(雨) → 雨天路滑，扭伤了脚 → 扭伤

*congest [kənˈdʒest] *v.* (使)充血（to cause the accumulation of excessive blood or tissue fluid in vessel or organ）; (使)堵塞
【记】con (全部) + gest(管道，带来) → 全部进入血管 → 充血
【派】congestion(*n.* 充血；堵塞)

acrophobia [ˌækrəʊˈfəʊbjə] *n.* 恐高症（fear of heights）
【记】acro(高) + phob(憎恨) + ia(病) → 憎恨高的病 → 恐高症

infection [ɪnˈfekʃn] *n.* 传染，感染（an act or process of infecting）
【反】free of infection(未受感染的) → septic(*adj.* 腐烂的)
【派】infectious(*adj.* 传染的)

injection [ɪnˈdʒekʃn] *n.* 注射（an act or instance of injecting）; 注射剂（sth that is injected）
【记】来自inject(*vt.* 注射), in(进) + ject(扔) → 扔进去 → 注射

inoculate [ɪˈnɑːkjuleɪt] *vt.* 预防接种（to inject a serum or vaccine to create immunity）
【记】in(进入) + ocul(萌芽；眼睛) + ate → 在萌芽时期进入 → 预防接种

stutter [ˈstʌtər] *n./v.* 口吃，结巴（to speak with involuntary disruption of speech）

stammer ['stæmər] *n./v.* 口吃，结巴（to make involuntary stops and repetitions in speaking）

balm [bɑːm] *n.* 香油，药膏（any fragrant ointment or aromatic oil）；镇痛剂

【记】来自balsam（*n.* 香油；香脂）

【反】irritant（*n.* 刺激物）

deranged [dɪ'reɪndʒd] *adj.* 精神错乱的，有精神病的（insane）

【记】de（去掉）+ rang（看做range，排列）+ ed → 没有顺序的 → 精神错乱的

frenetic [frə'netɪk] *adj.* 狂乱的，发狂的（frantic; frenzied）

【记】fren（=phren心灵）+ etic → 心智错乱 → 狂乱的

irremediable [ˌɪrɪ'miːdiəbl] *adj.* 无法治愈的（incurable; not remediable）；无法纠正的，不能补救的

【记】ir（不）+ remedi（=remedy治疗）+ able（可…的）→ 无法治愈的

remedial [rɪ'miːdiəl] *adj.* 治疗的；补救的，矫正的

salvageable ['sælvɪdʒəbl] *adj.* 可抢救的

spasmodic [spæz'mɑːdɪk] *adj.* 痉挛的（of a spasm）；间歇性的（intermittent）

【例】It was an involuntary and *spasmodic* pain.

therapy ['θerəpi] *n.* 治疗，疗法（any treatment designed to relieve or cure an illness or a disability）

【例】have / undergo *therapy* 接受治疗

traumatic [trɔː'mætɪk] *adj.* 外伤的，创伤的

wan [wæn] *adj.* 虚弱的（feeble）；呈病态的（sickly pallid）

【例】a *wan* complexion

depressant [dɪ'presnt] *adj.* 有镇静作用的 *n.* 镇静剂（substance that reduces mental or physical activity）

【记】de（向下）+ press（按压）+ ant → 把人（躁动的心情）往下压的东西 → 镇静剂

anorexia [ˌænə'reksiə] *n.* 厌食症（an eating disorder or aversion to food）

【记】an + orex（胃口）+ ia → 无胃口的病 → 厌食症

antibody ['æntibɑːdi] *n.* 抗体（身体中的抗病物质）

【反】antigen（*n.* 抗原）

arthritis [ɑːr'θraɪtɪs] *n.* 关节炎（an inflammation of the joints）

【记】arthr（连结；关节）+ itis（炎症）→ 关节炎

concussion [kən'kʌʃn] *n.* 脑震荡；强烈震动（a violent shaking）

【记】con（共同）+ cuss（震动）+ ion → 强烈震荡

diagnose [ˌdaɪəɡ'noʊs] *vt.* 判断，诊断 (to find out the nature of an illness by observing its symptoms)

【记】dia(穿过) + gnos(知道) + e → 穿过(身体)知道 → 诊断

mania ['meɪnɪə] *n.* 癫狂 (wild or violent mental disorder); 狂热 (an excessive, persistent enthusiasm)

【记】比较记忆：kleptomania(*n.* 盗窃狂)；bibliomania(*n.* 爱书癖)

myopia [maɪ'oʊpɪə] *n.* 近视；缺乏远见 (lack of foresight or discernment)

【记】myo(肌肉) + p(看做op，眼) + ia(病) → 眼病 → 近视

【反】prescience(*n.* 远见)

【派】myopic(*adj.* 近视的；缺乏远见的)

relapse [rɪ'læps] *n.* 旧病复发 (a recurrence of symptoms of a disease); 再恶化 (the act or an instance of backsliding, worsening) *vi.* 旧病复发；再恶化 (to slip or fall into a former worse state)

【记】re + lapse(滑) → (身体状况)再次下滑 → 旧病复发

sterilize ['sterəlaɪz] *v.* 使不育；杀菌，消毒 (to make sterile)

【反】contaminate(*vt.* 污染)

【派】sterilization(*n.* 杀菌)

stimulant ['stɪmjələnt] *n.* 兴奋剂，刺激物 (an agent that produces a temporary increase of the functional activity) *adj.* 刺激的

【记】stimul(刺激) + ant → 刺激物

【反】soporific(*n.* 催眠药 *adj.* 催眠的)

convalesce [ˌkɑːnvə'les] *vi.* 康复，复原 (to regain strength and health)

【记】con + val(强壮) + esce(开始…的) → 开始强壮 → 康复

convalescent [ˌkɑːnvə'lesnt] *adj./n.* 康复中的(病人) ((a person who is) recovering from illness)

diabetes [ˌdaɪə'biːtiːz] *n.* 糖尿病

【记】dia(穿过) + betes → 总觉得有尿要穿过 → 多尿症 → 糖尿病

claustrophobia [ˌklɔːstrə'foʊbɪə] *n.* 幽闭恐惧症 (fear of being locked in)

【记】claus(close，关闭) + tro + phob(憎恨) + ia(病) → 幽闭恐惧症

abrade [ə'breɪd] *vt.* 擦伤，磨损 (to scrape or rub off)

【记】ab(离去) + rad(磨擦) + e → 擦伤，磨损

【派】abraded(*adj.* 擦伤的，磨损的)

fester ['festər] *v.* (使)化脓 (to decay)

【例】It's lucky that the wound did not *fester*.

autopsy	['ɔːtɑːpsi] *n.* 验尸，尸体解剖
	【例】One of the pigs was killed and *autopsied*.
hypochondriac	[ˌhaɪpə'kɑːndriæk] *n.* 忧郁症患者 *adj.* 忧郁症的
liniment	['lɪnəmənt] *n.* 搽剂（尤指油质去痛剂）
opiate	['oʊpiət] *n.* 鸦片制剂（any medicine containing opium）；安眠药
	【记】来自opium（*n.* 鸦片）
placebo	[plə'siːboʊ] *n.* 安慰剂（sth tending to soothe）
	【记】plac(平静)+ ebo → 安慰剂
salubrious	[sə'luːbriəs] *adj.* (空气等)有益健康的（promoting health; salutary）
	【记】salubr(健康)+ ious → 有益健康的
	【反】unhealthy(*adj.* 不利健康的)；virulent(*adj.* 剧毒的)；deleterious (*adj.* 有害的)
nostrum	['nɑːstrəm] *n.* 家传秘方（quack medicine）；万灵丹（panacea）
	【记】nost(家)+ rum → 家传秘方
abscission	[æb'sɪʒn] *n.* 切除，截去（removal）；【植】脱离，（幼果）脱落(the natural separation of flowers, fruit, or leaves from plants at a special separation layer)
	【记】ab(离去)+ sciss(切，割)+ ion → 切除，截去
anatomical	[ˌænə'tɑːmɪkl] *adj.* 解剖学的（of or relating to anatomy）
	【记】来自anatomy(*n.* 解剖学)
apoplectic	[ˌæpə'plektɪk] *adj.* 中风的 （of, relating to, or causing stroke）；愤怒的 (furious)
	【记】来自apoplexy(*n.* 中风)
	【反】calm(*adj.* 平静的)
asphyxiate	[æs'fɪksieɪt] *vt.* 使无法呼吸，使窒息而死（to suffocate）
	【记】a（不）+ sphyx(跳动)+ iate → 使脉搏不再跳动 → 使窒息而死
	【例】The smoke *asphyxiated* the victim.
asthma	['æzmə] *n.* 哮喘症（an illness involving difficulty in breathing）
	【记】as + th(看做the)+ ma(拼音：妈) → 像有哮喘病的大妈 → 哮喘症
cornea	['kɔːrniə] *n.* 角膜
cranial	['kreɪniəl] *adj.* 头盖的，头盖形的
coma	['koʊmə] *n.* 昏迷状态（deep, prolonged unconsciousness）
dyslexia	[dɪs'leksiə] *n.* 阅读障碍（impairment of the ability to read）
	【记】dys(不良)+ lex(词语)+ ia(病) → 阅读障碍

dyspeptic [dɪs'peptɪk] *adj.* 消化不良的（indigestible）；不高兴的，阴郁的（morose; grouchy）

【反】genial(*adj.* 快乐的)

gerontology [ˌdʒerən'tɑːlədʒi] *n.* 老年病学（the scientific study of aging and of the problems of the aged people）

【记】geront(老人，老年) + ology → 老年病学

hemophilia [ˌhiːmə'filiə] *n.* 血友病

【记】hemo(血) + phil(爱) + ia(病) → 爱出血的病 → 血友病

hemorrhage ['hemərɪdʒ] *n.* 出血(尤指大出血)(heavy bleeding)

【记】hemo(血) + rrhage(超量流出) → 超量流血 → 大出血

hemostat ['hiːməstæt] *n.* 止血器；止血剂(sth that hastens clotting)

【记】hemo(血) + stat(站住) → 止血器；止血剂

hypertension [ˌhaɪpər'tenʃn] *n.* 高血压(abnormally high blood pressure)；过度紧张

【记】hyper(超过) + tension(紧张，压力) → 高血压；过度紧张

lancet ['lænsɪt] *n.* 柳叶刀，刺血针（a sharp-pointed surgical instrument used to make small incisions）

【记】lance（长矛）+ t → 像长矛般锋利的手术刀 → 柳叶刀

narcotic [nɑːr'kɑːtɪk] *n.* 催眠药 *adj.* 催眠的

【记】narcot(睡眠) + ic → 催眠的

pediatrics [ˌpiːdi'ætrɪks] *n.* 儿科学(a branch of medicine dealing with diseases of children)

【记】ped(儿童) + iatrics(医学科) → 儿科学

rabies ['reɪbiːz] *n.* 狂犬病；恐水症

【记】当心那些婴儿们(babies)感染上狂犬病(rabies)

septic ['septɪk] *adj.* 受感染的，腐败的(causing infection)

【记】sept(细菌；腐烂) + ic → 腐败的

【反】free of infection(未受感染的)

*cerebral [sə'riːbrəl] *adj.* 大脑的（of the brain）；深思的（of the intellect rather than the emotions）

【记】cerebr(脑) + al → 大脑的

*gall [gɔːl] *n.* 胆汁(bile)；怨恨(hatred; bitter feeling)

【记】一头撞到墙(wall)上，心中充满怨恨(gall)

girth [gɜːrθ] *n.* (树干、腰身等的)周长，围长(circumference)

rind [raɪnd] *n.* (瓜果的)外皮(hard or tough outer layer)

【记】找到(find)果皮(rind)

aorta [eɪˈɔːrtə] *n.* 主动脉（the main artery of the body）

【记】把r置前，单词变成raota（拼音：绕它）→ 主动脉在身体中弯曲盘缠 → 主动脉

dimple [ˈdɪmpl] *n.* 酒窝，笑靥（a small dent or pucker, especially in the skin of one's cheeks or chin）

【记】d + imp（小精灵）+ le → 像小精灵一样微笑 → 笑靥

fetus [ˈfiːtəs] *n.* 胎儿

【记】fet(=foet胎儿) + us → 胎儿

freckle [ˈfrekl] *n.* 雀斑，斑点（a small, brownish spot on the skin）

【记】和heckle（*vt.* 诘问，责问）一起记

knuckle [ˈnʌkl] *n.* 指关节；（猪等四足动物的）膝关节；（供食用的）肘，蹄

【例】Our fingers bend at the *knuckle*.

stature [ˈstætʃər] *n.* 身高，身材（nature height in an upright position）

【记】stat（站）+ ure（状态）→ 站的状态 → 身高

auricular [ɔːˈrɪkjələr] *adj.* 耳的（of the ear）

【记】aur（耳，听）+ icular → 耳的

cephalic [sɪˈfælɪk] *adj.* 头的，头部的（of the head or skull）

【记】cephal（头）+ ic → 头的

incisor [ɪnˈsaɪzər] *n.* 门牙（any of the four anterior teeth）

【记】in（进入）+ cise（切）+ or → 将进来的东西切断 → 门牙

intestine [ɪnˈtestɪn] *n.* 肠 *adj.* 内部的（internal）

【记】in（内）+ test（外壳）+ ine → 在外壳之内 → 肠

visage [ˈvɪzɪdʒ] *n.* 脸，面貌（the face, countenance, or appearance）

【记】vis（看）+ age → 脸，面貌

pulmonary [ˈpʌlməneri] *adj.* 肺的，与肺有关的，有肺的（pertaining to the lungs）

练 习 题

填空题

amputate	bruise	congest	contuse	deranged
frenetic	remedial	therapy	traumatic	infection
infusion	inoculate	diagnose	paralysis	paranoid
relapse	convalesce	sprain	salubrious	septic

1. The strike caused total _____ in the city.
2. She had slipped and badly _____ her face.
3. The company needs an _____ of new blood.
4. Difficulty and failure don't _____ his passion.
5. My _____ ankle has been acting up badly all week.
6. The highway was _____ with cars.
7. She's getting really _____ about what other people say about her.
8. People catch all kinds of _____ in the winter.
9. The disease can now be prevented by _____.
10. He seemed to be on the verge of total _____.
11. She rushes from job to job at a _____ pace.
12. We had to move to a house in a less _____ area.
13. A dirty cut may go _____.
14. Two days after leaving the hospital she _____ into a coma.
15. The building needs urgent _____ work to make it safe.
16. Most leukaemia patients undergo some sort of drug _____.
17. The illness was _____ as cancer.
18. She is _____ at home after her operation.
19. Divorce can be _____ for everyone involved.
20. He had to have both legs _____.

配对题

1. munity	恐高症	11. bloodstream	疟疾
2. malaria	抗凝血剂	12. painkiller	易感性
3. psychiatry	香油	13. paranoia	镇静剂
4. psychotherapy	(体内循环的)血流, 血液	14. acrophobia	偏执狂
5. caffeine	咖啡因	15. injection	瘟疫
6. anticoagulant	泻药	16. stutter	生理学
7. immunology	止痛药	17. incisor	精神病学
8. physiology	厌食症	18. balm	精神疗法
9. pestilence	免疫学	19. depressant	口吃
10. cathartic	注射	20. anorexia	门牙

练习题答案

填空题答案

1. The strike caused total <u>paralysis</u> in the city.
2. She had slipped and badly <u>bruised</u> her face.
3. The company needs an <u>infusion</u> of new blood.
4. Difficulty and failure don't <u>contuse</u> his passion.
5. My <u>sprained</u> ankle has been acting up badly all week.
6. The highway was <u>congested</u> with cars.
7. She's getting really <u>paranoid</u> about what other people say about her.
8. People catch all kinds of <u>infections</u> in the winter.
9. The disease can now be prevented by <u>inoculation</u>.
10. He seemed to be on the verge of total <u>derangedment</u>.
11. She rushes from job to job at a <u>frenetic</u> pace.
12. We had to move to a house in a less <u>salubrious</u> area.
13. A dirty cut may go <u>septic</u>.
14. Two days after leaving the hospital she <u>relapsed</u> into a coma.
15. The building needs urgent <u>remedial</u> work to make it safe.
16. Most leukaemia patients undergo some sort of drug <u>therapy</u>.
17. The illness was <u>diagnosed</u> as cancer.
18. She is <u>convalescing</u> at home after her operation.
19. Divorce can be <u>traumatic</u> for everyone involved.
20. He had to have both legs <u>amputated</u>.

配对题答案

1. munity	易感性	11. bloodstream	(体内循环的)血流, 血液
2. malaria	疟疾	12. painkiller	止痛药
3. psychiatry	精神病学	13. paranoia	偏执狂
4. psychotherapy	精神疗法	14. acrophobia	恐高症
5. caffeine	咖啡因	15. injection	注射
6. anticoagulant	抗凝血剂	16. stutter	口吃
7. immunology	免疫学	17. incisor	门牙
8. physiology	生理学	18. balm	香油
9. pestilence	瘟疫	19. depressant	镇静剂
10. cathartic	泻药	20. anorexia	厌食症

Word List 8
人类学·社会学·考古学

人类学

*eurocentric [ˌjurəˈsentrɪk] *adj.* 以欧洲为中心的

*juvenile [ˈdʒuːvənaɪl] *adj.* 青少年的 (adolescent; young) *n.* 未成年人，少年
【记】juven(年青) + ile → 青少年的
【例】The clerk directed Jane and her mother to the *juvenile* clothing section of the store.

ethnic [ˈeθnɪk] *adj.* 种族的 (racial; national)
【记】ethn(种族) + ic → 种族的
【例】The chef prepared many *ethnic* dishes.

**interracial [ˌɪntəˈreɪʃl] *adj.* 种族间的 (between or involving different races)
【例】*interracial* conflict

*filial [ˈfɪliəl] *adj.* 子女的
【记】fil(儿子) + ial → 儿子的 → 子女的

*semihuman [ˌsemɪˈhjuːmən] *adj.* 半人类的
【例】The kangaroo is one of the "evolved" animals, genetic upgrades that are permitted to live *semihuman* lives and do society's grunt work.

*humanlike [ˈhjuːmənlaɪk] *adj.* 人类的；似人类的 (hominoid)
【例】Scientists digging in a Kenyan desert have found what they believe to be the oldest *humanlike* footprints.

**humanoid [ˈhjuːmənɔɪd] *adj.* 像人的 (man-like)
【例】On its last trip, it delivered a new storage compartment packed with supplies and a *humanoid* robot.

**longevity [lɔːnˈdʒevəti] *n.* 长寿
【记】long(长) + ev(时间) + ity → 活得时间长 → 长寿

antecedent [ˌæntɪˈsiːdnt] *n.* 前事 (a preceding event, condition or cause)；前辈
adj. 在前的，先行的 (preceding in time and order)

*anthropology [ˌænθrə'pɑːlədʒi] n. 人类学

*anthropocentric [ˌænθrəpə'sentrɪk] adj. 以人类为中心的，以人类观点解释宇宙万物的

【例】But the persistence of this attitude felt stale and charged with *anthropocentric* assumptions and a lack of scientific objectivity.

*matriarchal [ˌmeɪtri'ɑːrkl] adj. 母系氏族的

【例】The mythical origin of the Gelede is said to reflect the transformation from a *matriarchal* society into a patriarchal society.

maternal [mə'tɜːrnl] adj. 母性的

【记】matern(母亲) + al → 母性的

progeny ['prɑːdʒəni] n. 后代，子女(descendants; children)

【记】pro(前) + gen(产生) + y → 前人所生下的 → 后代

*matriarchy ['meɪtriɑːrki] n. 母系社会；母权制

【记】matr(母) + i + archy(统治) → 母权制

【派】matriarchal(adj. 母系氏族的)

*patriarchy ['peɪtriɑːrki] n. 父系社会

【例】It's about having an ongoing conversation about how we rethink gender and sexuality and *patriarchy* within the black community.

**posterity [pɑː'sterəti] n. 后代(offspring; descendant)

【记】post(后) + erity → 后代

**ancestral [æn'sestrəl] adj. 祖先的；祖传的(patrimonial)

【例】Using DNA markers and mathematical time-clock calculations, researchers have identified our *ancestral* Adam and Eve.

ancestry ['ænsestri] n. 祖先，血统(forbear)

【例】The most interesting results may come from investigations into human, rather than personal, *ancestry*.

forebear ['fɔːrber] n. 祖宗，祖先

【例】He was given the name in honour of his illustrious *forebear*.

*progenitor [proʊ'dʒenɪtər] n. (人或动植物的)祖先；(思想、学术或政治运动的)创始人，先驱

【例】Marx was the *progenitor* of Communism.

**predecessor ['predəsesər] n. (职务或职位的)前任者(a person who held an office or position before sb else)

【例】The decision was made by my *predecessor*.

*celibacy ['selɪbəsi] *n.* 独身（bachelorhood）

【例】"I do think that our clergy have this particular quality because of their *celibacy*," he said.

polygamist [pə'lɪgəmɪst] *n.* 一夫多妻者，一夫多妻论者

【例】The *polygamist* leader was hospitalized at least once before during his two years in jail.

*genealogy [ˌdʒiːni'ælədʒi] *n.* 家谱；家系；家系学

【记】gene(基因) + alogy(=ology学科) → 关于基因的研究 → 家系学

*ethicist ['eθɪsɪst] *n.* 伦理学家

*groom [gruːm] *n.* 马夫；新郎（bridegroom）

【记】g(哥哥) + room(房间) → 哥哥进新娘房间 → 新郎

*demography [dɪ'mɑːgrəfi] *n.* 人口统计学

【记】demo(人) + graphy(写) → 写出人口有多少 → 人口统计学

**census ['sensəs] *n.* 人口普查

【记】cens(评估) + us → 评估人口 → 人口统计

**aboriginal [ˌæbə'rɪdʒənl] *n.* 土著 *adj.* 土著的；原来的（native）

【记】ab + original(原来的) → 原来的

**descent [dɪ'sent] *n.* 血统（ancestry）

*hybrid ['haɪbrɪd] *n.* 杂种；混血儿

*ethnicity [eθ'nɪsəti] *n.* 种族划分

*grownup ['grəʊnˌʌp] *n.* 成年人（adult）

【例】He was a *grownup* and knew that it would have insulted her to say that he had noticed nothing.

*mustache ['məstɑːʃ] *n.* 胡子（moustache）

【例】The *mustache* remains popular abroad, especially in the Middle East and in Southeast Asia.

社 会 学

conventional [kən'venʃənl] *adj.* 传统的，习俗的（traditional; customary）

【例】Mary thought marriage and family was too *conventional* so she joined the army.

*hierarchical [ˌhaɪə'rɑːrkɪkl] *adj.* 分层的，等级体系的（layered）

【例】It has an uncomfortable connection to old *hierarchical* codes at odds with our democratic values.

*democratic [ˌdemə'krætɪk] *adj.* 民主的，民主政体的（based on the principles of democracy）

【例】*democratic* rules

*humanistic [ˌhjuːmə'nɪstɪk] *adj.* 人文主义的

【例】The code of the communist ethics included not all main aspects of the European *humanistic* one.

*genteel [dʒen'tiːl] *adj.* 上流社会的，有教养的（well-bred; courteous）

【记】和gentle（*adj.* 温柔的）一起记

*exotic [ɪg'zɑːtɪk] *adj.* 外来的；有异国风味的（unusual; foreign）

【记】exo（外面）+ tic → 外来的

【例】Susan and Bill love to eat spicy and *exotic* food.

*rustic ['rʌstɪk] *adj.* 乡村的（rural）；质朴的（unsophisticated）

【记】rust（乡村）+ ic → 乡村的

*companionable [kəm'pæniənəbl] *adj.* 好交往的，友善的（amicable）

【例】She made chickens seem less like livestock and more like useful and *companionable* creatures.

*colonial [kə'loʊniəl] *adj.* 殖民地的；占有殖民地的 （of, relating to or possessing a colony or colonies）

【例】France was once a *colonial* power.

convention [kən'venʃn] *n.* 传统

【例】Chinese people have the *convention* of shaking hands.

*folkway ['foʊkweɪ] *n.* 民风，社会习俗（tradition）

subcultural [ˌsʌb'kʌltʃərəl] *n.* 亚文化 （behaviour, practices, etc associated with a group within a society）

【例】the teenage *subculture*

strata ['streɪtə] *n.* （单数为stratum）层次，社会阶层

【例】the privileged *stratum*

**phenomenology [fɪˌnɑːmə'nɑːlədʒi] *n.* 现象学

phenomenon [fə'nɑːmɪnən] *n.* 现象 （fact or occurrence, especially in nature or society, that can be perceived by the senses）

【例】Bankruptcy is a common *phenomenon* in an economic recession.

destitute ['destɪtuːt] *adj.* 贫乏的（being without; lacking）；穷困的

【记】de（无）+ stitute（建立）→ 没有建立 → 穷困的

existential	[ˌegzɪˈstenʃəl] *adj.* (有关)存在的；存在主义的
	【记】来自动词exist(*v.* 存在)
*grassroot	[ˈɡrɑːsˌruːt] *n.* 草根
*famine	[ˈfæmɪn] *n.* 饥荒
	【记】family(家庭)处于饥荒(famine)中
*asylum	[əˈsaɪləm] *n.* 精神病院，收容所；安全，庇护 (safety; refuge)
	【例】be granted political *asylum*
epistemology	[ɪˌpɪstəˈmɑːlədʒi] *n.* 认识论
*commercialization	[kəˌmɜːrʃəlaɪˈzeɪʃn] *n.* 商品化
philosophy	[fəˈlɑːsəfi] *n.* 哲学 (search for knowledge and understanding of the nature and meaning of the universe and of human life)
	【例】moral *philosophy*
hedonistic	[ˌhiːdəˈnɪstɪk] *adj.* 快乐主义者的
	【例】Scott Fitzgerald's lustrous stretch of shoreline is still attractive to those seeking mild winters and *hedonistic* lifestyles.
materialism	[məˈtɪriəlɪzəm] *n.* 物质享乐主义(obsession with material possessions, bodily comforts, etc, while neglecting spiritual values)
	【例】the rampant *materialism* of modern society
metaphysical	[ˌmetəˈfɪzɪkl] *adj.* 形而上学的，玄学的(of metaphysics)
	【记】meta(变化，超过) + physic(看做physics，物理) + al → 在物理之上的 → 形而上学的，玄学的
ethos	[ˈiːθɑːs] *n.* (个人、团体或民族的)道德风貌，思潮，信仰
	【记】eth (=ethn种族) + os → 种族气氛 → 民族精神
*dentistry	[ˈdentɪstri] *n.* 牙科学
	【例】The student is Michele McAuley, who is in the first year of a course in *dentistry*.
*elitist	[eɪˈliːtɪst] *n.* 优秀人才，杰出人物
	【例】He argued that Bloomberg was an *elitist*, out of touch with regular New Yorkers.
*pluralism	[ˈplʊrəlɪzəm] *n.* 多元论
**aviation	[ˌeɪviˈeɪʃn] *n.* 航空学，航空(science or practice of flying aircraft)
*slum	[slʌm] *n.* 贫民窟 (house or rooms in a street, alley, etc of badly-built, over-crowded buildings)
	【例】brought up in a *slum*

zeitgeist	['zaɪtgaɪst] n. 时代精神 （spirit of a particular period of history as shown by the ideas, beliefs, etc. of the time）
Arabian	[ə'reɪbiən] adj. 阿拉伯的，阿拉伯人的 （of Arabia or the Arabs） n. 阿拉伯人
	【例】the *Arabian* Sea
proletarian	[ˌprəʊlə'teriən] adj. 无产阶级的
	【例】As the population exploded, *proletarian* families built rickety shacks inside the courtyards, many of which are now hardly recognizable.
Thai	[taɪ] n. 泰国人；泰国语 adj. 泰国的；泰国人的

考 古 学

**artifact	['ɑːrtɪfækt] n. 人造物品，手工艺品
**antiquity	[æn'tɪkwəti] n. 古代；古老；古代的遗物
**antique	[æn'tiːk] n. 古物，古董
**antiquated	['æntɪkweɪtɪd] adj. 陈旧的，过时的（obsolete; old-fashioned）
**archaic	[ɑːr'keɪɪk] adj. 古的（old）
	【记】arch(古) + aic → 古的
	【例】The *archaic* ship was just like the ones used centuries earlier.
**archaeology	[ˌɑːrki'ɑːlədʒi] n. 考古学 （the scientific study of material remains of past human life and activities）
	【记】archae(古) + ology(学科) → 考古学
	【派】archaeological(adj. 考古学的)
**porcelain	['pɔːrsəlɪn] n. 瓷器（china）
**ascend	[ə'send] vi. 追溯
	【例】His ancestors *ascend* to the 18th century.
*remnant	['remnənt] n. 残余，遗迹（remains; leftover; vestige）
	【例】No *remnants* of the settlement of Roanoke, Virginia were found by the next group of colonists.
*tomb	[tuːm] n. (尤指有石碑的)坟，墓
*excavate	['ekskəveɪt] vt. 挖掘（to dig; delve）
	【记】ex + cav(洞) + ate → 挖出洞 → 挖掘
	【例】They *excavated* a huge hole for the foundation of the building.
hoary	['hɔːri] adj. (头发)灰白的（gray）；古老的（very old）
	【记】发音似"好理" → 头发灰白，该好好整理了 → 头发灰白

genesis [ˈdʒenəsɪs] *n.* 创始，起源(beginning; origin)

【记】gene（产生；基因）+ sis → 创始；大写 Genesis专指《圣经》中的《创世纪》

hieroglyph [ˈhaɪərəglɪf] *n.* 象形文字，图画文字(a picture or symbol representing a word)

【记】hiero(神) + glyph(写，刻) → 神写的字 → 象形文字

unearth [ʌnˈɜːrθ] *vt.* 挖掘，发现(to uncover; exhume)

【记】un + earth(土地) → 弄开土 → 挖掘

【例】A recent excavation *unearthed* a pottery of Ming dynasty.

exhume [ɪgˈzuːm] *vt.* 挖掘(尸体)，掘出(to excavate; dig)

【记】ex(出) + hume(土) → 出土 → 掘出

【例】The coroner *exhumed* the body in order to perform tests regarding the cause of death.

annals [ˈænlz] *n.* 编年史(a record of events arranged in yearly sequence)

【记】ann(年) + als → 编年史

antediluvian [ˌæntidɪˈluːviən] *adj.* (《圣经》中所说的)大洪水前的，史前的 (of the time before the Biblical Flood)；陈旧的(old fashioned, or primitive)

【记】ante + diluv(洪水) + ian → 大洪水以前的

练 习 题

填空题

aboriginal	ancestral	colonial	companionable	democratic
descent	exotic	filial	genteel	hierarchical
humanistic	humanlike	humanoid	interracial	juvenile
longevity	posterity	predecessor	rustic	semihuman

1. I suspect you're of Jewish _____.
2. We should study our _____ achievements.
3. We wish you both health and _____.
4. The Indians are the _____ Americans.
5. Most of the suspects were _____ under the age of 17.
6. She had done her _____ respect to her mother.
7. The kangaroo is one of the "evolved" animals, genetic upgrades that are permitted to live _____ lives and do society's grunt work.
8. An omniscient and omnipotent God must be above such _____ constraints.
9. Civil services are organized in _____ structures of offices.
10. They are aiming to make the institutions of the EU truly _____.
11. Roman republican law upheld a _____ view of marriage.
12. Her _____ accent irritated me.
13. She travels to all kinds of _____ locations all over the world.
14. The village had a certain _____ charm.
15. They sat together in _____ silence.
16. Tunisia achieved independence from French _____ rule in 1956.
17. Kennedy's _____ as president was the war hero Dwight Eisenhower.
18. _____ will remember him as a great man.
19. In 1967, 16 states still had laws against _____ marriage, but attitudes were changing.
20. A new method was presented, which can analyze the kinematics of _____ running robot.

配对题

1. census	以人类为中心的	11. remnant	古代
2. eurocentric	人类学	12. porcelain	史前的
3. anthropology	残余	13. antiquity	母系氏族的
4. anthropocentric	瓷器	14. antique	母系社会;母权制
5. matriarchal	古物	15. archaeology	考古学
6. matriarchy	航空学,航空	16. artifact	父系社会
7. patriarchy	人造物品	17. tomb	现象学
8. progenitor	人口普查	18. antediluvian	祖先;创始人,先驱
9. aviation	坟,墓	19. hieroglyph	创始,起源
10. phenomenology	以欧洲为中心的	20. genesis	象形文字

练习题答案

填空题答案

1. I suspect you're of Jewish <u>descent</u>.
2. We should study our <u>ancestral</u> achievements.
3. We wish you both health and <u>longevity</u>.
4. The Indians are the <u>aboriginal</u> Americans.
5. Most of the suspects were <u>juveniles</u> under the age of 17.
6. She had done her <u>filial</u> respect to her mother.
7. The kangaroo is one of the "evolved" animals, genetic upgrades that are permitted to live <u>semihuman</u> lives and do society's grunt work.
8. An omniscient and omnipotent God must be above such <u>humanlike</u> constraints.
9. Civil services are organized in <u>hierarchical</u> structures of offices.
10. They are aiming to make the institutions of the EU truly <u>democratic</u>.
11. Roman republican law upheld a <u>humanistic</u> view of marriage.
12. Her <u>genteel</u> accent irritated me.
13. She travels to all kinds of <u>exotic</u> locations all over the world.
14. The village had a certain <u>rustic</u> charm.
15. They sat together in <u>companionable</u> silence.
16. Tunisia achieved independence from French <u>colonial</u> rule in 1956.
17. Kennedy's <u>predecessor</u> as president was the war hero Dwight Eisenhower.
18. <u>Posterity</u> will remember him as a great man.
19. In 1967, 16 states still had laws against <u>interracial</u> marriage, but attitudes were changing.
20. A new method was presented, which can analyze the kinematics of <u>humanoid</u> running robot.

配对题答案

1. census	人口普查	11. remnant	残余
2. eurocentric	以欧洲为中心的	12. porcelain	瓷器
3. anthropology	人类学	13. antiquity	古代
4. anthropocentric	以人类为中心的	14. antique	古物
5. matriarchal	母系氏族的	15. archaeology	考古学
6. matriarchy	母系社会；母权制	16. artifact	人造物品
7. patriarchy	父系社会	17. tomb	坟，墓
8. progenitor	祖先；创始人，先驱	18. antediluvian	史前的
9. aviation	航空学，航空	19. hieroglyph	象形文字
10. phenomenology	现象学	20. genesis	创始，起源

Word List 9

语言学·文学

语言学

*pun [pʌn] *n.* 双关语

figurative [ˈfɪɡərətɪv] *adj.* 比喻的，借喻的（metaphoric）
【记】figur(e)(象征) + ative → 象征性的 → 比喻的
【例】language used in a *figurative* or nonliteral sense

*metaphorical [ˌmetəˈfɔːrɪkl] *adj.* 比喻的，隐喻的
【例】The English edition therefore becomes a *metaphorical* bridge towards international institutions, private committees and individual citizens.

**succinct [səkˈsɪŋkt] *adj.* 简明的，简洁的（terse; concise）

*symbolize [ˈsɪmbəlaɪz] *vt.* 象征
【例】Fairly or not, lobbyist Jack Abramoff has come to *symbolize* Washington at its worst.

*cogent [ˈkoʊdʒənt] *adj.* 强有力的，有说服力的（convincing; compelling）
【例】The defense attorney's *cogent* argument was persuasive.

cognate [ˈkɑːɡneɪt] *adj.* 同词源的（related through the same source）；同类的（having the same nature or quality）
【记】cogn(认识) + ate → 认识的 → 同类的

*linguistic [lɪŋˈɡwɪstɪk] *adj.* 语言的（of language）
【记】lingu(语言) + istic → 语言的

multilingual [ˌmʌltiˈlɪŋɡwəl] *adj.* 多语的；能使用多种语言的（speaking or using many languages）
【例】India is a *multilingual* country.

**jargon [ˈdʒɑːrɡən] *n.* 暗语（confused language）；术语，行话（the technical terminology）
【记】jar(大罐) + go(走) + (on)(在…上) → 大罐走在上面 → 暗语

glossary [ˈglɑːsəri] *n.* 词汇表

【记】gloss(舌头，语言) + ary → 词汇表

*personification [pərˌsɑːnɪfɪˈkeɪʃn] *n.* 典型，化身，完美榜样（a perfect example; embodiment; incarnation）

【例】Obviously, this man is the *personification* of evil.

irony [ˈaɪrəni] *n.* 反话（the opposite of the literal meaning）；出人意料的事情或情况（the opposite of what is expected）

paradigm [ˈpærədaɪm] *n.* 范例，示范（a typical example or archetype）

【记】para(旁边) + digm(显示) → 显示给旁边的看 → 示范

【派】paradigmatic(*adj.* 作为示范的，典范的）

*dialect [ˈdaɪəlekt] *n.* 方言，土语（vernacular; jargon）

【记】dia + lect(说) → 方言

【例】John's Southern *dialect* is hard for me to understand.

adage [ˈædɪdʒ] *n.* 格言，谚语（proverb）

【例】Isn't there an old *adage* that a stitch in time saves nine?

*maxim [ˈmæksɪm] *n.* 格言，箴言（proverb; motto）

【记】比较：maximum(最大值) → minimum(最小值)

**nomenclature [nəˈmenklətʃər] *n.* 名称，术语，专业名词（terminology; system of names）

【例】She struggled to master scientific *nomenclature*.

*simile [ˈsɪməli] *n.* 明喻（comparison of one thing with another）

【记】simil(相类似的) + e → 把相类似的事物进行比较 → 明喻

*acronym [ˈækrənɪm] *n.* 首字母缩略词

【记】acro(高) + nym(名称) → 把高出小写字母的大写字母放在一起，如GRE, TOEFL, USA → 首字母缩略词

terminology [ˌtɜːrməˈnɑːlədʒi] *n.* 术语，术语学（the technical or special terms）

【记】term(术语) + in + ology(…学) → 术语(学)

alliteration [əˌlɪtəˈreɪʃn] *n.* 头韵（repetition of beginning sound in poetry）

*euphemism [ˈjuːfəmɪzəm] *n.* 婉言，委婉的说法

【记】eu(好) + phem(出现) + ism → 以好的语言出现 → 委婉的说法

*fiction [ˈfɪkʃn] *n.* 小说

【记】fict(做) + ion → 做出的故事 → 小说

***rhetoric [ˈretərɪk] *n.* 修辞；修辞学；浮夸的言语（insincere or grandiloquent language）

【记】来自Rhetor(古希腊的修辞学教师，演说家）

*fable ［ˈfeɪbl］ *n.* 寓言，传说（allegory）

【例】Many *fables* were first told by an old Greek story-teller named Aesop.

*excerpt ［ˈeksɜːrpt］ *n.* 摘录（selection; extract）

【例】The actor auditioned by performing an *excerpt* from the play.

satire ［ˈsætaɪər］ *n.* 讽刺，讥讽（attacking foolish or wicked behavior by making fun of it）

【例】Is there too much *satire* in his article?

*palindrome ［ˈpælɪndroʊm］ *n.* 回文（正读反读皆同的词，如madam）

*paradox ［ˈpærədɑːks］ *n.* 似非而是的隽语，看似矛盾而实际（或可能）正确的说法（statement that seems to be absurd or contradictory but is or may be true）

【例】"More haste, less speed" is a well-known *paradox*.

argot ［ˈɑːrɡət］ *n.* 隐语，黑话（slang; speech spoken by only a small group of people）

【反】standard language（标准语言）; common verbalism（一般用语）

parenthesis ［pəˈrenθəsɪs］ *n.* 插入语；插曲；圆括号

【记】par(=para旁边) + en(进入) + thesis(放) → 插入语

【例】The careless student always uses the *parenthesis* without any definite pause.

*tag ［tæɡ］ *n.* 附加语；标签（label; tab）

*cognizance ［ˈkɑːɡnɪzəns］ *n.* 认识，认知（knowledge; awareness）

【记】cogn(知道) + izance → 认识，认知

genre ［ˈʒɑːnrə］ *n.* (文艺作品的)体裁，风格（style; manner）

【例】His six String Quartets is the most important works in the *genre* since Beethoven's.

*circumlocution ［ˌsɜːrkəmləˈkjuːʃn］ *n.* 迂回累赘的陈述，婉转曲折的说法，遁词（a roundabout, lengthy way of expressing sth）

【记】circum(绕圈) + locu(说话) + tion → 说话绕圈子 → 迂回累赘的陈述

【反】succinctness(*n.* 简洁)

【派】circumlocutory(*adj.* 迂回累赘的)

*lexis ［ˈleksɪs］ *n.* 词汇，词语（vocabulary）

adapt ［əˈdæpt］ *vt.* 改编，改写（to revise; amend）

**articulate ［ɑːrˈtɪkjuleɪt］ *v.* 清晰地说(话)、发(音)（to express clearly）

【派】articulation(*n.* 清晰说话、发音)

**compile [kəmˈpaɪl] vt. 汇编，编纂（to collect; put together）

【记】com(共同) + pile(堆) → 将资料堆在一起 → 汇编

【例】The scientists *compiled* a great amount of data to help develop their theory.

*abridge [əˈbrɪdʒ] vt. 缩短，删节（to shorten; condense; abbreviate）

【记】a(使) + bridge(桥) → 桥使路程变短 → 缩短

【例】This book might be more readable if the obscure parts in it is *abridged*.

*paraphrase [ˈpærəfreɪz] vt. 意译，改写，转述（to rewrite）

【记】para(旁边) + phrase(词句) → 在旁边用不同的词写 → 改写

【例】Would you please *paraphrase* the speech in colloquial English?

abstract [æbˈstrækt] v. 做(…的)摘要

【记】abs + tract(拉) → 从原文中拉出来 → 摘要

bilingual [ˌbaɪˈlɪŋgwəl] adj. (说)两种语言的（of two languages）

【记】bi(两个) + lingu(语言) + al → (说)两种语言的

parlance [ˈpɑːrləns] n. 说法，用语，语调（manner of speaking; idiom）

【记】parl(说话) + ance(方式) → 说法

alphabetical [ˌælfəˈbetɪkl] adj. 按字母顺序排列的（in the order of the alphabet）

【记】由希腊字母α, β 的发音而来

monosyllabic [ˌmɑːnəsɪˈlæbɪk] adj. 单音节的

*orthographical [ˌɔːrθəˈgræfɪkəl] adj. 拼字正确的

verbatim [vɜːrˈbeɪtɪm] adj. 逐字的，照字面的 （being in or following exact words; word for word）

【记】verb(词语) + atim → 逐字的

*neuter [ˈnjuːtər] adj. (指词)中性的（of a word neither masculine nor feminine in gender）

【例】a *neuter* noun

cognitive [ˈkɑːgnətɪv] adj. 认识的，认知的

*unpersuasive [ˌʌnpərˈsweɪsɪv] adj. 无说服力的（lame）

【例】Even as I made the argument, I knew that it was *unpersuasive*.

*vernacular [vərˈnækjələr] n. 本国语，地方语（dialect）

farce [fɑːrs] n. 闹剧

ellipsis [ɪˈlɪpsɪs] n. 省略（the omission of words）

【记】el(出) + lipsis(离开) → 使离去 → 省略

cant [kænt] n. 隐语，术语，黑话（jargon）vi. 使用黑话或隐语

【记】把can't中的 ’ 拿掉就是cant

neologism [ni'ɑːlədʒɪzəm] *n.* 新词，新义（a new word or phrase）

【记】neo(新) + log(话语) + ism → 新话语 → 新词

assonance ['æsənəns] *n.* 半谐音（两个词或音节的元音类似或辅音类似，如 sharper 和 garter 或 killed 和 cold）

*syncopate ['sɪŋkəpeɪt] *vt.* 词中省略，省去（中间字母或音节）

phylum ['faɪləm] *n.* 语系，语群（a large division of possibly genetically related families of languages or linguistic stocks）

etymology [ˌetɪ'mɑːlədʒi] *n.* 词源学（the branch of linguistics dealing with word origin and development）

【记】来自 etymon(*n.* 词源，词根)

innuendo [ˌɪnju'endoʊ] *n.* 含沙射影，暗讽（an indirect remark, gesture, or reference, usually implying sth derogatory; insinuation）

【记】innu(在内) + endo(内部) → 包含在内的讽刺 → 暗讽

malapropism ['mæləprɑːpɪzəm] *n.* 字的误用（ludicrous misuse of words）

【记】mal(坏，不) + aprop(恰当) + ism → 用字不恰当 → 字的误用；源自 Malaprop，爱尔兰喜剧《情敌》中的人物马勒普太太，以荒唐地误用词语而出名

philology [fɪ'lɑːlədʒi] *n.* 语文学，文学语言学

【记】phil(爱) + ology(语言) → 语文学

solecism ['sɑːlɪsɪzəm] *n.*（尤指显示某人为外国人或社会阶层低下的）语言错误，语病（mistakes in the use of language, especially one that shows sb to be foreign or of low social class）

tirade ['taɪreɪd] *n.* 长篇的攻击性演说（a long and angry speech）

【记】tir(拉) + ade → 拉长的话 → 长篇的攻击性演说

【反】dispassionate speech(心平气和的演说)

homograph ['hɑːməɡræf] *n.* 同形异义字（one of two or more words spelled alike but different in meaning or derivation or pronunciation）

【记】homo(相同) + graph(写) → 写起来相同但意义不同的词 → 同形异义字

monogram ['mɑːnəɡræm] *n.* 由姓与名的第一个字母编制而成的图案（design composed of one or more initials of a name）

orthography [ɔːr'θɑːɡrəfi] *n.* 正确拼字，拼字法，正字法（correct spelling）

asterisk ['æstərɪsk] *n.* 星号（a mark like a star used to draw attention）

【记】aster(星星) + isk → 星号

coeval ［koʊˈiːvl］ *adj.* 同时代的（existing at the same time）
【记】co(共同) + ev(时代) + al → 同时代的

neolithic ［ˌniːəˈlɪθɪk］ *adj.* 新石器时代的
【记】neo(新) + lith(石头) + ic → 新石器时代的

paleolithic ［ˌpæliʊˈlɪθɪk］ *adj.* 旧石器时代的
【记】paleo(古) + lith(石头) + ic → 旧石器时代的

prehistoric ［ˌpriːhɪˈstɔːrɪk］ *adj.* 史前的（of a time before recorded history）
【记】pre(前) + historic(历史的) → 史前的

preliterate ［priːˈlɪtərət］ *adj.* 文字出现以前的（antedating the use of writing）
【记】pre(前) + liter(文字) + ate → 文字出现以前的

provenance ［ˈprɑːvənəns］ *n.* (艺术等的)出处，起源（origin; source）
【记】pro(前面) + ven(来) + ance → 前面来的东西 → 起源

runic ［ˈruːnɪk］ *adj.* 北欧古代文字的

文 学

**reportage ［rɪˈpɔːrtɪdʒ］ *n.* 报道，报道的消息，报告文学（the act or process of reporting news）
【记】来自report(*n./v.* 报道)

**scenario ［səˈnærioʊ］ *n.* 剧情梗概（an outline or synopsis of a play）；剧本（screenplay）
【记】scen(=scene场景) + ario → 剧情梗概

*epigram ［ˈepɪɡræm］ *n.* 讽刺短诗，警句（terse, witty statement）
【记】epi(在…旁边) + gram(写) → 旁敲侧击的东西 → 讽刺短诗

burlesque ［bɜːrˈlesk］ *n.* 讽刺滑稽作品（derisive caricature; parody）
【记】burl(玩笑，讽刺) + esque → 讽刺滑稽作品

*epistolary ［ɪˈpɪstəleri］ *adj.* 书信的，书信体的
【例】*Epistolary* romance in the movies means listening to letters in voice-over, rather than studying live flesh in close-up.

*ballad ［ˈbæləd］ *n.* 歌谣，民歌（a song or poem that tells a story in short stanzas）
【记】ball(球) + ad → 像球一样一代代传下来 → 歌谣

parody ［ˈpærədi］ *n.* 讽刺性模仿文章或表演（article or performance in which the style of an author or work is closely imitated for comic effect or in ridicule）；拙劣的模仿（a feeble or ridiculous imitation）
【记】par(=para旁边) + ody(=ode唱) → 在旁边学着唱 → 拙劣的模仿

*analogy [əˈnælədʒi] *n.* 相似（partial resemblance）；类比（the likening of one thing to another）

【记】ana(并列)+log(说话)+y → 放在一起说 → 类比

【反】lacking similarity(缺乏相似性)

epic [ˈepɪk] *n.* 叙事诗，史诗(a long narrative poem) *adj.* 英雄的；史诗的；大规模的，壮丽的(of great size)

【反】modest(*adj.* 一般的；适度的；谦逊的)

saga [ˈsɑːgə] *n.* 英雄故事，长篇冒险小说（any long story of adventure or heroic deeds）

【记】注意不要和sage(*adj.* 智慧的)相混

**allegory [ˈæləgɔːri] *n.* 寓言(fable)

【记】al(=all)+leg(讲)+ory → 讲的全部都是小故事 → 寓言

parable [ˈpærəbl] *n.* 寓言(a short fictitious story that illustrates a moral attitude or a religious principle)；比喻

【记】par(平等)+able → 能够平行比较 → 比喻

precept [ˈpriːsept] *n.* 规范，准则，箴言，格言（moral instruction; rule or principle that teaches correct behavior）

【记】pre(预先)+cept(拿住) → 预先接受的话 → 格言

*autobiography [ˌɔːtəbaɪˈɑːgrəfi] *n.* 自传（the story of a person's life written by that person）

【记】auto(自己)+bio(生命)+graphy(写) → 写自己的一生 → 自传

【派】autobiographical(*adj.* 自传的；有关自传的)

annotate [ˈænəteɪt] *v.* 注解(to provide critical or explanatory notes)

【记】an+not(标示)+ate → 注解

【派】annotated(*adj.* 注释过的，评注的)；annotation(*n.* 注解)

limerick [ˈlɪmərɪk] *n.* 五行打油诗(a nonsense poem of five anapestic lines)

【记】源自爱尔兰一首歌曲中连唱五遍的叠句：Will you come up to Limerick?(Limerick为城市名)

metaphor [ˈmetəfər] *n.* 隐喻，暗喻

【记】meta(变化)+phor(带有) → 以变化的方式表达 → 隐喻

astrology [əˈstrɑːlədʒi] *n.* 占星术，占星学(primitive astronomy)

【记】astro(星)+(o)logy → 占星学

【派】astrologer(*n.* 占星家)

trilogy [ˈtrɪlədʒi] *n.* 三部曲(a group of three related books)

【记】tri(三)+logy(说话)+y → 三步讲的故事互相联系 → 三部曲

epitaph ['epɪtæf] *n.* 墓志铭(an inscription on a tomb or gravestone)

【记】epi(在…上) + taph(=tomb 墓) → 在墓碑上刻的字 → 墓志铭

*eulogy ['juːlədʒi] *n.* 颂词，颂文(high speech or commendation)

【反】denunciation(*n.* 谴责); diatribe(*n.* 恶骂); defamation(*n.* 诋毁)

paean ['piːən] *n.* 赞美歌，颂歌(a song of joy, praise, triumph)

【记】和hymn(*n.* 赞美歌)一起记忆

【反】harsh lampoon(激烈讽刺文章)

panegyric [ˌpænə'dʒɪrɪk] *n.* 颂词，颂扬(elaborate praise)

【记】pan(全部) + egyric(集中) → 把赞扬的话集中 → 颂扬

【反】anathema(*n.* 诅咒)

dissertation [dɪsər'teɪʃn] *n.* 专题论文(long essay on a particular subject)

【记】dis(加强) + sert(断言) + ation → 加强言论，说明主题 → 专题论文

doggerel ['dɔːɡərəl] *n.* 歪诗，打油诗

【例】The *doggerel* doesn't filiate itself.

aphorism ['æfərɪzəm] *n.* 格言(maxim; adage)

【记】a + phor(带来) + ism → 带来智慧的话 → 格言

【派】aphoristic(*adj.* 格言(似)的; 简短的)

canto ['kæntoʊ] *n.* (长诗的)篇(division of a long poem)

【记】can(能) + to(到) → 能拿到舞台上朗诵的 → (长诗的)篇

lampoon [læm'puːn] *n.* 讽刺文章(a broad satirical piece of writing) *vt.* 讽刺(to ridicule or satirize)

【记】lamp(灯) + oon → 用灯照别人的缺点 → 讽刺

【反】paean(*n.* 赞歌)

【派】lampooner(*n.* 讽刺作家)

libretto [lɪ'bretoʊ] *n.* (歌剧等的)歌词(the words of an opera, etc); (歌剧等的)剧本

【记】libre(书) + tto → 剧本

madrigal ['mædrɪgl] *n.* 抒情短诗; 情歌，小曲

【记】madri(看做Madrid) + gal → 马德里是个浪漫的城市，经常能听到情歌 → 情歌

picaresque [ˌpɪkə'resk] *adj.* (指文学作品)以无赖和流浪汉为题材的

slanguage ['slæŋgwɪdʒ] *n.* 使用俚语的表现法; 多俚语的作品

backdrop ['bækdrɑːp] *n.* (事件的)背景; 背景幕布(printed cloth hung at the back of a theatre)

【记】back(后面) + drop(后面挂下的幕布) → 背景幕布

valediction [ˌvælɪˈdɪkʃn] *n.* 告别；告别演说，告别辞（an address or statement of farewell）

【记】vale（告别）+ diction（讲话）→ 告别辞

【反】greeting（*n.* 欢迎词）

eclogue [ˈeklɔg] *n.* 田园诗，牧歌（a short, usually pastoral poem）

【记】ec（环境）+ log（说话）+ ue → 关于自然环境的话 → 田园诗；诗人维吉尔的一本诗歌集名为*Eclogue*

**concordance [kənˈkɔːrdəns] *n.* （作家作品中的重要词语）按字母顺序排列的索引；和谐，一致性

【例】a *concordance* to Shakespeare

A man is not old as long as he is seeking something. A man is not old until regrets take the place of dreams.

只要一个人还有所追求，他就没有老。直到后悔取代了梦想，一个人才算老。

——美国演员 巴里穆尔（J. Barrymore, American actor）

练 习 题

填空题

abridge	adapt	articulate	cogent	epic
compile	parody	lampoon	dialect	concordance
backdrop	euphemism	linguistic	maxim	metaphorical
neuter	paradox	paraphrase	epistolary	succinct

1. The mountains provided a dramatic _____ for our picnic.
2. The *Iliad* and *Odyssey* are _____.
3. There is reasonable _____ between the two sets of results.
4. His cartoons mercilessly _____ the politicians of his time.
5. His personality made him an easy subject for _____.
6. She struggled to _____ her thoughts.
7. Keep your answers as _____ as possible.
8. They are _____ statistics for a report on traffic accidents.
9. The word has a _____ as well as a literal meaning.
10. Most of this famous writer's novels have been _____ into films.
11. She put forward some _____ reasons for abandoning the plan.
12. Their language and _____ competence should be improved.
13. There are _____ differences from one area of the country to another.
14. "Waste not, want not" is her favorite _____.
15. _____ romance in the movies means listening to letters in voice-over, rather than studying live flesh in close-up.
16. It is a curious _____ that professional comedians often have unhappy personal lives.
17. She has been asked to _____ the novel for radio.
18. Try to _____ the question before you answer it.
19. The _____ for the prison camps was "retraining centres".
20. There are three genders in German: masculine, feminine and _____.

配对题

1. orthographical	按字母顺序排列的索引	11. palindrome	拼字正确的
2. rhetoric	暗语；术语，行话	12. tag	认识，认知
3. jargon	报道，报告文学	13. cognizance	首字母缩略词
4. nomenclature	词汇，词语	14. circumlocution	术语，专业名词
5. pun	典型，化身，完美榜样	15. lexis	双关语
6. personification	讽刺短诗，警句	16. reportage	小说
7. acronym	附加语；标签	17. scenario	修辞；修辞学；浮夸的言语
8. fiction	歌谣，民歌	18. concordance	迂回累赘的陈述
9. fable	回文	19. epigram	寓言，传说
10. excerpt	剧情梗概	20. ballad	摘录

练习题答案

填空题答案

1. The mountains provided a dramatic <u>backdrop</u> for our picnic.
2. The *Iliad* and *Odyssey* are <u>epics</u>.
3. There is reasonable <u>concordance</u> between the two sets of results.
4. His cartoons mercilessly <u>lampooned</u> the politicians of his time.
5. His personality made him an easy subject for <u>parody</u>.
6. She struggled to <u>articulate</u> her thoughts.
7. Keep your answers as <u>succinct</u> as possible.
8. They are <u>compiling</u> statistics for a report on traffic accidents.
9. The word has a <u>metaphorical</u> as well as a literal meaning.
10. Most of this famous writer's novels have been <u>adapted</u> into films.
11. She put forward some <u>cogent</u> reasons for abandoning the plan.
12. Their language and <u>linguistic</u> competence should be improved.
13. There are <u>dialectal</u> differences from one area of the country to another.
14. "Waste not, want not" is her favorite <u>maxim</u>.
15. <u>Epistolary</u> romance in the movies means listening to letters in voice-over, rather than studying live flesh in close-up.
16. It is a curious <u>paradox</u> that professional comedians often have unhappy personal lives.
17. She has been asked to <u>abridge</u> the novel for radio.
18. Try to <u>paraphrase</u> the question before you answer it.
19. The <u>euphemism</u> for the prison camps was "retraining centres".
20. There are three genders in German: masculine, feminine and <u>neuter</u>.

配对题答案

1. orthographical	拼字正确的	11. palindrome	回文
2. rhetoric	修辞；修辞学；浮夸的言语	12. tag	附加语；标签
3. jargon	暗语；术语，行话	13. cognizance	认识，认知
4. nomenclature	术语，专业名词	14. circumlocution	迂回累赘的陈述
5. pun	双关语	15. lexis	词汇，词语
6. personification	典型，化身，完美榜样	16. reportage	报道，报告文学
7. acronym	首字母缩略词	17. scenario	剧情梗概
8. fiction	小说	18. concordance	按字母顺序排列的索引
9. fable	寓言，传说	19. epigram	讽刺短诗，警句
10. excerpt	摘录	20. ballad	歌谣，民歌

Word List 10
艺术

艺 术

***portrait** [ˈpɔːrtrət] *n.* 肖像，画像；描写

***aesthetic** [esˈθetɪk] *adj.* 审美的，美学的（artistic）
【记】a + esthe(感觉) + tic → 对美有感觉的 → 美学的
【例】I added an *aesthetic* touch to the living room with silk flowers.

fresco [ˈfreskoʊ] *n.* 壁画
【记】fres(看做fresh，新鲜的) + co(看做cool，凉爽的) → 画在凉爽、新鲜的灰泥上 → 壁画

*crayon** [ˈkreɪən] *n.* 彩色蜡笔、粉笔；用彩色蜡笔、粉笔作的画
【记】和canyon(*n.* 峡谷)一起记

*sculpture** [ˈskʌlptʃər] *n.* 雕塑术，雕刻术（carving, engraving）；雕塑品，雕刻品
【例】*Sculpture* is the art of shaping solid materials.

*statuary** [ˈstætʃueri] *n.* 雕塑术（the art of making statues）；[总称] 雕塑，塑像（a collection of statues）
【记】来自statue(*n.* 雕像)

palette [ˈpælət] *n.* 调色板；调色板上的一套颜料

*silhouette** [ˌsɪluˈet] *n.* 黑色轮廓，侧影（dark outline of sb/sth seen against a light background）
【例】the *silhouettes* of the trees against the evening sky

*inscription** [ɪnˈskrɪpʃn] *n.* 铭刻；题献
【记】in(进入) + script(写，刻) + ion → 刻写进去 → 铭刻

collage [kəˈlɑːʒ] *n.* 拼贴画

*hue** [hjuː] *n.* 色彩，色泽（color）
【例】Her face has returned to its rosy pink *hue*.

*pigment** [ˈpɪgmənt] *n.* 干粉颜料；天然色素
【记】pig(猪) + ment(看做meat，猪肉) → 染色的猪肉是上了干粉颜料 → 干粉颜料

*miniature ［ˈmɪnətʃər］ *n.* 小画像；缩影

【记】mini(小) + ature(看做picture) → 小画像

figurine ［ˌfɪɡjəˈriːn］ *n.* 小塑像，小雕像

【记】来自figure(*n.* 塑像)

*archetype ［ˈɑːkitaɪp］ *n.* 原始模型，原型(prototype)

embroider ［imˈbrɔɪdər］ *v.* 绣(花)，在…上刺绣

【记】em + broider(刺绣) → 在…上刺绣

【例】Susan *embroidered* the edges of all her pillowcases.

ceramic ［səˈræmɪk］ *n.* 陶瓷制品(the making of pots or tiles by shaping pieces of clay and baking them) *adj.* 陶器的(made of clay and permanently hardened by heat)

rendition ［renˈdɪʃn］ *n.* 表演，扮演，演奏，演唱(the act or result of rendering)

repertoire ［ˈrepərtwɑːr］ *n.* (剧团等的)常备剧目(the complete list or supply of dramas, operas, or musical works)

【记】汇报(report)演出需要常备节目(repertoire)

thespian ［ˈθespiən］ *adj.* 戏剧的，演戏的(relating to drama; dramatic)

【记】来自古希腊悲剧创始者Thespis

*sitcom ［ˈsɪtkɑːm］ *abbr.* 情景喜剧(situation comedy)

*surrealistic ［səˌriːəˈlɪstɪk］ *adj.* 超现实主义的

【例】Maybe it's like what all these people say, just a bunch of *surrealistic* nonsense.

**picturesque ［ˌpɪktʃəˈresk］ *adj.* 如画般的，生动的(vivid)

【记】picture(图画) + sque → 如画般的

【例】City dwellers would sometimes long for a *picturesque* and serene rural life.

*vivid ［ˈvɪvɪd］ *adj.* 生动的(lively; active)

【例】David's *vivid* description seems to bring the students to the real battle field.

*histrionic ［ˌhɪstriˈɑːnɪk］ *adj.* 演戏的；剧院的

【记】histrion(演员) + ic → 演戏的；注意不要和historic(*adj.* 历史的)相混

charade ［ʃəˈreɪd］ *n.* 用动作等表演文字意义的字谜游戏

*monologue ［ˈmɑːnəlɔːɡ］ *n.* (戏剧等的)独白(soliloquy)；个人长篇演说(a prolonged discourse)

【记】mono(单独) + logue(说话) → 一个人说话 → 独白

prologue [ˈproulɔːg] *n.* 开场白；序幕；序言

【记】pro(在前) + logue(话语) → 前面说的话 → 开场白

【反】epilogue(*n.* 后记)

**folklore [ˈfouklɔːr] *n.* 民间传说；民俗学

【记】folk(乡民) + lore(传说，学问) → 民间传说；民俗学

prelude [ˈpreljuːd] *n.* 前奏，序幕(preface)

【记】pre(先) + lud(玩，演奏) + e → 先演奏 → 前奏

*vaudeville [ˈvɔːdəvɪl] *n.* 杂耍表演；轻歌舞剧

*tableau [ˈtæblou] *n.* 活人扮演的静态画面或场景，舞台造型

*pantomime [ˈpæntəmaɪm] *n.* 哑剧；哑剧演员

【记】panto(神话剧) + mime(哑剧) → 哑剧

mime [maɪm] *n.* 哑剧表演；哑剧(演员)(pantomime or an actor in a mime) *v.* 模仿；哑剧表演

【记】比较记忆：pantomime(*n.* 哑剧)；mimic(*v.* 模仿，戏弄)

*folktale [ˈfəukteɪl] *n.* 民间故事

cursive [ˈkɜːrsɪv] *adj.* 草书的

【记】curs(跑) + ive → (写字)像跑一样 → 草书的

*calligraphy [kəˈlɪgrəfi] *n.* 书法(beautiful handwriting)

*printmaking [ˈprɪntˌmeɪkɪŋ] *n.* 版画复制

【例】The gallery will show stages in the development of individual prints during Picasso's golden years of *printmaking*.

**bust [bʌst] *n.* 半身(雕)像

artisan [ˈɑːrtəzn] *n.* 技工，工匠(a skilled workman or craftsman)

【例】an *artisan* in leatherwork

*colossus [kəˈlɑːsəs] *n.* 巨人；巨型雕像

*ensemble [ɑːnˈsɑːmbl] *n.* 合奏；大合唱

【记】en + semble(相同) → 唱相同(的歌) → 大合唱

【反】solo(*n.* 独唱)

**renaissance [ˈrenəsɑːns] *n.* 文艺复兴

【记】re(重新) + naiss(出生) + ance → 新生 → 文艺复兴

*choreography [ˌkɔːriˈɑːgrəfi] *n.* 舞蹈(dancing)；舞蹈编排

【记】chore(歌舞) + o + graphy(写) → 为歌舞编排动作 → 舞蹈编排

*artistry [ˈɑːrtɪstri] *n.* 艺术技巧(skill of an artist)

【记】artist(艺术家) + ry → 艺术技巧

torso [ˈtɔːrsoʊ] *n.* (没有头和四肢的)躯干雕像；(人体的)躯干(the main part of the human body)

*baroque [bəˈroʊk] *n./adj.* 巴洛克风格(的)；(艺术、建筑等)过分雕琢(的) (gaudily ornate)

【记】由17世纪"巴洛克"艺术而来，以大胆的曲线结构、复杂的装饰和完全不同部分之间的整体协调为特色

【反】austere(*adj.* 简朴的)

*theatricality [θiˌætrɪˈkæləti] *n.* 戏剧风格，不自然，夸张(dramatic)

【例】The long wait is justified by the ritualistic *theatricality* of the murderous climax.

**chase [tʃeɪs] *v.* 雕镂(to make a groove in)；追捕，追寻(to follow rapidly)

【例】They are very interested in the *chased* silver.

**inscribe [ɪnˈskraɪb] *vt.* 刻，雕；题写

【记】in(进入) + scribe(写) → 刻写进去 → 刻，雕

*travesty [ˈtrævəsti] *v./n.* 拙劣模仿；歪曲，曲解 (a distorted or grossly inferior imitation)

【记】tra(横) + vest(穿衣) + y → 横过来穿衣 → 拙劣模仿

【反】paragon(*n.* 模范典型)

**conjure [ˈkʌndʒər] *vt.* 用魔术变出

【例】I don't know how I'll *conjure* up the money, but I'll pay rent tomorrow.

**mural [ˈmjʊrəl] *adj.* 墙壁的(of a wall) *n.* 壁画

【记】mur(墙) + al → 墙壁的

cameo [ˈkæmioʊ] *n.* 浮雕宝石 (jewel carved in relief)；生动刻画；(演员的)出演

【记】came(来) + o → 来哦 → 演员来哦 → 演员的出演

montage [ˌmɑːnˈtɑːʒ] *n.* 蒙太奇 (a literary, musical, or artistic composite of juxtaposed more or less heterogeneous elements)；拼贴画 (a composite picture made by combining several separate pictures)

opus [ˈoʊpəs] *n.* 艺术作品，(尤指)乐曲(work especially musical composition)

portray [pɔːrˈtreɪ] *vt.* 绘制(to delineate; depict)

【例】His work *portrays* the beautiful view of his hometown.

sartorial [sɑːrˈtɔːriəl] *adj.* 裁缝的，缝制的 (of or relating to a tailor or tailored clothes)

【记】sartor(裁缝) + ial → 裁缝

sphinx [sfɪŋks] *n.* 斯芬克斯（埃及的狮身人面或狮身兽面石像）；内心世界不外露的人，谜一样的人（a person who keeps his thoughts and feelings secret; enigmatic person）

【例】I've always found her rather *sphinx*-like.

*cello ['tʃelou] *n.* 大提琴

*cellist ['tʃelɪst] *n.* 大提琴演奏家

*clarinet [klærə'net] *n.* 单簧管，竖笛

**trumpet ['trʌmpɪt] *n.* 喇叭，小号（a brass wind instrument）

*saxophone ['sæksəfoun] *n.* 萨克斯管（铜管乐器）

*microphone ['maɪkrəfoun] *n.* 麦克风，话筒

harpsichord ['hɑːrpsɪkɔːrd] *n.* 键琴（钢琴前身）

【记】harp(竖琴) + si + chord(琴弦) → 键琴

*choir ['kwaɪər] *n.* (教堂的)唱诗班，圣乐团

*chorus ['kɔːrəs] *n.* 合唱团（choir; ensemble）

【例】A *chorus* accompanied the orchestra.

unison ['juːnɪsn] *n.* 齐奏，齐唱；一致，协调（complete accord）

**aria ['ɑːriə] *n.* 独唱曲，咏叹调

*recital [rɪ'saɪtl] *n.* 独奏(会)；吟诵

【记】来自recite(v. 背诵)，re + cite(唤起) → 重新引出 → 背诵

【派】recitalist(n. 独奏家)

descant ['deskænt] *n.* 高音部伴奏或伴唱

*duet [du'et] *n.* 二重唱

**orchestra ['ɔːrkɪstrə] *n.* 管弦乐队（band; ensemble）

*bandleader ['bændliːdər] *n.* 领队

**melodrama ['melədrɑːmə] *n.* 情节剧；音乐剧

【记】melo(dy)(旋律) + drama(戏剧) → 音乐剧

epilogue ['epɪlɔːg] *n.* 收场白，尾声（a closing section）

【记】epi(在…后) + logue(说话) → 在后面说的话 → 尾声

【反】prologue(n. 开场白；序幕；序言)；preface(n. 前奏；序言)

cantata [kæn'tɑːtə] *n.* 清唱剧，大合唱（a vocal and instrumental piece composed of choruses, solos, and recitatives）

【记】cant(唱) + ata(表示音乐类作品) → 清唱剧

reverie ['revəri] *n.* 幻想，梦幻曲（daydream）

【记】rever(做梦) + ie → 幻想，梦幻曲

operetta	[ˌɑːpəˈretə] n. 小歌剧（a light and amusing opera）
	【记】oper(=opera歌剧) + etta(小) → 小歌剧
sonata	[səˈnɑːtə] n. 奏鸣曲（an instrumental musical composition）
	【记】son(声音) + ata (表示音乐类作品) → 奏鸣曲
dirge	[dɜːrdʒ] n. 哀歌（a funeral hymn）
lullaby	[ˈlʌləbaɪ] n. 摇篮曲（cradlesong）
	【记】lull(使安睡) + aby(看做baby，婴儿) → 摇篮曲
fantasia	[fænˈteɪziə] n. 幻想曲；组合乐曲（a medley of familiar tunes）
	【记】来自fantasy(n. 幻想，怪念头)
diva	[ˈdiːvə] n. 歌剧中的女主角
**symphony	[ˈsɪmfəni] n. 交响乐，交响曲
	【记】sym(共同) + phon(声音) + y → 交响乐
gamut	[ˈɡæmət] n. 全音阶（any complete musical scale）；整个领域，全部
*pean	[ˈpiːən] n. 赞颂歌，凯旋歌
vocalist	[ˈvoʊkəlɪst] n. 流行歌手，声乐家（singer）
	【记】voc(声音) + alist(表人) → 声乐家
**chord	[kɔːrd] n. 和弦，和音
*melody	[ˈmelədi] n. 旋律；歌曲
	【记】mel(甜) + ody(唱) → 旋律
	【派】melodious(adj. 旋律优美的，悦耳的)
*timbre	[ˈtɪmbər] n. 音色，音质（the quality given to a sound by its overtones）
	【记】做音色(timbre)好的乐器必须用好木材(timber)
	【例】The singer's voice had a pleasant timbre.
cadence	[ˈkeɪdns] n. 抑扬顿挫（rhythmic rise and fall）；节奏，韵律（rhythm）
	【记】cad(落下) + ence → 声音的落下上升 → 节奏，韵律
cadent	[ˈkeɪdənt] adj. 有节奏的（rhythmed; metronomic）
*harmonic	[hɑːrˈmɑːnɪk] n. 泛音 adj. 和声的
*rhythm	[ˈrɪðəm] n. 节奏，韵律
	【例】play the same tune in a different rhythm
finale	[fɪˈnæli] n. 最后，最终，结局（an ending to sth）；乐曲的最后部分，终曲，末乐章（the concluding part of a musical composition）
	【记】来自final(adj. 最后的)
reprise	[rɪˈpraɪz] n. （音乐剧中）乐曲的重复（musical repetition）；重复（repetition）
	【记】rep(看做red，红色) + rise(升起) → 红色太阳重复升起 → 重复

*stanza	[ˈstænzə] *n.* (诗的)节，段
	【记】stan(看做stand，站住) + za → 诗停止的地方 → 节，段
dulcet	[ˈdʌlsɪt] *adj.* (声音)美妙的，悦耳的 (soothing or pleasant to hear; melodious)
	【记】dulc(=sweet甜) + et → 声音甜的 → 悦耳的
	【反】cacophonous(*adj.* 刺耳的)
*acoustic	[əˈkuːstɪk] *adj.* 听觉的，有关声音的 (having to do with hearing or sound)
	【派】acoustics(*n.* 声学)
euphonious	[juːˈfoʊniəs] *adj.* 悦耳的(pleasing to the ear)
	【记】eu(好) + phon(声音) + ious → 悦耳的
	【例】Her praise is surely a *euphonious* song to me.
**melodious	[məˈloʊdiəs] *adj.* 悦耳的，旋律优美的
	【例】Could there be a downside to such *melodious* power over all of us?
crescendo	[krəˈʃendoʊ] *n.* (音乐)渐强，高潮(a gradual increase in loudness)
	【记】crescend(成长；上升) + o → (音乐)渐强
*harsh	[hɑːrʃ] *adj.* 刺耳的(hoarse; unpleasant)
	【例】The *harsh* words by Tom annoyed Mike.
staccato	[stəˈkɑːtoʊ] *adj.* (音乐)断音的，不连贯的(abrupt; disjointed)
	【记】st + acca + to，记住中间的acca，似乎呈断裂状态 → 断音的

Love and faithfulness meet together; righteousness and peace kiss each other.

慈爱和诚实，彼此相遇。公义和平安，彼此相亲。

——《圣经·旧·诗》85:10

练 习 题

填空题

aesthetic	archetype	rhythm	chase	epilogue
conjure	cadence	reverie	hue	finale
gamut	inscribe	chorus	recital	inscription
mural	picturesque	dulcet	melody	sculpture

1. The benefits of conservation are both financial and _____.
2. We were _____ by a bull while crossing the field.
3. The trophy was _____ with his name.
4. There is a large _____ in the temple.
5. He could _____ coins from behind people's ears.
6. The place is remarkable for its _____ scenery.
7. The sculptor is working on a _____ of Venus.
8. There are no _____ or markings to identify the tombs.
9. Her paintings capture the subtle _____ of the countryside in autumn.
10. She is the _____ of an American movie star.
11. Fortinbras speaks the _____ in Shakespeare's *Hamlet*.
12. She was jolted out of her _____ as the door opened.
13. She felt she had run the whole _____ of human emotions from joy to despair.
14. The _____ is then taken up by the flutes.
15. He delivered his words in slow, measured _____.
16. The boat rocked up and down in _____ with the sea.
17. The festival ended with a grand _____ in Hyde Park.
18. I thought I recognized your _____ tones.
19. Bill sang the verses and everyone joined in the _____.
20. She is going to give a piano _____.

配对题

1. portrait	半身(雕)像	11. chord	大提琴
2. renaissance	彩色蜡笔、粉笔	12. cello	大提琴演奏家
3. folklore	民间传说；民俗学	13. cellist	单簧管
4. palette	小画像；缩影	14. clarinet	独唱曲
5. bust	调色板；调色板上的一套颜料	15. aria	和弦
6. crayon	天然色素	16. symphony	交响乐
7. statuary	肖像；描写	17. trumpet	喇叭
8. silhouette	文艺复兴	18. melodrama	麦克风
9. pigment	黑色轮廓，侧影	19. saxophone	情节剧
10. miniature	雕塑术；雕塑	20. microphone	萨克斯管

练习题答案

填空题答案

1. The benefits of conservation are both financial and aesthetic.
2. We were chased by a bull while crossing the field.
3. The trophy was inscribed with his name.
4. There is a large mural in the temple.
5. He could conjure coins from behind people's ears.
6. The place is remarkable for its picturesque scenery.
7. The sculptor is working on a sculpture of Venus.
8. There are no inscriptions or markings to identify the tombs.
9. Her paintings capture the subtle hues of the countryside in autumn.
10. She is the archetype of an American movie star.
11. Fortinbras speaks the epilogue in Shakespeare's *Hamlet*.
12. She was jolted out of her reverie as the door opened.
13. She felt she had run the whole gamut of human emotions from joy to despair.
14. The melody is then taken up by the flutes.
15. He delivered his words in slow, measured cadences.
16. The boat rocked up and down in rhythm with the sea.
17. The festival ended with a grand finale in Hyde Park.
18. I thought I recognized your dulcet tones.
19. Bill sang the verses and everyone joined in the chorus.
20. She is going to give a piano recital.

配对题答案

1. portrait	肖像；描写		11. chord	和弦	
2. renaissance	文艺复兴		12. cello	大提琴	
3. folklore	民间传说；民俗学		13. cellist	大提琴演奏家	
4. palette	调色板；调色板上的一套颜料		14. clarinet	单簧管	
5. bust	半身(雕)像		15. aria	独唱曲	
6. crayon	彩色蜡笔、粉笔		16. symphony	交响乐	
7. statuary	雕塑术；雕塑		17. trumpet	喇叭	
8. silhouette	黑色轮廓，侧影		18. melodrama	情节剧	
9. pigment	天然色素		19. saxophone	萨克斯管	
10. miniature	小画像；缩影		20. microphone	麦克风	

Word List 11
政治

政 治

**arbitrary [ˈɑːrbətreri] *adj.* 专横的，武断的（discretionary; despotic; dictatorial）；
任意的，随意的
【记】arbitr（判断）+ ary → 自己作判断，完全不考虑其他人的建议
→ 武断的
【派】arbitrarily（*adv.* 随心所欲地，霸道地）

**hierarchy [ˈhaɪərɑːrki] *n.* 阶层；等级制度（a system of ranks）；僧侣统治
【记】hier（神圣）+ archy（统治）→ 僧侣统治

**anarchy [ˈænɑːrki] *n.* 无政府状态（absence of government）；政治混乱
（political disorder）
【记】an（不，无）+ archy（统治）→ 无统治 → 无政府状态
【派】anarchic（*adj.* 无政府的）

**nome [nəʊm] *n.* (古埃及的)省；(现代希腊的)州

**tyranny [ˈtɪrəni] *n.* 暴虐，残暴，专制（cruel, unjust or oppressive use of power
or authority）
【例】a lifelong hatred of *tyranny*

**diplomatic [ˌdɪpləˈmætɪk] *adj.* 外交的；有策略的（tactful）
【例】She is always *diplomatic* when she deals with angry students.

**anarchistic [ˌænərˈkɪstɪk] *adj.* 无政府主义的
【例】Suddenly the *anarchistic* tendencies don't seem as cool.

**parliamentary [ˌpɑːrləˈmentri] *adj.* 议会的，国会的；议会制度的
【例】But as things stand the most likely outcome is that the
Parliamentary Party splits three ways.

**authoritarian [əˌθɔːriːˈterian] *n.* 独裁主义者，极权主义者（person who believes in
complete obedience to authority）
【记】来自authority（*n.* 权威，权力）

demagogue [ˈdeməgɑːg] *n.* 蛊惑民心的政客（a political leader who tries to win people's support by using emotional and often unreasonable arguments）

【记】来自demagogy（*n.* 煽动，蛊惑民心），dem（人民，人们）+ agogy（教导，鼓动）→ 蛊惑民心

covenant [ˈkʌvənənt] *n.* 契约（a binding and solemn agreement）*v.* 立书保证（to promise by a covenant）

【记】co（一起）+ ven（来）+ ant → 来到一起立约 → 契约

lobby [ˈlɑːbi] *n.* 门厅，前厅；（对议员施加压力的）院外游说团 *v.* 对（议员等）进行游说支持或反对议案（to persuade a politician, etc to support or oppose proposed legislation）

【例】*lobby* for higher farm subsidies

dissemination [dɪˌsemɪˈneɪʃn] *n.* 宣传，散播（publicity）

【例】In December 1998 there will be a publication and *dissemination* of the edited city-templates.

confer [kənˈfɜːr] *vi.* 协商，商谈

【记】con（共同）+ fer（带来）→ 共同带来观点 → 协商

【例】I *conferred* with my friends about what we should eat for dinner.

maneuver [məˈnuːvər] *v.* 调遣（部队等）；操纵 *n.* 策略（move; step; tactic）

【记】man（手）+ euver（劳动）→ 用手劳动 → 操纵

【例】At the last moment, the basketball player made a clever *maneuver* that allowed a goal to be made.

autonomous [ɔːˈtɑːnəməs] *adj.* 自治的（self-governing）；自主的

scandalous [ˈskændələs] *adj.* 诽谤性的；令人愤慨的

nonpartisan [nɑnˈpɑːrtɪzn] *adj.* 无党派的 *n.* 无党派的人

【例】They're *nonpartisan* and unicameral, so they're unique in a couple of ways.

burgess [ˈbɜːrdʒɪs] *n.* <英>自由民，市民；议员；<美>（殖民地时期弗吉尼亚或马里兰州的）下议院议员

deserter [dɪˈzɜːrtər] *n.* 背弃者，逃亡者（a person who deserts）

protégé [ˈproʊtəʒeɪ] *n.* 受有权势人物提携的人，门徒

【例】Only the old politician and his *protégé* were invited.

partisanship [ˈpɑːrtəznʃɪp] *n.* 党派性，党派偏见

【例】Besides, Obama had delivered a promissory note to the American people that he would overcome *partisanship*.

*amendment [ə'mendmənt] *n.* （议案等的）修正案；改善，改正

*Congo ['kɑːŋgoʊ] *n.* 刚果

*franchise ['fræntʃaɪz] *n.* 公民权，选举权；特许经营权 （the right granted by authority）

【例】 The city issued a *franchise* to the company to operate surface transit lines on the streets for ninety-nine years.

*nationality [ˌnæʃə'næləti] *n.* 国籍

【记】 nation（国家）+ ality → 国籍

*concourse ['kɑːŋkɔːrs] *n.* （车站、机场等的的）中央大厅；广场

【例】 The ticket office is at the rear of the station *concourse*.

*puppet ['pʌpɪt] *n.* 傀儡；木偶

【例】 a *puppet* theatre

*clique [kliːk] *n.* 朋党派系，小集团（snobbish or narrow coterie）

*treaty ['triːti] *n.* （国家之间的）条约，协定（an agreement made between countries）；（人与人之间的）协议（agreement between people）

【记】 treat（处理）+ y → 做出处理的文件 → 条约

*utopia [juː'toʊpiə] *n.* 乌托邦 （imaginary place or state of things in which everything is perfect）

【例】 create a political *Utopia*

*suffrage ['sʌfrɪdʒ] *n.* 选举权，投票权（the right of voting）

【记】 suf + frage（表示拥护的喧闹声）→ 投票表示拥护 → 投票权

【例】 grant *suffrage* to women

*ideology [ˌaɪdi'ɑːlədʒi] *n.* 意识形态

【记】 ide(o)（意识）+ ology（学科）→ 意识形态

*inning ['ɪnɪŋ] *n.* 执政期

*supremacy [suː'preməsi] *n.* 至高无上，最高权力（the quality or state of being supreme）

*reunification [ˌriːˌjuːnɪfɪ'keɪʃn] *n.* 重新统一

【例】 If this target is met it would be the best result since Germany's *reunification* in 1990.

*sovereign ['sɑːvrən] *n.* 最高统治者，元首（one that exercises supreme authority）

【记】 sove(= over在上面）+ reign（统治）→ 高高在上的统治者 → 最高统治者

*deliverance [dɪ'lɪvərəns] *n.* 获得释放，被拯救（being freed or rescued）

【例】 They prayed for an early *deliverance* from captivity.

*bureaucratization [ˌbjʊəˌrɒkrətaɪˈzeɪʃən] *n.* 官僚化

*constituency [kənˈstɪtʃʊənsi] *n.* 选区；全体选民；（一批有共同利益的）支持者，拥护者，追随者（a group of people with the same interests that one can turn to for support）

【例】Mr. Jones has a natural *constituency* among steel workers.

*agitate [ˈædʒɪteɪt] *vt.* 鼓动，煽动（to argue publicly or campaign for/against sth）；使不安，使焦虑（to cause anxiety）

【记】ag（做）+ itate（表示不断的动作）→ 不断地做 → 鼓动，煽动

*depose [dɪˈpəʊz] *v.* 罢免，免职（to remove from office or a position of power）；宣誓作证（to state by affidavit）

【记】de + pose（放）→ 放下去 → 免职

*dispel [dɪˈspel] *vt.* 驱散，消除（to scatter and drive away; disperse）

【记】dis（分开）+ pel（推）→ 推开 → 驱散

*emigrate [ˈemɪɡreɪt] *v.* （使）移居（外国或外部地区）

【记】e（出）+ migr（移）+ ate → 移出 → 移居

【例】Mary *emigrated* from Germany to France during World War I.

*enfranchise [ɪnˈfræntʃaɪz] *vt.* 给予…选举权（to endow with the right to vote）；解放

【记】en（加强）+ franch（=frank，公开表达思想感情的）+ ise（使）→ 给予…选举权；解放

【反】enfetter（*vt.* 束缚）；resubject（*vt.* 使臣服）；subjugate（*vt.* 使屈从，镇压）

*inspect [ɪnˈspekt] *vt.* 检查（to examine; survey）；视察

【记】in（内）+ spect（看）→ 看里面 → 检查

【例】The general *inspected* the troops.

*exile [ˈeksaɪl] *vt.* 流放（to banish; deport）*n.* 放逐；流亡者

【例】The king was *exiled* when his expire was taken over.

*oust [aʊst] *vt.* 驱逐（to dismiss; throw out）

【例】He was *ousted* from his position as chairman.

*banish [ˈbænɪʃ] *vt.* 驱逐，赶走，放逐（to exile; expel）

【例】The naughty child was *banished* to his room until dinner.

*reign [reɪn] *vt.* 统治（to govern; rule）

【例】The old king has been *reigning* the nation for 30 years.

*poll [pəʊl] *n.* 民意测验；选举投票

【记】比较记忆：loll（*v.* 懒散地倚靠）；doll（*n.* 洋娃娃）

apolitical [ˌeɪpəˈlɪtɪkl] *adj.* 不关心政治的，不涉及政治的（not interested or involved in politics）

extradition [ˌekstrəˈdɪʃn] *n.* （根据条约或法令对逃犯等的）引渡（surrender of prisoner by one state to another）

hegemony [hɪˈdʒeməʊni] *n.* 霸权，领导权（the leadership or dominance）
【记】来自希腊语hegemon（领导）；he + ge（看做get）+ mony（看做 money）→ 他想通过霸权聚敛钱财 → 霸权
【反】lack of authority（缺乏权威）

enclave [ˈenkleɪv] *n.* 飞地（被他国领土包围的一片领土），被包围的领土（territory enclosed within an alien land）
【记】en（在内）+ clav(=close包围) → 被包围的领土

plutocracy [pluːˈtɑːkrəsi] *n.* 财阀统治（government by the wealthy）
【记】pluto（财富）+ cracy（统治）→ 财阀统治；来自Plutus（希腊神话中的财神）

dissident [ˈdɪsɪdənt] *n.* 唱反调者（a person who disagrees; dissenter）
【记】dis（分开）+ sid（坐）+ ent → 分开坐的人 → 唱反调者

oligarchy [ˈɑːləɡɑːrki] *n.* 寡头政治（a form of government in which power is concentrated in the hands of a few persons）
【记】olig（少）+ archy（统治）→ 少数人统治 → 寡头政治

monarchy [ˈmɑːnərki] *n.* 君主政体，君主政治，君主国

firebrand [ˈfaɪərbrænd] *n.* 火把（a piece of burning wood）；（社会或政治动乱的）挑动者（a person who stirs up trouble or kindles a revolt）
【记】fire（火）+ brand（打火印）→ 用火把过火印 → 火把

theocracy [θiˈɑːkrəsi] *n.* 神权政治（government of a state by immediate divine guidance）
【记】theo（神）+ cracy（统治）→ 神权政治

ascendancy [əˈsendənsi] *n.* 统治权，支配力量（supremacy; domination）

protocol [ˈproʊtəkɔːl] *n.* 外交礼节（official etiquette）；协议，草案（an original draft of a document or transaction）
【记】proto（首要）+ col（胶水）→ 礼节很重要，把人凝聚（粘）到一起 → 外交礼节

realm [relm] *n.* 王国；领域（field; domain）

interregnum [ˌɪntəˈreɡnəm] *n.* （新王尚未登基旧王统治已结束的）空位期，无王时期
【记】inter（在…之间）+ reg（国王）+ num → 在两个国王统治之间的时期 → 无王时期

anarchist [ˈænərkɪst] *n.* 无政府主义者（a person who believes in, advocates, or promotes anarchism or anarchy）

affidavit [ˌæfəˈdeɪvɪt] *n.* 宣誓书（a written statement made under oath）
【记】af(加强) + fid(相信) + avit(表名词) → 让人相信的东西 → 宣誓书

junta [ˈdʒʌntə] *n.* （在革命中以武力夺取政权并统治国家的）军人集团（a group, especially of military officers, who rule a country after taking power by force in a revolution）

incumbent [ɪnˈkʌmbənt] *n.* 在职者，现任者（the holder of an office or benefice）*adj.* 负有责任的，义不容辞的（obligatory）
【记】in + cumb(躺) + ent → 躺在(职位)上的人 → 在职者

caucus [ˈkɔːkəs] *n.* 政党高层会议（a private meeting of leaders of a political party）

agent [ˈeɪdʒənt] *n.* 间谍，特工；代理人，经纪人
【例】work as a secret *agent* // an insurance *agent*

amnesty [ˈæmnəsti] *n.* 大赦（尤指对国家所犯的罪行）（general pardon, especially for offences against the State）
【例】An *amnesty* has been declared.

entitlement [ɪnˈtaɪtlmənt] *n.* 权利（rights）；津贴（pension）
【例】Social Security is the country's largest *entitlement* program, making it one of the most politically popular.

regime [reɪˈʒiːm] *n.* 政体，政权（method or system of government）
【例】a socialist, fascist, etc *regime*

address [əˈdres] *vt.* 处理，对付，着手解决（to tackle）；向…致词（to deliver a formal speech to）

extrude [ɪkˈstruːd] *v.* 挤出，逐出（to force or push out; thrust out）；突出（to protrude）
【记】ex(出) + trude(伸) → 伸出 → 挤出

emancipate [ɪˈmænsɪpeɪt] *vt.* 解放，解除（to free from restraint）
【记】e + man(手) + cip(落下) + ate → 手(从锁链中)落下 → 解放
【反】shackle(*vt.* 给…戴上枷锁；束缚)

expatriate [ˌeksˈpeɪtriət] *v.* 驱逐，流放（to banish; exile）；移居国外（to withdraw from residence in one's native country）
【记】ex(出) + patri(父亲，引申为国家) + ate → 移居国外

accede [əkˈsiːd] *vi.* 同意（to give assent; consent）

【记】ac + cede(走) → 走到一起 → 同意

【例】She can't *accede* to the proposal on any account.

【反】demur(*vi.* 反对)

convoke [kənˈvouk] *vt.* 召集（to summon to assemble; convene）

【记】con + vok (喊) + e → 喊到一起 → 召集

【反】adjourn(*v.* 休会，中止)

exploit [ɪkˈsplɔɪt] *vt.* 剥削；开发（to explore）

【记】ex + ploit(重叠) → 从重叠中拿出 → 开发

【例】The company *exploited* the workers by falsely promising them pay raises.

abdicate [ˈæbdɪkeɪt] *v.* 放弃（权力等）（to abandon）；退位，辞职

【记】ab(表否定) + dic(说话，命令) + ate → 不再命令 → 放弃权力

【例】King Edward *abdicated* in 1936.

impel [ɪmˈpel] *vt.* 驱使（to compel; urge）

【记】im(进入) + pel(推动) → 驱使

【例】He was *impelled* by a strong passion to save the diseased boy.

cabal [kəˈbæl] *n.* 阴谋；政治阴谋小集团（a conspiratorial group of plotters）

【记】发音似"叩拜儿" → 在一起叩拜搞阴谋 → 政治阴谋小集团

propaganda [ˌprɑːpəˈɡændə] *n.* 宣传，传播（publicity that is intended to spread ideas or information which will persuade or convince people）

【例】There has been so much *propaganda* against smoking that many people have given it up.

sectarian [sekˈteriən] *adj.* 派别的，宗派的，（尤指）教派的（of a sect or sects）

【例】*Sectarian* politics are ruining the country's economy.

oratory [ˈɔːrətɔːri] *n.* 演讲术（the art of making good speeches）

【记】来自orate(*vi.* 演讲)

referendum [ˌrefəˈrendəm] *n.* 公民复决；公民复决投票；（外交使节致本国政府的）请示书

triumvirate [traɪˈʌmvərət] *n.* 三人统治集团，三人领导小组（ruling group of three people）

【例】The company is run jointly by a *triumvirate* of directors.

autocracy [ɔːˈtɑːkrəsi] *n.* 独裁政府（government by one person that with unlimited power）

【记】auto(自己) + cracy(统治) → 自己一个人统治 → 独裁政府

coercion	[koʊˈɜːrʒn] *n.* 强制，强迫（the act, process, or power of coercing）；高压统治

gerontocracy	[ˌdʒerənˈtɑːkrəsi] *n.* 老人统治的政府（social organization in which a group of old men dominates）

【记】geront(老人) + o + cracy(统治) → 老人统治的政府

malpractice	[ˌmælˈpræktɪs] *n.* 玩忽职守，渎职（failure to carry out one's professional duty）

【记】mal(坏) + practice(行为) → 玩忽职守

gynaecocracy	[ˌɡaɪnɪˈkɑːrəsi] *n.* 妇女当政（government by women）

【记】gynaeco(女人) + cracy(统治) → 妇女当政

polyandry	[ˌpɑːliˈændri] *n.* 一妻多夫制（the state or practice of having more than one husband）

【记】poly(多) + andry(男人) → 多个男人 → 一夫多妻制

plebiscite	[ˈplebɪsɪt] *n.* 公民投票，公民表决（direct vote by the entire electorate）

municipality	[mjuːˌnɪsɪˈpæləti] *n.* 市；市政当局

【记】来自municipal(*adj.* 市政的)

commonwealth	[ˈkɑːmənwelθ] *n.* 共和国，联邦（an organization of independent states）

【记】common(共同的) + wealth(财产) → 共同拥有国家财产 → 共和国

**deprive	[dɪˈpraɪv] *vt.* 剥夺，使丧失

**totalitarian	[toʊˌtæləˈteriən] *adj.* 极权主义的（authoritarian; dictatorial）

【记】total(全部) + itarian → 将权力都掌握在手中 → 极权主义的

**unconventional	[ˌʌnkənˈvenʃənl] *adj.* 不依惯例的，不寻常的

**faction	[ˈfækʃn] *n.* 派系；派系斗争（partisan conflict）

**partisan	[ˈpɑːrtəzn] *adj.* 党派的，派系性强的

【例】Her *partisan* speech angered the opposing party.

**ideological	[ˌaɪdiəˈlɑːdʒɪkl] *adj.* 思想的，意识形态的

【例】Here is a case in which, unlike in the Sharif stabbing, the *ideological* motive is undoubted.

*immigrant	[ˈɪmɪɡrənt] *adj.* （从外国）移来的，移民的，移居的

*parade	[pəˈreɪd] *n.* 游行（procession; march）

*reactionary	[riˈækʃəneri] *adj.* 反动的，反动主义的，反对进步的，极端保守的（ultraconservative in politics）

【记】re(反) + action(动) + ary → 反对进步的

servitude	[ˈsɜːrvətuːd] *n.* 奴役，劳役（a condition in which one lacks liberty especially to determine one's course of action or way of life）
bicameral	[ˌbaɪˈkæmərəl] *adj.* 两院制的，有两个议院的（two-chambered as a legislative body）
potent	[ˈpoʊtnt] *adj.* 有全权的，有权势的；强有力的（cogent; powerful） 【例】His *potent* speech impressed all the people present.
authoritative	[əˈθɔːrəteɪtɪv] *adj.* 官方的，当局的；权威性的，可信赖的 【例】Make sure you ask an *authoritative* source for directions.
imperial	[ɪmˈpɪriəl] *adj.* 帝王的，至尊的（of an emperor or its ruler）
manumit	[ˌmænjuˈmɪt] *vt.* 解放（奴隶）（to free from slavery） 【记】manu(手) + mit(放) → 把手放开 → 解放 【反】enslave(*vt.* 使奴役)
coronation	[ˌkɔːrəˈneɪʃn] *n.* 加冕典礼（the act or ceremony of crowning a sovereign or the sovereign's consort）

When an end is lawful and obligatory, the indispensable means to it are also lawful and obligatory.

如果一个目的是正当而必须做的，则达到这个目的的必要手段也是正当而必须采取的。

——美国政治家 林肯（Abraham Lincoln, American statesman）

练 习 题

填空题

amendment	anarchistic	anarchy	arbitrary	autonomous
confer	deserter	diplomatic	dispel	franchise
hierarchy	ideology	nonpartisan	parliamentary	partisanship
scandalous	sovereign	supremacy	treaty	tyranny

1. The choice of players for the team seemed completely _____.
2. She's high up in the management _____.
3. The overthrow of the military regime was followed by a period of _____.
4. The children had no protection against the _____ of their father.
5. Attempts are being made to settle the dispute by _____ means.
6. Guilds can be democratic, _____, totalitarian, or some other type of government.
7. He was adopted as a Liberal _____ candidate.
8. He wanted to _____ with his colleagues before reaching a decision.
9. Teachers aim to help children become _____ learners.
10. His speech _____ any fears about his health.
11. It is _____ that he has not been punished.
12. They're _____ and unicameral, so they're unique in a couple of ways.
13. He is a craven _____.
14. The main obstacle is not _____, but individualism.
15. She made several minor _____ to her essay.
16. The 1918 Reform Act extended the _____ to women over 30.
17. Under the terms of the _____, La Rochelle was ceded to the English.
18. His attitude to ownership is rooted in communist _____.
19. The company has established total _____ over its rivals.
20. King George was then the _____ of England.

配对题

1. nome	独裁主义者	11. nationality	执政期
2. authoritarian	官僚化	12. concourse	院外游说团
3. demagogue	自由民，市民	13. puppet	调遣（部队等）
4. covenant	朋党派系	14. clique	国籍
5. lobby	中央大厅；广场	15. utopia	（古埃及的）省
6. dissemination	刚果	16. suffrage	门徒
7. maneuver	契约	17. inning	傀儡；木偶
8. burgess	获得释放	18. reunification	重新统一
9. protégé	蛊惑民心的政客	19. deliverance	选举权
10. Congo	宣传	20. bureaucratization	乌托邦

练习题答案

填空题答案

1. The choice of players for the team seemed completely <u>arbitrary</u>.
2. She's high up in the management <u>hierarchy</u>.
3. The overthrow of the military regime was followed by a period of <u>anarchy</u>.
4. The children had no protection against the <u>tyranny</u> of their father.
5. Attempts are being made to settle the dispute by <u>diplomatic</u> means.
6. Guilds can be democratic, <u>anarchistic</u>, totalitarian, or some other type of government.
7. He was adopted as a Liberal <u>parliamentary</u> candidate.
8. He wanted to <u>confer</u> with his colleagues before reaching a decision.
9. Teachers aim to help children become <u>autonomous</u> learners.
10. His speech <u>dispelled</u> any fears about his health.
11. It is <u>scandalous</u> that he has not been punished.
12. They're <u>nonpartisan</u> and unicameral, so they're unique in a couple of ways.
13. He is a craven <u>deserter</u>.
14. The main obstacle is not <u>partisanship</u>, but individualism.
15. She made several minor <u>amendments</u> to her essay.
16. The 1918 Reform Act extended the <u>franchise</u> to women over 30.
17. Under the terms of the <u>treaty</u>, La Rochelle was ceded to the English.
18. His attitude to ownership is rooted in communist <u>ideology</u>.
19. The company has established total <u>supremacy</u> over its rivals.
20. King George was then the <u>sovereign</u> of England.

配对题答案

1. nome	（古埃及的）省	11. nationality	国籍
2. authoritarian	独裁主义者	12. concourse	中央大厅；广场
3. demagogue	蛊惑民心的政客	13. puppet	傀儡；木偶
4. covenant	契约	14. clique	朋党派系
5. lobby	院外游说团	15. utopia	乌托邦
6. dissemination	宣传	16. suffrage	选举权
7. maneuver	调遣（部队等）	17. inning	执政期
8. burgess	自由民，市民	18. reunification	重新统一
9. protégé	门徒	19. deliverance	获得释放
10. Congo	刚果	20. bureaucratization	官僚化

Word List 12

法律

**legitimate [lɪˈdʒɪtɪmət] *adj.* 法定的；依法的；合法的(in accordance with the law or rules; lawful)

【例】the *legitimate* heir

**abolition [ˌæbəˈlɪʃn] *n.* 废除，废止(the state of being abolished; prohibition)

【派】abolitionist(*n.* 废奴主义者)

**nefarious [nɪˈferiəs] *adj.* 违法的，不法的；邪恶的(extremely wicked; evil)

【记】ne(=not) + far(公正) + ious → 违法的

【反】above reproach(无可责备)；virtuous(*adj.* 美德的，正直的)

**indictment [ɪnˈdaɪtmənt] *n.* 起诉，控告；起诉书

【例】bring in an *indictment* against sb // The fact that these children cannot read is a damning *indictment* of our education system.

**venue [ˈvenjuː] *n.* 作案现场，案件发生地；审判管辖区，审判地点

【例】He requested a change of *venue*.

**legislate [ˈledʒɪsleɪt] *vi.* 立法(to make law)

【记】legis(法律) + late(放) → 放出法律 → 立法

【例】It is impossible to *legislate* for every contingency.

**denounce [dɪˈnaʊns] *vt.* 告发

【记】de(坏) + nounce(讲话) → 讲坏话 → 告发

【例】Jane loudly *denounces* anyone who litters.

commit [kəˈmɪt] *vt.* 托付给(to consign)；使作出承诺(to bind or obligate)；犯(罪)(to perpetrate)

【记】com(一起) + mit(送) → 一起送给 → 托付给

【例】If you love each other, you should *commit* yourselves to each other.

perjure [ˈpɜːrdʒər] vt. 使作伪证，使发假誓 (to tell a lie under oath)

【记】per(假，坏) + jure(发誓) → 使发假誓

【反】depose(vi. 宣誓作证)

culprit [ˈkʌlprɪt] n. 犯罪者 (one who is guilty of a crime)

maleficent [məˈlefɪsnt] adj. 犯罪的 (doing evil); 有害的

【记】male(坏) + fic(做) + ent → 做坏事的 → 有害的

mayhem [ˈmeɪhem] n. 严重伤害罪 (the intentional mutilation of another's body)

【记】may(也许) + hem(边缘) → 也许会使人处于生命垂危的边缘 → 严重伤害罪

*unauthorized [ʌnˈɔːθəraɪzd] adj. 非法的，未被授权的

【例】Apple says consumers should contact their credit-card company for a chargeback for any *unauthorized* transactions.

*litigious [lɪˈtɪdʒəs] adj. 好诉讼的，好争论的 (of or relating to litigation)

【例】Egypt is an extremely *litigious* society, and its Byzantine laws allow unusual cases to be brought.

*mandatory [ˈmændətɔːri] adj. 法定的，强制的 (obligatory; compulsory)

【例】It's *mandatory* to pay taxes.

*illegal [ɪˈliːgl] adj. 不合法的，违法的 (against the law)

【记】il(不) + legal(合法的) → 不合法的

【派】illegality(n. 非法，违法)

*responsible [rɪˈspɑːnsəbl] adj. 有责任的

*defendant [dɪˈfendənt] n. 被告 (a person required to make answer in a legal action or suit)

【记】defend(防御) + ant → 需要自我防御 → 被告

*outlaw [ˈaʊtlɔː] n. 歹徒，亡命之徒

【例】He is a kind of *outlaw*, rebel, or robber.

*arbitration [ˌɑːrbɪˈtreɪʃn] n. 调停，仲裁

【记】来自arbitrate(v. 调停，仲裁)

【例】The matter was sent into *arbitration* to avoid the costs of a court trial.

*tribunal [traɪˈbjuːnl] n. 法庭，审判场所 (a court or forum of justice)

【记】来自tribune(n. 古罗马护民官)

*discontinuance [ˌdɪskənˈtɪnjuəns] n. 废止，中止; 撤销诉讼

【例】You agree that SYM Stationary shall not be liable to you or to any third party for any modification, suspension or *discontinuance* of the Services.

*accountability [əˌkaʊntə'bɪləti] *n.* 负有责任(responsibility)

【派】accountable(*adj.* 应负责任的)

*inheritance [ɪn'herɪtəns] *n.* 继承, 遗传; 遗产

【例】From early on, he said, Lewis schemed several different ways to get the *inheritance* money.

*inheritor [ɪn'herɪtər] *n.* 继承人, 后继者

*plea [pliː] *n.* 恳求(appeal)

*illegibility [ɪˌledʒə'bɪləti] *n.* 模糊, 不清不楚, 无法辨认

*conviction [kən'vɪkʃn] *n.* 判罪(the act of convicting someone who is guilty of a crime); 坚信(a strong belief; certainty of opinion)

【反】skepticism(*n.* 怀疑)

indict [ɪn'daɪt] *vt.* 控告, 起诉(to charge; accuse)

【记】in + dict(言, 说) → 说出缘由 → 起诉

*prosecution [ˌprɑːsɪ'kjuːʃn] *n.* 起诉(the act or process of prosecuting); 实行, 执行(carrying out or being occupied with sth)

【记】来自prosecute(*vt.* 起诉, 检举)

*trial ['traɪəl] *n.* 审判(hearing; inquisition)

【例】The scandal put the president on *trial*.

*jurisdiction [ˌdʒʊrɪs'dɪkʃn] *n.* 司法权

【记】juris(法律) + dict(说, 命令) + ion → 法律上命令 → 司法权

litigation [ˌlɪtɪ'geɪʃn] *n.* 诉讼(the process of making and defending claims in a court)

【记】litig(打官司) + ation → 诉讼

*infraction [ɪn'frækʃn] *n.* 违法(violation; infringement)

【记】in(使) + fract(破裂) + ion → 使(法律)破裂 → 违法

*penalty ['penəlti] *n.* 刑罚, 处罚(punishment for breaking a law or contract)

*query ['kwɪri] *n.* 质问, 询问(inquiry) *v.* 询问

【例】He couldn't bear his wife's daily *queries* about where he had been and he demanded a divorce.

*immure [ɪ'mjʊr] *vt.* 监禁(to imprison; confine; seclude)

【记】im(进入) + mure(墙) → 进入墙围着的空间 → 监禁

【反】release(*vt.* 释放)

*sue [suː] *v.* 控告, 对…提起诉讼(to make a legal claim against)

【例】If you don't complete the work, I will *sue* you for damages.

*pinch [pɪntʃ] *vt.* 勒索, 诈取

【记】粉红色的(pink)信封是勒索(pinch)的证据

*exonerate [ɪɡˈzɑːnəreɪt] *vt.* 使免除责任(to relieve from an obligation); 证明…无罪(to clear from guilt; absolve)

【记】ex(出) + oner(负担) + ate → 走出负担 → 使免除责任

【反】prove guilty(证明有罪); inculpate(*vt.* 使负罪); censure(*vt.* 责难); incriminate(*vt.* 控告)

【派】exoneration(*n.* 免罪)

*infringe [ɪnˈfrɪndʒ] *v.* 侵犯(to encroach; intrude); 违反

【例】Your book *infringes* on my copyright.

*flee [fliː] *v.* 逃跑, 逃离(to escape)

【例】When the rain began, we *fled* for cover.

*scalp [skælp] *vt.* 剥下…的头皮(to take the scalp from) *n.* 头皮

*dispossess [ˌdɪspəˈzes] *vt.* 没收, 夺走(财产、土地、房屋等)(to take away property, land, a house, etc from)

【例】The nobles were *dispossessed* of their estates after the revolution.

*reaffirm [ˌriːəˈfɜːrm] *vt.* 重申, 再确认(to affirm again)

【例】She *reaffirmed* that she was prepared to help.

*abolish [əˈbɑːlɪʃ] *vt.* 废除, 取消(to abandon; annul; terminate)

【例】If I were the king, I would *abolish* taxes.

proscribe [proʊˈskraɪb] *vt.* 禁止(to ban; forbid; forestall)

【记】pro(前) + scribe(写) → 写在前面 → 禁止

【例】The sale of opium is *proscribed* by law.

incriminate [ɪnˈkrɪmɪneɪt] *vt.* 控告(to accuse); 使负罪

【记】in(进入) + crimin(罪行) + ate → 使负罪

【例】He was *incriminated* of murder.

*interrogate [ɪnˈterəɡeɪt] *vt.* 审问, 质问

【记】inter(中间) + rog(问) + ate → 审问

【例】The police *interrogated* Sally about the robbery.

*invalidate [ɪnˈvælɪdeɪt] *vt.* 使作废, 使无效(to nullify)

【例】Economists differ as to whether the many other influences on inflation *invalidate* the idea of an unemployment-inflation.

*empower [ɪmˈpaʊər] *vt.* 授权; 使能够

【记】em + power(权力) → 授权

【例】The owner *empowered* Jane to hire new employees for the store.

*verify [ˈverɪfaɪ] *vt.* 验证(to confirm; substantiate)

【例】Your signature here will *verify* that you understand the terms of the agreement.

stipulate [ˈstɪpjuleɪt] *vt.* 约定，规定(to set; specify)

【例】The workers' contract *stipulated* that they couldn't smoke on the job.

*substantiate [səbˈstænʃieɪt] *vt.* 证实(to corroborate; verify)

【例】Evidences *substantiated* that he was the murderer.

*enact [ɪˈnækt] *vt.* 制定(法律)

【记】en + act(行为) → 制定法律，规范行为 → 制定(法律)

【例】Congress *enacted* the new crime bill.

*reprieve [rɪˈpriːv] *v./n.* 缓刑 (to delay the punishment of); 暂时解救 (to give relief for a time)

【记】re(重新)+prieve(拿) → 重新从刑场带回来 → 不执行死刑 → 缓刑

liability [ˌlaɪəˈbɪləti] *n.* 责任，义务(the state of being liable); 债务(obligation; debt)

【记】来自liable(*adj.* 有责任的)

【反】asset(*n.* 资产); immunity(*n.* 免债务)

*behoove [bɪˈhuːv] *v.* 理应，有必要(to be right or necessary to)

*extenuate [ɪkˈstenjueɪt] *vt.* 使(罪过等)显得轻微(to diminish; lessen)

【记】ex + tenu(细薄) + ate → 使显得轻微

【例】"Your money cannot help to *extenuate* your crime," said the judge.

*saddle [ˈsædl] *vt.* 使负担(to burden; load)

【例】The landowner *saddled* his tenants with heavy taxes.

unruly [ʌnˈruːli] *adj.* 难驾驭的，不守规矩的，不守法的(disorderly)

【记】un(不) + rul(e)(控制；规则) + y → 难驾驭的，不守规矩的

retroactive [ˌretrouˈæktɪv] *adj.* 可追溯的，有追溯效力的(effective from a certain date in the past)

【例】*retroactive* tax increase

illicit [ɪˈlɪsɪt] *adj.* 违法的(unlawful; illegal)

obligatory [əˈblɪgətɔːri] *adj.* 义务的；必须的(compulsory; necessary)

【记】oblig(强迫) + atory → 必须的

【例】Wearing seat belts while driving is *obligatory* in most states.

retribution [ˌretrɪˈbjuːʃn] *n.* 报答，回报；报应，惩罚(sth given as punishment)

【记】re (返回) + tribut(给予) + ion → 反过来给予 → 报答；报应

default [dɪˈfɔːlt] *n.* 不履行义务，拖欠 (nonfulfilment); 缺席 *v.* 不履行义务，拖欠；缺席；疏忽职责

【记】de(犯) + fault(错误) → 犯错误 → 疏忽职责

【例】If they can't raise the money to pay the debt, they will have to *default*.

statute [ˈstætʃuːt] *n.* 法规，法令(a law enacted by the legislative branch)

【记】stat(站) + ute → 站着的规矩 → 法规，法令

edict	['i:dɪkt] n. **法令**(an official public proclamation or order); **命令**(any command or order)
	【记】e + dict(说) → 说出 → 命令; 注意不要和addict(vt. 使上瘾, 使沉溺)相混
ordinance	['ɔːrdɪnəns] n. **法令, 条例**(a governmental statute of regulation)
	【记】ord(看做order, 命令) + inance → 命令, 条例; 注意不要和ordnance(n. 大炮)相混
jurisprudence	[ˌdʒʊrɪs'pruːdns] n. **法律学**
	【记】juris(法律) + prudence(谨慎; 智慧) → 法律学
inquisitor	[ɪn'kwɪzɪtər] n. **检察官; 询问者, 审问者**
impeach	[ɪm'piːtʃ] vt. **弹劾; 控告**(to accuse)
	【记】im(进入) + peach(告发) → 控告
	【例】The Congress has the right to *impeach* a president.
disenfranchise	[ˌdɪsɪn'fræntʃaɪz] vt. **剥夺…的公民权**
codify	['kɑːdɪfaɪ] vt. **将（法律、规则等）编成法典**(to arrange laws, rules systematically into a code); **整理, 编纂**
	【记】来自code(n. 法典)
	【派】codification(n. 编纂, 整理)
*polygraph	['pɑːlɪɡræf] n. **测谎器; 复写器**
*aboveground	[ə'bʌvˌɡraʊnd] n. **合法天地, 公开活动**
acquittal	[ə'kwɪtl] n. **宣告无罪, 无罪开释**(a setting free from the charge of an offense by verdict, or other legal process)
enactment	[ɪ'næktmənt] n. **制定, 颁布; 法律, 法规**
exculpate	['ekskʌlpeɪt] vt. **开脱, 申明…无罪**(to free from blame; declare or prove guiltless)
	【记】ex(出) + culp(罪行) + ate → 开脱
	【反】attribute guilt(归罪); indict(vt. 控告); inculpate(vt. 控告)
felon	['felən] n. **重罪犯**(a person guilty of a major crime)
	【记】fel(=fell 倒下) + on → 倒在罪恶之上 → 重罪犯
forensic	[fə'rensɪk] adj. **法庭的; 辩论的**(of public debate or formal argumentation)
	【记】来自forum(n. 罗马用于公开讨论的广场, 讨论会)
impunity	[ɪm'pjuːnəti] n. **免罚**
	【记】im(不) + pun(罚) + ity → 免罚
	【例】You can not do this with *impunity*.
incarcerate	[ɪn'kɑːrsəreɪt] vt. **使下狱, 监禁**(to imprison; confine)
	【记】in(进入) + carcer(监狱) + ate → 使下狱
	【反】liberate(vt. 释放)

– 115 –

recidivism [rɪˈsɪdɪvɪzəm] *n.* 累犯，重犯（a person relapsing into criminal behavior）

【例】Even more shocking is the fact that the rate of *recidivism* is more than 20 percent.

subpoena [səˈpiːnə] *n.* （法庭）传票（a written order requiring a person to appear in court）*vt.* 传讯（to summon with a writ of subpoena）

【记】sub（下面）+ poena（= penalty 惩罚）→ 在惩罚下 → 传讯

*apprehend [ˌæprɪˈhend] *vt.* 逮捕（to capture or arrest）；恐惧，担忧（to anticipate with anxiety; dread）

【记】ap + prehend（抓住）→ 逮捕

【派】apprehension（*n.* 焦虑，担忧）；apprehensive（*adj.* 恐惧的）→ intrepid（*adj.* 无畏的）

litigant [ˈlɪtɪɡənt] *n.* 诉讼当事人（one engaged in a lawsuit）

【记】litig（打官司）+ ant → 打官司的人 → 诉讼当事人

alibi [ˈæləbaɪ] *n.* 不在犯罪现场的申辩或证明（formal statement that a person was in another place at the time of a crime）；借口（excuse of any kind）

【记】ali（其他）+ bi（看做be=being，存在）→ 存在于其他地方 → 不在犯罪现场的申辩或证明；注意alibi（拉丁文）=elsewhere

bail [beɪl] *n.* 保释，保释金（security given for the release of a prisoner on bail）*vt.* 保释（to release under bail）

【例】The *bail* is a hundred thousand dollars.

demurrable [dɪˈmɜːrəbl] *adj.* 可抗辩的

inculpate [ˈɪnkʌlpeɪt] *vt.* 连累；控告；归咎于（to incriminate）

【记】in（使）+ culp（错，罪）+ ate → 使有罪 → 连累；控告

【反】exonerate（*vt.* 证明…无罪）；absolve（*vt.* 使免受惩罚）

treason [ˈtriːzn] *n.* 叛国罪（violation of allegiance toward one's country or sovereign）

【例】You'll hang for high *treason*.

manacle [ˈmænəkl] *n.* 手铐

【记】man（手）+ acle（东西）→ 戴在手上的东西 → 手铐

onus [ˈoʊnəs] *n.* 责任，义务，负担（a difficult, unpleasant task）

【记】on + us → 在我们身上 → 责任

练 习 题

填空题

abolish	abolition	conviction	denounce	dispossess
exonerate	flee	immure	indictment	infringe
interrogate	legislate	legitimate	mandatory	nefarious
prosecution	reaffirm	responsible	sue	unauthorized

1. Their business operations are perfectly _____.
2. Few people would not exult at the _____ of slavery.
3. He was universally feared because of his many _____ deeds.
4. The fact that these children cannot read is a damning _____ of our education system.
5. They promised to _____ to protect people's right to privacy.
6. She publicly _____ the government's handling of the crisis.
7. _____ personnel are not allowed on the premises.
8. The offence carries a _____ life sentence.
9. Even where parents no longer live together, they each continue to be _____ for their children.
10. She has six previous _____ for theft.
11. _____ for a first minor offence rarely leads to imprisonment.
12. At the age of 86 he was _____ in his house by infirmity.
13. They threatened to _____ if the work was not completed.
14. The police report _____ Lewis from all charges of corruption.
15. Two of the projects are deemed to _____ EU legislation.
16. He _____ to London after an argument with his family.
17. Many black South Africans had been _____ of their homes.
18. The President _____ his commitment to democratic elections.
19. This tax should be _____.
20. He was _____ by the police for over 12 hours.

配对题

1. scalp	负有责任	11. inheritance	好诉讼的
2. venue	调停	12. inheritor	歹徒
3. litigious	被告	13. plea	刑罚
4. illegal	废止	14. illegibility	勒索，诈取
5. defendant	违法的	15. trial	恳求
6. outlaw	模糊	16. jurisdiction	质问
7. arbitration	违法	17. infraction	剥…的头皮
8. tribunal	继承	18. penalty	审判
9. discontinuance	继承人	19. query	法庭
10. accountability	司法权	20. pinch	作案现场

练习题答案

填空题答案

1. Their business operations are perfectly <u>legitimate</u>.
2. Few people would not exult at the <u>abolition</u> of slavery.
3. He was universally feared because of his many <u>nefarious</u> deeds.
4. The fact that these children cannot read is a damning <u>indictment</u> of our education system.
5. They promised to <u>legislate</u> to protect people's right to privacy.
6. She publicly <u>denounced</u> the government's handling of the crisis.
7. <u>Unauthorized</u> personnel are not allowed on the premises.
8. The offence carries a <u>mandatory</u> life sentence.
9. Even where parents no longer live together, they each continue to be <u>responsible</u> for their children.
10. She has six previous <u>convictions</u> for theft.
11. <u>Prosecution</u> for a first minor offence rarely leads to imprisonment.
12. At the age of 86 he was <u>immured</u> in his house by infirmity.
13. They threatened to <u>sue</u> if the work was not completed.
14. The police report <u>exonerated</u> Lewis from all charges of corruption.
15. Two of the projects are deemed to <u>infringe</u> EU legislation.
16. He <u>fled</u> to London after an argument with his family.
17. Many black South Africans had been <u>dispossessed</u> of their homes.
18. The President <u>reaffirmed</u> his commitment to democratic elections.
19. This tax should be <u>abolished</u>.
20. He was <u>interrogated</u> by the police for over 12 hours.

配对题答案

1. scalp	剥…的头皮	11. inheritance	继承
2. venue	作案现场	12. inheritor	继承人
3. litigious	好诉讼的	13. plea	恳求
4. illegal	违法的	14. illegibility	模糊
5. defendant	被告	15. trial	审判
6. outlaw	歹徒	16. jurisdiction	司法权
7. arbitration	调停	17. infraction	违法
8. tribunal	法庭	18. penalty	刑罚
9. discontinuance	废止	19. query	质问
10. accountability	负有责任	20. pinch	勒索，诈取

Word List 13
军事

军　事

**onslaught [ˈɑːnslɔːt] n. 猛攻，猛袭 (a fierce attack)
【记】on + slaught(打击) → 猛攻，猛袭

**clandestine [klænˈdestɪn] adj. 秘密的，暗中的 (secret; covert)
【记】clan(宗派) + destine(打算) → 各宗派打算秘密独立 → 秘密的
【例】Some angry peasants had a *clandestine* plan to overthrow the leader.

**mandate [ˈmændeɪt] n. 命令；要求 (command)
【记】mand(命令) + ate → 命令

**tactics [ˈtæktɪks] n. 战术，用兵学
【记】tact(机智) + ics → 机智地用兵 → 战术

**raid [reɪd] n./v. 袭击 (to attack; foray)
【例】Air *raids* involved in the war destroyed many families.

**siege [siːdʒ] n./vt. 围困，围攻 (to besiege; encircle)
【例】During the enemy's *siege*, no one could leave or enter the city.

**munition [mjuːˈnɪʃn] n. 军火，弹药 (weapons and ammunition)
【记】muni(礼物) + tion → 送给敌人的礼物 → 军火

**garrison [ˈɡærɪsn] n. 卫戍部队，守备部队，警备部队 (troops stationed in a town or fort)
【例】Half the *garrison* is/are on duty.

**decipher [dɪˈsaɪfər] vt. 解开(疑团) (to make out the meaning of)；破译(密码) (to decode)
【记】de(去掉) + cipher(密码) → 破译(密码)

**entrench [ɪnˈtrentʃ] v. 挖(壕沟)；确立 (to establish firmly)
【记】en(使) + trench(壕沟) → 挖壕沟

*nonmilitary [ˌnɑːnˈmɪləteri] adj. 非军事的

*naval ['neɪvl] *adj.* 海军的；舰队的

【记】来自 navy(*n.* 海军；海军舰队)

*seafaring ['si:ferɪŋ] *adj.* 航海的，跟航海有关的（of or relating to the use of the sea for travel or transportation）*n.* 海上航行

【记】来自 seafarer(*n.* 水手，海员)，sea(海) + fare(过日子) + r → 在海上生活的人 → 水手，海员

*aggressive [ə'gresɪv] *adj.* 侵略的，好斗的（militant; assertive）；进取的（full of enterprise and initiative）

*militant ['mɪlɪtənt] *adj.* 好战的，富有战斗性的（aggressive, and often combative）

【记】milit(军事，打斗) + ant → 好战的

*bellicose ['belɪkoʊs] *adj.* 好战的，好斗的(eager to fight; warlike; belligerent)

【记】bell(战争) + icose → 好战的

【反】pacific(*adj.* 爱好和平的)

【派】bellicosity(*n.* 好斗，好战性)

*trajectory [trə'dʒektəri] *n.* （抛射物的）轨道，弹道（the curve that a body describes in space）

【记】tra(横) + ject(扔) + ory → （抛射物的)轨道

*disarmament [dɪs'ɑːrməmənt] *n.* 裁军；解除武装

【例】Separately, international diplomacy aimed at restarting nuclear *disarmament* talks with the North is continuing.

*missile ['mɪsl] *n.* 发射物(a thrown object or weapon)；导弹

【记】miss(发送) + ile(物体) → 发送出去的东西 → 发射物

*spaceflight ['speɪsflaɪt] *n.* 航天，宇宙飞行

*trophy ['troʊfi] *n.* 奖品，战利品(sth gained or given in victory or conquest)

【记】比较记忆：atrophy(*n.* 萎缩)；trophic(*adj.* 营养的)

*arsenal ['ɑːrsənl] *n.* 军械库（a place where weapons and ammunition are stored）

【记】arsen（热，火） + al → 带火的东西 → 军械库；也是英超阿森纳足球队的名字

*stratagem ['strætədʒəm] *n.* 谋略，策略(a cleverly contrived trick or scheme)

【记】strata(层次) + gem → 有层次的计划 → 谋略

*bombardment [bɑːm'bɑːrdmənt] *n.* 炮击，炮轰(attack as with missiles or bombs)

【记】来自 bombard(*vt.* 炮轰)

*truce [truːs] *n.* 停战，休战（协定)(agreement between enimies to stop fighting for a certain period)

【反】resumed fighting(继续战斗)

skirmish ['skɜːrmɪʃ] *n.* 小规模战斗；小争执，小争吵（a minor dispute or contest）

【记】skir(挥舞武器)+mish(防御) → 小规模战斗

*battlefield ['bætlfiːld] *n.* 战场

*radar ['reɪdɑːr] *n.* 雷达装置

【例】Enemy ships were detected on the *radar* screen.

*encroach [ɪn'kroʊʃ] *vi.* 蚕食，侵占（to intrude; trespass）

【记】和crochet(*v.* 用钩针编织)一起记

【例】The troops *encroached* on the neighbor's land // The reporter *encroached* on my privacy.

*besiege [bɪ'siːdʒ] *vt.* 围攻(to enclose and attack)；包围

【记】be + siege(围攻) → 围攻

【例】Troy was *besieged* by the Greeks. // The speaker was *besieged* with questions.

*exterminate [ɪk'stɜːrmɪneɪt] *vt.* 消灭，根除(to eradicate; eliminate)

【记】ex + termin(范围) + ate → 清除出范围 → 消灭

【例】The landlord *exterminated* the rats in the cellar.

*recruit [rɪ'kruːt] *vt.* 征募(新兵)(to enlist; enroll)

【记】He was *recruited* into the army.

*enlist [ɪn'lɪst] *vt.* 征召，招募(to enroll)

【记】en + list(列入名单) → 招募

【例】They *enlisted* four hundred recruits for the navy. // I *enlisted* Mary and Bill to help decorate the party room.

impinge [ɪm'pɪndʒ] *vi.* 侵犯(to infringe; encroach)；撞击(to collide with)

【记】im(进入) + pinge(固定) → 进入并固定里面的事物 → 侵犯

【例】Do not *impinge* on my privacy.

martial ['mɑːrʃl] *adj.* 战争的，军事的(of or suitable to war and soldiers)

【记】mar(毁坏) + tial → 战争常常意味着毁灭 → 战争的；Mars是罗马神话中的战神

espionage ['espiənɑːʒ] *n.* 间谍活动(the act of spying)

【记】来自法语，e + spion(=spy 看) + age → 出去看 → 间谍活动

armada [ɑːr'mɑːdə] *n.* 舰队(a fleet of warships)

【记】arm(武装) + ada(舰队) → 舰队

aggressor [ə'gresər] *n.* 侵略者，攻击者(one that commits or practices aggression)

encroachment [ɪnˈkroʊtʃmənt] n. 侵入，侵犯（gradual intrusion）

【记】来自encroach(vi. 侵占)

encipher [ɪnˈsaɪfər] vt. 将…译成密码（to convert a message into cipher）

【记】en(进入) + cipher(密码) → 将…译成密码

feint [feɪnt] v./n. 佯攻，佯击（a pretended attack or blow）

【记】和faint(adj. 头晕的；虚弱的)一起记

beset [bɪˈset] vt. 包围（to besiege; surround）

【例】The small town was *beset* by enemy troops.

absorb [əbˈsɔːrb] vt. 并吞；吸收

【记】ab + sorb(吸) → 吸收

【例】Large nations *absorbed* smaller ones.

***bushwhack** [ˈbʊʃwæk] vt. 奇袭

martyr [ˈmɑːrtər] n. 烈士，殉道者（any of those persons who choose to suffer or die rather than give up their faith or principles）

【记】像战神(Mars)一样的烈士(martyr)

fortify [ˈfɔːrtɪfaɪ] v. 修筑防御工事；加强防卫（to strengthen a place against attack）

【记】fort(强大) + ify(使) → 加强防卫

【反】sap(v. 削弱); enervate(vt. 使衰弱); vitiate(v. 损害); debilitate (vt. 使衰弱)

massacre [ˈmæsəkər] n. 大屠杀（the indiscriminate, merciless killing of a number of human beings）

【记】mass(大批) + acre(英亩) → 把一大批人在一英亩的地方杀掉 → 大屠杀

holocaust [ˈhɑːləkɔːst] n. 大屠杀，浩劫（great or total destruction of life）

【记】holo(全部) + caust(烧) → 全部烧掉 → 大屠杀

incursion [ɪnˈkɜːrʒn] n. 侵犯，入侵（a hostile entrance into a territory）

【记】in + curs(跑) + ion → 跑进来 → 入侵

【反】retreat(n. 撤退)

bastion [ˈbæstiən] n.（可扩大射击范围的）棱堡, 堡垒, 阵地工事（stronghold; something seen as a source of protection）

【例】the last *bastion* of male chauvinism

cipher [ˈsaɪfər] n. 暗号，密码（code）

【例】Spies intercepted the *cipher* but could not decode it.

【派】encipher(vt. 将…译成密码); decipher(vt. 破译(密码))

barrage [bəˈrɑːʒ] *n.* 弹幕(a curtain of artillery fire)
【记】bar(障碍) + rage(大怒) → 障碍后面的怒火 → 弹幕

array [əˈreɪ] *n.* (军队中的)队列, 排列(order; display) *vt.* 整(队)
【例】His soldiers were *arrayed* along the river bank.

***moat** [moʊt] *n.* 壕沟(a deep, wide trench); 护城河
【例】She hurdled over the *moat* in a leap.

***posse** [ˈpɑːsi] *n.* 一队, 一团 (a group of men gathered together by a sheriff to help keep order); 民防团
【记】民防团(posse)摆姿势(pose)

armistice [ˈɑːrmɪstɪs] *n.* 休战, 停战(a temporary stopping of warfare; a truce)
【记】armi(武器) + stice(停止) → 停止使用武器 → 休战, 停战

brunt [brʌnt] *n.* 冲击, 撞击; 正面的冲击 (main impact or shock); 主要的压力
【例】These exhausted men carried the *brunt* of the war. // bore the *brunt* of the household chores

fusillade [ˌfjuːsəˈleɪd] *n./vt.* (枪炮)齐射, 连发 (a simultaneous or rapid and continuous discharge of many firearms)
【记】fus(流, 泻) + ill(伤害) + ade → (枪炮)齐射

***parachute** [ˈpærəʃuːt] *n.* 降落伞
【例】land by *parachute*

caliber [ˈkælɪbər] *n.* 口径

***platoon** [pləˈtuːn] *n.* 排(军队中连的下一级)

grapple [ˈɡræpl] *v.* 格斗, 扭打(to wrestle; come to grips with; take hold of and struggle with)
【例】He *grappled* with the burglar and overpowered him.

conscript [kənˈskrɪpt] *vt.* 征募, 征召 (to enroll for compulsory service in the armed forces; draft)
【记】con + script(写) → 把(名字)写入名单 → 征召

beleaguer [bɪˈliːɡər] *vt.* 围攻(to besiege by encircling); 骚扰, 使烦恼(to harass)
【记】be + leaguer(围攻的部队或兵营) → 围攻
【反】delight(*vt.* 使高兴)

***despoil** [dɪˈspɔɪl] *vt.* 夺取, 掠夺
【例】The region is *despoiled* of its scenic beauty by unchecked development.

dissimulate [dɪ'sɪmjuleɪt] *v.* 假装，掩饰（to disguise; dissemble）

【记】和simulate(*vt.* 假装；模仿)一起记

【例】The soldiers *dissimulated* themselves by wearing white garments in the snow.

accouter [ə'kuːtər] *vt.* 装备，供以军用品

detonation [ˌdetə'neɪʃn] *n.* 引爆，爆炸，爆炸声（explosion）

【记】来自detonate(*v.* 引爆，爆炸)

***reconnaissance** [rɪ'kɑːnɪsns] *n.* 侦察，预先探索（a preliminary survey to gain information）

【记】注意不要和renaissance(*n.* 复兴，复活)相混

【例】make an aerial *reconnaissance* of an island // Austin did some *reconnaissance* work at Tony's penthouse last night.

deploy [dɪ'plɔɪ] *v.* (使)展开，(使)部署（to spread out strategically）

【记】和employ(*vt.* 雇用)一起记

【反】concentrate(*v.* 集中)

catapult ['kætəpʌlt] *n.* 弹弓(slingshot); 弹射器(hurling machine)

【记】cata(向下) + pult(弹) → 弹射器

cavalcade [ˌkævl'keɪd] *n.* 骑兵队伍(a procession of horsemen or carriages)

【记】caval(骑马) + cade → 骑兵队伍

centurion [sen'tʃʊriən] *n.* 古罗马的百人队队长（ancient Roman officer commanding a unit of 100 soldiers）

【记】和century(*n.* 世纪)一起记

holster ['hoʊlstər] *n.* 手枪皮套(a pistol case)

【记】和bolster(*n.* 垫子；支持物)一起记

onset ['ɑːnset] *n.* 攻击(attack)

【记】来自词组set on(攻击)

【例】The *onset* of arthritis stopped the old lady from doing needlework.

pugnacity [pʌg'næsəti] *n.* 好斗性(combativeness; disposition to fight)

scabbard ['skæbərd] *n.* (刀剑的)鞘(a sheath or case to hold the blade of a sword or dagger)

【记】scab(疤) + bard(马的铠甲) → 拔剑出鞘，伤人留疤 → 鞘

waylay [weɪ'leɪ] *v.* 埋伏，伏击(to lie in wait for and attack from ambush)

【记】way(路) + lay(躺) → 躺路边 → 埋伏

rampart ['ræmpɑːrt] *n.* 壁垒(a protective barrier); 城墙(a broad embarkment raised as a fortification)

armory	[ˈɑːrməri] *n.* 军械库(a place where arms and armor are kept)
battalion	[bəˈtæliən] *n.* 营，军队 (a considerable body of troops organized to act together)
	【记】battal(看做battle，战争) + ion → 军队
belligerence	[bəˈlɪdʒərəns] *n.* 交战(the state of being at war)；好战性，斗争性(an aggressive attitude, atmosphere, etc)
	【记】bell(战斗) + iger + ence → 交战；好战性
militia	[məˈlɪʃə] *n.* 民兵部队(an army composed of ordinary citizens)
	【记】milit(军事，战斗) + ia → 战斗的人民 → 民兵部队
warmonger	[ˈwɔːrmʌŋɡər] *n.* 好战者，战争贩子(one who urges to stir up war)
	【记】war(战争) + monger(商人，贩子) → 战争贩子
	【反】pacifist(*n.* 和平主义者)；dove(*n.* 和平鸽；主和派人物)
torpedo	[tɔːrˈpiːdoʊ] *n.* 鱼雷(underwater explosive apparatus)

Before his downfall a man's heart is proud, but humility comes before honor.

败坏之先，人心骄傲。尊荣以前，必有谦卑。

——《圣经·旧·箴》18:12

填空题

aggressive	skirmish	impinge	fortify	bellicose
besiege	clandestine	decipher	disarmament	encroach
entrench	exterminate	militant	naval	nonmilitary
onslaught	raid	seafaring	siege	stratagem

1. Several people were killed in _____ during the night.
2. China also has been very active in enforcing its claims via _____ means.
3. An individual's rights end when they _____ on the safety and rights of others.
4. Beiyang Navy is the earliest _____ force of China.
5. Britain has always been a _____ nation.
6. As a teenager Sean was _____ and moody.
7. Some trade unions have a more _____ approach to pay negotiations.
8. His _____ disposition alienated his friend.
9. The early Christians held _____ meetings in caves.
10. I don't go along with her views on nuclear _____.
11. The town survives the _____ of tourists every summer.
12. They have worked out the _____ to attack the enemy.
13. They carried out a bombing _____ on enemy bases.
14. The police placed the city center under a virtual state of _____.
15. Can anyone _____ his handwriting?
16. This idea had firmly _____ itself in his consciousness.
17. He _____ himself against the cold with a hot drink.
18. He never allows work to _____ upon his family life.
19. Paris was _____ for four months and forced to surrender.
20. Staff use the poison to _____ moles and rabbits.

配对题

1. trajectory	征募(新兵)	11. tactics	军火
2. missile	战争的,军事的	12. radar	奇袭
3. spaceflight	间谍活动	13. garrison	雷达装置
4. trophy	军械库	14. recruit	烈士,殉道者
5. munition	舰队	15. martial	航天
6. arsenal	战场	16. espionage	战术
7. mandate	炮击	17. armada	大屠杀
8. bombardment	卫戍部队	18. bushwhack	(抛射物的)轨道,弹道
9. truce	命令	19. martyr	奖品
10. battlefield	发射物	20. massacre	停战,休战(协定)

练习题答案

填空题答案

1. Several people were killed in <u>skirmishes</u> during the night.
2. China also has been very active in enforcing its claims via <u>nonmilitary</u> means.
3. An individual's rights end when they <u>impinge</u> on the safety and rights of others.
4. Beiyang Navy is the earliest <u>naval</u> force of China.
5. Britain has always been a <u>seafaring</u> nation.
6. As a teenager Sean was <u>aggressive</u> and moody.
7. Some trade unions have a more <u>militant</u> approach to pay negotiations.
8. His <u>bellicose</u> disposition alienated his friend.
9. The early Christians held <u>clandestine</u> meetings in caves.
10. I don't go along with her views on nuclear <u>disarmament</u>.
11. The town survives the <u>onslaught</u> of tourists every summer.
12. They have worked out the <u>stratagem</u> to attack the enemy.
13. They carried out a bombing <u>raid</u> on enemy bases.
14. The police placed the city center under a virtual state of <u>siege</u>.
15. Can anyone <u>decipher</u> his handwriting?
16. This idea had firmly <u>entrenched</u> itself in his consciousness.
17. He <u>fortified</u> himself against the cold with a hot drink.
18. He never allows work to <u>encroach</u> upon his family life.
19. Paris was <u>besieged</u> for four months and forced to surrender.
20. Staff use the poison to <u>exterminate</u> moles and rabbits.

配对题答案

1. trajectory	(抛射物的)轨道, 弹道		11. tactics	战术	
2. missile	发射物		12. radar	雷达装置	
3. spaceflight	航天		13. garrison	卫戍部队	
4. trophy	奖品		14. recruit	征募(新兵)	
5. munition	军火		15. martial	战争的, 军事的	
6. arsenal	军械库		16. espionage	间谍活动	
7. mandate	命令		17. armada	舰队	
8. bombardment	炮击		18. bushwhack	奇袭	
9. truce	停战, 休战(协定)		19. martyr	烈士, 殉道者	
10. battlefield	战场		20. massacre	大屠杀	

Word List 14

经济·农业

经　济

***conversion [kən'vɜːrʒn] *n.* 折合，换算；转变，变换（converting or being converted）

【例】the *conversion* of a barn into a house, of pounds into dollars

**prosperous ['prɑːspərəs] *adj.* 繁荣的（thriving; flourishing）

**patronage ['pætrənɪdʒ] *n.* 赞助，资助

【记】来自patron（*n.* 赞助人）

prosperity [peɪɑ'sperəti] *n.* 繁荣（well-being）

【例】The *prosperity* of the society promises a rapid economic growth.

gratis ['grætɪs] *adj.* 免费的（free）

*pecuniary [pɪ'kjuːnieri] *adj.* 金钱的（monetary; financial）

【记】pecuni(钱财) + ary → 金钱的

【例】Dad refused me a *pecuniary* request of 100 pound.

*bankrupt ['bæŋkrʌpt] *adj.* 破产的（unable to pay debts; insolvent）

【记】bank(银行) + rupt(断) → 破产的

【派】bankruptcy(*n.* 破产) → solvency(*n.* 偿债能力)

insolvent [ɪn'sɑːlvənt] *adj.* 无力还债的，破产的（bankrupt）

*transnational [ˌtrænz'næʃnəl] *adj.* 跨国的，跨越国界的

【例】The aim of this initiative is to combat drug trafficking, *transnational* crime and money laundering.

*proprietary [prə'praɪəteri] *adj.* 私有的，私营的（privately owned and managed）

【记】propr(拥有) + iet + ary → 私有的

*merger ['mɜːrdʒər] *n.* (企业等的)合并，并购

*statement ['steɪtmənt] *n.* 报表，清单

collateral [kə'lætərəl] *n.* 抵押品

【例】The Smiths used valuable jewelry as *collateral* for their loan.

*invoice [ˈɪnvɔɪs] *n.* 发票；发货清单(bill) *vt.* 给…开发票(to send an invoice for or to)

【记】in + voice(声音) → 大声把人叫进来开发票 → 发票

**rebate [ˈriːbeɪt] *n.* 返回款；折扣(refund; repayment)

【记】和debate(*v.* 争论)一起记

【例】The government uses tax *rebate* as a means to attract investment on this line.

*payroll [ˈpeɪroʊl] *n.* 工资单

【例】The Official said he had been on the Central Intelligence Agency's *payroll*, providing help against the Taliban.

*dividend [ˈdɪvɪdənd] *n.* 股息，红利

*bonus [ˈboʊnəs] *n.* 红利；奖金(award; gift)

【例】At the end of the year, the employees all received cash *bonuses*.

***account [əˈkaʊnt] *n.* 户头；账目

【例】I have an *account* with the Midland Bank.

*lottery [ˈlɑːtəri] *n.* 奖券；抽奖

【例】"Marriage is just a *lottery*. Don't believe in love." said the old man.

*transaction [trænˈzækʃn] *n.* 交易(business; trade; deal)

【记】trans(交换) + action(活动) → 交易

expenditure [ɪkˈspendɪtʃər] *n.* 消耗，支出(amount expended)

*quotation [kwoʊˈteɪʃn] *n.* (股票等的)行情，报价

【例】the latest *quotations* from the Stock Exchange

*commission [kəˈmɪʃn] *n.* 佣金

【例】Our agents in other areas usually get a 3.5% *commission*.

check [tʃek] *n.* 支票

discount [ˈdɪskaʊnt] *n./v.* (打)折扣(reduction)

【例】Mary gets an employee *discount* at the department store.

purchase [ˈpɜːrtʃəs] *n./vt.* 购买(to buy)

*profitability [ˌprɑːfɪtəˈbɪləti] *n.* 收益性，利益率

【例】The purchase of Finansbank, says Mr. Arapoglou, will immediately increase NBG's *profitability* by 10%.

liquidate [ˈlɪkwɪdeɪt] *v.* 清算(to settle the affairs of a business by disposing of its assets and liabilities)；清偿债务(to pay or settle a debt)

【记】liquid(清澈的) + ate → 弄清 → 清算

【派】liquidation(*n.* 清算；停止营业)

reimburse [ˌriːɪmˈbɜːrs] *vt.* 偿还(to pay back; refund)

【记】re(重新) + im(=in 进入) + burse(钱包) → 偿还

【例】You should *reimburse* the taxi fee those strangers paid to get you to hospital.

*underestimate [ˌʌndərˈestɪmeɪt] *vt.* 低估(to undervalue)

【例】The value of the antique has long been *underestimated* before the recent investigation.

*consolidate [kənˈsɑːlɪdeɪt] *vt.* 合并(to merge); 巩固, 加强

【记】con + solid(固体的, 结实的) + ate → 巩固, 加强

【例】The two schools were *consolidated* to reduce costs.

defray [dɪˈfreɪ] *vt.* 为…付款(to provide for the payment of)

【记】def(看做deaf, 聋) + ray(光线) → 聋人得到光线 → 有人付款帮助治疗 → 为…付款

【例】The cost of the expedition was *defrayed* by the college.

suborn [səˈbɔːrn] *vt.* 收买, 贿赂, 教唆(to induce secretly to do an unlawful thing)

【记】sub(下面) + orn(装饰) → 在下面给人好处 → 贿赂

actuarial [ˌæktʃuˈeriəl] *adj.* 保险精算的, 保险统计的(calculating; pertaining to insurance statistics)

【记】actua(=actual 精确的; 实际的) + rial → 追求精确的 → 保险精算的

【派】actuary(*n.* 保险精算师)

remunerative [rɪˈmjuːnərətɪv] *adj.* 报酬高的, 有利润的(providing payment; profitable)

【记】remunerate(*vt.* 给…酬劳)

【反】unrequited(*adj.* 无报酬的)

【派】unremunerative(*adj.* 无报酬的, 利润低的)

underwrite [ˌʌndərˈraɪt] *vt.* (签名)同意负担…的费用(to support with money and take responsibility for possible failure); 为…保险(to take responsibility for fulfilling an insurance agreement)

【记】under(在…下) + write(写) → (签名)同意负担…的费用

*moneybag [ˈmʌnɪbæg] *n.* 钱袋; 财富

opulence [ˈɑːpjələns] *n.* 财富, 富裕(wealth; affluence)

【记】opul(财富) + ence → 财富

optional [ˈɑːpʃənl] *adj.* 可选择的, 随意的

【例】It also arrives with many features that are *optional* on other Mercedes models, like Bi-Xenon headlamps.

*consumerism [kənˈsuːmərɪzəm] *n.* 保护消费者利益运动，用户至上主义

【例】We just can't control ourselves with any kind of *consumerism*, be it food or anything else.

**residue [ˈrezɪdjuː] *n.* 残余（remains; leftover; remnant）；剩余财产

*surplus [ˈsɜːrpləs] *n.* 过剩，剩余；盈余，顺差 *adj.* 过剩的（extra; excess）

【记】sur（超过）+ plus（加）→ 过剩

【例】The farmer's *surplus* grain was stored in silos.

embargo [ɪmˈbɑːrɡoʊ] *n.* 禁运令，封港令（a legal prohibition on commerce）

【记】em + bar（阻挡）+ go（去）→ 阻拦（船等）进入 → 禁运令，封港令

redress [rɪˈdres] *n.* 补偿，赔偿

*confiscation [ˌkɑːnfɪˈskeɪʃn] *n.* 没收，征用，充公

【例】The *confiscation* of equipment, money and other materials is unacceptable and must end immediately.

penury [ˈpenjəri] *n.* 贫穷，拮据（destitution）

【记】penur（缺少）+ y → 贫穷，拮据

*cess [ses] *n.* 租税；税，税率

excise [ˈeksaɪz] *n.* 消费税

【例】the *excise* on beer

*option [ˈɑːpʃn] *n.* 选择，选择权，可选择的东西（choice; alternative）

*stake [steɪk] *n.* 股份；柱，桩 （a pointed piece of wood driven into the ground）；赌注（sth staked for gain or loss）

*lease [liːs] *n./v.* 出租（to lend; loan）

【记】l + ease（安心的）→ 房子租出去，开始收租金，终于安心了 → 出租

【例】The owner *leased* his spare houses to make a fortune.

*barter [ˈbɑːrtər] *n./v.* 拿…作易货交易，作物物交换（to trade; exchange）

【例】Before currency came into use, people used the *barter* system, exchanging goods directly for goods.

*opportunism [ˌɑːpərˈtjuːnɪzəm] *n.* 机会主义

【例】political *opportunism*

economy [ɪˈkɑːnəmi] *n.* 经济，节约（efficiency or conciseness in using something）

depreciate [dɪˈpriːʃieɪt] *v.* （使）贬值

【记】de（坏）+ preci（价值）+ ate → 贬值

【例】The US dollar has *depreciated* against the Japanese Yen.

*buck [bʌk] *n.* <俚>（美）元 *vi.* 反对（to oppose; resist）

【记】美国口语中一美元叫one buck

【反】assent to（同意）

bullion ['bʊliən] *n.* 金，银；金条，银条（gold or silver in the form of ingots）
【记】bull（公牛）+（1)ion（狮子）→ 卖公牛、狮子得金银（sell bulls to get bullions）

yen [jen] *n.* 日元

usury ['juːʒəri] *n.* 放高利贷（the lending of money at exorbitant interest rates）
【记】us(=use 用)+ury → 用钱生钱 → 放高利贷
【派】usurious（*adj.* 放高利贷的）

农　业

**indigenous [ɪn'dɪdʒənəs] *adj.* 土产的；当地的，土著的
【记】indi(内部)+gen(产生)+ous → 内部出产 → 土产的
【例】The *indigenous* people of the area know which plants are safe to eat and which are poisonous.

**barn [baːrn] *n.* 谷仓；畜棚，畜舍

granary ['grænəri] *n.* 谷仓，粮仓（a building for storing threshed grain）

【记】gran(=grain 谷物)+ary(表场所)→ 谷仓

*prolific [prə'lɪfɪk] *adj.* 多育的；多产的（productive）
【例】*prolific* animals // The *prolific* author published over 80 novels.

*fertile ['fɜːrtl] *adj.* 肥沃的，多产的（fruitful; rich）；生育力强的
【记】fert(=fer 带来)+ile → 能带来粮食 → 肥沃的
【例】The very *fertile* couple had six children in eight years.

fatten ['fætn] *v.* （使）长肥（to make or become fat）；使肥沃（to make fertile）；装满
【反】emaciate（*vt.* 使消瘦）

fecund ['fiːkənd] *adj.* 肥沃的，多产的（fruitful or fertile; productive）；生殖力强的
【记】发音似"翻垦" → 可翻垦的土地 → 肥沃的

loam [loʊm] *n.* 沃土，肥沃的土壤（a rich soil）

*weedy ['wiːdi] *adj.* 瘦弱的；似杂草的，杂草丛生的
【例】The seahorses did not survive, but the leafy and *weedy* sea dragons did, to everyone's surprise.

**infertile [ɪn'fɜːrtl] *adj.* 贫瘠的；不能生育的（not fertile; barren）
【例】*infertile* land

*infertility [ˌɪnfɜːrˈtɪləti] *n.* 不肥沃，贫瘠；不育

【例】Doctors do not know which types of *infertility* are highly unlikely to yield to technology.

flag [flæg] *vi.* 减弱，衰退(to lose strength)；枯萎(to droop)

【记】flag作为"旗，国旗"一意大家都熟悉

【反】wax(*vi.* 增强，增大)

flaggy [ˈflægi] *adj.* 枯萎的；松软无力的(lacking vigor or force)

sere [siər] *adj.* 干枯的，凋萎的(being dried and withered)

【记】和sear(*v.* 烧灼)一起记

【反】verdant(*adj.* 翠绿的)；lush(*adj.* 青翠的)；damp(*adj.* 潮湿的)

wilt [wɪlt] *v.* (使)凋谢，(使)枯萎(to lose vigor from lack of water)

【例】The rose has already begun to *wilt*.

acarpous [eɪˈkɑːrpəs] *adj.* 不结果实的(impotent to bear fruit)

shrivel [ˈʃrɪvl] *v.* (使)枯萎(to draw into wrinkles especially with a loss of moisture)

wizen [ˈwizən] *adj.* 凋谢的，枯萎的(that is wizened)

*irrigation [ˌɪrɪˈɡeɪʃn] *n.* 灌溉

【例】The water that does run off is collected and stored in tanks for *irrigation*.

*irrigate [ˈɪrɪɡeɪt] *vt.* 灌溉

【例】They *irrigated* the land in order to increase the produce.

*husbandry [ˈhʌzbəndri] *n.* 农事，耕种；饲养业；管理 (farming management)；节俭

【记】husband(丈夫)+ry → 丈夫主外 → 耕种

【例】He studied animal *husbandry* in college.

fallow [ˈfæloʊ] *n.* 休耕地(cultivated land that is allowed to lie idle during the growing season) *adj.* (土地)休耕的(left uncultivated or unplanted)

【记】和fellow(*n.* 伙伴，同伙)一起记

【反】in use(在使用中)

*maize [meɪz] *n.* 玉米(a type of tall plant grown for its ears of yellow seeds)

*swath [swɔθ] *n.* 收割的刈痕，收割的宽度；狭长的一条，细长的列

【例】Rebels hold a large *swath* of the east and a string of towns nearer the capital.

*sow [soʊ] *v.* 播(种)，播种于(土地等) *n.* 大母猪

【例】As you *sow*, so will you reap.

graft [grɑːft] v. 嫁接（to cause a scion to unite with a stock）n. 嫁接；嫁接用的嫩枝
【记】g(看做go) + raft(木筏) → 用木筏运送嫁接的树苗 → 嫁接
【反】abscission(n. 剪除)

*cultivate [ˈkʌltɪveɪt] vt. 耕种；培育，培养（to till; foster; train）
【记】cult(培养) + ivate → 培育，培养
【例】The botanist *cultivated* tropical flowers.

tiller [ˈtɪlər] n. 耕作者，农夫（farmer）
【例】land to the *tiller*

plough [plaʊ] n. 犁 v. 犁（地）（to work with a plow）

strew [struː] vt. 撒，散播（to spread randomly; scatter）

trough [trɔːf] n. 槽，水槽，饲料槽；木钵

*haystack [ˈheɪstæk] n. 干草堆

**poultry [ˈpoʊltri] n. 家禽

*pasture [ˈpæstʃər] n. 牧草；草原，放牧场

*squash [skwɑːʃ] n. 南瓜

fodder [ˈfɑːdər] n. 饲料，草料

*greenhouse [ˈɡriːnhaʊs] n. 温室，花房

agronomy [əˈɡrɑːnəmi] n. 农学，农艺学（science of controlling the soil to produce crops）
【记】agro(田地；农业) + nomy(学科) → 农学
【派】agronomist(n. 农学家)

graze [ɡreɪz] v.（牛羊等）吃草（to feed on growing grass）；放牧（to put livestock to eat grass）
【记】来自grass(n. 草)；和glaze(vt. 给…装玻璃；给…上釉彩)一起记

manure [məˈnʊr] n. 粪肥（waste matter from animals）vt. 给…施肥（to put manure on）

horticulture [ˈhɔːrtɪkʌltʃər] n. 园艺学
【记】horti(花园) + culture(培植) → 园艺学

prairie [ˈpreri] n. 大草原，牧场
【例】The car races across the open *prairie*.

conservatory [kənˈsɜːrvətɔːri] n. 温室（noncommercial greenhouse）；音乐学院（academy of music, art）
【记】conserv(e)(保存，保养) + atory(地方) → 保存植物、文化之地 → 温室；音乐学院

练 习 题

填空题

bankrupt	commission	consolidate	cultivate	dividend
fertile	indigenous	infertile	infertility	irrigate
patronage	pecuniary	profitability	prolific	proprietary
prosperous	sow	transaction	transnational	underestimate

1. Few composers can match his _____ output.
2. The city at one time must have been _____, for it enjoyed a high level of civilization.
3. We have irrigated the desert area to make it _____.
4. He was trying to get a _____ advantage for himself.
5. Nokia is a famous _____ corporation.
6. The company was declared _____ in the High Court.
7. The company has a _____ right to the property.
8. The kangaroo is _____ to Australia.
9. The farmers in this area have to struggle to wrest a living from the _____ soil.
10. There are many possible causes of _____ in women.
11. The company declared a large _____ at the end of the year.
12. He attends to the _____ of important business himself.
13. He earned 2,000 in _____ last month.
14. _____ of the arts comes mostly from businesses and private individuals.
15. The present director has presided over a rapid decline in the firm's _____.
16. The fields around had been _____ with wheat.
17. The statistics seriously _____ the number of people affected.
18. The land around here has never been _____.
19. _____ has increased the area of cultivable land.
20. With this new movie he has _____ his position as the country's leading director.

配对题

1. merger	户头；账目		11. quotation	（企业等的)合并，并购
2. consumerism	谷仓，畜棚		12. conversion	钱袋，财富
3. statement	红利；奖金		13. moneybag	工资单
4. residue	保护消费者利益运动		14. husbandry	家禽
5. invoice	折合，换算		15. weedy	瘦弱的；杂草丛生的
6. rebate	农事，耕种；饲养业		16. barn	（股票等的)行情
7. payroll	发票，发货清单		17. irrigation	返回款；折扣
8. bonus	灌溉		18. poultry	残余
9. account	奖券；抽奖		19. maize	报表，清单
10. lottery	玉米		20. swath	收割的刈痕，收割的宽度

练习题答案

填空题答案

1. Few composers can match his <u>prolific</u> output.
2. The city at one time must have been <u>prosperous</u>, for it enjoyed a high level of civilization.
3. We have irrigated the desert area to make it <u>fertile</u>.
4. He was trying to get a <u>pecuniary</u> advantage for himself.
5. Nokia is a famous <u>transnational</u> corporation.
6. The company was declared <u>bankrupt</u> in the High Court.
7. The company has a <u>proprietary</u> right to the property.
8. The kangaroo is <u>indigenous</u> to Australia.
9. The farmers in this area have to struggle to wrest a living from the <u>infertile</u> soil.
10. There are many possible causes of <u>infertility</u> in women.
11. The company declared a large <u>dividend</u> at the end of the year.
12. He attends to the <u>transaction</u> of important business himself.
13. He earned 2,000 in <u>commission</u> last month.
14. <u>Patronage</u> of the arts comes mostly from businesses and private individuals.
15. The present director has presided over a rapid decline in the firm's <u>profitability</u>.
16. The fields around had been <u>sown</u> with wheat.
17. The statistics seriously <u>underestimate</u> the number of people affected.
18. The land around here has never been <u>cultivated</u>.
19. <u>Irrigation</u> has increased the area of cultivable land.
20. With this new movie he has <u>consolidated</u> his position as the country's leading director.

配对题答案

1. merger	(企业等的)合并, 并购	11. quotation	(股票等的)行情
2. consumerism	保护消费者利益运动	12. conversion	折合, 换算
3. statement	报表, 清单	13. moneybag	钱袋, 财富
4. residue	残余	14. husbandry	农事, 耕种; 饲养业
5. invoice	发票, 发货清单	15. weedy	瘦弱的; 杂草丛生的
6. rebate	返回款; 折扣	16. barn	谷仓, 畜棚
7. payroll	工资单	17. irrigation	灌溉
8. bonus	红利; 奖金	18. poultry	家禽
9. account	户头; 账目	19. maize	玉米
10. lottery	奖券; 抽奖	20. swath	收割的刈痕, 收割的宽度

Word List 15

宗教·教育

宗 教

**icon ［ˈaɪkɑːn］ n. 圣像（an image or picture of Jesus, Mary, a saint, etc）; 偶像
【派】iconize（vt. 盲目崇拜）; iconoclasm（n. 打破圣像的理论/行动）

*inviolable ［ɪnˈvaɪələbl］ adj. 不可侵犯的（incapable of being violated）; 不可亵渎
的（sacred）
【记】in（不）+ viol（看做violate，违反，冒犯）+ able → 不可侵犯的
【反】profane（adj. 亵渎的）; impure（adj. 不纯的）

*sacrosanct ［ˈsækrousæŋkt］ adj. 神圣不可侵犯的（most sacred; inviolable）
【例】The brash insurance salesman invaded the *sacrosanct* privacy of
the office of the president of the company.

apotheosis ［əˌpɑːθiˈousɪs］ n. 神化（the act of raising a person to the status of a god;
deification）; 典范（a glorified ideal）
【记】apo + theo（神）+ sis → 神化

sacrosanctity ［ˌsækrouˈsæŋktəti］ n. 神圣不可侵犯

*consecration ［ˌkɑːnsɪˈkreɪʃn］ n. 神圣化，献祭（仪式）
【例】Wafers are deposited into a bowl for *consecration* during the Mass.

amoral ［ˌeɪˈmɔːrəl］ adj. 与道德无关的（having no moral standards at all）
【记】a（无）+ moral（道德的）→ 与道德无关的

blasphemy ［ˈblæsfəmi］ n. 亵渎（行为或言语）

*sacrilege ［ˈsækrəlɪdʒ］ n. 亵渎，冒犯神灵（outrageous violation of what is
sacred）
【反】respect（n./v. 尊敬）

profanity ［prəˈfænəti］ n. 亵渎；不敬的言语

sacrilegious ［ˌsækrəˈlɪdʒəs］ adj. 亵渎神圣的（treating a sacred thing or place with
disrespect）
【记】sacr（神圣的）+ i + leg（读，讲）+ ious → 说神的坏话 → 亵渎神圣的

*invocation ［ˌɪnvəˈkeɪʃn］ n. 祈祷（to plea; prayer）

*immerse [ɪˈmɜːrs] *vt.* 给…施洗礼；使浸没；使沉浸

【记】im(进) + merse(沉) → 沉进去 → 给…施洗礼

【例】I *immersed* myself in the hot bath and relaxed.

parochial [pəˈroʊkiəl] *adj.* 教区的(of or relating to a church parish)；地方性的，狭小的(restricted to a small area or scope; narrow)

【记】来自parish(*n.* 教区)

**sacred [ˈseɪkrɪd] *adj.* 上帝的，神圣的(holy; heavenly)

【例】In maternal tribes, *sacred* things were kept by the elderest woman.

*redemptive [rɪˈdemptɪv] *adj.* 赎回的，救赎的，救世的 (acting to save someone from error or evil)

*earthly [ˈɜːrθli] *adj.* 现世的，尘世的(of this world; not spiritual)

【记】来自earth(*n.* 土地；地球)

heterodox [ˈhetərədɑːks] *adj.* 异端的，非正统的(unorthodox)

【记】hetero(异种) + dox(思想) → 异端的

【反】canonical(*adj.* 正统的，规范的)

*earthbound [ˈɜːrθbaʊnd] *adj.* 只在地面的；向地球移动的

【例】The *earthbound* astronauts will have to deal with simulated emergencies and perhaps even real ones.

devotee [ˌdevoʊˈtiː] *n.* 爱好者(people who devotes to sth; enthusiast)

**pilgrim [ˈpɪlɡrɪm] *n.* 朝圣者，香客(one who travels to a shrine as a devotee)

*exodus [ˈeksədəs] *n.* 大批离去，撤离

【例】The refugees made an *exodus* to a safe place.

*inferno [ɪnˈfɜːrnoʊ] *n.* 火海，地狱般的场所(hell or any place characterized by great heat or flames)

【记】infern(地狱) + o → 地狱般的场所

*dogma [ˈdɔːɡmə] *n.* 教义，教条(belief; view)

【例】Tom rejected the *dogma* of his church and joined another.

*mosque [mɑːsk] *n.* 清真寺(伊斯兰教的寺庙)(a building used for public worship by Muslims)

anthem [ˈænθəm] *n.* 圣歌(a religious choral song)；赞美歌，国歌(a song of praise, as to a nation)

【记】an + them → 一首他们一起唱的歌 → 赞美歌

fatalism [ˈfeɪtəlɪzəm] *n.* 宿命论

【记】fat(=fate 命运) + alism(主义，论断) → 宿命论

**tenet ['tenɪt] *n.* 信念；信条；教义（a principle, belief, or doctrine generally held to be true）

【记】ten(握住)+et→(握住的)想法→信念

*credo ['kriːdoʊ] *n.* 信条（creed）

【记】cred(相信，信任)+o→信条

*confessional [kən'feʃənl] *n.*（教堂中神父听取忏悔的）告解室（private, usually enclosed, place in a church where a priest sits to hear confessions）

【例】the secrets of the *confessional*

*crescent ['kresnt] *n.* 新月形（物体），月牙形（物体）（narrow curved shape that is like the new moon）

*deify ['deɪfaɪ] *vt.* 将…奉为神（to worship as a god）；崇拜（to adore in an extreme）

atone [ə'toʊn] *v.* 赎（罪），补偿（to make amends for a wrongdoing）

【记】a+tone(看做stone，石头)→女娲用石头补天→补偿

【派】atonement(*n.* 赎罪，弥补)

**divine [dɪ'vaɪn] *v.* 推测，预言（to discover or guess by or as if by magic）*adj.* 神的，神性的；神授的

*demythologize [diːmi'θɒlədʒaɪz] *vt.* 除去…的神话色彩

【记】de(无)+myth(神话)+ologize(使)→除去…的神话色彩

【例】*Genesis I* can best be described as *demythologizing* what was a common cultural heritage.

*consecrate ['kɑːnsɪkreɪt] *vt.* 将…奉为神圣；献身于（to dedicate; devote）

【记】和sacred(*adj.* 神圣的)一起记

【例】The priest *consecrated* the water in the baptismal basin.

*invoke [ɪn'voʊk] *vt.* 恳求，祈求（to beg; pray）

【记】in+voke(喊)→恳求

【例】I *invoked* their forgiveness.

*preach [priːtʃ] *vt.* 说教，布道；鼓吹（to advocate）

【记】和reach(*v.* 到达)一起记

【例】He *preached* tolerance and peaceful coexistence.

ecclesiastic [ɪˌkliːzi'æstɪk] *n.* 神职者，牧师；教会 *adj.* 神职者的，牧师的；教会的（ecclesiastical; pertaining to the church）

seminary ['semɪneri] *n.* 神学院（an institution for the training of candidates for the priesthood）

【记】semin(种子)+ary→培养(上帝)种子的地方→神学院

redeem [rɪ'diːm] *vt.* 为…赎罪，救赎（to atone for; expiate）

【记】re（重新）+ deem（买）→ 重新买回 → 救赎

【派】redemption（*n.* 赎罪）

cathedral [kə'θiːdrəl] *n.* 总教堂，主教堂（the main church of a district under the care of a bishop）

【记】来自拉丁文cathedra，指主教坐的椅子

chapel ['tʃæpl] *n.* （附属于大教堂的）小教堂（a small church used for Christian worship）

gospel ['gɑːspl] *n.* [G-] 福音；教义，信条（any doctrine or rule widely or ardently maintained）

【记】来自《圣经·新约》中的"福音书"（Gospel）；god + spel（看做spell）→ 上帝的话 → 福音；信条

scripture ['skrɪptʃər] *n.* 经文，圣典（a body of writing considered sacred or authoritative）

【记】script（写）+ ure → 写出的东西 → 经文，圣典

*pious ['paɪəs] *adj.* 虔诚的（loyal; faithful）

【例】Those *pious* faithfuls are not allowed to take photos of themselves.

*devout [dɪ'vaʊt] *adj.* 虔诚的（pious; religious）；真诚的

【例】The *devout* worshiper attended church each week.

atheistic [ˌeɪθi'ɪstɪk] *adj.* 无神论（者）的（denying the existence of God）

【派】atheism（*n.* 无神论）；atheist（*n.* 无神论者）

*heretical [hə'retɪkl] *adj.* 异教的，异端邪说的（of heresy or heretics）

【记】here（异）+ tical → 异教的

heterodoxy ['hetərədɑːksi] *n.* 异端，异端邪说

【例】And as we grapple for solutions to the crisis, we must pay adequate attention to the importance of policy diversity—which has somewhat disparagingly been called "*heterodoxy*".

heresy ['herəsi] *n.* 异教；异端邪说

【记】here（异）+ sy → 异端邪说

impiety [ɪm'paɪəti] *n.* 无信仰，不虔诚（the quality or state of being impious）

【记】im（不）+ piety（虔诚）→ 不虔诚

【例】We must regard your blasphemy as an act of *impiety*.

【反】devoutness（*n.* 虔诚）

impious ['ɪmpiəs] *adj.* 不虔诚的

infidel [ˈɪnfɪdəl] n. 无宗教信仰之人（a person with no belief in a religion, especially in what is considered to be the true religion）

pagan [ˈpeɪgən] n. 没有宗教信仰的人（a person who has no religion）; 异教徒, 非基督教徒（heathen）
【记】pag（看做pig）+ an（一个）→ 异教徒被贬低为一头猪 → 异教徒
【派】paganism（n. 异教信仰）

recantation [ˌriːkænˈteɪʃn] n. 改变宗教信仰（statement that one's former beliefs were wrong）

atheism [ˈeɪθiɪzəm] n. 无神论, 不信神（the belief that there is no god）
【记】a（无）+ the（神）+ ism → 无神论
【派】atheistic（adj. 无神论的）

pastoral [ˈpæstərəl] adj. 乡村的, 田园生活的（idyllic; rural）; 宁静的（pleasingly peaceful and innocent）
【记】pastor（牧人）+ al → 乡村的, 田园生活的

astral [ˈæstrəl] adj. 星形的（relating to the stars）

*apocalyptic [əˌpɑːkəˈlɪptɪk] adj. 预示灾祸的; 启示的（prophetic）
【记】来自apocalypse（n. 天启, 启示）, apo（离开）+ calyps（盖上）+ e → 揭开 → 启示

*fiesta [fiˈestə] n.（西班牙语国家的）宗教节日

*talisman [ˈtælɪzmən] n. 避邪物, 护身符（an object held to act as a charm to avert evil and bring good fortune）
【记】talis（做仪式, 驱邪）+ man（人）→ 人在驱邪仪式上佩戴避邪物 → 避邪物, 护身符

anathema [əˈnæθəmə] n. 驱逐出教门; 极讨厌的人或事物（detested person or thing）
【例】Racial prejudice is an *anathema* to me.

*malediction [ˌmælɪˈdɪkʃn] n. 诅咒（curse; execration）
【记】male（坏）+ dict（说）+ ion → 说坏话 → 诅咒

**vestry [ˈvestri] n.（教堂的）法衣室

*lection [ˈlekʃn] n. 经文（scriptures）

*lustrate [ˈlʌstreɪt] vt. 举行宗教仪式驱除（邪恶等）

*enchant [ɪnˈtʃænt] vt. 施魔法于（to enthrall; fascinate）
【记】en + chant（歌曲）→ 通过吟唱施魔法于 → 施魔法于
【例】The witch *enchanted* the handsome knight, turning him into a frog.

anoint [əˈnɔɪnt] vt. 对…施以涂油礼(to apply oil to as a sacred rite especially for consecration)

ablution [əbˈluːʃn] n. (宗教的)净礼，沐浴(a washing of the body as a religious ceremony)

【记】ab + lut(冲，洗) + ion → (宗教的)净礼，沐浴；含有相同词根 lut 的词语：dilute(vt. 冲淡，稀释)；antediluvian(adj. 大洪水以前的)

cloister [ˈklɔɪstər] n. 修道院(monastery or convent; nunnery)

【记】cloist(=close) + er → 幽闭之地 → 修道院

【派】cloistered(adj. 隐居的)

proselytize [ˈprɑːsəlataɪz] v. (使)皈依，(使)改变信仰(to recruit or convert to a new faith)

【记】pros(靠近) + elyt(来到) + ize → 走到(佛祖)面前 → 皈依

sectarianism [sekˈteriənɪzəm] n. 宗派主义

【例】He condemned religious *sectarianism*.

sacrament [ˈsækrəmənt] n. 圣礼，圣事(any of certain rites instituted by Jesus)

【记】sacra(神圣) + ment → 圣礼

***sacrificial** [ˌsækrɪˈfɪʃl] adj. 牺牲的，献祭的(immolated)

教　育

rostrum [ˈrɑːstrəm] n. 讲台，讲坛(a raised place for a public speaker)

dais [ˈdeɪɪs] n. 台，讲台 (raised platform for speakers or other important people)

***ology** [ˈɑːlədʒi] n. 科学，学问

****pedagogy** [ˈpedəgɑːdʒi] n. 教育学；教学法(the art, science of teaching)

【记】ped(儿童) + agog(引导) + y → 引导儿童之学 → 教育学

****curriculum** [kəˈrɪkjələm] n. (pl. curricula)课程

***didactic** [daɪˈdæktɪk] adj. 教诲的，说教的(instructive)

【例】He started to know the real meaning of life from a *didactic* speech given by a celebrity.

***expertise** [ˌekspɜːrˈtiːz] n. 专门知识(special knowledge and skill)

【记】来自 expert(n. 专家)

【例】Do you have the *expertise* required to tune the piano?

***interface** [ˈɪntərfeɪs] n. (两学科等的)交叉以及相互影响之处

【例】at the *interface* of art and science

*reeducation [ˌriːedjuˈkeɪʃn] *n.* 再教育

【例】Prince also embarked on a company-wide cultural *reeducation* program, designed to prevent regulatory lapses from happening in the future.

**sermonize [ˈsɜːrmənaɪz] *v.* 说教，布道，讲道(to compose or deliver a sermon)

【记】来自sermon(*n.* 说教，布道)

*instruct [ɪnˈstrʌkt] *vt.* 教导

【例】She *instructed* me in the use of the telephone.

*edify [ˈedɪfaɪ] *vt.* 陶冶，教化(to enlighten; teach)

【例】A trip to the art museum *edified* the tourists and helped them understand the local culture better.

*instill [inˈstil] *vt.* 灌输(to infuse; impart)

【记】in(进入) + still(滴) → 灌输

【例】Courtesy must be *instilled* in childhood.

inculcate [ˈɪnkʌlˌkeɪt] *vt.* 反复灌输，谆谆教诲 (to impress upon the mind by persistent urging; implant)

【记】in(进入) + culc(=cult 培养，种植) + ate → 种进去 → 反复灌输

*enlightening [ɪnˈlaɪtnɪŋ] *adj.* 有启迪作用的 (giving spiritual and intellectual insight)；使人领悟的

**edifying [ˈedɪfaɪɪŋ] *adj.* 有益的，有教化意味的

【例】When she made remarks to this *edifying* effect, she had a firm little frown on her brow.

**enlightenment [ɪnˈlaɪtnmənt] *n.* 启迪，教化；启蒙运动

【例】Why, on the path to *enlightenment*, did so many people seem to yield power to Ray?

*admonish [ədˈmɑːnɪʃ] *vt.* 警告(to warn)

【记】ad(加强) + mon(警告) + ish → 告诫，警告

【例】Mary *admonished* the children not to talk to strangers.

**anthology [ænˈθɑːlədʒi] *n.* 诗集，文选(a collection of poems, stories or songs)

【记】anth(花) + ology → 像花一样的文章 → 诗集，文选

*discipline [ˈdɪsəplɪn] *n.* 学科

练 习 题

填空题

apocalyptic	confessional	consecrate	consecration	deify
demythologize	devout	divine	earthly	heretical
immerse	inviolable	invocation	invoke	pious
preach	redemptive	sacred	sacrosanct	tenet

1. Cows are _____ to Hindus.
2. Our _____ is "Client orineted, Faith is root".
3. She could _____ what he was thinking just by looking at him.
4. The people possess _____ rights.
5. I'll work till late in the evening, but my weekends are _____.
6. Easter Monday is generally regarded as an unofficial _____ of Spring.
7. His disciples gathered about him, reciting a sutra during the _____.
8. He _____ himself totally in his work.
9. God has _____ purposes in mind which will ultimately lead to Satan's defeat.
10. No _____ sovereign can do what he pleases.
11. Then I noticed this _____, like you see in Catholic churches.
12. Before them was an _____ landscape of burnt villages and bomb craters.
13. Primitive peoples _____ the sun.
14. Genesis I can best be described as _____ what was a common cultural heritage.
15. She _____ her life to God.
16. She _____ several eminent scholars to back up her argument.
17. The chaplain came and _____ to a packed church.
18. He dismissed his critics as _____ do-gooders.
19. It is my _____ hope that we can work together in peace.
20. Most blind beliefs in _____ ideas and various taboos originate in some religious mentality.

配对题

1. rostrum	灌输	11. ology	启迪，教化；启蒙运动
2. pedagogy	反复灌输，谆谆教诲	12. didactic	举行宗教仪式驱除(邪恶等)
3. expertise	讲台，讲坛	13. sermonize	诗集，文选
4. edify	教诲的，说教的	14. instill	说教，讲道
5. inculcate	教育学；教学法	15. admonish	陶冶，教化
6. anthology	经文	16. discipline	(两学科等的)交叉以及相互影响之处
7. enlightenment	劝诫，警告	17. interface	学科
8. curriculum	(宗教的)净礼，沐浴	18. sectarianism	专门知识
9. ablution	科学，学问	19. lustrate	宗教节日
10. lection	课程	20. fiesta	宗派主义

练习题答案

填空题答案

1. Cows are <u>sacred</u> to Hindus.
2. Our <u>tenet</u> is "Client orineted, Faith is root".
3. She could <u>divine</u> what he was thinking just by looking at him.
4. The people possess <u>inviolable</u> rights.
5. I'll work till late in the evening, but my weekends are <u>sacrosanct</u>.
6. Easter Monday is generally regarded as an unofficial <u>consecration</u> of Spring.
7. His disciples gathered about him, reciting a sutra during the <u>invocation</u>.
8. He <u>immersed</u> himself totally in his work.
9. God has <u>redemptive</u> purposes in mind which will ultimately lead to Satan's defeat.
10. No <u>earthly</u> sovereign can do what he pleases.
11. Then I noticed this <u>confessional</u>, like you see in Catholic churches.
12. Before them was an <u>apocalyptic</u> landscape of burnt villages and bomb craters.
13. Primitive peoples <u>deified</u> the sun.
14. Genesis I can best be described as <u>demythologizing</u> what was a common cultural heritage.
15. She <u>consecrated</u> her life to God.
16. She <u>invoked</u> several eminent scholars to back up her argument.
17. The chaplain came and <u>preached</u> to a packed church.
18. He dismissed his critics as <u>pious</u> do-gooders.
19. It is my <u>devout</u> hope that we can work together in peace.
20. Most blind beliefs in <u>heretical</u> ideas and various taboos originate in some religious mentality.

配对题答案

1. rostrum	讲台，讲坛	11. ology	科学，学问
2. pedagogy	教育学；教学法	12. didactic	教诲的，说教的
3. expertise	专门知识	13. sermonize	说教，讲道
4. edify	陶冶，教化	14. instill	灌输
5. inculcate	反复灌输，谆谆教诲	15. admonish	劝诫，警告
6. anthology	诗集，文选	16. discipline	学科
7. enlightenment	启迪，启蒙运动，教化	17. interface	(两学科等的)交叉以及相互影响之处
8. curriculum	课程	18. sectarianism	宗派主义
9. ablution	(宗教的)净礼，沐浴	19. lustrate	举行宗教仪式驱除(邪恶等)
10. lection	经文	20. fiesta	宗教节日

SAT
按意群分类
Analogous

Word List 16

正向评价(一)

慷 慨

*charitable [ˈtʃærətəbl] *adj.* 慷慨的，慈善的（generous; benevolent）

【例】Because it was Susan's first offense, the judge was *charitable* and gave her probation.

*unstinting [ʌnˈstɪntɪŋ] *adj.* 极为慷慨的，大方的（very generous）

【记】un（不）+ stint（吝惜，限制）+ ing → 极为慷慨的

*munificent [mjuːˈnɪfɪsnt] *adj.* 慷慨的（generous; liberal）

【记】muni（礼物）+ fic（做）+ ent → 做礼物给大家 → 慷慨的

*magnanimous [mægˈnænɪməs] *adj.* 宽宏大量的，慷慨的（noble in mind; high souled）

*magnanimity [ˌmægnəˈnɪməti] *n.* 宽宏大量，慷慨

【记】magn（大）+ anim（心胸，生命）+ ity → 心胸宽大 → 宽宏大量

*liberality [ˌlɪbəˈrælətɪ] *n.* 慷慨（generosity）；心胸开阔（quality of being tolerant and open-minded）

【记】来自liberal（*adj.* 慷慨的；开明的），liber（自由）+ al → 开明的

**bounty [ˈbaʊnti] *n.* 慷慨，大方（generosity; liberality）

【例】a monarch famous for his *bounty*

altruistic [ˌæltruˈɪstɪk] *adj.* 无私的，利他主义的（unselfish regard for or devoted to the welfare of others）

节 俭

thrifty [ˈθrɪfti] *adj.* 节省的（marked by economy and good management）

【记】来自thrift（*n.* 节约）

*frugal [ˈfruːɡl] *adj.* 节约的（thrifty; economical）

spartan ['spɑːtn] *adj.* 斯巴达的，斯巴达式的；简朴的（of simplicity or frugality）；刻苦的（strict self-discipline or self-denial）

【记】来自Sparta(斯巴达)，古代希腊城邦，该地区的人都很简朴刻苦

【反】sybaritic / voluptuous / luxurious（*adj.* 奢侈的）；indulgent（*adj.* 放纵的）

*abstemious [æb'stiːmiəs] *adj.* 节俭的；有节制的(moderate in eating and drinking; temperate)

【记】abs(不) + tem(酒) + ious → 不喝酒 → 有节制的；注意tem来自拉丁文temetum(=mead 蜜酒)

**austerity [ɔː'sterəti] *n.* 节俭；朴素；苦行；严厉

【例】*Austerity* is the chosen lifestyle of a monk.

frugality [fruˈɡæləti] *n.* 节约，节俭(thrift; economy)

【例】His *frugality* deeply impressed us.

skimp [skɪmp] *vi.* 节省，节俭 *vt.* 舍不得给，克扣（to give barely sufficient funds for sth）

【例】They have to *skimp* on fuel in winter.

*ingenuous [ɪn'dʒenjuəs] *adj.* 纯朴的；单纯的(simple; artless)

【记】来自拉丁语ingenuus，意为"天真，诚实"

【反】cunning（*adj.* 狡猾的）；hypercritical（*adj.* 苛刻的）

**austere [ɔː'stɪr] *adj.* 朴素的(very plain; lacking ornament)；苦行的

【记】au + stere(冷) → 冷色调的穿着 → 朴素的

【反】baroque（*adj.* 过分装饰的）

artless ['ɑːrtləs] *adj.* 天真烂漫的，淳朴的

canny ['kæni] *adj.* 节俭的(frugal)

naivety [naɪ'iːvəti] *n.* 天真，纯朴 (unaffected simplicity)

【记】来自naive(*adj.* 天真的)，源自native(*adj.* 天然的，自然的)，也写成naivete

【派】naive(*adj.* 天真的) → worldly(*adj.* 善于处事的)

谦　虚

*modest ['mɑːdɪst] *adj.* 谦虚的，审慎的(humble; unassuming)；适度的，有节制的

【记】mod(方式) + est → 做事有规矩 → 审慎的

humility [hjuː'mɪləti] *n.* 谦逊，谦恭，谦卑(absence of pride or self-assertion)

【反】hubris / hauteur(*n.* 自大，傲慢)；panache(*n.* 炫耀，自负)

*unassuming	[ˌʌnə'suːmɪŋ] *adj.* 不摆架子的，不装腔作势的（not arrogant or presuming; modest）	

【记】 un(不) + assuming(傲慢的) → 不摆架子的

*unpretentious [ˌʌnprɪ'tenʃəs] *adj.* 谦虚的，含蓄的；不炫耀的，不铺张的（not attempting to seem special, important or wealthy）

【记】 un(不) + pretentious(自命不凡的) → 谦虚的

【反】 bombastic(*adj.* 夸大的)

谨 慎

*prudent ['pruːdnt] *adj.* 谨慎的（cautious）

【记】 prud(小心) + ent → 谨慎的

wary ['weri] *adj.* 谨慎的，小心的（looking out for danger）；谨防的，唯恐的

*circumspect ['sɜːkəmspekt] *adj.* 慎重的，仔细的，考虑周到的（prudent; cautious）

【记】 circum(绕圈) + spect(看) → 四处看 → 仔细的

【例】 Never very *circumspect* in expressing his views, Bill annoyed almost everyone at the party.

**meticulous [mə'tɪkjələs] *adj.* 细心的，一丝不苟的（taking extreme care about minute details; precise）

【记】 metic(害怕的) + ulous(多…的) → 非常害怕出错 → 一丝不苟的

**scrupulous ['skruːpjələs] *adj.* 严谨的，认真的（conscientious and exact）

【例】 The secretary is *scrupulous* about her dress.

*discretion [dɪ'skreʃn] *n.* 慎重，审慎（caution; prudence）

【例】 The decorator showed no *discretion* in her purchases for our new house, everything costing too much money.

prudence ['pruːdns] *n.* 谨慎，小心；精明（shrewdness）

punctilious [pʌŋk'tɪliəs] *adj.* 谨小慎微的（careful）

【记】 punct(点，尖) + ilious → 注意到每一点 → 谨小慎微的

【反】 slipshod(*adj.* 马虎的)；remiss(*adj.* 玩忽职守的)

studied ['stʌdid] *adj.* 深思熟虑的（carefully thought about or considered）

tender ['tendər] *adj.* 细心的，敏感的

vigilance ['vɪdʒɪləns] *n.* 警戒，警觉，警惕

【例】 Jean-Claude Trichet said the ECB was "in a posture of strong *vigilance*" against rising inflation.

gingerly [ˈdʒɪndʒərli] *adj./adv.* 轻手轻脚的(地)；小心谨慎的(地)(very careful or very carefully)

*cautious [ˈkɔːʃəs] *adj.* 小心的，谨慎的
【例】Be *cautious* when you approach strangers.

chary [ˈtʃeri] *adj.* 小心的，审慎的(careful; cautious)
【例】Be *chary* of catching cold!
【反】bold(*adj.* 鲁莽的)

*vigilant [ˈvɪdʒɪlənt] *adj.* 机警的，警惕的，清醒的(watchful; alert)
【例】The president's *vigilant* bodyguard immediately noticed the man with a gun.

**sanity [ˈsænəti] *n.* 神智清楚(saneness; rationality)

finicky [ˈfɪnɪki] *adj.* 苛求的，过分讲究的，过分挑剔的 (too particular or exacting; fussy)
【记】单词finical的变体，来自fine(*adj.* 精细的)

*cautionary [ˈkɔːʃəneri] *adj.* 警戒的，警告的(giving advice or a warning)
【记】来自caution(*n.* 小心，谨慎)

*formality [fɔːrˈmæləti] *n.* 形式；礼仪；拘谨
【记】form(形式)+ al + ity(表性质) → 形式

熟 练

*proficient [prəˈfɪʃnt] *adj.* 熟练的，精通的(skillful; expert)
【记】pro(在前)+ fic(做)+ ient → 做在别人前面的 → 熟练的
【派】proficiency(*n.* 熟练，精通)

seasoned [ˈsiːznd] *adj.* 经验丰富的，训练有素的(experienced)

deft [deft] *adj.* 灵巧的，机敏的，熟练的(skillful; adroit)
【例】The pianist's *deft* fingers were delightful to watch.

**empirical [ɪmˈpɪrɪkl] *adj.* 经验的，实证的(based on observation or experience)
【记】来自empiric，原指"单凭经验而行医的医生"，即"江湖医生"

*nimbly [ˈnɪmbli] *adv.* 敏捷地，机敏地(promptly; swiftly)
【例】Palin, who circulated *nimbly* through the room, and spoke admiringly of National Review, made a good impression.

*adept [əˈdept] *adj.* 擅长的，内行的，熟练的(adroit; apt)
【例】Mary is very *adept* at tuning pianos.

*stunt [stʌnt] *n.* 惊人的技艺(trick; feat)
【例】In the film he had to drive a car into the sea, and do other hair-raising *stunts*.

omniscient [ɑːmˈnɪsiənt] *adj.* 无所不知的，博识的(knowing all things)
【记】omni(全) + sci(知道) + ent → 全知道的 → 无所不知的

美　丽

debonair [ˌdebəˈner] *adj.* 温文尔雅的 (urbane)；和蔼的，友好的(affable; friendly)
【记】de + bon(好) + air(气氛) → 让气氛好的 → 和蔼的，友好的
【例】He strolled about, looking very *debonair* in his elegant new suit.

Lithe & limber

lissome [ˈlisəm] *adj.* (身体)柔软的(lithe; supple; limber)；敏捷轻快的
subtle [ˈsʌtl] *adj.* 微妙的；精巧的(delicate)
【反】palpable(*adj.* 明显的)；blatant(*adj.* 明显的；炫耀的)

*ineffable [ɪnˈefəbl] *adj.* 妙不可言的(inexpressible)
【记】in(不) + effable(可以表达的) → 难以表达的 → 妙不可言的

敏　锐

**acumen [ˈækjəmən] *n.* 敏锐，机智(acuteness)
【记】acu(尖端) + men → 敏锐
【例】Bill has a lot of business *acumen* and earns a high salary.

*sensitive [ˈsensətɪv] *adj.* 敏感的；灵敏度高的
*agile [ˈædʒl] *adj.* 敏捷的，灵活的(able to move quickly and easily)
*perspicacious [ˌpɜːrspɪˈkeɪʃəs] *adj.* 独具慧眼的，洞察力强的 (of acute mental vision or discernment)
【记】per(全部) + spic(=spect 看) + acious → 全部都看到 → 洞察力强的
【反】obtuse(*adj.* 迟钝的)；undiscerned(*a.* 无辨别力的)

celerity [sɪˈlerəti] *n.* 快速，迅速(swiftness in acting or moving; speed)
【记】celer(速度) + ity → 快速，迅速

*alacrity [əˈlækrəti] *n.* 敏捷，轻快 (promptness in response)；乐意，欣然 (cheerful readiness)
【例】The child obeyed with *alacrity*.
【反】hesitance(*n.* 犹豫)；reluctance(*n.* 不情愿)；recalcitrance(*n.* 不顺从)；dilatoriness(*n.* 迟缓，拖延)

活 泼

*vivacious [vɪˈveɪʃəs] *adj.* 活泼的，快活的（lively in temper, conduct, or spirit; sprightly）

【记】viv(生命) + acious → 有生命力的 → 活泼的

【反】phlegmatic(*adj.* 冷漠的); languid(*adj.* 疲倦的)

*frisky [ˈfrɪski] *adj.* 活泼的，快活的，爱嬉闹的(playful; frolicsome; merry)

*frolicsome [ˈfrɑːlɪksəm] *adj.* 快活的，爱嬉闹的(full of gaiety or high spirits)

animated [ˈænɪmeɪtɪd] *adj.* 活泼的，生动的，栩栩如生的（full of vigor and spirit）

vitality [vaɪˈtæləti] *n.* 活力，生命力(capacity to live and develop)

spry [spraɪ] *adj.* 精神好的，活泼的，敏捷的(vigorously active; nimble)

【例】She was eighty years old, yet still *spry* and alert.

*animate [ˈænɪmeɪt] *adj.* 活的，有生命力的(living; having life)

【例】The dog lay so still and it scarcely seemed *animate*.

*vibrant [ˈvaɪbrənt] *adj.* 振动的; (色彩)明快的(bright); 生机勃勃的，精力充沛的(pulsating with life; energetic)

【记】vibr(振动) + ant → 振动的

【反】ponderous(*adj.* 沉闷的)

**flourish [ˈflɜːrɪʃ] *vi.* (植物)繁茂; 昌盛，兴旺(to develop well and be successful); 活跃而有影响力(to be very active and influential)

【记】flour(=flor 花) + ish → 像花一样开放 → 昌盛，兴旺

【反】waste away(衰退)

verve [vɜːrv] *n.* 热忱(vivacity); (人的)生机，精力(energy; vitality)

忠 诚

*heartfelt [ˈhɑːrtfelt] *adj.* 衷心的，真心真意的(earnest)

rectitude [ˈrektɪtjuːd] *n.* 诚实，正直，公正(moral integrity; righteousness)

【记】rect(直) + itude → 正直

【反】inequity(*n.* 不公正)

allegiance [əˈliːdʒəns] *n.* 忠诚，拥护(loyalty or devotion to a cause or a person)

【记】al(加强) + leg(法律) + iance → 拥护法律 → 拥护

adherence [ədˈhɪrəns] *n.* 坚持；信奉，忠诚

*committed [kəˈmɪtɪd] *adj.* (对事业、本职工作等)尽忠的，坚定的(devoted to a cause)

【反】ambivalent(*adj.* 有矛盾情感的)

**dedication [ˌdedɪˈkeɪʃn] *n.* (对事业的)专心致力，献身(devotion to a cause or an aim)

【记】来自dedicate(*v.* 致力)，其反义词有 dabble(*vi.* 浅尝，涉足)

**fidelity [fɪˈdeləti] *n.* 坚贞，忠诚(loyalty; faithfulness)

【记】fid(相信) + elity → 坚贞，忠诚

upright [ˈʌpraɪt] *adj.* 垂直的 (straight up)；正直的(honest; fair)

【记】up(向上) + right(正面的) → 垂直的

【派】uprightness(*n.* 垂直) → list(*n.* 倾斜)

**disingenuous [ˌdɪsɪnˈdʒenjuəs] *adj.* 不坦率的，不真诚的(lacking in candor)

【记】来自 ingenuous(*adj.* 坦率的，真诚的)；与ingenious(*adj.* 灵巧的，聪慧的)区别记忆

guileless [ˈɡaɪlləs] *adj.* 不狡猾的，诚实的(frank; honest)

【例】His *guileless* smile disarmed us; we began to believe him.

勇　敢

mettle [ˈmetl] *n.* 勇气，斗志，毅力(courage and fortitude)

【记】和metal(金属，引申为钢铁)一起记，有着钢铁(metal)一般的毅力(nattle)；比较记忆：nettle(*n.* 荨麻 *vt.* 使恼火)；settle(*vt.* 使安定)

*undaunted [ˌʌnˈdɔːntɪd] *adj.* 吓不倒的，无畏的，勇敢的(intrepid; fearless)

*bold [bould] *adj.* 勇敢的，大胆的(daring; brave)

【例】The *bold* employee insisted on better working conditions.

**audacious [ɔːˈdeɪʃəs] *adj.* 大胆的，无畏的(daring; fearless; brave)；愚勇的，鲁莽的

【记】aud(大胆) + acious(多…的) → 大胆的

【反】circumspect(*adj.* 慎重的)；timid(*adj.* 胆小的)

【派】audacity(*n.* 大胆；鲁莽)

*poised [pɔɪzd] *adj.* 泰然自若的，镇定的

【例】They suggest that Latin America may have bottomed out and stands *poised* for a rebound.

*chivalrous ［ˈʃɪvlrəs］*adj.* 骑士的，侠义的；彬彬有礼的（gallant; courteous）

【记】chival（=caval 骑马）+ rous → 骑马的 → 骑士的

【例】I appreciate *chivalrous* acts such as holding doors open for ladies.

dauntless ［ˈdɔːntləs］*adj.* 勇敢的，吓不倒的

【记】daunt(吓到)+ less → 吓不倒的

【例】The *dauntless* pilot flew through the rough storms.

*valorous ［ˈvælərəs］*adj.* 勇敢的（brave）

【记】val(强大)+ orous → 勇敢的

【反】craven(*adj.* 懦弱的)

**intrepid ［ɪnˈtrepɪd］*adj.* 勇敢的（fearless; dauntless）

【记】in(不)+ trepid(害怕) → 勇敢的

【例】The *intrepid* explorers reached the South Pole.

enterprising ［ˈentərpraɪzɪŋ］*adj.* 有事业心的，有进取心的

【例】In economics, the United States has always been *enterprising* and market-driven.

*heroic ［həˈroʊɪk］*adj.* 有英雄气概的，英勇的（brave）

【例】*heroic* deeds

candor ［ˈkændə］*n.* 坦白，率直（frankness）

【记】cand(白)+ or(表状态) → 坦白

【反】artifice(*n.* 狡诈)

**prowess ［ˈpraʊəs］*n.* 勇敢，英勇（distinguished bravery）；非凡的能力（extraordinary ability）

【记】来自prow(*adj.* 英勇的)，是proud的变体

【反】timidity(*n.* 胆小)

*aplomb ［əˈplɑːm］*n.* 自信，沉着（confidence and self-control; poise）

【例】She performs the duties of a princess with great *aplomb*.

*valour ［ˈvælər］*n.* (尤指在战争中)勇武，英勇（bravery）

【例】display great *valour*

**embolden ［ɪmˈboʊldən］*vt.* 鼓励，给…壮胆（to give confidence to sb）

【记】em + bold(大胆)+ en → 使大胆 → 鼓励

【反】abash(*vt.* 使窘迫)；faze(*vt.* 烦扰)；cow(*vt.* 恐吓)；appall(*vt.* 使害怕)；boggle(*v.* 犹豫，迟疑)；daunt(*vt.* 威吓)

gamely ［ˈɡeɪmli］*adj.* 不屈地，勇敢地（in a spirited manner; with courage）

【例】fight *gamely* against a superior boxer

valor ['vælə] *n.* 英勇，勇气（bravery; courage）

【记】val(强大) + or → 英勇

【例】The terminally ill patient showed great *valor* in the last months of his life.

强 壮

**robust [roʊ'bʌst] *adj.* 强壮的，结实的（strong; sturdy）

【例】If you want to be healthy and *robust*, you need to exercise yourself routinely.

hardy ['hɑːrdi] *adj.* 强壮的（tough; rugged）；吃苦耐劳的

【例】Those *hardy* and stocky Eskimos have been living in this frozen world for centuries.

**stiff [stɪf] *adj.* 生硬的，僵直的；刚强的

virile ['vɪrəl] *adj.* 有男子气的，雄健的（masculine）

【记】vir(力量) + ile → 有力量的 → 雄健的

【例】Some people say it's the most *virile* sport.

stalwart ['stɔːlwərt] *adj.* 健壮的，结实的

【反】lank(*adj.* 瘦的)

burly ['bɜːrli] *adj.* 魁梧的，强壮的（husky; muscular）

【例】The *burly* mover lifted the packing crate with ease.

**vigorous ['vɪɡərəs] *adj.* 健壮的，精力充沛的

【例】Mary stretched her muscles before an hour of *vigorous* exercise.

填空题

acumen	audacious	austere	austerity	bounty
charitable	dedication	embolden	fidelity	flourish
frugal	intrepid	munificent	prowess	prudent
robust	scrupulous	stiff	vigilant	vigorous

1. Take _____ exercise for several hours a week.
2. I admire those _____ warriors from childhood.
3. He has always been hard-working and _____.
4. It might be more _____ to get a second opinion before going ahead.
5. The thief was spotted by _____ neighbors.
6. He enjoys being _____ on a princely scale.
7. His later years were devoted largely to _____ work.
8. Their clothes were always _____.
9. She was almost 90, but still very _____.
10. He was _____ in all his business dealings.
11. I've got a _____ neck.
12. He has an _____ disposition, and great strength.
13. His _____ to teaching gained the respect of his colleagues.
14. A sudden fit of fiscal _____ would be a mistake.
15. The firm's success is largely due to Brannon's commercial _____.
16. He was complimented on his _____ as an oarsman.
17. His _____ and industry brought him speedy promotion.
18. He is famous for his _____ to the poor.
19. The arts began to at _____ that time.
20. _____ by the wine, he went over to introduce himself to her.

配对题

1. ingenuous	节俭的；有节制的	11. meticulous	有男子气的，雄健的
2. unstinting	擅长的	12. cautious	宽宏大量的，慷慨的
3. unassuming	警戒的，警告的	13. abstemious	细心的，一丝不苟的
4. unpretentious	小心的，谨慎的	14. disingenuous	谦虚的；适度的
5. magnanimous	慎重的，仔细的	15. nimbly	敏捷地，机敏地
6. modest	慎重，审慎	16. virile	熟练的，精通的
7. cautionary	不坦率的，不真诚的	17. liberality	神智清楚
8. adept	形式；礼仪；拘谨	18. sanity	不摆架子的，不装腔作势的
9. circumspect	纯朴的，单纯的	19. discretion	炫耀的
10. proficient	心胸开阔	20. formality	极为慷慨的

练习题答案

填空题答案

1. Take <u>vigorous</u> exercise for several hours a week.
2. I admire those <u>audacious</u> warriors from childhood.
3. He has always been hard-working and <u>frugal</u>.
4. It might be more <u>prudent</u> to get a second opinion before going ahead.
5. The thief was spotted by <u>vigilant</u> neighbors.
6. He enjoys being <u>munificent</u> on a princely scale.
7. His later years were devoted largely to <u>charitable</u> work.
8. Their clothes were always <u>austere</u>.
9. She was almost 90, but still very <u>robust</u>.
10. He was <u>scrupulous</u> in all his business dealings.
11. I've got a <u>stiff</u> neck.
12. He has an <u>intrepid</u> disposition, and great strength.
13. His <u>dedication</u> to teaching gained the respect of his colleagues.
14. A sudden fit of fiscal <u>austerity</u> would be a mistake.
15. The firm's success is largely due to Brannon's commercial <u>acumen</u>.
16. He was complimented on his <u>prowess</u> as an oarsman.
17. His <u>fidelity</u> and industry brought him speedy promotion.
18. He is famous for his <u>bounty</u> to the poor.
19. The arts began to <u>flourish</u> at that time.
20. <u>Emboldened</u> by the wine, he went over to introduce himself to her.

配对题答案

1. ingenuous	纯朴的，单纯的	11. meticulous	细心的，一丝不苟的
2. unstinting	极为慷慨的	12. cautious	小心的，谨慎的
3. unassuming	不摆架子的，不装腔作势的	13. abstemious	节俭的；有节制的
4. unpretentious	不炫耀的	14. disingenuous	不坦率的，不真诚的
5. magnanimous	宽宏大量的，慷慨的	15. nimbly	敏捷地，机敏地
6. modest	谦虚的；适度的	16. virile	有男子气的，雄健的
7. cautionary	警戒的，警告的	17. liberality	心胸开阔
8. adept	擅长的	18. sanity	神智清楚
9. circumspect	慎重的，仔细的	19. discretion	慎重，审慎
10. proficient	熟练的，精通的	20. formality	形式；礼仪；拘谨

Word List 17

正向评价（二）

聪　颖

*intelligent ［ɪnˈtelɪdʒənt］*adj.* 聪明的，有才智的（ingenious; wise）

*sagacious ［səˈɡeɪʃəs］*adj.* 有洞察力的，睿智的（showing keen perception and foresight）

【记】来自sage（*n.* 智慧）

【反】without wisdom（无智慧）；puerile（*adj.* 幼稚的）

sagacity ［səˈɡæsəti］*n.* 聪慧，睿智

【例】My *sagacity* was not a fault.

scintillate ［ˈsɪntɪleɪt］*vi.* 火花闪烁；（谈吐）流露机智（to emit sparks; sparkle）

【记】scintill（火花）+ ate → 火花闪烁

sleight ［slaɪt］*n.* 巧妙手法，巧计；灵巧（dexterity; skill）

【记】sl（看做sly, 狡猾）+ eight → 八面玲珑，会用巧计 → 巧计

**finesse ［fɪˈnes］*n.* 技巧，计谋，巧妙的手段（adroitness and delicacy; the ability to handle delicate and difficult situations skillfully and diplomatically）

【记】fine（好，巧妙）+ sse → 巧妙的手段

【反】heavy handedness（笨手笨脚）；ineptitude（*n.* 笨拙）

*flair ［fler］*n.* 天赋，本领，才华（a natural talent or ability）

【记】没有本领（flair），哪能飞（fly）到天上去

**ingenuity ［ˌɪndʒəˈnjuːəti］*n.* 巧思，聪敏；独创性（cleverness; originality）

【记】来自ingenue（*n.* 天真少女）

【反】lack of inventiveness（缺乏创造性）

*astute ［əˈstjuːt］*adj.* 机敏的，聪敏的（shrewd, canny）

【例】The boss appreciated Mary's *astute* observations about how to improve the company's image.

adroit [əˈdrɔɪt] *adj.* 灵巧的，敏捷的（skillful; adept; deft）
【例】The elderly man couldn't walk, but he was still *adroit* with his hands.

exquisite [ɪkˈskwɪzɪt] *adj.* （指感觉、感受等）灵敏的，敏锐的
【例】The artists have an *exquisite* sense of color.

expeditious [ˌekspəˈdɪʃəs] *adj.* 敏捷的，迅速的（prompt; speedy）

ambidextrous [ˌæmbiˈdekstrəs] *adj.* 左右手都很灵巧的（very skillful or versatile）
【记】ambi（两个）+ dextr（右的）+ ous → 两只手都像右手一样灵巧 → 左右手都很灵巧的

versatile [ˈvɜːrsətl] *adj.* 通用的，万能的；多才多艺的，多面手的

sage [seɪdʒ] *adj.* 智慧的（wise; discerning）*n.* 智者（a very wise person）

tact [tækt] *n.* 老练；机智（diplomacy, thoughtfulness）

conversant [kənˈvɜːrsnt] *adj.* 精通的，熟知的（familiar or acquainted; versed）
【记】con + vers（转）+ ant → 全方位转 → 精通的；注意不要和conversation（*n.* 对话）相混
【派】conversance/conversancy（*n.* 精通）

witty [ˈwɪti] *adj.* 诙谐的；机智的

leery [ˈlɪri] *adj.* 机警的，猜疑的 （wary; cautious; suspicious）
【记】你送秋波（leer），我怀疑（leery）你的动机

shrewd [ʃruːd] *adj.* 精明的（clever; smart）
【例】The *shrewd* business owner made large profits.

judicious [dʒuˈdɪʃəs] *adj.* 有判断力的（having or showing sound judgment）；明智的（wise and careful）
【记】judic（判断）+ ious → 有判断力的
【反】unwise（*adj.* 不明智的）；daft（*adj.* 愚蠢的）

wit [wɪt] *n.* 风趣，机智；说话风趣的人
【例】have a ready *wit*

intelligible [ɪnˈtelɪdʒəbl] *adj.* 可理解的，明晰的（apprehensible）

sane [seɪn] *adj.* 理智的，明智的；心智健全的，神志正常的
【例】The nation's economy will only improve under *sane* policy.

和 蔼

genial [ˈdʒiːniəl] *adj.* 和蔼的，温和的（kindly; good natured）
【记】gen（产生）+ ial → 产生友情的 → 和蔼的

amiable [ˈeɪmɪəbl] *adj.* 和蔼的，亲切的（good natured; affable; genial）

【记】am(爱)＋iable → 和蔼的，亲切的

【反】inimical(*adj.* 敌意的)

【派】amiability(*n.* 友好，和蔼可亲)

*affable [ˈæfəbl] *adj.* 和蔼可亲的（genial; benevolent）

【记】af＋fable(说，讲) → 好说话的 → 和蔼可亲的

【例】Mary is quite *affable* and is always invited to parties.

*approachable [əˈproʊtʃəbl] *adj.* 可接近的，随和的

*benign [bɪˈnaɪn] *adj.* 亲切的，友好的，善良的（kind; benevolent）

【例】The poor farmer had a *benign* manner.

clemency [ˈklemənsi] *n.* 仁慈，宽厚（mercy）

【记】和cement(*n.* 水泥)一起记

**humane [hjuːˈmeɪn] *adj.* 仁慈的，富有同情心的（sympathetic; kind）

【记】human(人)＋e → 有人情味的 → 仁慈的

*beneficent [bɪˈnefɪsnt] *adj.* 仁慈的，乐善好施的（doing or producing good）

【记】bene(好，善)＋fic(做) → 做好事 → 乐善好施的

【反】noxious(*adj.* 有害的)

*moderate [ˈmɑːdərət] *adj.* 温和的，适度的（average; reasonable）

【记】moder(=mod 方式)＋ate → 方式正确 → 适度的

suavity [ˈswɑːvəti] *n.* 柔和，温和，愉悦

meek [miːk] *adj.* 温顺的（docile; submissive）；柔和的

*amicable [ˈæmɪkəbl] *adj.* 友好的（friendly in feeling; showing good will）

【记】am(爱)＋ic＋able(能) → 能带来爱的 → 友好的

*outgoing [ˈaʊtɡoʊɪŋ] *adj.* 友善的，好交际的（openly friendly; sociable）

*gracious [ˈɡreɪʃəs] *adj.* 有礼貌的，和善的（affable）；仁慈的

【记】grac(=grace 优雅，讲究礼仪)＋ious → 有礼貌的

【例】I thanked Jane for her *gracious* hospitality.

*affectionate [əˈfekʃənət] *adj.* 挚爱的，充满深情的（loving; genial）

【例】Jane gave her mother an *affectionate* hug.

*keen [kiːn] *adj.* 热切的，热情的，热心的（eager; enthusiastic）

【例】I'm not *keen* to go again.

amity [ˈæməti] *n.* 和睦，亲善，友爱关系（friendly relationship between people or countries）

【记】am(爱)＋ity → 友爱关系

*gentility ［dʒenˈtɪləti］ *n.* 有教养；优美，文雅

【例】These young ladies brought up with *gentility* showed great elegance in their behavior.

**philanthropic ［ˌfɪlənˈθrɑːpɪk］ *adj.* 博爱的

【记】phil(爱) + anthrop(人) + ic → 爱所有人的 → 博爱的

*outspoken ［aʊtˈspoʊkən］ *adj.* 坦率直言的（forthright, straight-forward）

【记】来自speak out(说出)

*endearing ［ɪnˈdɪrɪŋ］ *adj.* 讨人喜欢的

【记】en(进入) + dear(喜爱) + ing → 进入被喜爱的状态 → 讨人喜欢的

tractable ［ˈtræktəbl］ *adj.* 易驾驭的，温顺的（obedient）；容易处理的

【记】tract(拉) + able → 能拉得动的 → 易驾驭的

【例】Being *tractable* and loyal are essential qualities the owners ask for their slaves.

**congenial ［kənˈdʒiːniəl］ *adj.* 意气相投的 （compatible; agreeable; pleasant; pleasing）；友善的，同情的

【例】The Smiths are very *congenial* and accepting of others.

*charity ［ˈtʃærəti］ *n.* 慈悲，仁爱（benevolence; altruism）；慈善事业

【例】The *charity's* goal is to help people help themselves.

subdued ［səbˈduːd］ *adj.* (光、声等)柔和的，缓和的；(人)温和的，顺从的（unnaturally or unusually quiet in behavior）

【反】flamboyant(*adj.* 华丽的)；unruly(*adj.* 蛮横的)

*facile ［ˈfæsl］ *adj.* 随和的；轻而易举的，容易做的（easy; effortless）

【记】fac(做) + ile → 能做得出的 → 轻而易举的

【例】I'm bored at work because my boss only gives me *facile* assignments.

ductile ［ˈdʌktaɪl］ *adj.* 顺从的，易受影响的；柔软的，易延展的（plastic; malleable）

*facetious ［fəˈsiːʃəs］ *adj.* 幽默的，滑稽的（amusing; jesting）；开玩笑的

【例】Don't be offended; it was just a *facetious* remark.

品　质

*patriotic ［ˌpeɪtriˈɑːtɪk］ *adj.* 爱国的

【例】Very quickly what had begun as a business venture was transformed into a popular *patriotic* cause.

*straightforward [ˌstreɪt ˈfɔːrwərd] *adj.* 正直的，坦率的（honest and open）；易懂的（not difficult to understand）*adv.* 直截了当地（directly）

【反】tortuous（*adj.* 含糊的）；convoluted（*adj.* 费解的）；byzantine（*adj.* 错综复杂的）；equivocating（*adj.* 含糊其辞的）

*urbane [ɜːr ˈbeɪn] *adj.* 有礼貌的，温文尔雅的（having or showing refined manners, smooth elegance and sophistication）

【例】an *urbane* man

*righteous [ˈraɪtʃəs] *adj.* 正直的，公正的，正义的，正当的（upright; morally justifiable）

【例】Don't adopt that *righteous* tone of voice!

*decorously [ˈdekərəsli] *adv.* 有礼貌地，高雅地（politely; courteously）

【例】More *decorously*, the Venetians carted off anything of beauty they could find.

aptitude [ˈæptɪtuːd] *n.* 才能（talent; knack）

【记】apti(能力) + tude → 才能

【例】I have no musical *aptitude* and I can't even sing a simple tune.

volition [voʊ ˈlɪʃn] *n.* 决断力，意志力

【记】vol(意志) + ition → 决断力，意志力

【反】inability to choose（不能选择）

*temperament [ˈtemprəmənt] *n.* 气质，性情（disposition; nature）

【记】tempera(脾气) + ment → 气质，性情

serendipity [ˌserən ˈdɪpəti] *n.* 善于发掘新奇事物的天赋

【记】出自18世纪英国作家Horace的童话故事 *The Three Princes Of Serendip*（《锡兰三王子》），书中主人公具有随处发现珍宝的本领。

【派】serendipitous（*adj.* 偶然发现的）

**pluck [plʌk] *n.* (在困难面前表现出的)勇气，胆量，意志

【记】p(音似：不) + luck(运气) → 不靠运气靠勇气 → 勇气

【反】cowardice（*n.* 懦弱）

intellect [ˈɪntəlekt] *n.* 智力，思维能力；非凡的才智

*leniency [ˈliːniənsi] *n.* 宽厚，仁慈，温和（mercy; kindness）

【例】Other business owners say their *leniency* stems from memories of working for bullies or micromanagers.

*courtesy [ˈkɜːrtəsi] *n.* 礼貌，客气（courteous behavior; good manners）

【例】They didn't even have the *courtesy* to apologize.

— *manliness [ˈmænlinəs] n. 男子气概；勇敢，刚毅（bravery）

【例】With chiseled pecs and a bushy beard, George seemed like a model of *manliness*.

— *competency [ˈkɑːmpɪtənsi] n. (=competence)能力，资格（capacity; ability）

【例】Terrorism pushed Britain to start strictly enforcing a requirement for English-language *competency* for prospective citizens.

*tenacity [təˈnæsəti] n. 韧性，不屈不挠（toughness; perseverance）

【例】The officer received a commendation certificate for displaying *tenacity*, bravery and dedication to duty.

vigor [ˈvɪɡər] n. 精力（energy; enthusiasm）；气势，魄力

*expressive [ɪkˈspresɪv] adj. 表现感情或思想的，富有表现力的（showing one's feelings or thoughts）

【例】an *expressive* piece of music

**punctual [ˈpʌŋktʃuəl] adj. 守时的

【记】punct(点) + ual → 卡着点的 → 守时的

【例】Mary is *punctual*; she would never be late for an appointment.

stamina [ˈstæmɪnə] n. 体力，耐力（endurance）

【例】Wrestling tests one's agility and *stamina*.

公 正

*equitable [ˈekwɪtəbl] adj. 公平的，公正的（fair; just）

【例】Twenty dollars is an *equitable* price for this lamp.

*evenhanded [ˌiːvənˈhændɪd] adj. 公平的，不偏不倚的（fair and impartial）

【记】even(平的) + hand(手) + ed → 两手放得一样平 → 公平的

*detached [dɪˈtætʃt] adj. 公正的，超然的，不带感情的

**disinterested [dɪsˈɪntrəstɪd] adj. 无私的，公正的（impartial; unbiased）

【例】Mary is completely *disinterested* in the matter and can judge fairly.

**impartial [ɪmˈpɑːrʃl] adj. 公正的，无偏见的（fair; unbiased）

【例】The judge should make his appraisal *impartial*.

**conscientious [ˌkɑːnʃiˈenʃəs] *adj.* 认真的，谨慎的；勤勤恳恳的（diligent）

objective [əbˈdʒektɪv] *adj.* 客观的

【记】object（反对）＋ive → 反对主观 → 客观的

*decent [ˈdiːsnt] *adj.* 正派的；体面的，适当的（reasonable; proper）

【例】Don't walk around in your underwear. Go put on some *decent* clothes! // The house was in *decent* shape when we bought it.

*aboveboard [əˌbʌvˈbɔːrd] *adj./adv.* 光明正大的（地）（honest and open/honestly and openly）；率直的（地）

【记】above（在…上）＋board（会议桌）→ 可以放到桌面上谈 → 光明正大的（地）

【反】surreptitious（*adj.* 秘密的）

*candid [ˈkændɪd] *adj.* 无偏见的，公正的；坦白的，率直的

equity [ˈekwəti] *n.* 公平，公正（fairness; impartiality; justice）

【反】unfairness（*n.* 不公平）；discrimination（*n.* 歧视，偏见）

**integrity [ɪnˈtegrəti] *n.* 正直（honesty）

He who guards his lips guards his life, but he who speaks rashly will come to ruin.
谨守口的，得保生命。大张嘴的，必致败亡。

——《圣经·旧·箴》13:3

练 习 题

填空题

gentility	adroit	amiable	subdued	facetious
congenial	exquisite	humane	urbane	ingenuity
intelligible	facile	philanthropic	pluck	punctual
conversant	tractable	sage	tact	versatile

1. You need to become fully _____ with the company's procedures.
2. She has _____ taste in art.
3. She thinks expensive clothes are a mark of _____ .
4. He's a _____ actor who has played a wide variety of parts.
5. This approach helps to make the issues more _____ .
6. These regulations ensure the _____ treatment of all refugees.
7. The reception was a _____ affair.
8. The problem tested the _____ of even the most imaginative students.
9. The minister is _____ handling of the crisis.
10. A _____ has more than one teacher.
11. Settling the dispute required great _____ and diplomacy.
12. The child's speech was barely _____ .
13. Her parents seemed very _____ .
14. The old gentleman was renowned far and wide for his _____ generosity.
15. I met few people _____ to me in that city.
16. It takes a lot of _____ to do what she did.
17. She has been reliable and _____ .
18. It seems too _____ to blame everything on his mishandling of the crisis.
19. Stop being _____ ; this is serious.
20. He was charming and _____ , full of witty conversation.

配对题

1. intelligent	和蔼可亲的	11. affable	光明正大的(地)
2. sagacious	挚爱的, 充满深情的	12. approachable	聪明的, 有才智的
3. flair	有礼貌的, 和善的	13. benign	有判断力的
4. astute	可接近的, 随和的	14. beneficent	热切的, 热情的
5. expeditious	机敏的, 聪敏的	15. moderate	机警的, 猜疑的
6. leery	仁慈的, 乐善好施的	16. gracious	温和的, 适度的
7. judicious	亲切的, 友好的, 善良的	17. outgoing	友善的, 好交际的
8. wit	敏捷的, 迅速的	18. aboveboard	有洞察力的, 睿智的
9. sane	天赋, 本领, 才华	19. affectionate	理智的, 明智的
10. genial	和蔼的, 温和的	20. keen	风趣, 机智

练习题答案

填空题答案

1. You need to become fully <u>conversant</u> with the company's procedures.
2. She has <u>exquisite</u> taste in art.
3. She thinks expensive clothes are a mark of <u>gentility</u>.
4. He's a <u>versatile</u> actor who has played a wide variety of parts.
5. This approach helps to make the issues more <u>tractable</u>.
6. These regulations ensure the <u>humane</u> treatment of all refugees.
7. The reception was a <u>subdued</u> affair.
8. The problem tested the <u>ingenuity</u> of even the most imaginative students.
9. The minister is <u>adroit</u> handling of the crisis.
10. A <u>sage</u> has more than one teacher.
11. Settling the dispute required great <u>tact</u> and diplomacy.
12. The child's speech was barely <u>intelligible</u>.
13. Her parents seemed very <u>amiable</u>.
14. The old gentleman was renowned far and wide for his <u>philanthropic</u> generosity.
15. I met few people <u>congenial</u> to me in that city.
16. It takes a lot of <u>pluck</u> to do what she did.
17. She has been reliable and <u>punctual</u>.
18. It seems too <u>facile</u> to blame everything on his mishandling of the crisis.
19. Stop being <u>facetious</u>; this is serious.
20. He was charming and <u>urbane</u>, full of witty conversation.

配对题答案

1. intelligent	聪明的, 有才智的	11. affable	和蔼可亲的
2. sagacious	有洞察力的, 睿智的	12. approachable	可接近的, 随和的
3. flair	天赋, 本领, 才华	13. benign	亲切的, 友好的, 善良的
4. astute	机敏的, 聪敏的	14. beneficent	仁慈的, 乐善好施的
5. expeditious	敏捷的, 迅速的	15. moderate	温和的, 适度的
6. leery	机警的, 猜疑的	16. gracious	有礼貌的, 和善的
7. judicious	有判断力的	17. outgoing	友善的, 好交际的
8. wit	风趣, 机智	18. aboveboard	光明正大的(地)
9. sane	理智的, 明智的	19. affectionate	挚爱的, 充满深情的
10. genial	和蔼的, 温和的	20. keen	热切的, 热情的

Word List 18

负向评价（一）

草 率

*perfunctory [pər'fʌŋktəri] *adj.* 马虎的，敷衍的（characterized by superficiality）
【反】obsessional（*adj.* 沉迷的）

slapdash ['slæpdæʃ] *adv./adj.* 草率地（的），马虎地（的）（haphazard; slipshod）
【记】slap（拍打）+ dash（溅）→ 拍打把水溅出来 → 马虎地（的）

*scratchy ['skrætʃi] *adj.* 潦草的，信手而写的（rough-and-ready）
【例】*scratchy* handwriting

**reckless ['rekləs] *adj.* 鲁莽的（rash）
【记】reck（顾虑）+ less（少，无）→ 没有顾虑 → 鲁莽的
【例】The *reckless* driver drove above the speed limit.

*slipshod ['slɪpʃɑːd] *adj.* 马虎的，懒散的（not exact or thorough; careless; sloppy）；穿着邋遢的
【记】slip（滑）+ shod（穿着鞋）→ 穿着松松的鞋，滑倒了 → 穿着邋遢的
【反】punctilious（*adj.* 细心的）

*imprudent [ɪm'pruːdnt] *adj.* 轻率的，不谨慎的（rash）
【记】im（不）+ prudent（谨慎的）→ 不谨慎的
【例】It is *imprudent* to accept a date with a stranger.

*brusque [brʌsk] *adj.* 唐突的，鲁莽的（rough or abrupt; blunt）
【记】发音似"不如屎壳（郎）"→ 鲁莽的

*lax [læks] *adj.* 不严格的，疏忽的（not sufficiently strict or severe; negligent）；散漫的，放纵的
【例】He's too *lax* with his pupils.

*headlong ['hedlɔːŋ] *adj./adv.* 轻率的（地），迅猛的（地）（hasty; rash）
【记】head + long → 头很长 → 做事长驱直入不假思索 → 轻率地，迅猛地

indiscretion [ˌɪndɪ'skreʃn] *n.* 不谨慎，轻率之举
【例】This is my first *indiscretion*.

*temerity [tə'merəti] n. 鲁莽，大胆（audacity; rashness; recklessness）

【记】temer(轻率) + ity → 鲁莽

【反】circumspection(n. 谨慎); pusillanimity(n. 胆怯)

*levity ['levəti] n. 轻率(lack of seriousness); 轻浮(flippancy)

【记】lev(升起) + ity → 升起的状态 → 轻浮

【反】seriousness(n. 严肃); gravity(n. 庄重)

*wildcat ['waɪldkæt] n. 野猫；暴躁莽撞的人 adj. 不可靠的；未经允许的 n. 盲目开掘

【例】But like many other wildcat miners in this region, they're taking a gamble on striking gold.

impudent ['ɪmpjədənt] adj. 鲁莽的，无礼的(rude; rash)

【记】im(不) + pud(谦虚，小心) + ent → 不小心的 → 鲁莽的

witless ['wɪtləs] adj. 无知的，轻率的；发疯的

**unwitting [ʌn'wɪtɪŋ] adj. 无心的，不经意的(not intended; inadvertent; unaware)

【记】un (不) + witting(知道的，有意的) → 不经意的

inadvertently [ˌɪnəd'vɜːtəntli] adv. 不小心地，非故意地(by accident)

【记】来自advertent(adj. 留意的)

*obtrusive [əb'truːsɪv] adj. 冒失的，莽撞的，强迫人的（tending to push self-assertively forward）

【例】Urbane and smooth, he preferred to go about his daily affairs unencumbered by obtrusive bodyguards.

*flippant ['flɪpənt] adj. 无礼的(frivolous and disrespectful); 轻浮的(lacking proper seriousness)

【反】earnest(adj. 认真的)

*indiscriminate [ˌɪndɪ'skrɪmɪnət] adj. 不加鉴别的，任意而为的(given or done without careful judgement, or at random)

【例】indiscriminate praise

*brash [bræʃ] adj. 盛气凌人的，自以为是的(impudently self-assertive); 性急的，无礼的

【例】His brash answers annoyed the interviewers.

scamp [skæmp] n. 顽皮的孩子(mischievous child)

【例】That little scamp Jimmy has hidden my slippers again!

**impetuous [ɪm'petʃuəs] adj. 性急的，鲁莽的，冲动的(impulsive)

*impulsive [ɪmˈpʌlsɪv] *adj.* 易冲动的

【例】On seeing the poor little girl, he made an *impulsive* decision to adopt her.

bandy [ˈbændi] *vt.* 漫不经心地谈论(to discuss in a frivolous manner)

giddy [ˈɡɪdi] *adj.* 轻浮的, 不严肃的(not serious; frivolous); *dizzy*

【反】grave(*adj.* 严肃的, 庄重的); serious(*adj.* 严厉的)

粗 野

*churlish [ˈtʃɜːrlɪʃ] *adj.* 粗野的, 没有礼貌的 (lack of civility or graciousness; boorish; rude)

【反】complaisance (*adj.* 彬彬有礼的); genteel (*adj.* 文雅的)

*boorish [ˈbʊrɪʃ] *adj.* 粗野的, 笨拙的(rude; insensitive); 土里土气的

gauche [ɡoʊʃ] *adj.* 笨拙的, 粗鲁的; 不善交际的(awkward; clumsy; unapt)

【例】People laugh at Forrest Gump's *gauche* behavior at the White House.

**coarse [kɔːrs] *adj.* 粗糙的(rough; crude); 粗野的, 粗俗的, 粗鄙的

【例】Bill's *coarse* manners were becoming quite offensive.

*abrasive [əˈbreɪsɪv] *adj.* 有磨损作用的(tending to abrade); 生硬粗暴的(harsh and offensive)

【记】来自abrade(*vt.* 磨损)

surly [ˈsɜːrli] *adj.* 脾气暴躁的(bad tempered); 阴沉的(sullen)

【记】sur(=sir 先生) + ly → 像高高在上的先生一般 → 脾气暴躁的

【例】a *surly* unforgiving old woman

*brutal [ˈbruːtl] *adj.* 野蛮的, 冷酷的

【例】The *brutal* beast tore the deer to pieces.

*truculence [ˈtrʌkjələns] *n.* 野蛮, 粗暴, 好斗 (obstreperous and defiant aggressiveness); 刻薄

【例】His *truculence* can make him very difficult to work with sometimes.

*vulgar [ˈvʌlɡər] *adj.* 无教养的, 粗俗的(morally crude; undeveloped)

【记】vulg(庸俗) + ar → 粗俗的

【派】vulgarity(*n.* 粗俗, 低级)

pert [pɜːrt] *adj.* (尤指女孩或年轻女子)无礼的, 冒失的(especially of a girl or young woman not showing respect; cheeky)

【例】a *pert* reply

*barbaric [bɑːr'bærɪk] *adj.* 野蛮人的，野蛮的；极其粗野的（extremely wild, rough, cruel or rude）

【例】The group of *barbaric* soldiers killed many people.

*audacity [ɔː'dæsəti] *n.* 大胆，厚颜无耻（aggressive boldness or unmitigated effrontery）

【例】He had the *audacity* to ask for an increase in salary.

*unscrupulous [ʌn'skruːpjələs] *adj.* 肆无忌惮的，不讲道德的（unprincipled）

【记】un(不) + scrupulous(正直的) → 不讲道德的

*unprincipled [ʌn'prɪnsəpld] *adj.* 无原则的，不讲道德的（without regard to moral values, standards of honorable behavior）

【记】un(不) + principle(原则) + d → 无原则的

foolhardy ['fuːlhɑːrdi] *adj.* 鲁莽的，有勇无谋的（foolishly adventurous and bold; rash）

【记】fool(笨) + hardy(勇敢的) → 有勇无谋的

【例】a *foolhardy* soldier

peremptory [pə'remptəri] *adj.* 不容反抗的；专横的；强制的

【记】per(向四面八方) + emptory(看做empty，空的) → 把反对的人全部清空 → 专横的

【反】open to challenge(愿意接受挑战的)

ribald ['rɪbld] *adj.* 下流的，粗鄙的（crude; using coarse indecent humor）

【记】ri(拼音：日) + bald(光秃的) → 白天光着 → 下流的

【反】seemly(*adj./adv.* 得体的/地)

【派】ribaldry(*n.* 粗俗下流的言词或笑话)

unlettered [ˌʌn'letərd] *adj.* 未受教育的，文盲的

胆 小

*timorous ['tɪmərəs] *adj.* 胆小的，胆怯的（of timid disposition; fearful）

【记】tim(胆怯) + orous → 胆怯的

【反】intrepid(*adj.* 无畏的); scrappy(*adj.* 好斗的)

pusillanimous [ˌpjuːsɪ'lænɪməs] *adj.* 胆小的，懦弱的，优柔寡断的（lacking courage; cowardly; lacking resolution）

【记】pusill(虚弱的) + anim(生命，精神) + ous → 胆小的

【反】dauntless(*adj.* 大胆的); stouthearted(*adj.* 大胆的)

timidity [tɪ'mɪdəti] *n.* 胆怯，羞怯

【记】来自timid(*adj.* 胆小的)

【反】effrontery(*n.* 厚颜无耻)

craven [ˈkreɪvn] *adj.* 懦弱的，畏缩的(cowardly)

【记】c + raven(乌鸦) → 像乌鸦一样胆小 → 懦弱的

【反】valorous(*adj.* 勇敢的)

*cowardice [ˈkaʊərdɪs] *n.* 懦弱(lack of courage or resolution)

【例】I've been accused of many things in my life, but never of *cowardice*.

【反】pluck (*n.* 勇气)

flinch [flɪntʃ] *v.* 畏缩，退缩(to draw back; wince; cower)

【记】fl(看做fly) + inch(寸) → 一寸一寸向后飞 → 退缩

*tremulous [ˈtremjələs] *adj.* 颤动的，颤抖的(trembling); 胆小的，害怕的

**eerie [ˈɪri] *adj.* 可怕的，阴森恐怖的(weird; causing fear)

【记】一二瑞，真怪异，不是读一二三吗 → 可怕的

coy [kɔɪ] *adj.* 腼腆的，忸怩的(shrinking from contact with others; shy)

【记】和boy及toy一起记：A coy boy plays toys. (害羞男孩玩玩具。)

*abash [əˈbæʃ] *vt.* 使害羞，使尴尬(to make embarrassed)

【记】ab + ash(灰) → 灰头灰脸 → 使尴尬

【反】embolden(*vt.* 使大胆)

蠢 笨 傻

*clumsy [ˈklʌmzi] *adj.* 笨拙的 (lacking grace; awkward); 拙劣的 (ill-constructed)

**ponderous [ˈpɑːndərəs] *adj.* 沉重的，笨重的(heavy)

ungainly [ʌnˈɡeɪnli] *adj.* 笨拙的，(动作)不雅的(lacking in smooth or dexterity; clumsy)

【记】un + gainly(优雅的) → 不雅的

【反】lissome(*adj.* 动作优雅的); adroit(*adj.* 机敏的)

*awkward [ˈɔːkwərd] *adj.* 笨拙的，不熟练的 (clumsy; inept); 尴尬的，窘迫的

【例】The growing teenager went through an *awkward* stage.

*blunt [blʌnt] *adj.* 钝的，不锋利的；迟钝的 *vt.* 使钝；使迟钝

【例】The knife was too *blunt* to cut through the tough meat.

*logy [ˈloʊɡi] *adj.* 迟缓的，迟钝的(slow; tardive)

【例】They gave her drugs that made her feel *logy* and sleep a lot.

laggard [ˈlæɡərd] *adj.* 缓慢的(slow or late); 落后的(falling behind) *n.* 落后者(one that lags or lingers)

【记】lag(落后) + gard → 落后的

*obtuse [ɒbˈtuːs] *adj.* 愚笨的(dull or insensitive)；不尖的(blunt)；钝角的

【记】发音似"我不吐丝"→ 而别的蚕都吐 → 愚笨的

**awkwardness [ˈɔːkwərdnəs] *n.* 尴尬；笨拙(clumsiness)

【例】She questioned her aides, one of whom tried to explain the *awkwardness* of the situation.

*booby [ˈbuːbi] *n.* 笨人，呆子，傻子(a foolish person)

【例】He's a great *booby*!

maladroit [ˌmæləˈdrɔɪt] *adj.* 笨拙的，不机敏的(awkward; clumsy; bungling)

【记】mal(坏，不)+ adroit(机敏的)→ 不机敏的

*vacuous [ˈvækjuəs] *adj.* 发呆的，愚笨的，空虚的 (marked by lack of ideas or intelligence; stupid)

【记】来自vacuum(*n.* 真空)

【反】intelligent(*adj.* 睿智的)

【派】vacuity(*n.* (想像力等)贫乏，无聊，空白)

asinine [ˈæsɪnaɪn] *adj.* 驴的，驴似的；愚笨的，顽固的(of asses; stupid; silly)

【记】as(=ass 驴子)+ in + in + e → 笨得像驴 → 愚笨的

dolt [dəʊlt] *n.* 傻瓜(a stupid, slow witted person)

【记】像玩偶(doll)一样无头脑的傻瓜(dolt)

*folly [ˈfɑːli] *n.* 愚蠢(lack of wisdom)；荒唐事

【记】来自fool(*n.* 白痴；受骗者)

【反】sagacity(*n.* 睿智)

fatuous [ˈfætʃuəs] *adj.* 愚昧的(vacuously foolish; stupid; indolent)

【记】fatu(笨)+ ous → 愚昧的

oaf [əʊf] *n.* 傻瓜，笨蛋(stupid, clumsy and awkward person)

【例】Why did she marry that great *oaf*?

uncouth [ʌnˈkuːθ] *adj.* (言语行为) 粗野的，无教养的 (boorish; clumsy in speech or behavior)

【记】来自couth(*adj.* 文雅的)

【反】seemly(*adj.* 适宜的)

cumbersome [ˈkʌmbərsəm] *adj.* 笨重的，难处理的 (hard to handle or deal with; clumsy; heavy)

【记】来自cumber(*vt.* 拖累，妨碍)

unwieldy [ʌnˈwiːldi] *adj.* 笨重的，庞大的，难使用的(not easily managed or used; cumbersome)

【记】来自 wieldy(*adj.* 易使用的，易操作的)

**pedantic [pɪ'dæntɪk] *adj.* 书生气的，迂腐的，卖弄学问的

【例】Vanity has given her a *pedantic* and conceited manner.

lumber ['lʌmbər] *vi.* 笨重地移动 (to move with heavy clumsiness) *n.* 杂物 (miscellaneous discarded household articles); 木材 (timber)

【反】glide(*v./n.* 滑行)

inert [ɪ'nɜːrt] *adj.* 不活动的 (immobile; inactive); 迟钝的，呆滞的

【记】in(不) + ert(动) → 不活动的

*uninitiated [ˌʌnɪ'nɪʃieɪtɪd] *adj.* 外行的，缺乏经验的 (inexperienced)

【记】un(不) + initiate(传授) + d → 没有被传授的 → 外行的

*ignorant ['ɪɡnərənt] *adj.* 无知的，不了解的 (unaware)

【例】He who is *ignorant* of the situation can't really understand me.

gullible ['ɡʌləbl] *adj.* 易受骗的 (easily cheated or tricked; credulous)

【派】gullibility(*n.* 受骗，上当)

botch [bɑːtʃ] *vt.* (笨手笨脚地)弄坏 (to mismanage)

patch

【记】比较记忆：notch(*n.* 凹痕，刻痕); patch(*n.* 补丁); ditch(*n.* 壕沟); hatch(*n.* 船舱口 *v.* 孵化)

bovine ['bəʊvaɪn] *adj.* (似)牛的 (of an ox); 迟钝的 (slow; stolid)

【记】bov(牛) + ine → 牛的

gawk [ɡɔːk] *vi.* 呆呆地看着，张口瞠目地看着 (to stare foolishly; look in open-mouthed awe)

【例】The country boy *gawked* at the skyscrapers and neon lights of the big city.

refractory [rɪ'fræktəri] *adj.* 倔强的，难驾驭的 (stubborn; unmanageable); (机体组织)麻木的，反应迟钝的 (unresponsive to stimulus)

【记】re + fract(断裂) + ory → 宁折不弯 → 难驾驭的

【反】responsive(*adj.* 回答的，反应快的)

*impressionable [ɪm'preʃənəbl] *adj.* 易受影响的 (easily affected by impressions)

【记】来自impress(*vt.* 给…留下印象)

hulk [hʌlk] *n.* 废船，船壳 (the hull of a dismantled ship); 笨重之人或物 (one that is bulky or unwieldy)

**hackneyed ['hæknid] *adj.* 陈腐的，平庸的 (made trite by overuse; trite)

【记】来自伦敦近郊城镇Hackney，以养马闻名，hack的意思是"出租的老马"，引申为"陈腐的"。

【反】original(*adj.* 有新意的); fresh(*adj.* 新的)

*gangling [ˈgæŋglɪŋ] *adj.* 瘦长得难看的 (tall, thin and awkward looking)
【记】来自gangly (*adj.* 瘦长的); 发音似"杠铃" → 像杠铃一样瘦长的 → 瘦长得难看的

lethargy [ˈleθərdʒi] *n.* 昏睡, 倦怠 (the state of being abnormally sleepy or unnaturally tired); 呆滞懒散 (the state of being lazy, sluggish)
【记】leth(死) + argy → 昏睡的样子像死去一样 → 昏睡
【反】vigor (*n.* 活力)

幼　稚

*puerile [ˈpjʊrəl] *adj.* 孩子气的, 幼稚的 (childish); 儿童的 (juvenile)
【记】puer (＝boy 男孩) + ile → 幼稚的
【反】sagacious (*adj.* 精明的)

*infantile [ˈɪnfəntaɪl] *adj.* 幼稚的, 孩子气的 (like or typical of a small child); 婴儿的, 幼儿的
【记】infant (婴儿) + ile → 婴儿的

callow [ˈkæloʊ] *adj.* (鸟) 未生羽毛的 (unfledged); (人) 未成熟的 (immature)
【记】cal (秃的, 光的) + low → 未生羽毛的
【反】mature (*adj.* 成熟的)

incipient [ɪnˈsɪpiənt] *adj.* 初期的, 刚出现的
【记】in (进入) + cip (拿, 取) + ient → 拿进去 → 刚出现的

卑　鄙

scurvy [ˈskɜːrvi] *adj.* 卑鄙的, 可鄙的 (despicable)
【记】和scurry (*vi.* 急赶) 一起记

*vile [vaɪl] *adj.* 邪恶的, 卑鄙的, 可耻的 (morally despicable or abhorrent); (语言) 污秽的

*pitiable [ˈpɪtiəbl] *adj.* 可鄙的 (deserving contempt)
【例】a *pitiable* attempt to save himself from disgrace

*despicable [dɪˈspɪkəbl] *adj.* 可鄙的, 卑劣的 (detestable; contemptible)
【记】来自despise (*vt.* 鄙视, 看不起)
【例】That *despicable* child trampled my flowers.

*underhanded [ˌʌndəˈhændɪd] *adj.* 不光明的，卑鄙的（marked by secrecy and deception）

【记】under + handed → 在下面做手脚 → 不光明的

brazen [ˈbreɪzn] *adj.* 厚脸皮的，厚颜无耻的（showing no shame; impudent）

【记】braz（=brass 黄铜）+ en → 脸皮厚得像黄铜一样 → 厚颜无耻的

【反】modest（*adj.* 谦虚的）

**blatant [ˈbleɪtnt] *adj.* 厚颜无耻的，明目张胆的（brazen; completely obvious in a crass or offensive manner）

【记】blat(闲聊) + ant → 公然讨论别人的私事 → 明目张胆的

【反】unobtrusive（*adj.* 谦虚的）; inconspicuous（*adj.* 不显眼的）; unimpressive(*adj.* 无印象的); subtle(*adj.* 微妙的)

*ignominious [ˌɪɡnəˈmɪniəs] *adj.* 名誉不好的，不光彩的（disgraceful; humiliating）

【记】ig(不) + nomin(名字) + ious → 不好的名字 → 不光彩的

*nasty [ˈnæsti] *adj.* 令人不愉快的，令人厌恶的（unpleasant; disgusting）

【例】a *nasty* smell/taste/sight

effrontery [ɪˈfrʌntəri] *n.* 厚颜无耻，放肆（unashamed boldness; impudence）

【记】ef + front(脸，面) + ery → 不要脸面 → 厚颜无耻

【反】decorum(*n.* 得体); deference(*n.* 尊重); timidity(*n.* 胆怯)

*voluptuous [vəˈlʌptʃuəs] *adj.* 撩人的，性感的；沉溺于酒色的

【记】volupt(享乐，快感) + uous → 沉溺于酒色的

【反】ascetic（*adj.* 禁欲的）; spartan（*adj.* 简朴的）; self-contained（*adj.* 自制的）

【派】voluptuary(*n.* 耽于逸乐的人)

*smutty [ˈsmʌti] *adj.* 淫秽的，猥亵的（indecent; lewd）

*belittle [bɪˈlɪtl] *vt.* 轻视（to depreciate; despise）

【记】be + little(小) → 小看 → 轻视

【例】The reporter's comments *belittled* the candidate.

卑　贱

**menial [ˈmiːniəl] *adj.* 奴仆的；卑贱的，奴颜婢膝的（humble; mean）

abject [ˈæbdʒekt] *adj.* 极可怜的（miserable; wretched）；卑下的（degraded; base）

【记】ab + ject(抛，扔) → 被人抛弃 → 极可怜的

*servile [ˈsɜːrvl] *adj.* 奴性的，百依百顺的（meanly or cravenly submissive; abject）

【记】serv(服务) + ile → 奴性的

grovel [ˈɡrɑːvl] *vi.* 摇尾乞怜，卑躬屈膝(to behave humbly or abjectly; stoop)

【派】groveler(*n.* 乞怜者)

mendicant [ˈmendɪkənt] *adj.* 行乞的 *n.* 乞丐(beggar)

【记】mend(修补，改善) + icant → 生活需要改善的人 → 乞丐

servility [sɜːrˈvɪləti] *n.* 奴态，奴性，卑屈

*diffident [ˈdɪfɪdənt] *adj.* 缺乏自信的，怯懦的(not showing much belief in one's own abilities)

【记】dif(否定) + fid(相信) + ent → 缺乏自信的

【反】bold(*adj.* 大胆的)；brassy(*adj.* 厚颜无耻的)；expansive(*adj.* 豪爽的，胸襟开阔的)

严 酷

**nonchalant [ˌnɑːnʃəˈlɑːnt] *adj.* 冷漠的(not showing interest)

*ordeal [ɔːrˈdiːl] *n.* 严酷的考验(difficult experience; trial)

**callous [ˈkæləs] *adj.* 结硬块的(thick and hardened)；无情的，冷酷的(lacking pity; unfeeling)

【记】来自callus(*n.* 老茧)

sadistic [səˈdɪstɪk] *adj.* 施虐狂的 (inclined to cruelty)

【记】来自法国伯爵Sade，是虐待狂

**ruthless [ˈruːθləs] *adj.* 无情的，冷酷的(merciless; pitiless)

【例】The *ruthless* tyrant caused the deaths of millions of people.

*rigid [ˈrɪdʒɪd] *adj.* 严格的，僵化的(strict; fixed)

【例】Their *rigid* notion of true womanhood had been restricting women's life for centuries.

*stringent [ˈstrɪndʒənt] *adj.* 严格的，严厉的(strict; tight)

【例】Our company has a *stringent* policy against smoking.

**rigorous [ˈrɪɡərəs] *adj.* 严格的，严厉的；(气候等)严酷的，严峻的(harsh)；严密的，缜密的(rigidly accurate)

【记】rigor(发热前的寒战) + ous → (气候)严酷的

【例】The trainings soldiers received were *rigorous*.

bestial ［ˈbestʃəl］ *adj.* 野兽的，残忍的（beastlike; brutal）

【记】来自beast（*n.* 野兽）

draconian ［drəˈkoʊniən］ *adj.*（法律等）严厉的，严苛的（extremely severe）

【记】来自Draco（德拉古），雅典政治家，制定了雅典的法典，该法典因其公平受到赞扬，但因其严酷而不受欢迎

【反】indulgent（*adj.* 放纵的）；mild（*adj.* 温和的）

relentless ［rɪˈlentləs］ *adj.* 无情的，没有怜悯心的（merciless; ruthless）

【记】relent（怜悯）+ less（无）→ 没有怜悯心的

【例】The *relentless* bully beat Jimmy up.

*inhumane ［ˌɪnhjuːˈmeɪn］ *adj.* 不近人情的（cruel; brutal; unkind）

【记】来自humane（*adj.* 仁慈的，有人情味的）

**inexorable ［ɪnˈeksərəbl］ *adj.* 不为所动的，无情的（incapable of being moved or influenced）；坚决不变的，坚定不移的（that cannot be altered）

【记】in（不）+ exorable（可说服的）→ 不可说服的 → 不为所动的

*grueling ［ˈgruəlɪŋ］ *adj.* 繁重而累人的（punishing; exhausting）

【记】gruel（稀粥）+ ing → 喝着稀粥干活 → 繁重而累人的

【反】effortless（*adj.* 不费力气的）

exacting ［ɪgˈzæktɪŋ］ *adj.*（要求）严格的（demanding; rigorous）；（工作等）费力的，艰难的

【记】exact（精确的）+ ing → 要求精确的 →（要求）严格的

【例】Jane is very *exacting* in her work.

*intolerant ［ɪnˈtɑːlərənt］ *adj.* 不容忍的，不宽容的（not tolerant）

【例】*intolerant* of opposition

*unsmiling ［ʌnˈsmaɪlɪŋ］ *adj.* 严肃的，不笑的（serious; solemn）

【例】He was always *unsmiling* when his wife talked to him.

rigor ［ˈrɪgər］ *n.* 严格，严厉（rigidity）；（生活的）艰苦，（气候的）严酷（hardship）

【例】Those homeless children had to face the *rigors* of life by themselves.

*severity ［sɪˈverəti］ *n.* 严重；严格，严厉（roughness）；猛烈

【例】Smallpox can vary in its *severity*, with some strains killing many sufferers and others relatively few.

**ascetic ［əˈsetɪk］ *adj.* 苦行的（austere; rigorous; strict）

*obdurate ［ˈɑːbdərət］ *adj.* 固执的，顽固的（stubbornly persistent; inflexible）；冷酷的（hardened in feelings）

【记】ob(反) + dur(坚韧) + ate → 坚韧地对抗 → 固执的

【反】toward(*adj.* 温顺的)

*opinionated [əˈpɪnjəneɪtɪd] *adj.* 固执己见的（holding obstinately to one's own opinions）

【记】来自opinion(*n.* 观点)

**abusive [əˈbjuːsɪv] *adj.* 漫骂的（using harsh insulting language）；毁谤的（insulting）；虐待的(physically injurious)

【记】来自abuse(*vt.* 谩骂；虐待)

*trenchant [ˈtrentʃənt] *adj.* 一针见血的，锐利的(sharply perceptive; penetrating)

【记】trench(沟) + ant → 说话像挖沟，入木三分 → 锐利的

【反】vague(*adj.* 含糊的)；dull(*adj.* 迟钝的)

*magisterial [ˌmædʒɪˈstɪriəl] *adj.* 有权威的(authoritative; official)；威风的

【记】magister(=master 主人) + ial → 主人的 → 有权威的

solemnity [səˈlemnəti] *n.* 庄严，肃穆(formal or ceremonious observance)

【记】来自solemn(*adj.* 严肃的)

【反】jest(*n.* 笑话，开玩笑)

You have to believe in yourself. That's the secret of success.
人必须相信自己，这是成功的秘诀。

——美国演员 卓别林(Charles Chaplin, American actor)

练 习 题

填空题

abrasive	awkwardness	blatant	boorish	brash
gauche	trenchant	eerie	gawk	hackneyed
impetuous	imprudent	menial	obtrusive	pedantic
perfunctory	reckless	scratchy	slipshod	unscrupulous

1. He tried to smooth over the _____ of the situation.
2. The country boy _____ at the skyscrapers and neon lights of the big city..
3. I found the silence underwater really _____.
4. He showed a _____ disregard for his own safety.
5. I have never encountered such _____ disregard for the Bill of Rights.
6. It would be foolish and _____ to resign over such a small matter.
7. He was shattered and bewildered by this _____ criticism.
8. He is learned, but neither stuffy nor _____.
9. This article is rather _____.
10. She hated such _____ tasks as washing the pots and pans.
11. The operator answered the phone with a _____ greeting.
12. She had scrawled me a note in her familiar _____ handwriting.
13. The work was done in a _____ manner.
14. It would be _____ to invest all your money in one company.
15. They tried to ensure that their presence was not too _____.
16. Beneath his _____ exterior, he's still a little boy inside.
17. People laugh at Forrest Gump's _____ behavior at the White House.
18. It's possible that he doesn't even realize how _____ his comments are.
19. Throughout his career he was known for his _____ manner.
20. He was utterly _____ in his dealings with rival firms.

配对题

1. brusque	使害羞，使尴尬	11. vulgar	轻率；轻浮
2. headlong	大胆，厚颜无耻	12. barbaric	鲁莽，大胆
3. temerity	野蛮人的，野蛮的	13. audacity	胆怯，羞怯
4. levity	唐突的，鲁莽的	14. unprincipled	繁重而累人的
5. wildcat	野蛮的，冷酷的	15. timidity	颤动的，颤抖的
6. flippant	懦弱	16. opinionated	野蛮，粗暴，好斗
7. indiscriminate	无礼的；轻浮的	17. grueling	固执己见的
8. impulsive	轻率的(地)，迅猛的(地)	18. cowardice	无原则的，不讲道德的
9. brutal	易冲动的	19. tremulous	无教养的，粗俗的
10. truculence	不加鉴别的，任意而为的	20. abash	野猫；暴躁莽撞的人

练习题答案

填空题答案

1. He tried to smooth over the <u>awkwardness</u> of the situation.
2. The country boy <u>gawked</u> at the skyscrapers and neon lights of the big city.
3. I found the silence underwater really <u>eerie</u>.
4. He showed a <u>reckless</u> disregard for his own safety.
5. I have never encountered such <u>blatant</u> disregard for the Bill of Rights.
6. It would be foolish and <u>impetuous</u> to resign over such a small matter.
7. He was shattered and bewildered by this <u>trenchant</u> criticism.
8. He is learned, but neither stuffy nor <u>pedantic</u>.
9. This article is rather <u>hackneyed</u>.
10. She hated such <u>menial</u> tasks as washing the pots and pans.
11. The operator answered the phone with a <u>perfunctorily</u> greeting.
12. She had scrawled me a note in her familiar <u>scratchy</u> handwriting.
13. The work was done in a <u>slipshod</u> manner.
14. It would be <u>imprudent</u> to invest all your money in one company.
15. They tried to ensure that their presence was not too <u>obtrusive</u>.
16. Beneath his <u>brash</u> exterior, he's still a little boy inside.
17. People laugh at Forrest Gump's <u>gauche</u> behavior at the White House.
18. It's possible that he doesn't even realize how <u>boorish</u> his comments are.
19. Throughout his career he was known for his <u>abrasive</u> manner.
20. He was utterly <u>unscrupulous</u> in his dealings with rival firms.

配对题答案

1. brusque	唐突的，鲁莽的		11. vulgar	无教养的，粗俗的
2. headlong	轻率的(地)，迅猛的(地)		12. barbaric	野蛮人的，野蛮的
3. temerity	鲁莽，大胆		13. audacity	大胆，厚颜无耻
4. levity	轻率；轻浮		14. unprincipled	无原则的，不讲道德的
5. wildcat	野猫；暴躁莽撞的人		15. timidity	胆怯，羞怯
6. flippant	无礼的；轻浮的		16. opinionated	固执己见的
7. indiscriminate	不加鉴别的，任意而为的		17. grueling	繁重而累人的
8. impulsive	易冲动的		18. cowardice	懦弱
9. brutal	野蛮的，冷酷的		19. tremulous	颤动的，颤抖的
10. truculence	野蛮，粗暴，好斗		20. abash	使害羞，使尴尬

Word List 19

负向评价（二）

奢 侈

**luxurious [lʌɡˈʒʊriəs] *adj.* 奢侈的，豪华的(expensive; costly)

**extravagant [ikˈstrævəɡənt] *adj.* 奢侈的，浪费的(wasteful)

【记】extra + vag(走) + ant → 游走外面的世界 → 奢侈的

【例】The accountant warned the owner against *extravagant* purchases.

profligacy [ˈprɑːflɪɡəsi] *n.* 无耻放荡；肆意挥霍

【例】In other words, a little well-placed *profligacy* might yet do the world some good.

profuse [prəˈfjuːs] *adj.* 充沛的(bountiful)；十分慷慨的(giving freely and abundantly)

【记】pro(向前) + fuse(流) → 多得向外流 → 充沛的

【反】scant(*adj.* 不足的)；scanty(*adj.* 不足的)

prodigal [ˈprɑːdɪɡl] *adj.* 浪费的，挥霍的(extravagant, wasteful)；丰富的；慷慨的

【例】Nature is *prodigal* of her gifts.

sumptuous [ˈsʌmptʃuəs] *adj.* 华贵的，奢华的(expensive and grand)

【记】sum(总数) + ptuous → 总数很大 → 奢华的

【反】sober(*adj.* 节制的；朴素的)

profligate [ˈprɑːflɪɡət] *adj.* 肆意挥霍的，挥金如土的(wildly extravagant) *n.* 挥霍者；放荡的人

【记】pro(向前) + flig(搅，拌) + ate → 向前搅拌，撒了出去都不可惜 → 肆意挥霍的

【反】parsimonious(*adj.* 小气的)；provident(*adj.* 节俭的)；barren(*adj.* 贫瘠的)

【派】profligacy(*n.* 肆意挥霍)

improvident [ɪmˈprɑːvɪdənt] *adj.* 无远见的；浪费的（thriftless; wasteful）

【记】im(无) + provident(前瞻的) → 无远见的

*lavish [ˈlævɪʃ] *adj.* 浪费的，奢侈的（wasteful）；无节制的

【记】lav(洗) + ish → 冲掉 → 浪费的

【例】My neighbors spoiled their children with *lavish* gifts.

**flamboyant [flæmˈbɔɪənt] *adj.* 华丽的，浮夸的（dazzling; showy）

**pampered [ˈpæmpərd] *adj.* 饮食过量的；娇惯的

【例】It denoted a history of tradition, superior quality, and often a *pampered* buying experience. // The *pampered* cat refused to eat food without meat.

squander [ˈskwɑːndər] *vt.* 浪费，挥霍（to dissipate; waste）

【例】He was not at all shameful when *squandering* his family fortune on gambling.

腐 败

addle [ˈædl] *v.* (使)腐坏（to make rotten）；(使)昏乱（to become muddled or confused）

【记】add (增加) + le → 事情增加容易混乱 → 使昏乱

【派】addled(*adj.* 头脑混乱的)

putrefy [ˈpjuːtrɪfaɪ] *v.* (使)腐烂（to make putrid）；(使)堕落

【记】putr(腐烂) + efy → 使腐烂；注意不要和petrify(*vt.* 使石化)相混

【派】putrefaction(*n.* 腐坏，腐败；堕落)

*deterioration [dɪˌtɪriəˈreɪʃn] *n.* 恶化；堕落（the action or process of deteriorating）

【反】improvement(*n.* 改进)

贪 婪

ravenous [ˈrævənəs] *adj.* 饿极的，狼吞虎咽的；贪婪的

avid [ˈævɪd] *adj.* 渴望的，贪心的（having an ardent desire）

*acquisitive [əˈkwɪzətɪv] *adj.* 渴望得到的，贪得无厌的（covetous; greedy）

【记】ac + quisit(得到) + ive → 一再要得到 → 渴望得到的

【例】Jane has an *acquisitive* nature and will probably want a new car just like yours.

– 183 –

rapacious [rə'peɪʃəs] *adj.* 强夺的，贪婪的（taking by force; avaricious; covetous）

【记】rap(抓，夺) + acious → 强夺的

*greedy ['griːdi] *adj.* 贪婪的（voracious; insatiable）

cupidity [kjuː'pɪdəti] *n.* 贪婪，（尤指）贪财物（greed, especially for money or possessions）

avarice ['ævərɪs] *n.* 贪婪，贪财（greed; lust）

【记】来自avid(*adj.* 渴望的，贪心的)

【例】*Avarice* has caused the downfall of many people.

*insatiable [ɪn'seɪʃəbl] *adj.* 不能满足的，贪心的（very greedy）

【记】in(不) + sati(满) + able → 不能满足的

**voracious [və'reɪʃəs] *adj.* 狼吞虎咽的；贪婪的（excessively eager; insatiable）

【记】vor(吃) + acious → 吃得多的 → 狼吞虎咽的

【反】lack of appetite(没有胃口的)

venal ['viːnl] *adj.* 惟利是图的，贪赃枉法的（characterized by or associated with corrupt bribery）

【反】incorruptible(*adj.* 廉洁的)；unsusceptible of bribery(不怀疑受贿的)

【派】venality(*n.* 惟利是图)

erotic [ɪ'rɑːtɪk] *adj.* 性爱的，色情的；好色的

【记】来自希腊神话中的爱神Eros(厄洛斯)

*gloat [gloʊt] *vi.* 沾沾自喜，得意洋洋；幸灾乐祸（to express or feel selfish delight at one's own success or good fortune or sb else's failure）

【例】Stop *gloating* just because you won the game!

懒 惰

sluggish ['slʌgɪʃ] *adj.* 迟钝的，懒惰的(lethargic; listless; slow)

【例】The snake was *sluggish* because of the cold weather.

**slack [slæk] *adj.* 懒散的，懈怠的；马虎的（sluggish; inactive; careless）；(绳)松弛的(loose) *v.* 松懈，怠惰

【反】taut(*adj.* 绷紧的；紧张的)

slothful ['sloʊθfl] *adj.* 偷懒的，怠惰的

| indolence | ['ɪndələns] *n.* 懒惰，懒散 |

【例】Lawson tried to excuse his *indolence*.

| sluggard | ['slʌɡərd] *n.* 懒鬼（a habitually lazy person） |

【记】slug（蛞蝓：一种行动缓慢的虫）+ gard → 懒鬼

| indolent | ['ɪndələnt] *adj.* 懒惰的，懒散的（lazy; slothful） |

| loll | [lɑːl] *v.* 懒洋洋地坐、卧或依靠（to sit or lie in a very lazy and relaxed way） |

【记】发音似"老哦"→ 老了，不爱动 → 懒洋洋地坐、卧或依靠；和 lull（*v./n.* 安静）一起记

【反】move vigorously（充满活力地走动）

| ennui | ['ɑːnwiː] *n.* 倦怠，无聊（weariness of mind） |

【反】excitement（*n.* 兴奋）；exuberance（*n.* 充满活力）；keen interest（强烈的兴趣）；energy（*n.* 精力）；enthusiasm（*n.* 热情）

| lackadaisical | [ˌlækə'deɪzɪkl] *adj.* 无精打采的（listless; languid）；无兴趣的（showing lack of interest） |

【记】lack（缺少）+ a + daisi（=daisy 第一流人物）+ cal → 缺少第一流人物的聚会显得很无趣 → 无兴趣的

| sloth | [sloʊθ] *n.* 怠惰，懒惰 |

【派】slothful（*adj.* 怠惰的）

| desultory | ['desəltɔːri] *adj.* 不连贯的（disconnected; not methodical）；散漫的，无计划的（random） |

【记】de + sult（跳）+ ory → 跳来跳去 → 不连贯的

【反】strictly methodical（有条不紊的）

| *idle | ['aɪdl] *adj.* 无所事事的（avoiding work）；无用的（useless）*v.* 懒散，无所事事（to do nothing） |

【记】发音似"爱斗"→ 无所事事的才爱斗 → 无所事事的

| **sedentary | ['sednteri] *adj.* 需要（或惯于）久坐的（requiring much sitting） |

【记】sed（坐）+ entary → 久坐的

【反】migratory（*adj.* 迁徙的）

| *inertia | [ɪ'nɜːrʃə] *n.* 迟钝，不活动；惯性，惰性 |

| torpor | ['tɔːrpər] *n.* 死气沉沉，没有活力（extreme sluggishness of function）；（动物）冬眠 |

【反】extreme excitability（极其激动）；zeal（*n.* 热情）；animation（*n.* 活泼）

doodle ['du:dl] *vi.* 胡画（to make meaningless drawings）; 混时间（to kill time）
【记】吃着面条（noodle）混时间（doodle）

挑 剔

captious ['kæpʃəs] *adj.* 吹毛求疵的（quick to find fault; carping）
【记】capt（拿）+ ious → 拿（别人的缺点）说事 → 吹毛求疵的
【派】captiously（*adv.* 吹毛求疵地）

censorious [sen'sɔːriəs] *adj.* 挑剔的，苛刻批评的（critical）
【记】来自censure（*v.* 指责，谴责）; censor（审查官）+ ious → 总是像审查官一样 → 苛刻批评的
【例】*Censorious* people delight in casting blame.
【反】eulogistic（*adj.* 赞美的）

cavil ['kævl] *v.* 挑毛病，吹毛求疵（to object when there is little reason to do so; quibble）
【记】和civil（*adj.* 文明的，有礼貌的）一起记，文明（civil）人不会无端挑剔别人毛病（cavil）
【例】I don't think this is the time to *cavil* at the wording of the report.

平 庸

**mediocrity [ˌmiːdi'ɑːkrəti] *n.* 平庸，碌碌无为（mediocre abilities or attainment）
【记】来自mediocre（*adj.* 普通的，平庸的）
【反】virtuosity（*n.* 精湛的技艺）

*nearsighted [ˌnɪr'saɪtɪd] *adj.* 近视的; 没有远见的
【例】Flat-footed as well as *nearsighted*, he had little interest in sports, and he read voraciously. // No doubt the committee will wave aside his *nearsighted* view.

banal [bə'nɑːl] *adj.* 陈腐的（dull or stale; commonplace; insipid）
【记】ban（禁止）+ al → 应该禁止的 → 陈腐的
【反】arresting（*adj.* 引人注意的，醒目的）; novel（*adj.* 新奇的）

trite [traɪt] *adj.* 陈腐的，陈词滥调的（hackneyed or boring）
【反】original（*adj.* 有新意的）; unbanal（*adj.* 不迂腐的）

粗　俗

bedizen [bɪˈdɪzən] *vt.* 俗丽地穿着或装饰(to dress with vulgar finery)

【记】bed(床) + izen → 把床装饰得华丽 → 俗丽地穿着或装饰

**bungle [ˈbʌŋgl] *v.* 粗制滥造；笨手笨脚地做 (to act or work clumsily and awkwardly)

【记】比较记忆：jungle(*n.* 丛林)；tangle(*v.*/*n.* 纠缠)

【反】bring off(顺利完成)

【派】bungler(*n.* 笨手笨脚的人)

earthy [ˈɜːrθi] *adj.* 粗俗的，粗陋的(rough, plain in taste)

【记】earth(土地) + y → 土的 → 粗俗的

*tawdry [ˈtɔːdri] *adj.* 华而不实的，俗丽的(cheap but showy)

secular [ˈsekjələr] *adj.* 世俗的，尘世的(of the worldly or temporal)

【例】It's the last *secular* music we recall.

**mundane [mʌnˈdeɪn] *adj.* 现世的，世俗的(relating to the world; worldly)；平凡的，平淡的

【反】exotic(*adj.* 奇异的)；unearthly(*adj.* 超脱自然的)

*specious [ˈspiːʃəs] *adj.* 似是而非的 (having a false look of truth or genuineness)；华而不实的(having deceptive attraction or allure)

【记】spec(看) + ious → 用来看的 → 华而不实的

【反】valid(*adj.* 正确的)；veritable(*adj.* 真实的)

好　色

carnal [ˈkɑːrnl] *adj.* 肉体的，肉欲的，色欲的 (fleshly; sensual; concerning the desires of the body)

*sensual [ˈsenʃuəl] *adj.* 肉欲的，淫荡的(carnal)

【记】sens(感觉，感官) + ual → 注重肉体感官 → 肉欲的

*raunchy [ˈrɔːntʃi] *adj.* 淫秽的，猥亵的(coarse or obscene)

【例】a *raunchy* joke, story, etc

bawdy [ˈbɔːdi] *adj.* 淫猥的，下流的 (indecent; obscene; humorously coarse)

【记】来自bawd(*n.* 鸨母；妓女)

【反】decorous(*adj.* 端庄的)

*licentious [laɪˈsenʃəs] *adj.* 纵欲的，放荡的 (lascivious)；放肆的，漠视规范的 (marked by disregard for strict rules of correctness)

【记】licent(允许) + ious → 得到特别允许的 → 放肆的

lewd [luːd] *adj.* 淫荡的，猥亵的

【例】a story full of *lewd* innuendos

lechery [ˈletʃəri] *n.* 色欲，淫荡（excessive interest in sexual pleasure）

prurient [ˈprʊriənt] *adj.* 好色的，迷恋淫欲的（having or showing excessive interest in sexual matters）

【例】She showed a *prurient* interest in the details of the rape case.

incontinent [ɪnˈkɑːntɪnənt] *adj.*（尤指性方面）缺乏自制力的（lacking self-control, especially in sexual matters）

philander [fiˈlændər] *vi.*（指男子）挑逗女子，与女子调情（to amuse oneself by flirting with women）

【例】He spent his time *philandering* with the girls in the village.

狡 猾

wily [ˈwaɪli] *adj.* 狡猾的，诡计多端的（full of wiles; crafty）

【记】来自wile(*n.* 诡计)

【例】a *wily* fraud(狡猾的骗子)

*cunning [ˈkʌnɪŋ] *adj.* 狡猾的，奸诈的(sly; tricky)

【例】The successful owner had developed a *cunning* business sense.

*politic [ˈpɑːlətɪk] *adj.* 精明的，圆滑的，有策略的；狡猾的，不择手段的

【例】The *politic* governor didn't give the definite answer.

【反】unsophisticated(*adj.* 不世故的); injudicious(*adj.* 缺乏判断力的)

*chicanery [ʃɪˈkeɪnəri] *n.* 诡计，狡诈(deception by artful sophistry; trickery)

【记】chic(聪明) + anery → 耍聪明 → 诡计

【反】aboveboard action(光明正大的行为); honest dealing(诚实对待)

**subterfuge [ˈsʌbtərfjuːdʒ] *n.* 借口，托辞 (a deceptive device or stratagem); 手段，诡计

【记】subter(私下) + fuge(逃跑) → 找借口避开 → 借口，托辞

guile [gaɪl] *n.* 欺诈，狡猾(deceit; cunning)

【记】gui (拼音：贵) + le (拼音：了) → 东西买贵了 → 被欺骗了 → 欺诈

【反】artlessness(*n.* 淳朴)

*duplicitous [duːˈplɪsɪtəs] *adj.* 搞两面派的，口是心非的，奸诈的 (marked by duplicity); 双重的

【记】du(二) + plic(重叠) + itous → 有双重态度 → 口是心非的

*tricky [ˈtrɪki] adj. 机警的，狡猾的

【例】But renting could prove *tricky* for firms that have little experience as property managers.

glib [glɪb] adj. 能说会道的；油嘴滑舌的（speaking or spoken in a smooth, fluent, easy manner）

【反】labored（adj. 费力的）；awkward（adj. 笨拙的）

**insidious [ɪnˈsɪdiəs] adj. 阴险的，隐藏诡计的（more dangerous than seems evident）

【记】insid(看做inside，内部的) + ious → 阴险的

*duplicity [duːˈplɪsəti] n. 欺骗，口是心非（hypocritical cunning or deception）；二重性

【记】du(二) + plic(重叠) + ity → 有两层态度 → 口是心非

pitfall [ˈpɪtfɔːl] n. 陷阱(trap)；未料到的危险或困难(a hidden or not easily recognized danger or difficulty)

【记】pit(坑，洞) + fall(落下) → 不留心会落入的坑 → 陷阱

ruse [ruːz] n. 骗术，诡计，花招（trick to deceive; stratagem）

【记】用玫瑰(rose)来骗取(ruse)姑娘的芳心

*oily [ˈɔɪli] adj. (似)油的；油嘴滑舌的

【例】an *oily* liquid // I don't like *oily* shop assistants.

**artifice [ˈɑːrtɪfɪs] n. 奸诈，欺骗；诡计（a sly trick）

【记】arti(技巧) + fic(做) + e → 做的技巧 → 诡计

【反】candor（n. 坦白）

unctuous [ˈʌŋktʃuəs] adj. 油的，油质的；油腔滑调的（fatty; oily）

【记】unct(油) + uous → 油的

残 忍

**atrocity [əˈtrɑːsəti] n. 残暴，暴行（brutality; cruelty）

【例】*Atrocity* and terror are not political weapons.

*brutality [bruːˈtæləti] n. 残忍，野蛮行为（the trait of extreme cruelty）

*ferocity [fəˈrɑːsəti] n. 凶猛，残忍，狂暴的行为（the quality or state of being ferocious）

【记】来自ferocious（adj. 残暴的）

*brute [bruːt] n./adj. 野兽(的)(beast)；残忍的(人)（a person who is brutal）

【派】brutal（adj. 野蛮的，残忍的）

truculent	['trʌkjələnt] *adj.* 残暴的，凶狠的 (feeling or displaying ferocity; cruel)

【记】truc(凶猛) + ulent → 凶狠的

【反】gentle(*adj.* 温柔的)；pacific(*adj.* 平静的)

*feral | ['ferəl] *adj.* 凶猛的，野生的(wild or savage)

【反】cultivated(*adj.* 驯化的)

*vicious | ['vɪʃəs] *adj.* 残酷的，邪恶的(savage; fierce)

【记】来自vice(*n.* 邪恶)

*gruff | [grʌf] *adj.* (指人、声音)粗野的(rough; hoarse)

自 私

skinflint | ['skɪnflɪnt] *n.* 吝啬鬼(miser; niggard)

【记】来自词组：skin a flint → 刮石头皮 → 爱钱如命 → 吝啬鬼

miserly | ['maɪzərli] *adj.* 吝啬的(stingy)

**grudging | ['grʌdʒɪŋ] *adj.* 勉强的(reluctant)；吝啬的

【例】So I've got to give a little *grudging* credit to the way they've pulled it off.

*individualistic | [ˌɪndɪˌvɪdʒuə'lɪstɪk] *adj.* 个人主义的；利己主义的(selfish)

【例】Geoff was too *individualistic* and subjective to be a team captain.

*egocentric | [ˌiːɡoʊ'sentrɪk] *adj.* 利己的；以自我为中心的(self-centred)

egoism | ['iːɡoʊɪzəm] *n.* 利己主义(a doctrine that self-interest is the valid end)

【记】ego(自我) + ism(主义) → 利己主义

willful | ['wɪlfl] *adj.* 任性的(perversely self-willed)；故意的(intentional)

【记】来自will(*n.* 意愿，意向)

【例】You were like a *willful* child.

noncommittal | [ˌnɒnkə'mɪtəl] *adj.* 态度暧昧的 (giving no clear indication of attitude or feeling)；不承担义务的

【记】non(不) + committal(义务) → 不承担义务的

**ingratitude | [ɪn'ɡrætɪtuːd] *n.* 忘恩负义(lack of gratitude)

parsimony | ['pɑːrsəmoʊni] *n.* 过分节俭，吝啬(the quality of being parsimonious)

【记】parsi(发音似"怕失") + mony(看做money, 钱) → 怕失去钱 → 吝啬

【反】largesse(*n.* 慷慨)

THIS IS MINE!

偏　狭

*provincial ［prəˈvɪnʃl］*adj.* 省的；地方性的；偏狭的，粗俗的（limited in outlook; narrow）

【记】province（省）+ ial → 地方性的 → 偏狭的

jaundiced ［ˈdʒɔːndɪst］*adj.* 有偏见的（prejudiced）

【记】jaundice（黄疸；偏见）+ d → 有偏见的

*bias ［ˈbaɪəs］*n.* 偏见（prejudice; partiality）

【例】The classical music reviewer had a *bias* against rock music.

*prejudice ［ˈpredʒudɪs］*n.* 偏见，成见（opinion, or like or dislike of sb/sth that is not founded on experience or reason）*vt.* 使产生偏见（to cause to have prejudice）

【记】pre（预先）+ judice（判断）→ 预先判断 → 偏见

partiality ［ˌpɑːrʃiˈæləti］*n.* 偏袒，偏心（state of being partial; bias）

【记】来自partial（*adj.* 偏袒的）

**cramped ［kræmpt］*n.* 狭促的，狭窄的（confined; incommodious）

【反】commodious（*adj.* 宽敞的）

tendentious ［tenˈdenʃəs］*adj.* 有偏见的，有倾向性的（marked by a tendency in favor of a particular point of view; biased）

【记】tendent（趋势，倾向）+ ious → 有倾向性的

【反】unbiased（*adj.* 无偏见的）

inequity ［ɪnˈekwəti］*n.* 不公正，不公平（injustice; unfairness）

【记】in（不）+ equi（平等）+ ty → 不公平

nepotism ［ˈnepətɪzəm］*n.* 裙带关系（patronage or favoritism based on family relationship）

【记】nepot（=nephew 侄甥）+ ism → 裙带关系

coterie ［ˈkoʊtəri］*n.* （有共同兴趣的）小团体，圈内人（a close circle of friends who share a common interest or background; clique）

【记】cote（小屋，笼）+ rie → 一个小屋子的人 → 小团体

顽　固

*cussed ［ˈkʌsɪd］*adj.* （指人）执拗的，固执的，好作对的（obstinate）

【例】She's so *cussed* that she always does the opposite of what you ask.

*impenitent [ɪmˈpenɪtənt] *adj.* 不悔悟的 （without regret; unrepentant）

【记】im(不) + penitent(悔恨的) → 不悔悟的

【反】rueful(*adj.* 悔恨的)

**unyielding [ʌnˈjiːldɪŋ] *adj.* 不屈的，固执的(obdurate)

【记】un(不) + yielding(柔顺的) → 不屈的，固执的

*intransigent [ɪnˈtrænzɪdʒənt] *adj.* 不妥协的(uncompromising)

【记】in(不) + transigent(妥协的) → 不妥协的

【反】open to compromise(寻求和解的); tractable(*adj.* 易管教的)

*obstinate [ˈɑːbstɪnət] *adj.* 固执的(stubborn); 不屈服的

【记】ob + stin(站) + ate → 坚决站着 → 固执的; 不屈服的

*intractable [ɪnˈtræktəbl] *adj.* 倔强的 （unruly or stubborn）; 难管的 （not easily managed）

【记】in(不) + tract(拉) + able → 拉不动的 → 倔强的

*adamant [ˈædəmənt] *adj.* 强硬的 （too hard to be broken）; 固执的(unyielding; inflexible）

【记】adam(亚当) + ant(蚂蚁) → 亚当和蚂蚁都很固执 → 固执的

【反】vacillatory(*adj.* 犹豫不决的); moved(*adj.* 被打动的)

**headstrong [ˈhedstrɔːŋ] *adj.* 顽固的(obstinate; stubborn)

*dogged [ˈdɔːɡɪd] *adj.* 顽强的(determined; tenacious); 固执的(stubborn)

【记】dog(狗) + ged → 像狗一样顽强 → 顽强的

【反】yielded （*adj.* 屈服的）; easily-discouraged(容易气馁的)

pertinacious [ˌpɜːrtnˈeɪʃəs] *adj.* 固执的; 无法驾驭的 (insubordinate); 不妥协的(intransigent)

【记】per + tin(拿住) + acious → 始终拿住不放 → 固执的

【反】vacillation(*n.* 犹豫); tractable(*adj.* 温顺的)

【派】pertinacity(*n.* 顽固)

bigotry [ˈbɪɡətri] *n.* 顽固，偏狭(stubborn; intolerance)

【记】big + (g)ot + ry → 得到不放的人 → 顽固

虚　假

*insincere [ˌɪnsɪnˈsɪr] *adj.* 不真诚的，不诚恳的

affected [əˈfektɪd] *adj.* 装模作样的，不自然的(behaving in an artificial way)；假装的(assumed)

【记】受到好的影响(affect)就充满爱(affection)，受到不好的影响(affect)就装模作样(affected)

【例】I don't wish to look *affected*.

【反】natural(*adj.* 自然的)

contrived [kənˈtraɪvd] *adj.* 不自然的，做作的(not spontaneous or natural)

【记】来自contrive(*v.* 设计，图谋)

【例】a novel with a *contrived* ending

*spurious [ˈspjʊriəs] *adj.* 假的(false)；伪造的(falsified; forged)

【记】spuria(伪造的作品) + ous → 伪造的

【反】genuine(*adj.* 真正的)

*sanctimonious [ˌsæŋktɪˈmoʊniəs] *adj.* 假装虔诚的，假装神圣的(hypocritically pious or devout)

【记】sancti(神圣) + mon(警告) + ious → 因为你是假神圣，所以要警告你 → 假装虔诚的

**hypocritical [ˌhɪpəˈkrɪtɪkl] *adj.* 虚伪的(of hypocrisy or a hypocrite)

【记】hypo(下面) + critical(评论的；批评的) → 在背后批评的 → 虚伪的

bravado [brəˈvɑːdoʊ] *n.* 故作勇敢，虚张声势(pretended courage)

【记】brava(喝彩声) + do(作) → 故意大声喝彩 → 虚张声势

sham [ʃæm] *n.* 虚假，欺骗(hypocrisy; hoax)；赝品 *v.* 伪装(to feign)

【记】把shame(害臊)的e去掉成sham → 不知害臊地虚假 → 虚假

bluff [blʌf] *n./v.* 虚张声势，吓唬(pretense of strength)

【记】发音似"布老虎" → 布老虎和纸老虎都只是虚张声势

【例】He *bluffed* the police into thinking that he had a gun.

*hypocrisy [hɪˈpɑːkrəsi] *n.* 伪善，虚伪(insincerity)

*disguise [dɪsˈgaɪz] *vt.* 假扮；掩饰，隐瞒(to obscure real nature of)

【记】dis + guise(外观；伪装) → 假扮；掩饰；注意guise本身是一个单词

mannered ［ˈmænərd］*adj.* 做作的，矫揉造作的（having an artificial or stilted character）

【记】manner(风格；态度)＋ed→太过讲究风格的→矫揉造作的

【反】natural(*adj.* 自然的)

untenable ［ʌnˈtenəbl］*adj.* 防守不住的；站不住脚的（not able to be defended）

*unwarranted ［ʌnˈwɔːrəntɪd］*adj.* 没有根据的（unwelcome and done without good reason）

【记】un(不)＋warrant(理由，根据)＋ed→没有根据的

The ideals which have lighted my way, and time after time have given me new courage to face life cheerfully have been kindness, beauty and truth.

有些理想曾为我指引过道路，并不断给我新的勇气以欣然面对人生，那些理想就是——真、善、美。

——美国科学家　爱因斯坦（Albert Einstein, American scientist）

填空题

artifice	atrocity	bungle	extravagant	flamboyant
gloat	grudging	ingratitude	insidious	luxurious
mediocrity	mundane	pampered	sedentary	slack
specious	subterfuge	tawdry	bluff	voracious

1. His acting career started brilliantly, then sank into _____.
2. I lead a pretty _____ life; nothing interesting ever happens to me.
3. Residents were warned not to be _____ with water, in view of the low rainfall this year.
4. He's been very _____ in his work lately.
5. He _____ the police into thinking that he had a gun.
6. I am shocked by the _____ of this man's crimes.
7. This car is our most _____ model.
8. Penny has red hair and a rather _____ appearance.
9. The _____ cat refused to eat food without meat.
10. Some animals feed _____ in summer and hibernate in winter.
11. His lameness made him fond of _____ occupation.
12. The gang spent a year planning the robbery and then _____ it.
13. Journalists often use _____ to obtain material for stories.
14. The impostor will not get away with his _____ wiles.
15. Pretending to faint was merely (an) _____.
16. She always has a feeling of _____ admiration and desire to have something possessed by her friends around.
17. Her help was met with _____ and unkindness.
18. She was still _____ over her rival's disappointment.
19. She saw herself as shallow, _____.
20. Do not be misled by such _____ arguments.

配对题

1. lavish	渴望得到的, 贪得无厌的	11. cunning	无所事事的; 懒散
2. deterioration	残忍, 野蛮行为	12. politic	迟钝, 不活动
3. acquisitive	不自然的, 做作的	13. chicanery	不能满足的, 贪心的
4. greedy	诡计, 狡诈	14. duplicitous	浪费的, 奢侈的
5. insatiable	狡猾的, 奸诈的	15. intractable	纵欲的; 放肆的
6. idle	恶化; 堕落	16. sanctimonious	(似)油的; 油腔滑调的
7. inertia	搞两面派的; 双重的	17. oily	精明的, 圆滑的, 有策略的
8. sensual	假装虔诚的	18. brutality	淫秽的, 猥亵的
9. raunchy	凶猛, 残忍	19. ferocity	肉欲的, 淫荡的
10. licentious	贪婪的	20. contrived	倔强的; 难管的

练习题答案

填空题答案

1. His acting career started brilliantly, then sank into <u>mediocrity</u>.
2. I lead a pretty <u>mundane</u> life; nothing interesting ever happens to me.
3. Residents were warned not to be <u>extravagant</u> with water, in view of the low rainfall this year.
4. He's been very <u>slack</u> in his work lately.
5. He <u>bluffed</u> the police into thinking that he had a gun
6. I am shocked by the <u>atrocity</u> of this man's crimes.
7. This car is our most <u>luxurious</u> model.
8. Penny has red hair and a rather <u>flamboyant</u> appearance.
9. The <u>pampered</u> cat refused to eat food without meat.
10. Some animals feed <u>voraciously</u> in summer and hibernate in winter.
11. His lameness made him fond of <u>sedentary</u> occupation.
12. The gang spent a year planning the robbery and then <u>bungled</u> it.
13. Journalists often use <u>subterfuge</u> to obtain material for stories.
14. The impostor will not get away with his <u>insidious</u> wiles.
15. Pretending to faint was merely (an) <u>artifice</u>.
16. She always has a feeling of <u>grudging</u> admiration and desire to have something possessed by her friends around.
17. Her help was met with <u>ingratitude</u> and unkindness.
18. She was still <u>gloating</u> over her rival's disappointment.
19. She saw herself as shallow, <u>tawdry</u>.
20. Do not be misled by such <u>specious</u> arguments.

配对题答案

1. lavish	浪费的，奢侈的	11. cunning	狡猾的，奸诈的
2. deterioration	恶化；堕落	12. politic	精明的,圆滑的,有策略的
3. acquisitive	渴望得到的,贪得无厌的	13. chicanery	诡计，狡诈
4. greedy	贪婪的	14. duplicitous	搞两面派的；双重的
5. insatiable	不能满足的，贪心的	15. intractable	倔强的，难管的
6. idle	无所事事的；懒散	16. sanctimonious	假装虔诚的
7. inertia	迟钝，不活动	17. oily	(似)油的；油腔滑调的
8. sensual	肉欲的，淫荡的	18. brutality	残忍，野蛮行为
9. raunchy	淫秽的，猥亵的	19. ferocity	凶猛，残忍
10. licentious	纵欲的；放肆的	20. contrived	不自然的，做作的

Word List 20
属性（一）

比较概念

*prior ［ˈpraɪər］ *adj.* 优先的；在先的（before）

【例】*Prior* to the epidemic, public heath was largely the province of state and local authorities.

*primal ［ˈpraɪml］ *adj.* 主要的，首要的；最初的，根本的（fundamental; primary）

【例】of *primal* importance

*inferior ［ɪnˈfɪriər］ *adj.* （等级、社会地位、重要性、质量等）较低的，次要的，较差的（lower in rank, social position, importance, quality, etc）

【例】A captain is *inferior* to a major.

*incomparable ［ɪnˈkɑːmprəbl］ *adj.* 无比的，无双的，不可比拟的（beyond comparison）

【例】*incomparable* singing／hospitality／food

**outlive ［ˌaʊtˈlɪv］ *vt.* 比…活得久（to live longer than sb）

【例】He *outlived* his wife by three years.

**outsmart ［ˌaʊtˈsmɑːrt］ *vt.* 比…精明，智胜（to outwit）

【例】We *outsmarted* them and got there first by taking a shorter route.

*outsell ［ˌaʊtˈsel］ *vt.* 比…销售得多

【例】The Japanese can *outsell* any competitor in the market.

*outweigh ［ˌaʊtˈweɪ］ *vt.* （在重量、价值或重要性上）超过（to be greater in weight, value or importance than sth）

【例】This *outweighs* all other considerations.

*outperform ［ˌaʊtpərˈfɔːrm］ *vt.* （在操作或性能上）胜过，比…做得好（to exceed）

【例】But summer Olympics generally *outperform* those in the winter, which fetch lower rights fees as well.

precedence ['presɪdəns] *n.* 领先，居先；优先权（right to come before sb/sth in time, order, rank, etc）

【例】The longest-serving officer always takes *precedence*.

*vantage ['væntɪdʒ] *n.* 优势，有利地位（superiority in a contest）

commensurate [kə'menʃərət] *adj.* 同样大小的（equal in measure）；相称的，成比例的（proportionate）

【记】com + mensur(测量) + ate → 测量相同 → 相称的

【例】These employees perform services *commensurate* with their training.

【反】preponderant(*adj.* 占优势的)

**preceding [prɪ'siːdɪŋ] *adj.* 在前的(prior)

【例】Countries belonging to confederations that hosted the two *preceding* tournaments are barred from applying.

neutral ['nuːtrəl] *adj.* 中性的；中立的(nonaligned)

【记】neutr(中) + al → 中性的

*subplot ['sʌbplɑːt] *n.* 次要情节

【记】sub(在下面) + plot(情节) → 在主要情节之下的 → 次要情节

**resemble [rɪ'zembl] *vt.* 像，类似

【例】Mary *resembles* her mother in many ways.

*untended [ˌʌn'tendɪd] *adj.* 被忽略了的，未受到照顾的

【例】We found her in a semi-comatose state, completely *untended* by the same family members she had been supporting for years.

*untrustworthy [ʌn'trʌstwɜːrði] *adj.* 靠不住的，不能信赖的(unreliable)

【例】He couldn't stand *untrustworthy* women, and he's not ashamed to be a bit of a bastard.

*subcommittee ['sʌbkəmɪti] *n.* （由大委员会的委员组成的）小组委员会，附属委员会

【记】sub(在下面) + committee(委员会) → 在主要委员会下面的 → 小组委员会

*counterpoint ['kaʊntərpɔɪnt] *n.* 对比物，相互作用物

【例】The dark curtains make an interesting *counterpoint* to the lighter walls.

*subfield ['sʌbfiːld] *n.* 子域，分区

【例】The largest *subfield* of physics today is Condensed Matter Physics.

*sidetrack [ˈsaɪdtræk] *n.* 旁轨，(铁路)侧线 *v.* (将火车)导入侧线(to switch a railroad car to a siding)；转移目标(to divert from a main issue)；使受牵制

inferiority [ɪnˌfɪriˈɔːrəti] *n.* 自卑；劣等，次等

microcosm [ˈmaɪkroʊkɑːzəm] *n.* 小天地，小宇宙，缩影 (thing being regarded as representing the universe, or mankind, on a small scale; miniature representation of a system, etc)
【例】This town is a *microcosm* of our world.

合　适

*felicitous [fəˈlɪsɪtəs] *adj.* (话语等)适当的，得体的(used or expressed in a way suitable to the occasion; appropriate)
【记】felic(幸福)+ itous → (讲话)使人幸福的 → 得体的

seemly [ˈsiːmli] *adj.* (言行举止)得体的，适宜的(pleasing by being suitable to an occasion)
【记】seem(看起来)+ ly → 看起来很美丽 → 得体的
【反】indecorous(*adj.* 无礼的)；uncouth(*adj.* 笨拙的)；ribald(*adj.* 下流的)

*opportune [ˌɑːpərˈtjuːn] *adj.* (时间、事物等)合适的，适当的 (right for the purpose)
【记】op(进入)+ port(港口)+ une → 进入港口避风雨 → 适当的
【反】inconvenient(*adj.* 不适当的)

rationalize [ˈræʃnəlaɪz] *vt.* 使合理化；找借口，自圆其说，文过饰非
【记】来自rational(*adj.* 理性的，合理的)
【例】She *rationalized* her decision to abandon her baby by saying she could not afford to keep it.

apposite [ˈæpəzɪt] *adj.* 恰当的，相关的(appropriate; apt; relevant)
【记】ap + pos (放)+ ite → 放在恰当的地方 → 恰当的；注意不要和 opposite(*adj.* 相反的)相混淆
【反】opposite(*adj.* 相反的)；extraneous(*adj.* 外来的；无关的)

pertinent [ˈpɜːrtnənt] *adj.* 恰当的，切题的，相关的(relevant)
【例】It might be *pertinent* for you to make the suggestion to your boss.

**plausible [ˈplɔːzəbl] *adj.* 貌似合理的(seemingly reasonable)
【例】Susie's story about how she lost her books sounded *plausible*, but it wasn't actually true.

apropos [ˌæprə'pou] *adj./adv.* 恰当的(地)，适宜的(地)(seasonable)；相关的(地)(with reference to; regarding)

【记】a + prop(看做proper, 适当的) + os → 适宜的

【例】I thought her remarks were very *apropos*.

*propriety [prə'praiəti] *n.* 适当，妥当，得体(correctness)

qualified ['kwɑːlifaid] *adj.* 合格的，胜任的

**viable ['vaiəbl] *adj.* 可行的 (having a reasonable chance of succeeding)；(胎儿)能成活的，(蛋)能孵化的，(种子)能萌芽的(capable of living)

【记】via(道路) + (a)ble → 有路可走 → 可行的

*feasible ['fiːzəbl] *adj.* 切实可行的(practical; possible; viable)

【记】feas(做) + ible(能) → 能够做的 → 切实可行的

【例】Before you carry out the plan, make sure it is *feasible*.

*methodical [mə'θɑːdikl] *adj.* (办事)有条理的，有方法的(systematic)

【记】method(方法) + ical → 有方法的

orthodox ['ɔːrθədɑːks] *adj.* 正统的 (conforming to the usual beliefs of established doctrines)

【记】ortho(正) + dox(观点) → 观点正统的 → 正统的

practicable ['præktikəbl] *adj.* 可以实施的，行得通的(workable)

【例】a *practicable* scheme

coincidence [kou'insidəns] *n.* 巧合(的事)(occurrence of similar events or circumstances at the same time by chance)

【例】By a strange *coincidence* we happened to be travelling on the same train.

**moderation [ˌmɑːdə'reiʃn] *n.* 温和，适度，节制(avoiding extreme)

【例】They showed a remarkable degree of *moderation* in not quarrelling publicly on television.

**coincide [ˌkouin'said] *vi.* 相符合，相巧合；同时发生

【记】co(共同) + in + cid(落下) + e → 共同落下 → 同时发生

【例】Our vacations *coincided*, so we traveled together.

*expedient [ik'spiːdiənt] *adj.* 权宜的；方便的(suitable; convenient)

【例】*Expedient* solutions rarely solve long-term problems.

apt: 1. be apt to do sth. have a natural tendency to do sth.

2. appropriate

不合适

*inapt [in'æpt] *ad.* 不相干的，不合适的，无用的（not relevant, appropriate or useful）

【例】an *inapt* remark

*nonstandard [ˌnɑːn'stændərd] *adj.* 不标准的

【记】来自standard（*adj.* 标准的）

【例】"There are a lot of things about these settlements that are *nonstandard*," said Schlanger.

inopportune [ɪnˌɑːpər'tjuːn] *adj.*（时间、事物等）不合适的，不适当的（untimely; poorly chosen）

【例】Susan picks this *inopportune* moment to wake up.

*unseemly [ʌn'siːmli] *adj.*（言行举止）不得体的，不适宜的（unsuited; incongruous）

【例】Jane was regretful for her *unseemly* behavior at the grand party.

*inappropriate [ˌɪnə'proupriət] *adj.* 不恰当的，不适合的（not suitable or appropriate for sb/sth）

【例】an *inappropriate* comment / name / moment

impropriety [ˌɪmprə'praɪəti] *n.*（言行举止）不得体，不适当

【记】im（不）+ propriety（得体）→ 不得体

*irrational [ɪ'ræʃənl] *adj.* 没有道理的，不合逻辑的，荒谬的（illogical, absurd）

【例】*irrational* fears

preposterous [prɪ'pɑːstərəs] *adj.* 荒谬的，可笑的（contradictory to nature or common sense; absurd）

【记】pre（前）+ post（后）+ erous →"前、后"两个前缀放在一起了 → 荒谬的

【反】commonsensical（*adj.* 有基本常识的，明智的）

*inconvenient [ˌɪnkən'viːniənt] *adj.* 不方便的，打扰的，令人为难的（awkward）

【例】They arrived at an *inconvenient* time we had just started the meal.

*unconstitutional [ˌʌnkɑːnstə'tuːʃənl] *adj.* 违反宪法的

【例】Does the Constitution oblige him to order his solicitor general to defend an *unconstitutional* law?

**simplistic [sɪm'plɪstɪk] *adj.*（使困难的问题、事情、意见等）显得过于简单的，过分简单化的（over-simplifying）

【例】a rather *simplistic* assessment of a complex situation

*nonconformity [ˌnɑːnkən'fɔːrmɪti] *n.* 不信奉国教；不一致；不墨守成规

【例】Instead, he teaches that there are prices to pay for *nonconformity*, and that it's not easy.

*monotony [mə'nɑːtəni] *n.* 单调，千篇一律(tedious sameness)

**unsubstantiated [ˌʌnsəb'stænʃieɪtɪd] *adj.* 未经证实的，无事实根据的

【记】un(不) + substantiate(证实) + d → 未经证实的

【反】verified(*adj.* 证明的)

重　要

*indelible [ɪn'deləbl] *adj.* 擦拭不掉的，不可磨灭的(incapable of being erased)

【记】in + del(=delete 擦掉) + ible → 擦拭不掉的

pivotal ['pɪvətl] *adj.* 关键的；枢纽的

【记】来自pivot(*n.* 枢纽；关键)

【例】Chairman of the board is the *pivotal* figure among the managing board.

**elementary [ˌelɪ'mentri] *adj.* 基本的，初级的

【例】I took a course in *elementary* chemistry.

fundamental [ˌfʌndə'mentl] *adj.* 基础的，基本的(essential; elementary)

【例】The refugees were too poor to meet their *fundamental* needs of life.

*momentous [moʊ'mentəs] *adj.* 极重要的(important; critical)

【记】moment(时刻) + ous → 刻不容缓的 → 极重要的

**unprecedented [ʌn'presɪdentɪd] *adj.* 前所未有的(never having happened before)

【记】un(无) + precedent(先例) + ed → 前所未有的

*cardinal ['kɑːrdɪnl] *adj.* 首要的，基本的(essential)

【记】cardi(铰链；要点) + nal → 首要的

【例】To study hard is our *cardinal* thing to do.

**newsworthy ['nuːzwɜːrði] *adj.* 有报道价值的

【例】This question is all the more *newsworthy* because of the crisis that has overtaken journalism.

**significant [sɪɡ'nɪfɪkənt] *adj.* 有意义的；重要的(important; meaningful)

underlying [ˌʌndər'laɪɪŋ] *adj.* 在下面的；基本的，根本的

【记】under(在下面) + lying(位于) → 在下面的

*dominant ['dɑːmɪnənt] *adj.* 占优势的，主导的(predominant; prevalent)

【例】The *dominant* color in the design is red.

optimum [ˈɑːptɪməm] *adj.* 最优的(best)

【记】optim(最好) + um → 最优的

【例】Under *optimum* conditions, these cultivated grass grow best.

**paramount [ˈpærəmaʊnt] *adj.* 最重要的；至高无上的，最高权力的(supreme; dominant)

【记】par(超过) + amount(数量) → 在量上超过别的 → 最重要的

material [məˈtɪriəl] *adj.* 重要的，关键的，实质性的(important; essential; relevant)

【例】*material* evidence

**noteworthy [ˈnoʊtwɜːrði] *adj.* 值得注意的，显著的(marked; outstanding)

【例】What's *noteworthy* here is that I don't like or even admire all these movies.

*essentialism [ɪˈsenʃəlɪzəm] *n.* 本质先于存在论；实在说；基本教育论

【例】Belief in *essentialism* starts early.

*elite [ɪˈliːt] *n.* 精华，精英，中坚(best)

【记】e(出) + lite(=lig 选) → 精心选出的(人物) → 精英

【例】The movie star felt like one of the *elite*.

motif [moʊˈtiːf] *n.* 主题(theme; subject)；主旨

【例】The composer's symphony had an obvious waltz *motif*.

*staple [ˈsteɪpl] *n.* 主要产品 (the chief commodity or production)；主食

【记】满街的苹果(apple)是当下的主要产品(staple)

【例】Parched corn was a *staple* of the Indian diet.

*underscore [ˌʌndərˈskɔːr] *vt.* 在…之下划线 (to draw a line under a word to show its importance)；强调(to give force to)

【记】under(在下面) + score(划线) → 在…之下划线

*predominate [prɪˈdɑːmɪneɪt] *v.* 占优势，占主导地位；支配(to prevail)

【记】pre + domin(统治) + ate → 占优势

【例】Cheap and inferior commodities often *predominate* the morning market.

forte [fɔːrt] *n.* 长处(strong point)

【记】fort(强) + e → 强大 → 长处

linchpin [ˈlɪntʃpɪn] *n.* 轮辖，制轮楔；(组织、计划等中的)关键性的人或事物 (person or thing that is vital to an organization, plan, etc)

【例】Controlling wages is the *linchpin* of the government's policies.

rationale [ˌræʃə'næl] *n.* 基本原理，理论基础（fundamental reason for or logical basis of sth）

【例】the *rationale* behind a decision

*unheeded [ʌn'hiːdɪd] *adj.* 被忽视的，未被注意的（ignored; neglected）

【例】Unfortunately, the absence of Western resolve signals that this warning, too, will go *unheeded*.

*picayune [ˌpɪkə'juːn] *adj.* 不值钱的，微不足道的（cheap）

【例】Indeed, he considers much of modern Islam to be a tyranny of the *picayune*.

*milestone ['maɪlstoʊn] *n.* 里程碑；转折点

【记】mile(里) + stone(石头) → 标志里程的石头 → 里程碑

*breakthrough ['breɪkθruː] *n.* 突破（a penetration of a barrier）；物价暴涨

**gist [dʒɪst] *n.* 主旨，要点，大意（theme）

*tenor ['tenər] *n.* 要旨，要义（nature）

【例】The *tenor* of this speech is to pursue a noble life.

不重要

**inconsequential [ɪnˌkɑːnsɪ'kwenʃl] *adj.* 不重要的，微不足道的（unimportant; trivial）

【记】in(不) + consequential(重要的) → 不重要的

【反】crucial(*adj.* 至关重要的)

*nonsensical [nɑːn'sensɪkl] *adj.* 荒唐的，无意义的（having no meaning or conveying no intelligible ideas）

*periphery [pə'rɪfəri] *n.* 外围（the external boundary or surface of a body）；不重要的部分（part of minor importance）

【记】peri(周围) + pher(带) + y → 带到周围 → 外围

bauble ['bɔːbl] *n.* 花哨的小玩意儿；没价值的东西

【记】发音似"泡沫儿" → 泡沫 → 没价值的东西

*trifle ['traɪfl] *n.* 微不足道的事情，琐事；小玩意儿（sth of little value, substance, or importance）

【例】He told her not to pester him with *trifles*.

*minutia [mi'njuːʃiə] *n.* (*pl.* minutiae)细枝末节，细节（small or trifling matters）

【记】min(小) + utia → 细小之处 → 细节

【反】essential point(重点)；vital feature(重要特征)

inane [ɪˈneɪn] *adj.* 无意义的(lacking sense; silly); 空洞的(empty; void)

【派】inanity(*n.* 无意义，无聊)

【反】meaningful(*adj.* 有意义的); pregnant(*adj.* 意味深长的)

peripheral [pəˈrɪfərəl] *adj.* 周围的，外围的 (of a periphery or surface part; auxiliary); 不重要的

【记】来自periphery(*n.* 外围)

【反】peripheral element(不重要因素)→ crux(*n.* 关键)

piecemeal [ˈpiːsmiːl] *adj./adv.* 逐个的(地)，零碎的(地)(done, or made piece by piece or in a fragmentary way)

*banality [bəˈnæləti] *n.* 平凡，陈腐

【记】来自banal(*adj.* 陈腐的)

venial [ˈviːniəl] *adj.* (错误等)轻微的，可原谅的(forgivable; pardonable)

【记】ven(看做Venus，维纳斯)+ ial → 出于爱而原谅的 → 可原谅的

一　致

**congruent [ˈkɑːŋgruənt] *adj.* 全等的 (having identical shape and size); 一致的

【记】con + gru(看做agree，一致)+ ent → 一致的

【派】congruity(*n.* 全等；一致)

*identical [aɪˈdentɪkl] *adj.* 同一的，同等的(tantamount; same)

【记】iden(相同)+ tical → 同等的

【例】Bill and John have *identical* briefcases, and sometimes Bill picks up John's briefcase by mistake.

*corresponding [ˌkɔːrəˈspɑːndɪŋ] *adj.* 一致的(consistent); 对应的，相当的

【例】Australia's Peter Leek won the *corresponding* men's race, breaking his own world record by five seconds.

**conformity [kənˈfɔːrməti] *n.* 一致，符合

【记】来自conform(*vi.* 遵守；相符合)

*homogenize [həˈmɑːdʒənaɪz] *vt.* 使均匀，使一致 (to reduce to small particles of uniform size and distribute evenly usually in a liquid)

【反】stratify(*vt.* 使分层)

【派】homogenization(*n.* 均匀化，纯一化)

*jibe [dʒaɪb] *vi.* 与…一致，符合(to be in harmony, agreement, or accord)

【记】jibe的"嘲笑"之意大家较为熟悉，但"符合"之意在GRE考试中更为重要

【反】conflict(*v./n.* 冲突)

**correspond [ˌkɔːrəˈspɑːnd] *vi.* 相一致，相符合(to be in agreement)；相应

【例】Your account of events *corresponds* with hers.

**divisive [dɪˈvaɪsɪv] *adj.* 造成不和的，导致分裂的（causing disagreement or disunity among people）

【例】a *divisive* influence

equilibrium [ˌiːkwɪˈlɪbriəm] *n.* 平衡状态(balance)

【例】The gymnast has perfect *equilibrium*.

异 同

**approximate [əˈprɑːksɪmət] *adj.* 大约的，大概的；接近的，近似的(proximate)

【记】ap + proxim(接近) + ate → 接近的，近似的

【例】What is the *approximate* travel time from your house to your job?

*homogeneous [ˌhouməˈdʒiːniəs] *adj.* 同类的；相似的(uniform; same)

【记】homo(同) + gene(产生) + ous → 产生于相同的来源 → 同类的

【例】The population of the small town was *homogeneous*, mostly merchants and laborers.

*heterogeneous [ˌhetərəˈdʒiːniəs] *adj.* 异类的，不同的（dissimilar; incongruous; foreign）

【记】hetero(异) + gene(产生；基因) + ous → 异类的

diverse [daɪˈvɜːrs] *adj.* 不同的，各种各样的(different; various)

【例】Jane made a pretty bouquet of *diverse* flowers.

*uneven [ʌnˈiːvn] *adj.* 不一致的；不相等的；有差异的(not uniform or equal; varying)

【例】Emotion made his voice *uneven*.

**disparate [ˈdɪspərət] *adj.* 迥然不同的（essentially not alike; distinct or different in kind）

【记】dis(不) + par(平等) + ate → 不等的 → 迥然不同的

【反】homogeneous(*adj.* 同类的；相似的)

*disparity [dɪˈspærəti] *n.* 不同，差异(inequality or difference)

*diversify [daɪˈvɜːrsɪfaɪ] *vt.* 使多样化(to vary)

【例】That factory has *diversified* its products.

multiplicity [ˌmʌltɪˈplɪsəti] *n.* 多样性(large number or great variety)

异 常

*anomalous [əˈnɑːmələs] *adj.* 反常的（inconsistent with or deviating from what is usual, normal, or expected）；不规则的（irregular）

anomaly [əˈnɑːməli] *n.* 异常（事物），反常（现象）(sth anomalous)
【记】a（不）+ nomal（看做normal，正常的）+ y → 异常
【反】typical（*adj.* 典型的）；normal（*adj.* 正常的）

aberrant [əˈberənt] *adj.* 越轨的，脱离常轨的（turning away from what is right）；异常的（deviating from what is normal）
【记】ab + err（错误）+ ant → 走向错误 → 越轨的
【派】aberrance（*n.* 越轨；异常）

grotesque [grouˈtesk] *adj.* (外形或方式)怪诞的，古怪的（bizarre; fantastic）
【记】grotto（岩洞）+ picturesque（图画的），原意为"岩洞里的图画" → 和平常的不一样 → 怪诞的

inconsistency [ˌɪnkənˈsɪstənsi] *n.* 不一致，易变
【例】Wait a minute; if you think it's murder, there's an *inconsistency* here.

**miraculous [mɪˈrækjələs] *adj.* 神奇的，超自然的，不可思议的（of the nature of a miracle; supernatural）；奇迹的，惊人的
【记】mir（惊奇）+ aculous → 神奇的
【反】ordinary（*adj.* 平常的）

*prodigy [ˈprɑːdədʒi] *n.* 奇事；奇观；奇才

vagary [ˈveɪɡəri] *n.* 奇想，异想天开（an erratic, unpredictable, or extravagant manifestation）
【记】vag（游移）+ ary → 游移的思想 → 奇想；发音似"无规律" → 奇想

练 习 题

填空题

coincide	congruent	dominant	expedient	feasible
incomparable	indelible	inferior	methodical	monotony
outsell	outsmart	precedence	predominate	preposterous
propriety	rationalize	resemble	seemly	underscore

1. Modern music is often considered _____ to that of the past.
2. Her latest book is _____ better than her earlier ones.
3. She always managed to _____ her political rivals.
4. This year the newspaper has _____ its main rival.
5. She had to learn that her wishes did not take _____ over other people's needs.
6. The plant _____ grass in appearance.
7. It was not considered _____ to talk in such a way in front of the children.
8. She _____ her decision to abandon her baby by saying she could not afford to keep it.
9. Nobody questioned the _____ of her being there alone.
10. It's just not _____ to manage the business on a part-time basis.
11. They sorted slowly and _____ through the papers.
12. The strike was timed to _____ with the party conference.
13. The government has clearly decided that a cut in interest rates would be politically _____.
14. It's _____ to suggest that everything was her fault!
15. She watches television to relieve the _____ of everyday life.
16. The experience made an _____ impression on me.
17. The firm has achieved a _____ position in the world market.
18. The names of the winners are _____ in red.
19. A small group has begun to _____ in policy-making.
20. The measures are _____ with the changes in management policy.

配对题

1. prior	巧合(的事)	11. viable	关键的；枢纽的
2. outlive	同样大小的	12. coincidence	貌似合理的
3. outperform	(话语等)适当的, 得体的	13. inapt	优先的；在先的
4. vantage	不相干的, 不合适的	14. inconvenient	合格的, 胜任的
5. commensurate	不方便的, 打扰的	15. unconstitutional	违反宪法的
6. untended	极重要的	16. nonconformity	未经证实的, 无事实根据的
7. untrustworthy	有报道价值的	17. unsubstantiated	被忽略了的, 未受到照顾的
8. felicitous	不信奉国教；不墨守成规	18. pivotal	靠不住的, 不能信赖的
9. plausible	比…活得久	19. momentous	优势, 有利地位
10. qualified	胜过；比…做得更好	20. newsworthy	可行的

练习题答案

填空题答案

1. Modern music is often considered <u>inferior</u> to that of the past.
2. Her latest book is <u>incomparably</u> better than her earlier ones.
3. She always managed to <u>outsmart</u> her political rivals.
4. This year the newspaper has <u>outsold</u> its main rival.
5. She had to learn that her wishes did not take <u>precedence</u> over other people's needs.
6. The plant <u>resembles</u> grass in appearance.
7. It was not considered <u>seemly</u> to talk in such a way in front of the children.
8. She <u>rationalized</u> her decision to abandon her baby by saying she could not afford to keep it.
9. Nobody questioned the <u>propriety</u> of her being there alone.
10. It's just not <u>feasible</u> to manage the business on a part-time basis.
11. They sorted slowly and <u>methodically</u> through the papers.
12. The strike was timed to <u>coincide</u> with the party conference.
13. The government has clearly decided that a cut in interest rates would be politically <u>expedient</u>.
14. It's <u>preposterous</u> to suggest that everything was her fault!
15. She watches television to relieve the <u>monotony</u> of everyday life.
16. The experience made an <u>indelible</u> impression on me.
17. The firm has achieved a <u>dominant</u> position in the world market.
18. The names of the winners are <u>underscored</u> in red.
19. A small group has begun to <u>predominate</u> in policy-making.
20. The measures are <u>congruent</u> with the changes in management policy.

配对题答案

1. prior	优先的；在先的	11. viable	可行的
2. outlive	比…活得久	12. coincidence	合（的事）
3. outperform	胜过；比…做得更好	13. inapt	相干的，不合适的
4. vantage	优势，有利地位	14. inconvenient	方便的，打扰的
5. commensurate	同样大小的	15. unconstitutional	违反宪法的
6. untended	被忽略了的, 未受到照顾的	16. nonconformity	不信奉国教；不墨守成规
		17. unsubstantiated	未经证实的，无事实根据的
7. untrustworthy	靠不住的，不能信赖的		
8 felicitous	（话语等）适当的，得体的	18. pivotal	关键的；枢纽的
9. plausible	貌似合理的	19. momentous	极重要的
10. qualified	合格的，胜任的	20. newsworthy	有报道价值的

Word List 21

属性(二)

精　巧

*ingenious [ɪnˈdʒiːniəs] *adj.* 制作精巧的；心灵手巧的，机敏的(clever; intelligent)

【记】in(内) + geni(产生) + ous → 品质自内部产生 → 制作精巧的

【例】By such *ingenious* adaptations, orchids can attract insects from afar to fertilize them.

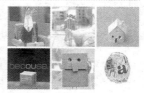

dexterous [ˈdekstrəs] *adj.* 灵巧的，熟练的(adroit; skillful)

【记】dexter(右边的) + ous → 左手和右手一样灵巧的 → 灵巧的

**crafty [ˈkræfti] *adj.* 巧妙的，狡诈的(cunning; sneaky)

【例】The spy thought of a *crafty* plan to steal the documents.

*elegant [ˈelɪɡənt] *adj.* (服饰等)雅致的(refined; exquisite; elaborate)；(举止)优雅的

【记】e(出) + leg(=lig 选) + ant → 精选出的 → 雅致的

【例】Successful women on political stage often have an *elegant* manner.

**polished [ˈpɑːlɪʃt] *adj.* 擦亮的；精练的，优美的，有教养的(highly developed, finished)

【例】The huge, *polished* wood table is neatly spread with the remains of breakfast.

【反】rustic(*adj.* 粗俗的)；untutored(*adj.* 无教养的)；gauche(*adj.* 笨拙的)

*elegance [ˈelɪɡəns] *n.* 典雅，高雅

【例】With a white gold face, blue hands and an alligator strap, it is masculine *elegance* personified.

*diaphanous [daɪˈæfənəs] *adj.* 精致的，透明的

【记】dia(通过) + phan(呈现) + ous → 透过该物体能看到对面 → 透明的

【反】opaque(*adj.* 不透明的)

*brittle [ˈbrɪtl] *adj.* 脆的，易碎的(fragile)

【例】Steel is not as *brittle* as cast iron; it doesn't break as easily.

精　确

*accuracy [ˈækjərəsi] *n.* 精确，准确(precision; exactness)

【记】ac + cur(关心) + acy → 不断关心才能保证精确 → 精确

nicety [ˈnaɪsəti] *n.* 准确，精确(precision; accuracy)；细微的区别

【记】来自nice(*adj.* 好的，精确的)

precise [prɪˈsaɪs] *adj.* (指人)周密的，精细的；精确的，清晰的(accurate; exact)

**sophisticated [səˈfɪstɪkeɪtɪd] *adj.* (仪器)精密的，复杂的(highly complicated)

【例】*sophisticated* devices used in spacecraft

数　量

*redundant [rɪˈdʌndənt] *adj.* 过多的，冗长的(unnecessary; superfluous)

replete [rɪˈpliːt] *adj.* 饱满的，充满的(fully provided; full)

【记】re + plet(满) + e → 充满的

【例】The book is *replete* with wisdom and insights.

【反】empty(*adj.* 空的)

*voluminous [vəˈluːmɪnəs] *adj.* 多卷的，长篇的；(指作家)多产的；大量的，庞大的

【记】volum(卷) + in + ous → 多卷的

【反】scanty(*adj.* 缺乏的)；scarce(*adj.* 不足的)

fraught [frɔːt] *adj.* 充满的，伴随的(full of)

【记】和freight(*n.* 装运的货物)一起记

【例】It was clearly not a job *fraught* with hope, but I have to take it for a living.

*abundant [əˈbʌndənt] *adj.* 充裕的(sufficient)

【记】a + bun(小圆面包) + d + ant(蚂蚁) → 蚂蚁有充裕的小圆面包 → 充裕的

【例】The *abundant* crops would feed the village throughout the winter.

*superfluous [suː'pɜːrfluəs] *adj.* 多余的，过剩的（exceeding what is needed）

【记】super（超过）+ flu（流）+ ous → 多得流了出来 → 多余的

【反】integral（*adj.* 构成整体所必需的）

*opulent ['ɑːpjələnt] *adj.* 富裕的（very wealthy）；充足的（profuse; luxuriant）

【记】opul（财富）+ ent → 富裕的

【派】opulence（*n.* 富裕；充足）

ample ['æmpl] *adj.* 充足的，足够的，大量的（enough; adequate）

【记】苹果（apple）在我国很充足（ample）

**myriad ['mɪriəd] *adj.* 许多的，无数的（innumerable）

【记】myria（许多）+ d → 许多的

multiform ['mʌltɪfɔːrm] *adj.* 多样的，多种形式的（diversiform; variant）

*miscellaneous [ˌmɪsə'leɪniəs] *adj.* 各种各样的，不同种类的（of various kinds）

【例】*miscellaneous* items

*incalculable [ɪn'kælkjələbl] *adj.* （数量）极大的，不可估量的，无数的（too large or great to be calculated）

【例】The scandal did *incalculable harm* to the president's reputation.

bountiful ['baʊntɪfl] *adj.* 慷慨的；丰裕的，充足的（generous; showing bounty）

【例】She distributed gifts in a *bountiful* and gracious manner.

*bumper ['bʌmpər] *adj.* 异常巨大的，较丰富的（unusually large or plentiful）

【例】a *bumper* crop/harvest

**laden ['leɪdn] *adj.* 装满的，满载的（loaded or weighted）

【例】trees *laden* with apples

**affluence ['æfluəns] *n.* 充裕，富足（an abundant flow or supply）；富裕

【记】af + flu（流）+ ence → 富得流油 → 富裕

*mint [mɪnt] *n.* 大量，巨额（钱）；造币厂

【记】mint作为"薄荷（糖）"一义大家都熟悉

【反】modicum（*n.* 微量）

plenitude ['plenɪtuːd] *n.* 充实，丰富（the condition of being complete）；大量

【例】I can feel the *plenitude* and joy during my work every day.

*profusion [prə'fjuːʒn] *n.* 丰富，充沛（abundance）

【记】来自profuse（*adj.* 丰富的，充沛的）

【例】The *profusion* of wildlife has made the Luangwa Valley a dangerous place for humans.

*abound [ə'baʊnd] *vi.* 大量存在；充满，富于

【例】Opportunity *abounds* here.

【派】abundant(*adj.* 充裕的)

*suffuse [sə'fjuːz] *vt.* 充满(to fill)

【记】suf(到处) + fus(流) + e → 到处流 → 充满

【例】His eyes were *suffused* with tears.

copious ['koʊpiəs] *adj.* 丰富的，大量的(plentiful)；(作家)多产的

glut [glʌt] *vt./n.* 过多供应；供过于求，充斥(to flood (the market) with goods so that supply exceeds demand)

【记】来自glutton(*n.* 贪吃的人)

【反】dearth(*n.* 缺乏)

scad [skæd] *n.* 许多，大量(large numbers or amounts)

【例】*Scads* of people are in the hall.

ubiquitous [juː'bɪkwɪtəs] *adj.* 无所不在的(existing or being everywhere at the same time)

【记】ubi(=where) + qu(=any) + itous → anywhere → 无所不在的

【反】unique(*a.* 独特的)

*insufficient [ˌɪnsə'fɪʃnt] *adj.* 不足的，不够的(inadaquate)

*sporadic [spə'rædɪk] *adj.* 零星的，不定时发生的(irregular; intermittent)

【例】The gunfire was *sporadic* until midnight.

*inadequate [ɪn'ædɪkwət] *adj.* 不充分的，不足的(insufficient)；不适当的

【例】The safety precautions are totally *inadequate*.

**sparsely ['spɑːrsli] *adv.* 稀少地，稀疏地(thinly; scarcely)

**paucity ['pɔːsəti] *n.* 少量，缺乏(fewness; dearth)

【记】pauc(少) + ity → 少量

【反】slew(*n.* 大量)；profusion(*n.* 丰富)

**stime [staɪm] *n.* 少量，少许(bit)

【记】来自苏格兰语和爱尔兰语

【例】Human fingerprints differ from one another and are invariant alone *stime*.

infinitesimal [ˌɪnfɪnɪ'tesɪml] *adj.* 极微小的，无限小的(infinitely small) *n.* 无穷小

【记】infinite(无穷的) + simal(看做small, 小) → 无限小的

iota [aɪ'oʊtə] *n.* 极小量，极少(a very small quantity)

【记】来自希腊语第九个字母，相当于英语中的字母i，因其位置靠后而引申为"微小"

modicum [ˈmɑːdɪkəm] *n.* 少量(a moderate or small amount)

【反】large amount(大量)

pittance [ˈpɪtns] *n.* 微薄的薪俸，少量的收入(small allowance or wage)

【记】原指"给和尚或穷人的食品施舍"，后引申为"少量津贴"

【反】cornucopia(*n.* 富饶)

*solitary [ˈsɑːləteri] *adj.* 隐居的，孤独的，独自的（lonesome; isolated）；单一的，唯一的

【记】solit(单独)+ary → 独自的

【例】He has taken a *solitary* approach to his pursuit of another basketball gold medal.

*multifaceted [ˌmʌltɪˈfæsɪtɪd] *adj.* 多层面的

【记】multi(多)+face(面)+ted → 多层面的

【例】Many countries and communities worldwide are considering how best to address this issue, which is complex and *multifaceted*.

multifarious [ˌmʌltɪˈferiəs] *adj.* （事物）多种的，各式各样的（numerous and varied）

【记】multi(多)+fari(=fact 做)+ous → 做的样子多 → 各式各样的

*sundry [ˈsʌndri] *adj.* （事物）各式各样的，杂七杂八的(miscellaneous; various)

【记】sun(太阳)+dry(干) → 太阳晒干各种东西 → 杂七杂八的

fulsome [ˈfʊlsəm] *adj.* 过度的，过多的；过分虚情假意的，过分恭维的（disgustingly insincere, excessively complimentary）

【记】ful(l)(满)+some(带有…的) → 过多的

*variegated [ˈverɪɡeɪtɪd] *adj.* 多种多样的；杂色的，斑驳的（marked irregularly with differently colored patches）

【例】This specimen is richly *variegated* in color.

**perimeter [pəˈrɪmɪtər] *n.* 周长(the boundary of a closed plane figure or the length of it)

【记】peri(周围)+meter(测量) → 周长

**triplet [ˈtrɪplət] *n.* 三胞胎中的一个

【例】His wife gave birth to *triplets*.

*multiply [ˈmʌltɪplaɪ] *v.* (使)相乘，(使)增加

bevy [ˈbevi] *n.* 一群(少女、鸟等)(a large group)

【例】The movie actor was surrounded by a *bevy* of starlets.

cornucopia [ˌkɔːrnjuˈkoʊpiə] *n.* 象征丰收的羊角(羊角装饰器内装满花、果、谷物等以示富饶)

【记】corn（玉米）+ ucopia（看做utopia，乌托邦）→ 很多玉米，美好的丰收景象 → 象征丰收的羊角

eon [ˈiːən] n.（=aeon）永世，无数的年代（long period of time; an age）
【例】It has taken *eons* for our civilization to develop.

horde [hɔːrd] n. 一大群，群；游牧部落

quorum [ˈkwɔːrəm] n. 法定最少人数（minimal number of members necessary to conduct a meeting）；被选出的一组人
【例】The senator asked for a roll call to determine whether a *quorum* was present.

sheaf [ʃiːf] n. 捆，束，扎

范　围

*inclusive [ɪnˈkluːsɪv] adj. 包含一切的，范围广的（including much or all）
【记】来自include（v. 包含，包括）

*interminable [ɪnˈtɜːrmɪnəbl] adj. 无尽头的，没完没了的（without end; lasting）
【记】in（不）+ termin（结束）+ able → 无尽头的

illimitable [ɪˈlɪmɪtəbl] adj. 无限的，无穷的
【例】He had caught a glimpse of the apparently *illimitable* vistas of knowledge.

**domain [doʊˈmeɪn] n. 领土（field; region）；领域

*dimensionality [dɪˌmenʃəˈnæləti] n. 维度；幅员，广延
【例】This high-speed flashing is not perceptible to the human eye but creates the perception of three-*dimensionality*.

extent [ɪkˈstent] n. 长度，面积，范围（length; area; range）
【例】From the roof we could see the full *extent* of the park.

**comprise [kəmˈpraɪz] vt. 包括（to constitute; contain; consist of; be made up of）
【例】The committee *comprises* seven persons.

**accommodate [əˈkɑːmədeɪt] vt. 容纳（to contain; load）；向…提供住处；使适应
【例】This elevator *accommodates* twelve people.

commodious [kəˈmoʊdiəs] adj. 宽敞的（spacious; capacious; roomy）
【记】com（共同）+ mod（范围）+ ious → 大家都有自己的空间范围 → 宽敞的

perspective [pər'spektɪv] n. (看待事物的)角度，观点(point of view); 透视法

【记】per+spect(看)+ive → 贯穿看 → 透视法

【例】I looked at everything from an entirely different *perspective*.

parish ['pærɪʃ] n. 教区；英国郡以下的行政区

communal [kə'mju:nl] adj. 全体共用的，共享的(held in common); 公共的，社区的

【记】com(共同) + mun(公共) + al → 公共的 → 全体共用的，共享的

precinct ['pri:sɪŋkt] n. 选区，(警力)管辖区(division of a city for election or police purposes); 建筑物周围的场地(space that surrounds a building)

【例】*precincts* of the college

tether ['teðər] vt. 用绳或链拴住(牲畜)(to tie an animal with a rope or tether) n. (拴牲畜的)绳或链(rope or chain); (能力、耐力等的)限度，范围(limit of one's endurance)

【反】detach(vi. 分割，分离); loose(v. 放松); tear(v. 撕破)

unilateral [ˌju:nɪ'lætrəl] adj. 单方面的，单边的；【植】单侧的

【记】uni(一个) + later(方面) + al → 单方面的

大

monumental [ˌmɑ:nju'mentl] adj. 极大的(massive; impressively large); 纪念碑的(built as a monument)

【记】monument(纪念建筑) + al → 纪念碑的

prodigious [prə'dɪdʒəs] adj. (数量)巨大的(colossal; enormous)

【记】prodig(巨大) + ious → 巨大的

【例】I have a *prodigious* amount of work to do before I leave.

mammoth ['mæməθ] adj. (体积、规模)巨大的，庞大的(gigantic; enormous)

【记】原指古代的猛犸象，十分巨大

colossal [kə'lɑ:sl] adj. 巨大的(immense; huge)

【记】源自希腊神话中名为Colossus的大力神

【例】Bill made a *colossal* mistake when he bought that used car.

**tremendous [trəˈmendəs] *adj.* (数量、程度等)巨大的，惊人的(huge; great)

**immense [ɪˈmens] *adj.* (面积、程度等)巨大的，无限的
【记】im(不) + mense(测量) → 不能测量 → 无限的

titanic [taɪˈtænɪk] *adj.* (体积、数量、力量等)巨大的(huge; immense)
【记】来自希腊神话中的提坦神(Titans)；美国影片《泰坦尼克号》英文为*Titanic*
【例】The politician tried to reduce the *titanic* deficit.

gargantuan [gɑːrˈgæntʃuən] *adj.* 巨大的，庞大的(of tremendous size or volume)
【记】来自法国作家拉伯雷《巨人传》中的巨人名字Gargantua

【反】minuscule(*adj.* 极小的)

monolithic [ˌmɑːnəˈlɪθɪk] *adj.* 独块巨石的；巨大的(huge; massive)
【记】mono(单个) + lith(石头) + ic → 独块巨石的

*expansive [ɪkˈspænsɪv] *adj.* 广阔的，辽阔的(extensive; large)；可扩张的，可膨胀的；广泛的
【记】来自expand(*v.* 扩张，展开，膨胀)
【例】The book's *expansive* index listed hundreds of important items.

*oceanic [ˌoʊʃiˈænɪk] *adj.* 海洋的；广阔无垠的
【例】An *oceanic* white tip shark injured three Russians and a Ukrainian earlier this week.

capacious [kəˈpeɪʃəs] *adj.* 容量大的；宽敞的，宽广的(spacious)

*boundless [ˈbaʊndləs] *adj.* 无限的(limitless)
【记】bound(边界；限制) + less(少，无) → 无限的

peerless [ˈpɪrləs] *adj.* 无与伦比的(matchless; unparalleled)
【记】peer(同等) + less(少，无) → 无相提并论者 → 无与伦比的

*overwhelming [ˌoʊvərˈwelmɪŋ] *adj.* 压倒性的，势不可挡的(so strong as to be irresistible)
【例】Their dominance was *overwhelming* and they outshot their opponents 38-11 in the first two periods.

*mountainous [ˈmaʊntənəs] *adj.* 多山的(full of mountains)；像山一般的，巨大的(very large)
【记】mountain(山) + ous → 多山的

impregnable [ɪmˈpregnəbl] *adj.* 攻不破的，征服不了的(not capable of being captured or entered by force)
【记】im(不) + pregn(拿住) + able(能) → 拿不住的 → 征服不了的

小

*minuscule ['mɪnəskjuːl] *adj.* 极小的(tiny); 小写字的
【记】min(小) + uscule → 极小的

*minimal ['mɪnɪməl] *adj.* （量或程度）最小的, 最低的 （smallest in amount or degree）
【例】We stayed with friends, so our expenses were *minimal*.

slight [slaɪt] *adj.* 少量的, 微小的(tiny; microscopic); 微不足道的

minute [maɪ'njuːt] *adj.* 微小的(tiny; minuscule)
【记】min(小) + ute → 微小的

*diminutive [dɪ'mɪnjətɪv] *adj.* 微小的(small; tiny) *n.* 微小的人或物
【记】di + min(小) + utive → 微小的
【例】The child placed the cute, *diminutive* furniture in a dollhouse.

granulate ['grænjuleɪt] *vt.* 使成颗粒状; 使表面粗糙

*granular ['grænjələr] *adj.* (似)粒状的, 含颗粒的(like, containing or consisting of small hard pieces)
【例】a *granular* substance

lilliputian [ˌlɪlɪ'pjuːʃn] *adj.* 微型的, 极小的(on a small scale; tiny)
【例】a model railway layout peopled with *lilliputian* figures

trifling ['traɪflɪŋ] *adj.* 微小的, 不重要的(insignificant; trivial)
【记】来自trifle(*n.* 小事, 琐事; 少量)

trivial ['trɪviəl] *adj.* 琐碎的, 微不足道的(unimportant; trifling)
【例】I didn't bother Bob with my *trivial* concerns because he was busy.

*nuance ['nuːɑːns] *n.* 细微的差异
【反】patent difference(明显的差异)

*negligible ['neglɪdʒəbl] *adj.* 可以忽略的, 不予重视的(insignificant; minimal)
【记】来自neglect(*vt.* 忽视, 忽略)

*feeble ['fiːbl] *adj.* 微弱的(weak; infirm); 虚弱的, 衰弱的

paltry ['pɔːltri] *adj.* 无价值的, 微不足道的(trashy; trivial; petty)
【记】pal(=pale 白) + try(努力) → 白努力 → 无价值的
【反】significant(*adj.* 重要的)

ignoble [ɪg'nəʊbl] *adj.* 卑微的, 低下的(despicable; dishonorable)
【记】ig(不) + noble(高贵) → 卑微的

*petty ['peti] *adj.* 琐碎的(trivial; unimportant)；气量小的

【派】petty-minded(*adj.* 心胸狭窄的)

*minimize ['mɪnɪmaɪz] *vt.* 把…减至最小数量或最低程度

【反】exaggerate(*vt.* 夸大)；overestimate(*vt.* 高估)；inflate(*v.* 膨胀，扩大)

*trivialize ['trɪvɪəlaɪz] *vt.* 使琐碎；使平凡

【记】来自trivial(*adj.* 琐碎的)

【例】Does that *trivialize* the serious work of electing a leader of the free world?

*tenuous ['tenjuəs] *adj.* 纤细的；稀薄的(thin; weak)

【记】ten(细，薄)+ uous → 纤细的；稀薄的

【例】The precious jewel was hung only with a *tenuous* thread that appeared very fragile.

空

*void [vɔɪd] *adj.* 空的(invalid; null) *n.* 真空，空白；空虚感

【例】His wife's death left a painful *void* in his life.

*vacant ['veɪkənt] *adj.* 空的；未被占用的(unoccupied; empty)

【记】vac(空)+ ant → 空的

*vacuum ['vækjuəm] *n.* 真空(gap; void)；空虚

*insubstantial [ˌɪnsəb'stænʃl] *adj.* 非实体的(immaterial)；薄弱的(frail)

【记】in(不)+ substantial(坚固的，实质的) → 非实体的

纯

*sheer [ʃɪr] *adj.* 纯粹的，全然的(pure; total)

【例】Don't believe him; his words are *sheer* nonsense.

*impeccable [ɪm'pekəbl] *adj.* 无瑕的，无懈可击的(faultless; stainless)

【记】im(无)+ pecc(斑点)+ able → 无瑕的

chaste [tʃeɪst] *adj.* 贞洁的，纯正的(pure; virtuous)

【例】The students were advised to remain *chaste* until marriage.

virtuous ['vɜːrtʃuəs] *adj.* 贞洁的；善良正直的(moral; righteous)

pellucid [pə'luːsɪd] *adj.* 清晰的，清澈的（transparent; clear）

【记】pel(=per 全部) + lucid(清澈的) → 清澈的

【反】murky(*adj.* 模糊的)

*translucent [træns'luːsnt] *adj.* 半透明的

**stainless ['steɪnləs] *adj.* 不锈的；纯洁的，无瑕疵的（pure）

旧

*outmoded [ˌaʊt'məʊdɪd] *adj.* 不再流行的，过时的（no longer in fashion; obsolete）

【记】out(出) + mode(时尚，流行) + d → 不再流行的

【反】original(*adj.* 创新的)

cliché [kliː'ʃeɪ] *adj.* 陈腐的 *n.* 陈词滥调（phrase or idea which is used so often that it has become stale or meaningless）

【例】Compositions are often marred by such *cliché*s as "strong as an ox".
// *Cliché* is a feature of bad journalism.

*fossilize ['fɑːsəlaɪz] *vt.* 使…成为化石（to cause sth to become a fossil）；使…过时(to make sth out of date)

【记】来自fossil(*n.* 化石)

*timeworn ['taɪmwɔːrn] *adj.* 陈旧的，老朽的（hackneyed; stale）

【记】time(时间) + worn(陈旧的) → 老朽的

Without wood a fire goes out; without gossip a quarrel dies down.

火缺了柴，就必熄灭。无人传舌，争竞便止息。

——《圣经·旧·箴》26:20

练 习 题

填空题

abundant	accuracy	communal	comprise	domain
fulsome	impeccable	incalculable	inclusive	ingenious
insufficient	minimal	miscellaneous	monumental	overwhelming
polished	redundant	sheer	vacant	void

1. She's very _____ when it comes to finding excuses.
2. She gave a _____ performance on the piano.
3. She hits the ball with great _____.
4. The picture has too much _____ detail.
5. We have _____ evidence to prove his guilt.
6. She gave me some money to cover any _____ expenses.
7. The oil spill has caused _____ damage to the environment.
8. There are fears that the existing flood barrier may prove _____.
9. He was _____ in his praise of the Prime Minister.
10. The rent is _____ of water and heating.
11. The care of older people is being placed firmly within the _____ of the family.
12. The committee is _____ of representatives from both the public and private sectors.
13. The property was owned _____.
14. We must act now to avert a disaster of _____ proportions.
15. The _____ majority of those present were in favour of the plan.
16. The work was carried out at _____ cost.
17. Her face was _____ of all interest.
18. The seat next to him was _____.
19. We were impressed by the _____ size of the cathedral.
20. Her written English is _____.

配对题

1. dexterous	慷慨的; 丰裕的	11. interminable	多种的, 各式各样的
2. elegant	宽敞的	12. extent	准确, 精确
3. voluminous	灵巧的, 熟练的	13. commodious	海洋的; 广阔无垠的
4. nicety	(服饰等)雅致的	14. precinct	选区, (警力)管辖区
5. sophisticated	长度, 面积, 范围	15. mammoth	饱满的, 充满的
6. replete	多卷的, 长篇的	16. oceanic	少量的, 微小的
7. superfluous	(似)粒状的, 含颗粒的	17. impregnable	(仪器)精密的
8. bountiful	攻不破的, 征服不了的	18. slight	稀少地, 稀疏地
9. sparsely	无尽头的	19. granular	多余的, 过剩的
10. multifarious	(体积、规模)巨大的, 庞大的	20. trivial	琐碎的, 微不足道的

练习题答案

填空题答案

1. She's very <u>ingenious</u> when it comes to finding excuses.
2. She gave a <u>polished</u> performance on the piano.
3. She hits the ball with great <u>accuracy</u>.
4. The picture has too much <u>redundant</u> detail.
5. We have <u>abundant</u> evidence to prove his guilt.
6. She gave me some money to cover any <u>miscellaneous</u> expenses.
7. The oil spill has caused <u>incalculable</u> damage to the environment.
8. There are fears that the existing flood barrier may prove <u>insufficient</u>.
9. He was <u>fulsome</u> in his praise of the Prime Minister.
10. The rent is <u>inclusive</u> of water and heating.
11. The care of older people is being placed firmly within the <u>domain</u> of the family.
12. The committee is <u>comprised</u> of representatives from both the public and private sectors.
13. The property was owned <u>communally</u>.
14. We must act now to avert a disaster of <u>monumental</u> proportions.
15. The <u>overwhelming</u> majority of those present were in favour of the plan.
16. The work was carried out at <u>minimal</u> cost.
17. Her face was <u>void</u> of all interest.
18. The seat next to him was <u>vacant</u>.
19. We were impressed by the <u>sheer</u> size of the cathedral.
20. Her written English is <u>impeccable</u>.

配对题答案

1. dexterous	灵巧的，熟练的	11. interminable	无尽头的
2. elegant	（服饰等）雅致的	12. extent	长度，面积，范围
3. voluminous	多卷的，长篇的	13. commodious	宽敞的
4. nicety	准确，精确	14. precinct	选区，（警力）管辖区
5. sophisticated	（仪器）精密的	15. mammoth	（体积、规模）巨大的，庞大的
6. replete	饱满的，充满的	16. oceanic	海洋的；广阔无垠的
7. superfluous	多余的，过剩的	17. impregnable	攻不破的，征服不了的
8. bountiful	慷慨的；丰裕的	18. slight	少量的，微小的
9. sparsely	稀少地，稀疏地	19. granular	（似）粒状的，含颗粒的
10. multifarious	多种的，各式各样的	20. trivial	琐碎的，微不足道的

Word List 22
属性（三）

整 洁

immaculate [ɪˈmækjələt] *adj.* 洁净的，无瑕的（perfectly clean; unsoiled; impeccable）
【记】im(不) + macul(斑点) + ate → 无斑点的

sanitary [ˈsænəteri] *adj.* 卫生的，清洁的

**slippery [ˈslɪpəri] *adj.* 滑的，容易使人滑跤的（slick; smooth）

natty [ˈnæti] *adj.* 整洁的，潇洒的（neatly or trimly smart）
【反】sloppy(*adj.* 邋遢的)

prim [prɪm] *adj.* 端庄的，整洁的（neat; trim; decorous）
【记】本身是词根prim(最初的，最好的)
【例】She's much too *prim* and proper to enjoy such a rude joke.

肮 脏

rubbish

*grubby [ˈgrʌbi] *adj.* 肮脏的，不洁的（dirty; unwashed）
【例】*grubby* hands 脏手

seamy [ˈsiːmi] *adj.* 污秽的，恶劣的（unpleasant; degraded; sordid）；有缝的
【记】seam(缝) + y → 有缝的
【反】decent and respectable(体面而值得尊敬的)

*dingy [ˈdɪndʒi] *adj.* 肮脏的，邋遢的（dirty-looking）；无生气的，无光泽的（not cheerful or bright; drab）；暗淡的，昏黑的
【例】a *dingy* room in a cheap hotel

*muddy [ˈmʌdi] *adj.* 多泥的（full of or covered with mud）；浑浊的，不纯的（lacking in clarity or brightness）
【记】来自mud(*n.* 泥，泥泞)

*foul [faʊl] *adj.* 肮脏的，污浊的；恶臭的，（食物）腐败的（stinking; loathsome）；邪恶的（very wicked） *vt.* 弄脏（to soil; defile） *n.* （体育等）犯规（an infraction of the rules, as of a game or sport）

*squalid [ˈskwɑːlɪd] *adj.* 污秽的，肮脏的，邋遢的 （filthy and degraded from neglect or poverty）
【反】pristine（*adj.* 纯洁的）

*blemish [ˈblemɪʃ] *n.* 污点，污垢；瑕疵，缺点 *vt.* 玷污；使有缺点 （to defect; flaw）
【记】blem（弄伤）+ ish → 使有缺点
【例】One illness will *blemish* your perfect attendance record.

*sully [ˈsʌli] *vt.* 玷污，污染（to make soiled or tarnished）；败坏，使受损
【例】His reputation is *sullied* by many crimes.

defile [dɪˈfaɪl] *vt.* 污损（to contaminate）；败坏，玷污
【记】de + file（=vile卑鄙）→ 玷污
【例】Watching too many violent TV shows *defiled* the child's mind.

bedraggle [bɪˈdrægl] *vt.* 拖脏，弄湿（to wet thoroughly）

*taint [teɪnt] *vt.* 玷污，败坏；使感染，使腐败（to corrupt） *n.* （道德）污点（a moral defect）；感染

dowdy [ˈdaʊdi] *adj.* 不整洁的，过旧的 （not neat or stylish; shabby）

grimy [ˈɡraɪmi] *adj.* 肮脏的，污秽的（dirty; filthy）
【记】来自grime（*n.* 污点，污垢）
【例】Of the 100 riel notes in circulation, many are old, *grimy* and beginning to deteriorate.

hovel [ˈhʌvl] *n.* 茅舍；肮脏的小屋（any small, miserable dwelling; hut）

*unpolished [ˌʌnˈpɑːlɪʃt] *adj.* 无光泽的，未擦亮的（crude）；未经润饰的
【例】He was a challenging guy, and his *unpolished*, idiosyncratic songs weren't easily digested.

insalubrious [ˌɪnsəˈluːbriəs] *adj.* 有损健康的，不卫生的（unhealthy）
【记】in(不) + salu(健康，卫生) + brious → 不卫生的
【例】*insalubrious* alleys and slums

seedy [ˈsiːdi] *adj.* 破旧的，破烂的 （run-down; decrepit; disreputable）；多籽的（having many seeds）
【例】I would rather stay in dormitory lodgings in a decent youth hostel than have a room of my own in a *seedy* downtown hotel.

squalor [ˈskwɑːlər] *n.* 不洁，污秽（的状况）（state of being squalid）

【记】来自squalid(*adj.* 肮脏的，污秽的)；发音似"四筐烂儿" → 四筐破烂儿 → 污秽

turbid [ˈtɜːrbɪd] *adj.* (水等)浑浊的，不清的（opaque or muddy; not clear）；紊乱的，混乱的（disordered or confused）

【例】the *turbid* floodwaters of the river // a *turbid* imagination

unkempt [ˌʌnˈkempt] *adj.* (衣服、头发等)不整洁的（messy; not combed）

【记】来自kempt(*adj.* 整洁的)

【反】dapper(*adj.* 整洁的)

*jagged [ˈdʒægɪd] *adj.* 锯齿状的，不整齐的（notched or ragged）

【记】jag(齿状) + ged → 锯齿状的

threadbare [ˈθredber] *adj.* (衣服)磨破的，穿旧的（worn off; shabby）；陈腐的（exhausted of interest or freshness）

【记】thread(线) + bare(露出) → 露出线头 → (衣服)磨破的

*obscene [əbˈsiːn] *adj.* 猥亵的（indecent; filthy）

【记】ob(不) + scene(场景) → 场景不堪入目的 → 猥亵的

*indecent [ɪnˈdiːsnt] *adj.* 不适当的，不礼貌的（improper; unacceptable）；污秽的，下流的

【记】in(不) + decent(合乎礼仪的) → 不礼貌的

salacious [səˈleɪʃəs] *adj.* (指言语、书籍、图画等) 猥亵的，污秽的（indecent; lewd）

*sanitize [ˈsænɪtaɪz] *vt.* 对…作卫生处理（to make a place hygienic）；审查，净化

【例】They've *sanitized* my report on army atrocities.

stigmatize [ˈstɪgmətaɪz] *vt.* 污蔑，玷污（to describe opprobrious terms）

【记】stigma(*n.* 耻辱的标志，污点)

dappled [ˈdæpld] *adj.* 有斑点的，斑驳的 （covered with spots of a different color）

【记】d + apple + d → 苹果上有斑点 → 有斑点的

sordid [ˈsɔːrdɪd] *adj.* 卑鄙的（marked by baseness）；肮脏的（dirty; filthy）

【记】发音似"扫地的" → 肮脏的

【例】*sordid* shantytowns

stigma [ˈstɪgmə] *n.* 耻辱的标志，污点（a mark of shame or discredit）

【反】mark of esteem(尊敬的标志)

模　糊

*ambiguous [æmˈbɪgjuəs] *adj.* 含糊的，不明确的（not clear; uncertain; vague）

【记】ambi(二) + guous(做…的) → 两件事都想做 → 含糊的

【反】watershed(*n.* 分水岭；转折点)

【派】ambiguity(*n.* 含糊不清)

subliminal [sʌbˈlɪmɪnl] *adj.* 潜意识的（existing or functioning below the threshold of consciousness）

【记】sub(下面) + limin(刺激阈) + al → 位于刺激阈下面的 → 潜意识的

【反】at a perceptible level(在感觉层次上)

subtlety [ˈsʌtlti] *n.* 隐约难辨，微妙；细微的差别

【例】The *subtlety* of his remarks was unnoticed by most of his audience.

*loom [luːm] *vi.* （威胁性地）隐约出现（to come into view in a massive and indistinct image）*n.* 织布机

【记】房间(room)里面有台织布机(loom)

【例】A gigantic image *loomed* in the room.

oracular [əˈrækjələr] *adj.* 意义模糊的，晦涩的 (obscure; enigmatic)；神谕的(of an oracle)

明　显

*overt [oʊˈvɜːrt] *adj.* 明显的，公然的

transcendent [trænˈsendənt] *adj.* 超越的，卓越的，出众的 (extremely great; supreme)

unobtrusive [ˌʌnəbˈtruːsɪv] *adj.* 不引人注目的(not very noticeable or easily seen)；不唐突的，不冒昧的

【记】un + obtrusive(突出的) → 不引人注目的

【反】blatant(*adj.* 显眼的)

titular [ˈtɪtʃələr] *adj.* 有名无实的，名义上的(existing in title only)

【记】只有个头衔(title)没有实权，可谓有名无实(titular)

**palpable [ˈpælpəbl] *adj.* 可触知的，明显的(tangible; perceptible; noticeable)

【记】palp(摸) + able(能) → 摸得到的 → 可触知的，明显的

【反】subtle(*adj.* 微妙的)

marked [mɑːrkt] *adj.* 有标记的；明显的，显著的（having a distinctive character）；被监视的（being an object of suspicion）

【记】mark(标记) + ed → 有标记的

salient [ˈseɪliənt] *adj.* 凸出的；显著的，突出的（noticeable; conspicuous; prominent）

【记】sal(跳) + ient → 跳起来 → 突出的

【反】unconspicuous(*adj.* 不引人注意的)

**emphatic [ɪmˈfætɪk] *adj.* 强调的，着重的；有力的（powerful）

【记】来自emphasize(*vt.* 强调)

【例】The supervisor's *emphatic* speech on worker productivity produced amazing results.

*compendious [kəmˈpendiəs] *adj.* 扼要的，简明的（giving a lot of information briefly）

【例】a *compendious* writer

*unmistakable [ˌʌnmɪˈsteɪkəbl] *adj.* 明白无误的，不会弄错的（recognizable; obvious）

【例】the *unmistakable* sound of an approaching train

*explicit [ɪkˈsplɪsɪt] *adj.* 明确的，清楚的（straightforward）

【例】The new tax law is *explicit*; that type of certificate is tax exempt.

*unremarkable [ˌʌnrɪˈmɑːrkəbl] *adj.* 平凡的，不显著的，不值得注意的

【例】Rove looks as *unremarkable* as his surroundings: an owlish fellow with a clipped professorial manner.

*unequivocal [ˌʌnɪˈkwɪvəkl] *adj.* 只有一种含义的，清楚明白的（clear and unmistakable）

【例】an *unequivocal* attitude

**crystallize [ˈkrɪstəlaɪz] *v.* (思想、计划等)清晰而具体化(to cause ideas, plans, etc to become clear and definite)

【例】His vague ideas *crystallized* into a definite plan.

definitive [dɪˈfɪnətɪv] *adj.* 明确的，有权威的（clear and having final authority）

【记】来自define(*vt.* 规定，使明确)

【反】provisional(*adj.* 临时的)

*exceeding [ɪkˈsiːdɪŋ] *adj.* 超越的，非常的；过度的

*laconic [ləˈkɑːnɪk] *adj.* (说话)简洁的，简明的（brief or terse in speech or expression; concise）

【记】来自古希腊王国Laconia(拉哥尼亚)，该国以说话简洁而闻名

【反】garrulous(*adj.* 多嘴的)；verbose(*adj.* 冗长的)；loquacious(*adj.* 多话的)；voluble(*adj.* 多话的)

latent [ˈleɪtnt] *adj.* 潜伏的（present but invisible; dormant; quiescent）

【记】有些病到(late)晚期才表现出来 → 潜伏的

transparent [trænsˈpærənt] *adj.* 透明的（clear; limpid）

【例】The sunset shined through the *transparent* glass.

legible [ˈledʒəbl] *adj.* 易读的（capable of being read easily）

【记】leg(读) + ible(能) → 易读的

downright [ˈdaʊnraɪt] *adj.* （指不喜欢的事物）彻底的，十足的，完全的（thorough; complete）；率直的，直截了当的

【例】a *downright* lie

*undecipherable [ˌʌndɪˈsaɪfərəbl] *adj.* 难辨认的，破译不出的

【例】"A-a-a-a-absolutely," spluttered Richardson, before winding up the interview with a question about the World Cup—the answer to which was *undecipherable*.

程　度

*egregious [ɪˈgriːdʒiəs] *adj.* （缺点等）过分的，惊人的（conspicuously bad; flagrant）

【记】e(出) + greg(团体，大众) + ious → 超出一般人 → 过分的

*dissolute [ˈdɪsəluːt] *adj.* 放荡的，无节制的（dissipated and immoral; profligate）

【记】dis(分开) + solute(溶解) → （精力）完全溶解掉 → 放荡的；注意不要和dissoluble(*adj.* 可溶解的)相混

*overly [ˈoʊvərli] *adv.* 过度地，极度地

【例】*overly* protective

exorbitant [ɪgˈzɔːrbɪtənt] *adj.* （要求、收费等）过分的，不合理的（excessive; unreasonable）

【例】I will not pay such an *exorbitant* price for these shoes!

*overdo [ˌoʊvərˈduː] *vt.* 将…做得过分，使…表现得过火（to exaggerate）

【例】She rather *overdid* the sympathy.

*overeat [ˌoʊvərˈiːt] *v.* (使)吃得过多（to eat more than one needs or more than is healthy）

【例】I *overate* at the party last night and got violent indigestion.

*overemphasize [ˌoʊvərˈemfəsaɪz] *vt.* 过分强调

【例】The President didn't *overemphasize* weapons of mass destruction as the only reason to go into Iraq.

*overreaction [ˌoʊvərɪˈækʃn] *n.* 过度反应

【例】It's not an *overreaction* to say we must make more sure those children are safe.

*overuse [ˌoʊvərˈjuːz] *vt./n.* 使用过度

【例】*Overuse* of antibiotics has made some strains tough to fight when they cause illness.

*overwrought [ˌoʊvərˈrɔːt] *adj.* 紧张过度的，过度兴奋的（very nervous or excited）

【记】over(过分) + wrought(兴奋的，精神的) → 过度兴奋的

unconscionable [ʌnˈkɑːnʃənəbl] *adj.* 昧着良心的，无理的；无节制的，过分的（excessive; unreasonable）

【记】un(不) + conscionable(合乎良心的) → 昧着良心的

*inordinate [ɪnˈɔːrdɪnət] *adj.* 无节制的，过度的（excessive; immoderate）；无规则的，紊乱的

【记】in(不) + ordin(正常) + ate → 过度的

*immoderate [ɪˈmɑːdərət] *adj.* 过度的，无节制的（extreme; excessive）

【例】*immoderate* eating/drinking habits

*blinking [ˈblɪŋkɪŋ] *adj.* 〈俚〉讨厌的，十足的（bloody）

【例】It's a *blinking* nuisance. 令人讨厌的事拖：人，く3る

*surfeit [ˈsɜːrfɪt] *n.* 过量，过度（an overabundant supply; excess）；饮食过量 *vt.* 使厌腻；使饮食过量

【记】sur(过分) + feit(做) → 做过了头 → 过度

【反】famish(*vt.* 使挨饿)；starve(*vt.* 使挨饿)；deprivation(*n.* 缺乏)；insufficient supply(供应不足)；deficiency(*n.* 不足)

*pamper [ˈpæmpər] *vt.* 纵容，过分关怀，娇养（to treat with excess or extreme care）

【记】比较记忆：hamper(*vt.* 妨碍)；tamper(*vt.* 损害，窜改)；camper(*n.* 露营者)

plethora [ˈpleθərə] *n.* 过量，过剩（excess; superfluity）

【记】pleth(满) + ora(嘴) → 嘴都塞满了 → 过剩

【反】dearth(*n.* 缺乏)；scarcity(*n.* 缺乏)

rhapsodize [ˈræpsədaɪz] *v.* 狂热地写或说；过分赞美（to speak or write in an exaggeratedly enthusiastic manner）

【例】She greatly enjoyed her Hawaiian vacation and *rhapsodized* about it for weeks.

*fervent [ˈfɜːrvənt] *adj.* 白热的；强烈的，热烈的(ardent)

【记】ferv(热) + ent → 热烈的

【例】Jenny is a *fervent* supporter of the feminist movement.

abysmal [əˈbɪzməl] *adj.* 极深的，深不可测的 (bottomless; unfathomable)；糟透的(wretched; immeasurably bad)

【记】来自abyss(*n.* 深渊，深坑)

absolute [ˈæbsəluːt] *adj.* 绝对的(sheer)

【记】和solute(*n.* 化学溶质)一起记

【例】The Prime Minister had *absolute* control of his cabinet.

*categorical [ˌkætəˈɡɔːrɪkl] *adj.* 绝对的，无条件的 (definite; positive; absolute; unconditional)

【例】The Japanese made a *categorical* surrendering to China in 1945 after 8 years of invasion.

substantial [səbˈstænʃl] *adj.* 相当的，大量的(plentiful; considerable)

【例】Mary has a *substantial* amount of money in the bank.

*utmost [ˈʌtmoʊst] *adj.* 最大的；最远的；极度的 (greatest; furthest; most extreme)

【例】in the *utmost* danger

*maturity [məˈtʃʊrəti] *n.* 成熟，完备(state of being mature)

*profoundly [prəˈfaʊndli] *adv.* 深刻地，深度地(deeply; greatly)

【记】来自profound(*adj.* 深刻的，深度的)

【例】Television programs with written subtitles help those *profoundly* deaf people to understand the world.

rampant [ˈræmpənt] *adj.* 繁茂的，蔓生的；猖獗的 (marked by a menacing wildness or absence of restraint)

【记】ram(羊) + pant(喘气) → 因为草生长猖獗，所以羊高兴得直喘气 → 猖獗的

**vehement [ˈviːəmənt] *adj.* 猛烈的，激烈的；感情热烈的(passionate; ardent)

unmitigated [ʌnˈmɪtɪɡeɪtɪd] *adj.* 未缓和的，未减轻的 (not lessoned or excused in any way)；全然的，十足的

【记】来自mitigate(*v.* 缓和，减轻)

exhaustive [ɪgˈzɔːstɪv] *adj.* 无遗漏的，彻底的，详尽的（comprehensive; thorough）

【例】The real-estate agent gave the prospective buyers an *exhaustive* tour of the new house.

*stark [stɑːrk] *adj.* 鲜明的，突出的；完全的（utter; sheer）

$stark\ spain$

【记】和start(*v.* 开始)一起记

【例】*stark* contrast // The firm got *stark* development.

**wondrous [ˈwʌndrəs] *adj.* 奇妙的，令人惊奇的，非常的（wonderful）

【例】No phenomenon illustrates this more clearly than the *wondrous*, illogical beast known as The Summer Jam.

*verbose [vɜːrˈboʊs] *adj.* 冗长的，啰嗦的 （containing more words than necessary）

【记】verb(词语) + ose(多…的) → 多词的 → 冗长的

【反】laconic(*adj.* 简洁的)

*consummate [ˈkɑːnsəmət] *adj.* 完全的，完善的 （complete or perfect）*vt.* 完成，实现(to finish; accomplish)

【记】con(共同) + sum(总数) + mate → 总数的，全数的 → 完全的

【派】consummation(*n.* 达到极点，完成)

**intact [ɪnˈtækt] *adj.* 完整的，未动过的(unimpaired; complete)

【记】in(不) + tact(接触) → 未接触过 → 完整的

【反】riven(*adj.* 被撕裂的)

*criterion [kraɪˈtɪriən] *n.* (*pl.* criteria)评判的标准，尺度

【记】crit(判断) + er(看做err, 错误) + ion → 判断对错的标准 → 评判的标准，尺度

**comprehensive [ˌkɑːmprɪˈhensɪv] *adj.* 综合的，广泛的；有理解力的

【例】A *comprehensive* survey was used to determine public opinion.

officious [əˈfɪʃəs] *adj.* 爱发命令的，好忠告的 （too ready or willing to give orders or advice）；过度殷勤的(meddlesome)

【记】来自officer(*n.* 官员)

【反】politic(*adj.* 慎重的，有策略的)

poignancy [ˈpɔɪnjənsi] *n.* 辛辣，尖锐

【记】来自poignant(*adj.* 尖锐的，切中要害的)

sophomoric [ˌsɒfəˈmɔːrɪk] *adj.* 大学二年级的；一知半解的，浅陋的(immature; shallow)

【例】The *sophomoric* students were playing an interesting game.

肯 定

**infallible [ɪnˈfæləbl] *adj.* 必然的，绝对不会错的

【记】in(无) + fall(跌倒) + ible(能) → 不会跌倒 → 绝对不会错的

*inevitable [ɪnˈevɪtəbl] *adj.* 不可避免的，必然的(unavoidable; certain)

【例】Death is the *inevitable* ending of life.

indubitable [ɪnˈdjuːbɪtəbl] *adj.* 不容置疑的(unquestionable)

【记】in(不) + dubit(怀疑) + able → 不容置疑的

【反】questionable(*adj.* 可疑的)

indisputable [ˌɪndɪˈspjuːtəbl] *adj.* 不容置疑的，无可否认的 (that cannot be disputed or denied)

【记】in(不) + disput(e)(质疑) + able → 不容置疑的

【例】One fact is *indisputable*: the essence of America is free enterprise and human rights.

*undeniable [ˌʌndɪˈnaɪəbl] *adj.* 无可争辩的，不可否认的 (plainly true)

【记】un(不) + deni(=deny否认) + able → 不可否认的

【例】His charm is *undeniable*, but I still mistrust him.

*undoubtedly [ʌnˈdaʊtɪdli] *adv.* 毋庸置疑地，的确(unquestionably; surely)

*justifiable [ˈdʒʌstɪfaɪəbl] *adj.* 有理由的，无可非议的(capable of being justified or defended as correct)

【记】来自justify(*vt.* 证明…是正当的)

*tenable [ˈtenəbl] *adj.* 站得住脚的，无懈可击的(defensible; reasonable)

【记】ten(拿住) + able → 能够拿住的 → 站得住脚的

【反】unjustified(*adj.* 未经证明的); unsound(*adj.* 靠不住的)

*affirmation [ˌæfərˈmeɪʃn] *n.* 断言，主张，肯定(positive assertion; confirmation)

*certitude [ˈsɜːrtɪtuːd] *n.* 确定无疑(certainty of act or event)

【记】cert(确定) + itude(状态) → 确定无疑

*undocumented [ʌnˈdɑːkjumentɪd] *adj.* 无事实证明的，无正式文件的

【例】*undocumented* income tax deductions // *undocumented* accusations

**yea [jeɪ] *adv.* 是的，确实是 *n.* 肯定，赞成；赞成票

*infallibility [ɪnfæləˈbɪlɪti] *n.* 绝无错误，无过失

【记】来自infallible(*adj.* 绝对不会错的)

【例】He remained loyal to Rome but still questioned some church doctrines, including papal *infallibility*.

encomium [en'koʊmiəm] *n.* 赞颂，颂辞（eulogy; panegyric）

【记】en（进来）+ com（=come来）+ ium → 进来说好话 → 赞颂

【反】diatribe（*n.* 恶骂）; harsh criticism（严厉批评）

【派】encomiast（*n.* 赞扬者；阿谀奉承者）; encomiastic（*adj.* 赞颂的，赞颂者的；阿谀的）

*ascertain [ˌæsər'teɪn] *vt.* 确定（to determine; make sure）

【记】as + certain（确信）→ 确定

【例】Did the doctor *ascertain* the cause of your sickness?

*indeterminate [ˌɪndɪ't3ːrmɪnət] *adj.* 不确定的，不明确的（not clearly seen as, or not fixed as）

【记】in（不）+ determin(e)（确定）+ ate → 不确定的

*discretionary [dɪ'skreʃəneri] *adj.* 自由决定的（left to one's own discretion or judgement）

【反】obligatory（*adj.* 强制性的）; preordained（*adj.* 预先决定的）

It is to his glory to overlook an offense.
宽恕人的过失，便是自己的荣耀。

——《圣经·旧·箴》19:11

练 习 题

填空题

blemish	consummate	criterion	crystallize	definitive
exorbitant	foul	inordinate	loom	overemphasize
palpable	pamper	sanitary	slippery	squalor
subtlety	sully	surfeit	unmistakable	unobtrusive

1. In places the path can be wet and _____.
2. Overcrowding and poor _____ conditions led to disease in the refugee camps.
3. _____ drinking water was blamed for the epidemic.
4. His reputation is without a _____.
5. By cheating they have _____ the good name of their country.
6. He had lost his job and was living in _____.
7. Some of the _____ of the language are lost in translation.
8. A dark shape _____ up ahead of us.
9. The service at the hotel is efficient and _____.
10. His statement is _____ nonsense.
11. Her accent was _____.
12. Our ideas began to _____ into a definite plan.
13. The _____ version of the text is ready to be published.
14. It's a good hotel but the prices are _____.
15. In the past the exam had been _____.
16. They spent an _____ amount of time and money on the production.
17. Indigestion can be brought on by a _____ of rich food.
18. _____ yourself with our new range of beauty treatments.
19. What _____ are used for assessing a student's ability?
20. He played the shot with _____ skill.

配对题

1. immaculate	含糊的, 不明确的	11. transcendent	明显的, 公然的
2. prim	讨厌的, 十足的	12. titular	过量, 过剩
3. grubby	扼要的, 简明的	13. compendious	端庄的, 整洁的
4. defile	污损; 败坏, 玷污	14. unequivocal	破旧的, 破烂的
5. seedy	放荡的, 无节制的	15. transparent	耻辱的标志, 污点
6. turbid	肮脏的, 不洁的	16. dissolute	有名无实的, 名义上的
7. obscene	洁净的, 无瑕的	17. overly	超越的, 卓越的
8. stigma	猥亵的	18. overreaction	透明的
9. ambiguous	过度地, 极度地	19. blinking	浑浊的, 不清的
10. overt	过度反应	20. plethora	只有一种含义的, 清楚明白的

练习题答案

填空题答案

1. In places the path can be wet and <u>slippery</u>.
2. Overcrowding and poor <u>sanitary</u> conditions led to disease in the refugee camps.
3. <u>Foul</u> drinking water was blamed for the epidemic.
4. His reputation is without a <u>blemish</u>.
5. By cheating they have <u>sullied</u> the good name of their country.
6. He had lost his job and was living in <u>squalor</u>.
7. Some of the <u>subtleties</u> of the language are lost in translation.
8. A dark shape <u>loomed</u> up ahead of us.
9. The service at the hotel is efficient and <u>unobtrusive</u>.
10. His statement is <u>palpable</u> nonsense.
11. Her accent was <u>unmistakable</u>.
12. Our ideas began to <u>crystallize</u> into a definite plan.
13. The <u>definitive</u> version of the text is ready to be published.
14. It's a good hotel but the prices are <u>exorbitant</u>.
15. In the past the exam had been <u>overemphasized</u>.
16. They spent an <u>inordinate</u> amount of time and money on the production.
17. Indigestion can be brought on by a <u>surfeit</u> of rich food.
18. <u>Pamper</u> yourself with our new range of beauty treatments.
19. What <u>criteria</u> are used for assessing a student's ability?
20. He played the shot with <u>consummate</u> skill.

配对题答案

1. immaculate	洁净的，无瑕的	11. transcendent	超越的，卓越的
2. prim	端庄的，整洁的	12. titular	有名无实的，名义上的
3. grubby	肮脏的，不洁的	13. compendious	扼要的，简明的
4. defile	污损；败坏，玷污	14. unequivocal	只有一种含义的,清楚明白的
5. seedy	破旧的，破烂的	15. transparent	透明的
6. turbid	浑浊的，不清的	16. dissolute	放荡的，无节制的
7. obscene	猥亵的	17. overly	过度地,极度地
8. stigma	耻辱的标志，污点	18. overreaction	过度反应
9. ambiguous	含糊的，不明确的	19. blinking	讨厌的,十足地
10. overt	明显的，公然的	20. plethora	过量,过剩

Word List 23
属性（四）

简　洁

*homespun ［'hoʊmspʌn］ *adj.* 家里纺织的；朴素的，简单的（domestic; spun or woven at home; simple and ordinary）
【例】We would say a plain and *homespun* word.

pithy ［'pɪθi］ *adj.* （讲话或文章）简练的，简洁有力的（tersely cogent; concise）
【反】prolix（*adj.* 冗长的）

**terse ［tɜːrs］ *adj.* （文笔等）精炼的，简明的（concise）
【记】诗歌（verse）力求简洁明了（terse）
【派】terseness（*n.* 简洁）

brevity ［'brevəti］ *n.* 简短，简洁（conciseness）
【记】来自brief（*adj.* 简短的，简洁的）

*lucid ［'luːsɪd］ *adj.* 表达清楚的，明白易懂的（well expressed and easy to understand）
【记】luc（光）＋id → 说话光亮清晰的 → 表达清楚的
【反】vague（*adj.* 模糊的）；murky（*adj.* 难懂的，隐晦的）
【派】lucidity（*n.* 清晰，明白）

*undemanding ［ˌʌndɪ'mændɪŋ］ *adj.* 容易的，要求不高的

schematic ［skiː'mætɪk］ *adj.* 纲要的，图解的（of or relating to an outline）
【记】来自schema（*n.* 图表，纲要）

冗　长

*tedious ［'tiːdiəs］ *adj.* 冗长乏味的，沉闷的（tiresome; boring）
【例】John's job at the factory is trivial and *tedious*.

drivel	['drɪvl] *n./vi.* 说废话，说傻话，胡说八道(to talk nonsense)
	【记】drive(开车)+l(拼音：聊) → 一边开车一边胡聊 → 胡说八道
prolixity	[prou'lɪksəti] *n.* 冗长，啰嗦(tedious wordiness; verbosity)
	【记】来自prolix(*adj.* 冗长的，啰嗦的)
	【反】extreme brevity(极为简洁)；conciseness(*n.* 简洁)；succinctness(*n.* 简洁)
verbiage	['vɜːrbiɪdʒ] *n.* 废话，空洞冗长的说辞(a profusion of words of little content)
	【记】verb(词语)+i+age → 话多 → 废话

虚　幻

**mythical	['mɪθɪkl] *adj.* 神话的；虚构的(legendary; fictitious)
*illusory	[ɪ'luːsəri] *adj.* 虚幻的，幻觉的(deceptive; unreal; illusive)；不实际的
*disillusionment	[ˌdɪsɪ'luːʒnmənt] *n.* 幻灭，觉醒
*fanciful	['fænsɪfl] *adj.* 富于想象力的，爱幻想的；奇怪的，稀奇的(whimsical; visionary; imaginary; produced by imagination)
	【例】*fanciful* scheme
*ostensible	[ɑː'stensəbl] *adj.* 表面上的，声称的，公开的 (apparent; seeming; professed)
	【记】ostens(显现)+ible → 显现出来的 → 表面上的
	【例】The *ostensible* reason was that private conduct was irrelevant.
intangible	[ɪn'tændʒəbl] *adj.* 不可触摸的，无实体的，无形的(incorporeal; impalpable)
	【记】in(不)+tang(可触摸的)+ible → 不可触摸的
	【反】corporeal(*adj.* 物质的)
*quixotic	[kwɪk'sɑːtɪk] *adj.* (=quixotical)堂吉诃德似的，不切实际的，空想的(foolishly impractical)
	【记】来自作家塞万提斯的名著*Don Quixote*《堂·吉诃德》
*fancy	['fænsi] *adj.* 奇特的，想象出来的，异想天开的 *vt.* 想象，设想；爱好 *n.* 爱好，迷恋(capricious liking)；想象力(imagination)
**mythological	[ˌmɪθə'lɑːdʒɪkl] *adj.* 神话的，虚构的
	【例】They recount Islamic and Gnostic poems and epics containing *mythological*, historical or legendary themes.
*mystic	['mɪstɪk] *adj.* 神秘的，不可思议的 *n.* 神秘主义者

arcane [ɑːˈkeɪn] *adj.* 神秘的，秘密的（mysterious; hidden or secret）

【记】arcan(秘密) + e → 神秘的

【反】well-known(*adj.* 众所周知的)

*angelic [ænˈdʒelɪk] *adj.* 天使的，似天使的；天国的

【记】来自angel(*n.* 天使)

【例】While moving with such force, he also has a kind of *angelic* calm.

ethereal [iˈθɪriəl] *adj.* 如空气般轻柔的，飘逸的（light; delicate）；天上的，非人间的

*clairvoyant [kleɪˈvɔɪənt] *adj.* 透视的；有洞察力的 *n.* 千里眼；有洞察力的人

【记】clair(看做clear，清楚的) + voy(看) + ant → 看得清楚的 → 有洞察力的

fictitious [fɪkˈtɪʃəs] *adj.* 虚构的（invented; imaginary）

【记】fict(做，造) + itious → 造出的，非自然的 → 虚构的

*disillusioned [ˌdɪsɪˈluːʒnd] *adj.* 大失所望的，幻想破灭的，醒悟的（disappointed）

【记】来自disillusion(*vt.* 使幻想破灭)

【例】*Disillusioned* voters want an alternative to the two main parties.

chimerical [kaɪˈmɪərɪkəl] *ad.* 荒诞不经的，梦幻的（fantastic; highly imaginative; created by wildly fanciful imagination）

【记】原指希腊神话中一种长着狮头、羊身、蛇尾会喷火的女妖怪

*rootless [ˈruːtləs] *adj.* 无根的，无所寄托的；无根据的（baseless）

【例】Our generation is a *rootless*, transient one, far more apt to move vast distances than our parents might have been, including my own.

*unrealistically [ˌʌnriːəˈlɪstɪkli] *adv.* 不切实际地，不现实地

【例】Property prices were *unrealistically* high and there was lots of speculation in the stock and property markets.

incarnation [ˌɪnkɑːˈneɪʃn] *n.* (突出表现某种品质的)典型人物，化身（a person that prominently displays a particular quality）

【例】She's the very *incarnation* of goodness.

advent [ˈædvent] *n.* 到来，来临（coming or arrival）

hallucination [həˌluːsɪˈneɪʃn] *n.* 幻觉，错觉（illusion of seeing or hearing）

【记】hall(大厅) + uci(发音相当于you see，你看) + nation(国家) → 你在大厅里看到了一个国家 → 幻觉

*dreamscape [ˈdriːmskeɪp] *n.* 梦幻景象，幻景

【记】dream(梦) + scape(花茎) → 梦中见到一个硕大的花茎 → 幻景

【例】Until that happens, our putative city of the future will exist more as *dreamscape* than reality.

superstition [ˌsuːpərˈstɪʃn] *n.* 迷信
【例】Fear of the number 13 is an old *superstition*.

nirvana [nɪrˈvɑːnə] *n.* 涅槃；极乐世界，天堂
【例】Despite his desire to achieve *nirvana*, the young Buddhist found that even the buzzing of a fly could distract him from his meditation.

mystical [ˈmɪstɪkl] *n.* 神秘的，神秘主义的（arcane; uncanny）
【例】A third of all adults report having had a *mystical* or religious experience.

*mystique [mɪˈstiːk] *n.* 神秘性（quality of sth which is not fully known about or understood but is seen to be admirable or special）
【例】the *mystique* of the British monarchy

*panacea [ˌpænəˈsiːə] *n.* 万灵药（cure-all）
【记】pan（全部）+ acea（治疗）→ 万灵药

elixir [ɪˈlɪksər] *n.* 万灵药，长生不老药（cure-all; panacea）
【记】源自阿拉伯人卖药时的喊叫"阿里可舍"，大致意思是：这个药好啊！

*vampire [ˈvæmpaɪər] *n.* 吸血鬼
【记】vamp（勾引男子的女人）+ ire → 吸血鬼总扮作美丽的女人魅惑男子 → 吸血鬼

*bugaboo [ˈbʌɡəbuː] *n.* 吓人的东西；妖怪
【记】发音似"八个婆"→ 八个老妖婆 → 妖怪

*incantation [ˌɪnkænˈteɪʃn] *n.* 咒语
【记】in + cant（黑话）+ ation → 咒语

*demon [ˈdiːmən] *n.* 恶魔，魔鬼（wicked or cruel spirit）
【例】medieval carvings of *demons*

mirage [məˈrɑːʒ] *n.* 海市蜃楼（optical illusion caused by hot air conditions）

*phantasm [ˈfæntæzəm] *n.* 幻象，幻影（illusion）；幽灵

*illusionist [ɪˈluːʒənɪst] *n.* 魔术师，幻术家（magician）；幻觉论者，爱幻想的人

**mysticism [ˈmɪstɪsɪzəm] *n.* 神秘主义者的信仰和体验，神秘主义（belief or experiences of a mystic）
【例】A strain of *mysticism* runs through his poetry.

necromancy [ˈnekroʊmænsi] *n.* 通灵术（art or practice of communicating by magic with the dead in order to learn about the future） wizardry ['wɪzərdri] n. 巫术，魔法（witchcraft）

figment ['fɪgmənt] n. 想像中的事物，虚构的事物（a thing that is not real but only imagined）

【例】a *figment* of someboby's imagination

nonentity [nɑ:'nentəti] n. 庸人，不重要的人（a person without any special qualities or achievements）；不存在，不存在的东西

【记】non(不)＋entity(实体)→被他人忽略，当作不存在→不重要的人

【例】How could such a *nonentity* become chairman of the company?

*conceive [kən'si:v] v. 想像，设想，构想（to devise; visualize）

【例】The inventor *conceived* a new gadget.

anthropomorphic [ˌænθrəpə'mɔ:rfɪk] adj. (将神、动物)拟人化的，赋予人的形体和性格的（having human form or characteristics）

【记】anthropo(人，人类)＋morph(形体)＋ic(…的)→拟人化的

demoniac [dɪ'moʊniæk] adj. 魔鬼的，恶魔的；着魔的，邪恶的（fiendish; cruel）n. 着魔的人

【记】来自demon(n. 恶魔)

真　实

*tangible ['tændʒəbl] adj. 可见的，有形的（touchable; substantial）；确实的，实际的

【记】tang(接触)＋ible(能)→可接触的→有形的

【例】One *tangible* benefit of my new job is a company car.

**authentic [ɔ:'θentɪk] adj. 真正的，非假冒的；可靠的，有根据的，真实的（genuine; real）

【记】aut(自己)＋hent(得到)＋ic→亲自得到→真实的

【例】Is your diamond ring *authentic*?

**unimpeachable [ˌʌnɪm'pi:tʃəbl] adj. 无可指摘的，无可置疑的（irreproachable; blameless）

【记】un(不)＋impeach(怀疑；控告)＋able(能)→无可置疑的

【反】open to question(易受质疑的)

**reliant [rɪ'laɪənt] adj. 依赖的，依靠的

【例】We don't need to be completely *reliant* on foreign oil but we choose to be.

*genuine ['dʒenjuɪn] adj. 真正的，非伪造的（authentic; real）；真诚的

【例】My necklace is made with *genuine* pearls.

*factual ['fæktʃuəl] *adj.* 真实的，事实的（restricted to or based on fact）

【记】来自fact（*n.* 事实，真相）

【反】fictitious（*adj.* 编造的）

*provable ['pruːvəbl] *adj.* 可证明的，可以查清的（evincible; certifiable）

【记】来自prove（*v.* 证明）

【例】The investor will have access to most of his money and a *provable* loss.

*undistorted [ˌʌndɪs'tɔːrtɪd] *adj.* 未失真的；不偏激的

【记】un（不）+ distort（歪曲）+ ed → 没被歪曲的 → 未失真的

【例】Callers sounded clear and *undistorted*, as if I were on a conventional phone line.

*verisimilitude [ˌverɪsɪ'mɪlɪtjuːd] *n.* 逼真，貌似真实（appearance or semblance of being true or real）

【记】veri（真的）+ simili（相似）+ tude → 逼真，真实

【例】These flower illustrations show the artist's concern for *verisimilitude*.

veracity [və'ræsəti] *n.* 真实性，精确性（truth）

【例】We have total confidence in the *veracity* of our research.

*reliability [rɪˌlaɪə'bɪləti] *n.* 可靠性

【记】来自reliable（*adj.* 可靠的）

【例】It will likely also have poor safety or *reliability* scores, although that's not a prerequisite.

verity ['verəti] *n.* (陈述等的)真实性；真理；基本事实（fundamental fact）

【例】universal *verities*

authenticate [ɔː'θentɪkeɪt] *vt.* 证明…为真（to prove or serve to prove the authenticity of）

【记】aut（自己）+ hent（得到）+ ic → 证明自己得到的是真品 → 证明…为真

truism ['truːɪzəm] *n.* 自明之理，真理（an undoubted or self-evident truth）

【记】tru（=true真实的）+ ism → 真理

perverse [pər'vɜːrs] *adj.* 刚愎自用的，倔强的；故意作对的（obstinate in opposing; wrongheaded）

【记】per（始终）+ verse（转）→ 始终和别人反着转 → 故意作对的

【派】perversity（*n.* 刚愎；悖理行为）

**inauthentic [ˌɪnɔːˈθentɪk] *adj.* 不真实的，不可靠的

【记】来自authentic(*adj.* 真实的，可靠的)

【例】If your brand feels *inauthentic* or contrived at any point of contact, people won't trust it.

*unconvincing [ˌʌnkənˈvɪnsɪŋ] *adj.* 不足以令人相信的

【记】un(不) + convinc(e)(令人信服) + ing → 不足以令人相信的

【例】The movie is *unconvincing* and graceless, and weirdly anachronistic and over explicit about gender issues.

*pragmatic [præɡˈmætɪk] *adj.* 实际的，实用主义的 (practical as opposed to idealistic)

【记】pragm(实际) + atic → 实际的

**uncensored [ʌnˈsensərd] *adj.* 未经审查的；无约束的

【记】un(不) + censor(审查) + ed → 未经审查的

*undisguised [ˌʌndɪsˈɡaɪzd] *adj.* 无伪装的，公开的

【记】un(不) + disguis(e)(伪装) + ed → 无伪装的

*unidentified [ˌʌnaɪˈdentɪfaɪd] *adj.* 不能辨认的，无法识别的(that cannot be identified)

【记】un(不) + identifi(=identify识别) + ed → 不能辨认的

【例】an *unidentified* species

*unbelievable [ˌʌnbɪˈliːvəbl] *adj.* 难以置信的，不可信的 (incredible; fabulous)

【记】un(不) + believ(e) + able → 难以置信的

【例】"He had to figure out another way now that mid-range is just *unbelievable*," Carter said.

*trusting [ˈtrʌstɪŋ] *adj.* 信任的，轻信的(naive; credulous)

【例】The most surprising result is that Americans are far more *trusting* than they say they are.

*outright [ˈaʊtraɪt] *adv.* 坦率地，诚实地，无保留地 (openly and honestly, with nothing held back)

【例】I told him *outright* what I thought of his behavior.

方　位

*concentric [kənˈsentrɪk] *adj.* (指数个圆)有同一中心的

【记】con(共同) + centr(中心) + ic → 有同一圆心的

orientation	[ˌɔːriənˈteɪʃn] *n.* 方向，定向
verge	[vɜːrdʒ] *n.* 边缘(border; edge; rim)
*frontal	[ˈfrʌntl] *adj.* 正面的，前面的(at, from, in, or of the front)
	【例】a *frontal* view
lateral	[ˈlætərəl] *adj.* 侧面的(of, at, from, or towards the side)
	【记】later(侧面) + al → 侧面的
**orient	[ˈɔːrient] *adj.* 上升的(rising) *vt.* 确定…方向(to ascertain the bearings of); 使熟悉情况(to acquaint with a particular situation)
	【记】ori(升起) + ent → 上升的
*skyward	[ˈskaɪwərd] *adj./adv.* 向上的(地); 向着天空的(地)
	【例】But when cotton prices kept rocketing *skyward*, he decided to revert to his usual mix.
zenith	[ˈziːnɪθ] *n.* 天顶(the highest point of the celestial sphere); 极点，最高点(the highest point)
	【反】nadir(*n.* 最低点); lowest point(最低点)
superimpose	[ˌsuːpərɪmˈpoʊz] *vt.* 把…放置在上面，叠加上去(to place or lay over or above sth)
	【记】super(在上面) + impose(强加) → 叠加上去
*juxtapose	[ˌdʒʌkstəˈpoʊz] *vt.* 将…并列，将…并置 (to put side by side or close together)
	【记】juxta(接近) + pose(放) → 挨着放 → 将…并列
**delimit	[diˈlɪmɪt] *vt.* 限定，给…划界(to fix the limits of)
	【记】de + limit(界限) → 给…划界

距　离

*contiguous	[kənˈtɪɡjuəs] *adj.* 接壤的，邻近的(near; adjacent)
	【记】con(共同) + tig(接触) + uous → 共同接触 → 接壤的
	【派】contiguity(*n.* 邻近，接壤)
**adjacent	[əˈdʒeɪsnt] *adj.* 邻近的，毗连的(adjoining; neighboring)
	【例】Tom's house is *adjacent* to the park.
propinquity	[prəˈpɪŋkwəti] *n.* (时间、地点上的)接近，邻近(nearness in space or time)
	【例】The neighbors lived in close *propinquity* to each other.

*equidistant [ˌiːkwɪˈdɪstənt] *adj.* 等距离的（at an equal distance）

【记】equi(相等) + distant(远的) → 等距离的

【例】Our house is *equidistant* from the two pubs in the village.

distant [ˈdɪstənt] *adj.* 远的(remote)

【例】My parents live in a *distant* state, and I rarely see them.

*cacumen [kəˈkjuːmən] *n.* 物体的顶端

首 尾

*primacy [ˈpraɪməsi] *n.* 首位，卓越；教皇的职责(地位或身份)

【记】prim(最初；首要，第一) + acy → 首位

primordial [praɪˈmɔːrdiəl] *adj.* 原始的；最初的，根本的(existing in the beginning)

【记】prim(最初；首要，第一) + ordial → 最初的，根本的

【例】There is a wild and *primordial* look in his eyes.

【反】most recent(最近的)

**precedent [ˈpresɪdənt] *n.* 先例，惯例；【律】判例

【例】I'm going to break the *precedent*.

gambit [ˈɡæmbɪt] *n.* （国际象棋）牺牲一子或数子以取得优势的开局棋法(opening in chess in which a piece is sacrificed)；开始的行动

【例】The player was afraid to accept his opponent's *gambit* because he feared a trap which as yet he could not see.

弯 曲

**lithe [laɪð] *adj.* 柔软的，易弯的(flexible; supple)

*supple [ˈsʌpl] *adj.* 柔软的，易弯的(flexible; lithe)

*pliable [ˈplaɪəbl] *adj.* 柔软的，易弯的(supple enough to bend freely; ductile)

【记】pli(=ply弯，折) + able(能) → 易弯的

【反】rigid(*adj.* 僵硬的)

limber [ˈlɪmbər] *adj.* 易弯曲的，灵活的，敏捷的(easily bent; flexible)

【记】limb(肢) + er → (四肢)易弯曲的

malleable [ˈmæliəbl] *adj.* 有延展性的，(指金属)可锻造的(pliable)；可塑的，易适应的

【记】malle(锤子) + able → 可锻的

*plasticity [plæ'stɪsəti] *n.* 可塑性(ability to be molded); 适应性

【记】来自plastic(*adj.* 可塑的)

【例】When clay dries out, it loses its *plasticity*.

【反】rigidity(*n.* 刚性, 硬度)

*pliant ['plaɪənt] *adj.* 易受影响的, 顺从的 (easily influenced); 易弯的, 柔软的(pliable)

【反】mulish (*adj.* 顽固的); intransigent (*adj.* 不妥协的); intractable (*adj.* 难对付的)

tortuous ['tɔːrtʃuəs] *adj.* (路)弯弯曲曲的(winding); 居心叵测的, 绕圈子的

【记】tort(弯曲) + uous → 弯弯曲曲的

【反】straightforward(*adj.* 直截了当的); direct(*adj.* 笔直的; 直接的)

*sinuous ['sɪnjuəs] *adj.* (河流等)蜿蜒的; 柔软的, 弯曲的

【记】sinu(弯曲) + ous → 弯曲的

【反】direct(*adj.* 笔直的)

askew [ə'skjuː] *adj./adv.* 歪斜的(地)(to one side; awry)

【记】a + skew(歪斜的) → 歪斜的

【反】aligned(*adj.* 排列成一行的)

*curved [kɜːrvd] *adj.* 弯曲的

【记】来自curve(*n.* 曲线, 弧线)

**detour ['diːtʊr] *n.* 弯路(a roundabout way); 绕行之路(a route used when the direct or regular route is not available) *v.* (使)绕道

【记】de + tour(旅行, 走) → 绕行之路

*contort [kən'tɔːrt] *v.* (使)扭曲(to deform); 曲解

【记】con + tort(弯曲) → 扭曲

【派】contortion(*n.* 扭曲; 曲解)

*distort [dɪ'stɔːrt] *vt.* 歪曲, 使变形(to misshape); 曲解(to misrepresent; twist)

【例】A painter may *distort* or exaggerate shapes and forms.

awry [ə'raɪ] *adj./adv.* 扭曲的, 走样的(not straight; askew)

【记】a + wry(歪的) → 扭曲的

【反】orderly(*adj.* 有序的); aligned(*adj.* 排成一行的)

练 习 题

填空题

brevity	concentric	contiguous	disillusioned	fictitious
frontal	genuine	mirage	intangible	pliable
gambit	precedent	primacy	rootless	superstition
tangible	tedious	terse	undemanding	veracity

1. The President issued a _____ statement denying the charges.
2. For the sake of _____, I'd like to make just two points.
3. She was a pleasant and _____ companion.
4. We had to listen to all the _____ details of his operation.
5. The old building had an _____ air of sadness about it.
6. All the places and characters in my novel are entirely _____.
7. I feel utterly _____ by his refusal to take any action.
8. She had had a _____ childhood moving from town to town.
9. High temperatures can cause _____.
10. According to _____, breaking a mirror brings bad luck.
11. We cannot accept his findings without _____ evidence.
12. Fake designer watches are sold at a fraction of the price of the _____ article.
13. Some people questioned the _____ of her story.
14. The revolving circle is _____ with the fixed outer circle.
15. Air bags are designed to protect the driver in the event of a severe _____ impact.
16. The two countries are _____.
17. This college emphasizes the _____ of teaching over research.
18. The ruling set a _____ for future libel cases.
19. The plant has long _____ stems.
20. The player was afraid to accept his opponent's _____ because he feared a trap which as yet he could not see.

配对题

1. homespun	邻近的，毗连的	11. nirvana	表达清楚的，明白易懂的
2. lucid	天使的；天国的	12. authentic	神话的；虚构的
3. schematic	有根据的，真实的	13. provable	涅槃；极乐世界，天堂
4. drivel	荒诞不经的，梦幻的	14. reliability	方向，定向
5. verbiage	梦幻景象，幻景	15. orientation	可塑性
6. mythical	说废话	16. lateral	原始的
7. fanciful	富于想象力的，爱幻想的	17. adjacent	可证明的，可以查清的
8. angelic	家里纺织的；朴素的，简单的	18. primordial	可靠性
9. chimerical	侧面的	19. lithe	纲要的，图解的
10. dreamscape	柔软的，易弯的	20. plasticity	废话，空洞冗长的说辞

- 246 -

练习题答案

填空题答案

1. The President issued a <u>terse</u> statement denying the charges.
2. For the sake of <u>brevity</u>, I'd like to make just two points.
3. She was a pleasant and <u>undemanding</u> companion.
4. We had to listen to all the <u>tedious</u> details of his operation.
5. The old building had an <u>intangible</u> air of sadness about it.
6. All the places and characters in my novel are entirely <u>fictitious</u>.
7. I feel utterly <u>disillusioned</u> by his refusal to take any action.
8. She had had a <u>rootless</u> childhood moving from town to town.
9. High temperatures can cause <u>mirage</u>.
10. According to <u>superstition</u>, breaking a mirror brings bad luck.
11. We cannot accept his findings without <u>tangible</u> evidence.
12. Fake designer watches are sold at a fraction of the price of the <u>genuine</u> article.
13. Some people questioned the <u>veracity</u> of her story.
14. The revolving circle is <u>concentric</u> with the fixed outer circle.
15. Air bags are designed to protect the driver in the event of a severe <u>frontal</u> impact.
16. The two countries are <u>contiguous</u>.
17. This college emphasizes the <u>primacy</u> of teaching over research.
18. The ruling set a <u>precedent</u> for future libel cases.
19. The plant has long <u>pliable</u> stems.
20. The player was afraid to accept his opponent's <u>gambit</u> because he feared a trap which as yet he could not see.

配对题答案

1. homespun	家里纺织的; 朴素的, 简单的		11. nirvana	涅槃; 极乐世界, 天堂
2. lucid	表达清楚的, 明白易懂的		12. authentic	有根据的, 真实的
3. schematic	纲要的, 图解的		13. provable	可证明的, 可以查清的
4. drivel	说废话		14. reliability	可靠性
5. verbiage	废话, 空洞冗长的说辞		15. orientation	方向, 定向
6. mythical	神话的; 虚构的		16. lateral	侧面的
7. fanciful	富于想象力的, 爱幻想的		17. adjacent	邻近的, 毗连的
8. angelic	天使的; 天国的		18. primordial	原始的
9. chimerical	荒诞不经的, 梦幻的		19. lithe	柔软的, 易弯的
10. dreamscape	梦幻景象, 幻景		20. plasticity	可塑性

Word List 24
属性(五)

先　后

anterior [ænˈtɪriər] *adj.* 较早的,以前的(previous; earlier)
【记】 ante(前的) + rior → 以前的
【反】 ensuing(*adj.* 跟着发生的)

*subsequent [ˈsʌbsɪkwənt] *adj.* 随后的,后来的(following; later)
【记】 sub(下面) + sequent(随着的) → 随后的
【例】 *Subsequent* events proved the man to be right.

antedate [ˌænti'deɪt] *vt.* (在信、文件上)写上较早日期;早于,先于
【记】 ante(前面) + date(日期) → 在现在的日期前面 → 早于

*ensue [ɪnˈsuː] *vi.* 继而发生,接踵而至(to happen afterwards)
【记】 en(进入) + sue(跟从) → 继而发生
【派】 ensuing(*adj.* 随后的) → anterior(*adj.* 以前的)

yore [jɔːr] *n.* 昔日,往昔
【例】 in days of *yore*

相　反

*inverse [ɪnˈvɜːrs] *adj.* (位置、方向、关系等)相反的,反向的(contrary; opposite)
【记】 in(反) + verse(转) → 反转的 → 相反的

antithesis [ænˈtɪθəsɪs] *n.* 对立,相对 (a contrast or opposition);对立面
【记】 anti(反) + thesis(放) → 反着放 → 对立
【派】 antithetic(*adj.* 对立的)

invert [ɪnˈvɜːrt] *vt.* 使倒转,使反向(to overturn; reverse)
【例】 I *inverted* the glasses so the water would drain out of them.

能　力

*omnipotent　[ɑːm'nɪpətənt] *adj.* 全能的，万能的(almighty; all-powerful)

【记】omni(全) + potent(有力的) → 全能的

*knack　[næk] *n.* 特殊本领；窍门(a clever, expedient way of doing sth)

【记】敲了敲(knock)脑袋，一下子想到了窍门(knack)

*incompetent　[ɪn'kɑːmpɪtənt] *adj.* 不称职的，不能胜任的，无能力的

【记】in(不) + competent(能干的) → 无能力的；来自compete(*v.* 竞争；比得上)

*inept　[ɪ'nept] *adj.* 不适宜的；无能的，笨拙的(incompetent; inefficient)

【记】in(不) + ept(熟练的) → 无能的

*solvent　['sɑːlvənt] *adj.* 有溶解力的；有偿付能力的 *n.* 溶剂；解决方法

**ineptitude　[ɪ'neptɪtuːd] *n.* 不适当；无能，笨拙 (the quality or state of being inept)

【反】bent(*n.* 天分); finesse(*n.* 灵巧)

legerdemain　['ledʒərdəmeɪn] *n.* 手法，戏法 (sleight of hand; tricks of a stage magician)

【记】leger (=light轻的) + de + main (手) → 手轻盈地变幻 → 手法；来自法语leger demain(=light of hand) → 手轻巧 → 手法

特　殊

**quaint　[kweɪnt] *adj.* 奇异的，不凡的，古色古香的 (queer; charmingly odd especially in an old-fashioned way)

*offbeat　[ɔːf'biːt] *adj.* 不规则的；不平常的，非传统的(unconventional)

【记】off(离开) + beat(节奏) → 无节奏 → 不规则的

【反】conventional(*adj.* 惯例的，常规的)

*distinctive　[dɪ'stɪŋktɪv] *adj.* 出众的，有特色的

【记】来自distinct(*adj.* 明显的，有区别的)

unique　[ju'niːk] *adj.* 独一无二的(unrivaled; matchless)

【例】The sales clerk showed me a most *unique* necklace.

*inimitable　[ɪ'nɪmɪtəbl] *adj.* 无法仿效的，不可比拟的 (incapable of being imitated or matched)

【记】in(不) + imit(模仿) + able(能) → 不可模仿的 → 无法仿效的

【反】ordinary(*adj.* 普通的); commonplace(*adj.* 普通的)

preternatural [ˌpriːtər'nætʃrəl] *adj.* 异常的（extraordinary）; 超自然的（existing outside of nature）

【记】preter(超) + natural(自然的) → 超自然的

【反】ordinary(*adj.* 常见的)

*specificity [ˌspesɪ'fɪsəti] *n.* 具体性，明确性；特异性，专一性

【例】The President claims that the two articles of impeachment are vague and lack of *specificity*.

*unanticipated [ˌʌnæn'tɪsɪpeɪtɪd] *adj.* 意料之外的

【记】un(不) + anticipat(e)(预料) + ed → 意料之外的

【例】He could get swamped by *unanticipated* problems or suffer from crippling flaws we haven't seen yet.

*unorthodox [ʌn'ɔːrθədɑːks] *adj.* 非正统的，非传统的（unconventional）

【记】来自orthodox(*adj.* 正统的)

【例】*unorthodox* beliefs

**idiosyncratic [ˌɪdiəsɪŋ'krætɪk] *adj.* 有特质的，独特的（peculiar; specific）

【例】Children are coming up with their own characters which are quite unique and *idiosyncratic*.

prerogative [prɪ'rɑːgətɪv] *n.* 特权（privilege; the discretionary power）

【记】pre(预先) + rog(要求) + ative → 预先要求的权力 → 特权

atypical [ˌeɪ'tɪpɪkl] *adj.* 非典型的（not normal; not typical）

【记】a(表否定) + typical(典型的) → 非典型的

**erratic [ɪ'rætɪk] *adj.* 飘忽不定的；古怪的，怪僻的（odd; eccentric）

【例】Bill's *erratic* moods upset everyone in our office.

**eccentric [ɪk'sentrɪk] *adj.* (人、行为等)古怪的，反常的（odd; erratic; bizarre）; 不同圆心的 *n.* 古怪的人

【记】ec(表否定) + centr(中心) + ic → 不同圆心的

【例】My neighbor's *eccentric* behavior is sometimes frightening.

*bizarre [bɪ'zɑːr] *adj.* 稀奇古怪的（odd; strikingly unconventional in style or appearance）

【例】*bizarre* behaviors or thoughts

**outlandish [aʊt'lændɪʃ] *adj.* 怪异的，古怪的（strikingly out of the ordinary）

【记】out(出) + land(国家) + ish → 从外国来的 → 怪异的

【例】*outlandish* clothes

*whimsical [ˈwɪmzɪkl] *adj.* 怪诞的，异想天开的（exhibiting whims）

【记】来自whim（*n.* 奇想，怪念头）

**esoteric [ˌesəˈterɪk] *adj.* 秘传的；神秘的；只限于小圈子内部的

【记】es（出）+ oter（看做outer）+ ic → 不出外面的 → 秘传的

【反】generally known（众所周知的）；common accepted（广为接受、认可的）

**twisted [ˈtwɪstɪd] *adj.* 扭曲的

【例】Bin Laden is using them as inspiration for his *twisted* holy war against the West.

*queer [kwɪr] *adj.* 奇怪的，古怪的（strange; fishy）

【记】奇怪的（queer）女王（queen）

*private [ˈpraɪvət] *adj.* 私人的，个人的（personal）

【例】my father's own *private* chair

*patent [ˈpætnt] *adj.* 公开的，显而易见的（readily visible obvious）*n.* 专利权（证书）

【记】专利（patent）一方面是起保护作用，另一方面也让大家都知道了知识产权保护是公开的（patent）

【反】not evident（不明显的）；abstruse（*adj.* 深奥的）；recondite（*adj.* 深奥的）；patent difference（明显差别）→ nuance（*n.* 细微差别）

【派】patency（*n.* 明显，显著性）

*prewar [ˌpriːˈwɔːr] *adj.* 战前的

【例】The postwar macro performance of the U. S. economy is in astonishing contrast to the *prewar* stagnation, deep depression, and falling prices.

singular [ˈsɪŋɡjələr] *adj.* （现象、事件等）异常的，奇怪的（unusual; strange）

【例】a *singular* occurrence

*unaccustomed [ˌʌnəˈkʌstəmd] *adj.* 不习惯的，不适应的（not used to）

【例】*Unaccustomed* to proclaiming her faith publicly, she found the prayer sessions unnerving at first.

*quintessential [ˌkwɪntɪˈsenʃl] *adj.* 精髓的，精粹的，典型的（extractive）

【记】来自quintessence（*n.* 第五元素）：quint（=fifth第五）+ essence（要素）；古代和中世纪哲学认为，构成宇宙的除了风、水、火、土这四大元素之外，还有第五种元素

【例】In nearly six decades of performing, Jackie McLean lived the *quintessential* jazz survivor's life.

**selective [sɪˈlektɪv] *adj.* 选择的，选择性的（using or based on selection）

【例】the *selective* training of recruits

erratically [ɪˈrætɪkli] *adv.* 飘忽不定地；怪异地

【记】来自 erratic（*adj.* 飘忽不定的；怪异的）

【例】In the summer of 1992, Gosinski began to notice that his boss was behaving *erratically*.

hallmark [ˈhɔːlmɑːrk] *n.* (金、银上的)纯度印记；特征(distinctive feature)

【记】mark（*n.* 标志；记号）

【反】uncharacteristic feature(无特点的标志)

idiosyncrasy [ˌɪdɪəˈsɪŋkrəsi] *n.* 个人特性，个人风格

【例】Tom has an *idiosycracy* of playing football all by himself.

birthright [ˈbɜːrθraɪt] *n.* 与生俱来的权利；长子继承权

【例】Freedom is our natural *birthright*.

characteristic [ˌkærəktəˈrɪstɪk] *n.* 特性，特征 *adj.* 特有的，典型的(distinctive; distinguishing)

quirk [kwɜːrk] *n.* 奇事(accident; vagary)；怪癖(a strange habit)

【例】They do have a certain *quirk*.

If you would go up high, then use your own legs! Do not let yourselves carried aloft; do not seat yourselves on other people's backs and heads.

如果你想要走到高处,就要使用自己的两条腿! 不要让别人把你抬到高处;不要坐在别人的背上和头上。

——德国哲学家 尼采(F. W. Nietzsche, German philosopher)

练 习 题

填空题

antithesis	birthright	characteristic	distinctive	eccentric
ensue	incompetent	inverse	invert	knack
patent	prerogative	preternatural	solvent	specificity
subsequent	twisted	unaccustomed	unique	unorthodox

1. Developments on this issue will be dealt with in a _____ report.
2. Bitter arguments _____ from this misunderstanding.
3. There is often an _____ relationship between the power of the tool and how easy it is to use.
4. There is an _____ between the needs of the state and the needs of the people.
5. In questions, the subject and verb are often _____.
6. He's got a real _____ for making money.
7. The Prime Minister was attacked as _____ to lead.
8. The male bird has _____ black and white markings on its head.
9. The city was _____ quiet.
10. The reporter's recommendations lack _____.
11. She has an _____ technique, but is an excellent player.
12. The Prime Minister exercised his _____ to decide when to call an election.
13. Most people considered him a harmless _____.
14. After the crash the car was a mass of _____ metal.
15. The device was protected by _____.
16. He was _____ to hard work.
17. Education is every child's _____.
18. She spoke with _____ enthusiasm.
19. The company managed to remain _____ during the recession.
20. The deal will put the company in a _____ position to export goods to Eastern Europe.

配对题

1. anterior	(在信、文件上)写上较早日期	11. idiosyncratic	手法，戏法
2. antedate	较早的，以前的	12. atypical	不规则的；不平常的
3. omnipotent	非典型的	13. erratic	全能的，万能的
4. whimsical	古怪的，怪僻的	14. esoteric	私人的，个人的
5. inept	秘传的；神秘的	15. private	精髓的，精粹的
6. legerdemain	有溶解力的	16. quintessential	奇事；怪癖
7. offbeat	有特质的，独特的	17. selective	选择的，选择性的
8. unique	不适宜的；无能的，笨拙的	18. solvent	意料之外的
9. inimitable	不凡的，古色古香的	19. quirk	独一无二的
10. unanticipated	无法仿效的，不可比拟的	20. quaint	怪诞的，异想天开的

练习题答案

填空题答案

1. Developments on this issue will be dealt with in a <u>subsequent</u> report.
2. Bitter arguments <u>ensued</u> from this misunderstanding.
3. There is often an <u>inverse</u> relationship between the power of the tool and how easy it is to use.
4. There is an <u>antithesis</u> between the needs of the state and the needs of the people.
5. In questions, the subject and verb are often <u>inverted</u>.
6. He's got a real <u>knack</u> for making money.
7. The Prime Minister was attacked as <u>incompetent</u> to lead.
8. The male bird has <u>distinctive</u> black and white markings on its head.
9. The city was <u>preternaturallly</u> quiet.
10. The reporter's recommendations lack <u>specificity</u>.
11. She has an <u>unorthodox</u> technique, but is an excellent player.
12. The Prime Minister exercised his <u>prerogative</u> to decide when to call an election.
13. Most people considered him a harmless <u>eccentric</u>.
14. After the crash the car was a mass of <u>twisted</u> metal.
15. The device was protected by <u>patent</u>.
16. He was <u>unaccustomed</u> to hard work.
17. Education is every child's <u>birthright</u>.
18. She spoke with <u>characteristic</u> enthusiasm.
19. The company managed to remain <u>solvent</u> during the recession.
20. The deal will put the company in a <u>unique</u> position to export goods to Eastern Europe.

配对题答案

1. anterior	较早的，以前的		11. idiosyncratic	有特质的，独特的
2. antedate	（在信、文件上）写上较早日期		12. atypical	非典型的
3. omnipotent	全能的，万能的		13. erratic	古怪的，怪僻的
4. whimsical	怪诞的，异想天开的		14. esoteric	秘传的；神秘的
5. inept	不适宜的；无能的，笨拙的		15. private	私人的，个人的
6. legerdemain	手法，戏法		16. quintessential	精髓的，精粹的
7. offbeat	不规则的；不平常的		17. selective	选择的，选择性的
8. unique	独一无二的		18. solvent	有溶解力的
9. inimitable	无法仿效的，不可比拟的		19. quirk	奇事；怪僻
10. unanticipated	意料之外的		20. quaint	不凡的，古色古香的

Word List 25
属性(六)

味　道

gustatory [ˈɡʌstətəri] *adj.* 味觉的；品尝的

relish [ˈrelɪʃ] *n.* 滋味，美味(pleasing flavor)；喜好(a strong liking) *v.* 喜欢，享受(to be gratified by; enjoy)；津津有味地吃

【记】rel(看做real)＋ish(看做fish)→真正的鱼→美味

aromatic [ˌærəˈmætɪk] *adj.* （植物）芬芳的，芳香的（having a strong pleasant smell）

*__fragrant__ [ˈfreɪɡrənt] *adj.* （花草）香的，芬芳的(aromatic)

*__redolent__ [ˈredələnt] *adj.* 芬芳的，芳香的(scented; aromatic; fragrant) *让人联想到...ch*

【记】red(=re反复)＋ol(=olfaction嗅觉)＋ent→反复闻→芳香的...ch

【反】unscented(*adj.* 无香味的)

*__cloying__ [ˈklɔɪɪŋ] *adj.* 甜得发腻的(too much of sweetness)

【记】来自cloy(*v.* 因过量吃甜的东西而发腻)

*__treacly__ [ˈtriːkli] *adj.* 糖蜜似的；甜蜜的

【例】The director might easily have made her a naively Candide-like figure, or a *treacly* Pollyannaish one.

palatable [ˈpælətəbl] *adj.* 味美的(savory; flavorous)

【记】palat(e)(上颚)＋able→美味可口的→味美的

luscious [ˈlʌʃəs] *adj.* 美味的，甘美多汁的（delicious）；肉感的，满足感官的（voluptuous）

【记】lu（看做lush，多汁的）＋scious（看做delicious，美味的）→甘美多汁的

musky [mʌski] *adj.* 麝香的，产生麝香的，麝香似的（having the odor of musk）

【记】来自musk(*n.* 麝香)

savory [ˈseɪvəri] *adj.* 美味可口的，芳香开胃的（appetizing to the taste or smell）

【例】 Lights were shining from every window, and there was a *savory* smell of roast goose.

【反】 noisome(*adj.* 有恶臭的)

*pungent ['pʌndʒənt] *adj.* (气味等)辛辣的，刺激性的(acrid; penetrating)

【记】 pung(刺) + ent → 刺激的

【例】 The aged cheese had a *pungent* taste.

piquant ['piːkənt] *adj.* 辛辣的，开胃的 (agreeably stimulating to the palate; spicy); 令人兴奋的，刺激的，有趣的(engagingly provocative)

【记】 piqu(刺激) + ant → 刺激的

*spice [spaɪs] *n.* 香料，调味品(从植物中提取而得，尤指粉状的)

【例】 Ginger, nutmeg, cinnamon, pepper and cloves are common *spices*.

*queasy ['kwiːzi] *adj.* 令人恶心的，感到反胃的 (experiencing nausea; nauseated); 充满疑虑的

【记】 que(拼音：缺) + easy(轻松) → 不轻松 → 感到反胃的

disgorge [dɪs'ɡɔːrdʒ] *v.* 呕出，吐出(to vomit); (水)喷出，流出(to pour forth)

【记】 dis(否定) + gorge(咽喉；胃) → 呕出

【反】 ingest(*vt.* 摄取，吸收); swallow(*vt.* 吞咽)

·musty ['mʌsti] *adj.* 发霉的，有霉臭的(stale in odor or taste; spoiled by age)

【记】 must(一定) + y → 一定发霉了 → 有霉臭的

odorous ['oʊdərəs] *adj.* 有显著(香的或臭的)气味的 (having a pleasant or unpleasant smell)

【记】 来自odor(*n.* 气味，香气，臭气)

*succulent ['sʌkjələnt] *adj.* 多汁的，多水分的(juicy; full of richness)

【例】 To some people, Florida citrus fruits are more *succulent* than those from California.

*insipid [ɪn'sɪpɪd] *adj.* 没有味道的，清淡的; 乏味的，枯燥的 (dull; vapid; banal)

【记】 in(进入) + sip(啜饮) + id → 不好喝的 → 没有味道的

*unpalatable [ʌn'pælətəbl] *adj.* 味道差的; 令人讨厌的(unpleasant and difficult for the mind to accept)

【记】 来自palatable(*adj.* 味美的)

savor ['seɪvər] *vt.* 品尝，欣赏(to taste; relish); 给…加调味品，使有气味 *n.* 滋味，气味

【例】 I want to *savor* this great moment of accomplishment.

fetid ['fetɪd] *adj.* (水等)有恶臭的(having a heavy offensive smell)

【记】fet(=feet脚)+ id(发音:一滴)→ 从脚上流出一滴恶臭的水!→ 有恶臭的

【反】having a pleasant smell(好闻的)

malodorous [ˌmælˈoʊdərəs] *adj.* 恶臭的(smelling unpleasant)

【记】mal(坏)+ odor(气味)+ ous → 恶臭的

【例】*malodorous* drains

mawkish ['mɔːkɪʃ] *adj.* 多愁善感的(sickly or puerilely sentimental);淡而无味的,令人作呕的(insipid or nauseating)

【记】maw(反刍动物的第四胃)+ kish → 令人作呕的

nauseate ['nɔːzieɪt] *v.* (使)作呕,(使)厌恶(to feel disgust)

【记】来自nausea(*n.* 作呕,恶心)

【派】nauseating(*adj.* 令人作呕的)

noisome ['nɔɪsəm] *adj.* 恶臭的 (foul smelling);讨厌的,令人不快的(highly obnoxious or objectionable);有害健康的

【记】noi(=annoy讨厌)+ some → 讨厌的,令人不快的

【反】appealing (*adj.* 吸引人的);beneficial (*adj.* 有益的);pleasant (*adj.* 令人愉快的);healthy(*adj.* 有益健康的)

putrid ['pjuːtrɪd] *adj.* 腐臭的(rotten)

【记】put(放)+ rid(清除)→ 冰箱里的肉都腐臭了,清除出去吧 → 腐臭的

【例】a pile of rotten, *putrid* fish

rancid ['rænsɪd] *adj.* 不新鲜的,变味的(rank; stinking)

【记】ran(跑)+ cid(看做acid,酸)→ 酸味跑出来了 → 变味的

reek [riːk] *vi.* 发出臭味 (to give off an unpleasant odor);冒烟 (to give out smoke)

危 险

*perilous ['perələs] *adj.* 危险的(dangerous; hazardous)

【记】来自peril(*n.* 危险)

**peril ['perəl] *n.* 危险,危机;危险的事物

**precarious [prɪˈkeəriəs] *adj.* 不稳定的,危险的(uncertain; unsafe)

【记】pre(前)+ car(汽车)+ ious → 在汽车前面 → 危险的

【反】safe（*adj.* 安全的）；secure（*adj.* 安全的）；stable（*adj.* 稳定的）

us ['hæzərdəs] *adj.* 危险的，冒险的（dangerous; perilous）

【例】People hesitated whether to begin the *hazardous* journey to the unknown west or not.

*deleterious [ˌdeləˈtɪriəs] *adj.* （对身心）有害的（harmful; detrimental）

*detrimental [ˌdetrɪˈmentl] *adj.* 有害的，有损的

【例】The *detrimental* newspaper article may lead to a lawsuit.

**jeopardize ['dʒepərdaɪz] *vt.* 危及，使濒于危险境地（to endanger）

【记】jeopard（看做leopard，豹）+ize → 环境污染导致这个地区的豹濒临灭绝 → 危及

【例】The security of the whole operation has been *jeopardized* by one careless person.

maim [meɪm] *vt.* 使残废（to disable; mutilate）

【记】和main（*adj.* 主要的）一起记

【例】He was seriously *maimed* in a car accident.

*impair [ɪmˈper] *vt.* 损害（to harm; damage）

【记】im（进入）+pair（坏）→ 使…坏 → 损害

【例】His misdeeds greatly *impaired* our friendship.

*emergent [iˈmɜːrdʒənt] *adj.* 紧急的，意外的；出现的，新兴的

【例】money laid aside for *emergent* contingencies // As it was, this undeniably brilliant staging fit an *emergent* pattern: arresting images, tenuous narrative.

exigency ['eksɪdʒənsi] *n.* 紧急（状态），危急（关头），事变（urgent situation）

【例】In this *exigency*, we must look for aid from our allies.

**mischief ['mɪstʃɪf] *n.* 恶作剧，捣蛋，顽皮；淘气鬼

【例】The child was a *mischief* in school.

*futility [fjuːˈtɪləti] *n.* 无用，无益

【记】futile（*adj.* 琐细无用的）

invulnerable [ɪnˈvʌlnərəbl] *adj.* 无法伤害的（incapable of being wounded or injured）

【记】in（不）+vulnerable（易受攻击的）→ 无法伤害的

*nihilistic [ˌnaɪɪˈlɪstɪk] *adj.* 虚无主义的；无政府主义的

【例】They became terrorists, providing an example of how passionate convictions can mutate into a *nihilistic* murderousness.

需　要

**indispensable　[ˌɪndɪˈspensəbl] *adj.* 不可缺少的，绝对必要的（essential; vital）

*basal　[ˈbeɪsl] *adj.* 基本的，基础的（basic; foundational）

【例】"These more ancient or *basal* species", she explained, "walk towards intruders and try to attack them."

requisite　[ˈrekwɪzɪt] *n.* 必需品（sth that is needed or necessary）*adj.* 必要的（required）

【记】re + quisite(寻求) → 反复寻求的 → 必要的

*requisition　[ˌrekwɪˈzɪʃn] *n.* 正式要求；(尤指军队)征用（official, usually written, demand for the use of property or materials by an army in wartime or by certain people in an emergency）

【例】make a *requisition* on headquarters for supplies

*dispensable　[dɪˈspensəbl] *adj.* 可有可无的，非必需的（unnecessary; unimportant）

【例】This magazine is *dispensable*, so let's discontinue our subscription.

*baseless　[ˈbeɪsləs] *adj.* 无根据的，无基础的

【例】Iranian Foreign Ministry spokesman Hamid-Reza Asefi has accused Israel of being behind the "*baseless* allegations".

壮　丽

*splendid　[ˈsplendɪd] *adj.* 灿烂的，辉煌的（magnificent）；极好的，令人极其满意的

【记】splend(明亮) + id → 灿烂的

【例】win a *splendid* victory // Thank you for cooking a most *splendid* meal tonight!

*regal　[ˈriːgl] *adj.* 帝王的（of a king）；华丽的（splendid）

【记】reg（统治）+ al → 帝王的；注意不要和 regale(*vt.* 款待)相混

【派】regality(*n.* 君权，王位)

**grandiose　[ˈgrændioʊs] *adj.* 宏伟的（impressive because of uncommon largeness）；浮夸的，夸大的（characterized by affectation or exaggeration）

【记】grandi(大的) + ose(多…的) → 多大的 → 宏伟的

*florid [ˈflɑːrɪd] adj. 华丽的(highly decorated; showy);(脸色)红润的(rosy; ruddy)

【记】flor(花)+ id → 像花一样的 → 华丽的

**resplendent [rɪˈsplendənt] adj. 华丽的，辉煌的(shining brilliantly)

【记】re + splend(明亮)+ ent → 不断发光 → 辉煌的

【反】dull(adj. 阴暗的)

*spectacular [spekˈtækjələr] adj. 引人注目的，惊人的;引人入胜的，壮观的(breathtaking; impressive; striking)

【例】The most *spectacular* thing that ever happened this century would be the introduction of computer.

*solemn [ˈsɑːləm] adj. 庄严的，隆重的(grave; somber)

**magnificent [mægˈnɪfɪsnt] n. 壮丽的，华丽的(gallant; splendid);高贵的，庄严的

【记】magn(大)+ ificent → 壮丽的

*pageant [ˈpædʒənt] n. 壮观的游行(a spectacular exhibition);露天历史剧

【记】page(页)+ ant(蚂蚁)→ 一页纸上蚂蚁浩浩荡荡爬过 → 壮观的游行

*glistening [ˈglɪːsnɪŋ] adj. 闪亮的，闪耀的(brilliant; shiny)

【记】来自glisten(v. 闪耀，发光)

【例】If you scrape the dirt away, you find the fiery brown nut, like a jewel, *glistening* within.

billowing [ˈbɪloʊɪŋ] adj. 如波浪般翻滚的，汹涌的(surgent; onrushing)

【例】Returning home after the handymen had gone, they saw smoke *billowing* from their house.

本　质

*intrinsical [ɪnˈtrɪnsɪkl] adj. 本质的，固有的，内在的(internal; substantive)

【例】Paying careful attention and responding quickly are *intrinsical* parts of good driving. // Thinking can indirectly and resumptively reflects *intrinsical* attribute and inherent rule of existent in the function of human brain.

*rudimentary [ˌruːdɪˈmentri] adj. 基本的，初步的;根本的，低级的，未发展完全的(undeveloped; elementary; primitive; unsophisticated)

【记】rudi(无知的)+ ment + ary → 无知的 → 低级的

【例】I took a *rudimentary* cooking class in high school.

inherent ［ɪnˈhɪrənt］*adj.* 固有的，内在的（innate; intrinsic）

【记】in（里面）+ her（粘连）+ ent → 在里面粘连 → 内在的

*foundational ［faʊnˈdeɪʃnəl］*adj.* 基础的，根本的（fundamental）

【例】When it came to something as *foundational* as that, we could not have dissension.

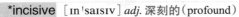

**abstruse ［æbˈstruːs］*adj.* 深奥的，难懂的（complicated; profound）

【记】abs + trus（走）+ e → 走不进去的 → 难懂的

*incisive ［ɪnˈsaɪsɪv］*adj.* 深刻的（profound）

【例】His *incisive* criticism gave us a thorough understanding of Dicksen's writings.

*substantive ［səbˈstæntɪv］*adj.* 实质性的（actual）

【例】An accident is just the appearance; a malicious murder is actually *substantive*.

innate ［ɪˈneɪt］*adj.* 与生俱来的，天生的（inborn; inherent）

【记】in（进）+ nate（生）→ 出生时一起来的 → 与生俱来的

【例】The singer had an *innate* talent for music.

*inborn ［ˌɪnˈbɔːrn］*adj.* 与生俱来的，天生的（innate）

【记】in（内）+ born（出生）→ 与生俱来的

【例】Man's ability to compute is far from *inborn*; you have to acquire after birth.

*crude ［kruːd］*adj.* 天然的，生的；未加工的，未提炼的（raw; unpolished; unprocessed）

*spontaneous ［spɑːnˈteɪniəs］*adj.* 自发的，本能的（impulsive; involuntary）

【记】spont（自然）+ aneous → 自然的 → 自发的

【例】There was a storm of *spontaneous* applause at the end of Mary's speech.

*inward ［ˈɪnwərd］*adj.* 内部的，里面的；（尤指）内心的，精神的（situated within; inner）

【例】*inward* thoughts / feelings / doubts

extrinsic ［eksˈtrɪnsɪk］*adj.*（指性质、价值等）非固有的，外来的，外在的（not belonging to or part of the real nature of a person or thing; coming from outside）

【例】information *extrinsic* to the situation

*bynature ［baɪˈneɪtʃər］*adv.* 生性地，天生地

*subconscious [ˌsʌb'kɑːnʃəs] *adj.* 下意识的，潜意识的（existing in the mind but not immediately available to consciousness）

【例】the *subconscious* self

效　果

effectual [ɪ'fektʃuəl] *adj.* 奏效的，有效的（efficient）

efficacy ['efɪkəsi] *n.* 功效，有效性（the power to produce an effect）

【记】ef(出)+fic(做)+acy → 做出了成绩 → 功效，有效性

*validate ['vælɪdeɪt] *vt.* 使生效（to make legally valid）

【记】来自valid(*adj.* 有效的)

valid ['vælɪd] *adj.* 有效的（soundly based; acceptable）

【例】The traveler's passport is *valid* within 10 months.

*impotent ['ɪmpətənt] *adj.* 无力的，虚弱的（lacking in power, strength）；无效的

【记】im(不)+potent(有力的) → 无力的

ineffectual [ˌɪnɪ'fektʃuəl] *adj.* 无效的，徒劳无益的（without effect）

【记】来自effectual(*adj.* 有效的)

*inefficacious [ˌɪnefɪ'keɪʃəs] *adj.* 无用的，无效果的（useless）

【记】来自efficacious(*adj.* 有效的)

unrequited [ˌʌnrɪ'kwaɪtɪd] *adj.* 无报答的（not reciprocated or returned in kind）

【反】remunerative(*adj.* 有报酬的)

*overarch [ˌoʊvər'ɑːrtʃ] *vt.* 在…上形成拱形

【记】来自arch(*n.* 拱形)

asymmetric [ˌeɪsɪ'metrɪk] *adj.* 不对称的（having sides that are not alike）

【记】a(不)+sym(相同)+metr(测量)+ic → 测量不同 → 不对称的

*impractical [ɪm'præktɪkl] *adj.* 不切实际的，无用的（unrealistic）

【例】It was *impractical* to think that we could build the house in one month.

forthright ['fɔːrθraɪt] *adv.* 径直地 *adj.* 直接的，直率的（frank; direct）

【例】The brave soldiers marched *forthright* with a knowledge that there would not be any enemy ahead.

*oblique [ə'bliːk] *adj.* 间接的，拐弯抹角的（not straightforward）；倾斜的（inclined）

【记】发音似"哦，不立刻" → 间接的

【反】direct(*adj.* 直接的)

附　属

*subordinate [səˈbɔːrdɪnət] *adj.* 次要的，附属的（inferior; secondary）

【记】sub（下面）+ ordin（顺序）+ ate → 顺序位于下面 → 附属的

【例】Pleasure should be *subordinate* to duty.

auxiliary [ɔːɡˈzɪliəri] *adj.* 辅助的，协助的（subordinate; additional; supplementary）

【记】aux（=aug提高）+ iliary → 帮助提高的 → 辅助的

*incidental [ˌɪnsɪˈdentl] *adj.* 附带的，伴随的（not essential; minor）；偶然的；容易发生的

accessory [əkˈsesəri] *adj.* 附属的，附加的（additional; supplementary; subsidiary）*n.* 附件，配件；小饰品

【反】primary（*adj.* 主要的，首要的）

*complement [ˈkɑːmplɪmənt] *n.* 补足物 [ˈkɑːmplɪment] *vt.* 补足

【记】和complete（*vt.* 使完整）一起记

adjunct [ˈædʒʌŋkt] *n.* 附加物，附件（sth joined or added to another thing but not essentially a part of it）

【记】ad + junct（结合，连接）→ 连在上面的东西 → 附加物

derivative [dɪˈrɪvətɪv] *adj.* 派生的 *n.* 派生物；【语】派生词

append [əˈpend] *vt.* 附加，添加（to attach）；悬挂

【例】I shall *append* this chart to my report.

codicil [ˈkɑːdəsl] *n.* 遗嘱的附录，附加条款（supplement to the body of a will; later addition to a will）

练 习 题

填空题

aromatic	disgorge	grandiose	indispensable	inherent
innate	invulnerable	inward	jeopardize	maim
mischief	perilous	piquant	pungent	queasy
rudimentary	solemn	splendid	spontaneous	substantive

1. The plant is strongly _____.
2. The air was _____ with the smell of spices.
3. A _____ bit of gossip is going on here among these ladies.
4. Travelling by boat makes me _____.
5. The pipe _____ sewage into the sea.
6. We came _____ close to disaster.
7. He would never do anything to _____ his career.
8. Hundreds of people are killed or _____ in car accidents every week.
9. Those children are always getting into _____.
10. The submarine is _____ to attack while at sea.
11. Cars have become an _____ part of our lives.
12. It will be a _____ opportunity to practise your Spanish.
13. The _____ scheme for a journey across the desert came to nothing.
14. She _____ promised not to say a word to anyone about it.
15. His understanding of the language is very _____.
16. Violence is _____ in our society.
17. The report concluded that no _____ changes were necessary.
18. He never lost his _____ sense of fun.
19. The audience burst into _____ applause.
20. Her calm expression hid her _____ panic.

配对题

1. relish	深奥的	11. emergent	本质的, 固有的
2. fragrant	生性地, 天生地	12. requisite	发霉的, 有霉臭的
3. cloying	甜得发腻的	13. dispensable	壮观的游行
4. palatable	(对身心)有害的	14. regal	味美的
5. spice	可有可无的	15. pageant	危险, 危机; 危险的事物
6. musty	紧急的, 意外的	16. intrinsic	帝王的; 华丽的
7. succulent	基础的, 根本的	17. foundational	滋味, 美味
8. peril	(花草)香的, 芬芳的	18. abstruse	必需品
9. deleterious	损害	19. inborn	香料, 调味品
10. impair	天生的	20. bynature	多汁的, 多水分的

练习题答案

填空题答案

1. The plant is strongly <u>aromatic</u>.
2. The air was <u>pungent</u> with the smell of spices.
3. A <u>piquant</u> bit of gossip is going on here among these ladies.
4. Travelling by boat makes me <u>queasy</u>.
5. The pipe <u>disgorges</u> sewage into the sea.
6. We came <u>perilously</u> close to disaster.
7. He would never do anything to <u>jeopardize</u> his career.
8. Hundreds of people are killed or <u>maimed</u> in car accidents every week.
9. Those children are always getting into <u>mischief</u>.
10. The submarine is <u>invulnerable</u> to attack while at sea.
11. Cars have become an <u>indispensable</u> part of our lives.
12. It will be a <u>splendid</u> opportunity to practise your Spanish.
13. The <u>grandiose</u> scheme for a journey across the desert came to nothing.
14. She <u>solemnly</u> promised not to say a word to anyone about it.
15. His understanding of the language is very <u>rudimentary</u>.
16. Violence is <u>inherent</u> in our society.
17. The report concluded that no <u>substantive</u> changes were necessary.
18. He never lost his <u>innate</u> sense of fun.
19. The audience burst into <u>spontaneous</u> applause.
20. Her calm expression hid her <u>inward</u> panic.

配对题答案

1. relish	滋味，美味	11. emergent	紧急的，意外的
2. fragrant	（花草）香的，芬芳的	12. requisite	必需品
3. cloying	甜得发腻的	13. dispensable	可有可无的
4. palatable	味美的	14. regal	帝王的；华丽的
5. spice	香料，调味品	15. pageant	壮观的游行
6. musty	发霉的，有霉臭的	16. intrinsic	本质的，固有的
7. succulent	多汁的，多水分的	17. foundational	基础的，根本的
8. peril	危险，危机；危险的事物	18. abstruse	深奥的
9. deleterious	（对身心）有害的	19. inborn	天生的
10. impair	损害	20. bynature	生性地，天生地

Word List 26

状态（一）

变 化

*amorphous [əˈmɔːrfəs] *adj.* 无定形的（without definite form; shapeless）

【记】a（表否定）+ morph（形状）+ ous → 无定形的

【派】amorphousness（*n.* 无定形）

caprice [kəˈpriːs] *n.* 奇思怪想，变化无常，任性（sudden change in attitude or behavior）

【记】cap（帽子）+ rice（米饭）→ 戴上帽子吃米饭 → 任性

**capricious [kəˈprɪʃəs] *adj.* 变化无常的，任性的（erratic; flighty）

【反】resolute（*adj.* 坚决的）；steadfast（*adj.* 不变的）

【派】capriciousness（*n.* 反复无常）

checkered [ˈtʃekərd] *adj.* （命运）盛衰无常的（with many changes of fortune）；有方格的

【记】来自checker（*n.* 棋盘上的方格或棋子），棋子一会儿就可能被吃掉，所以多变无常

【例】a family with a *checkered* past

**fickle [ˈfɪkl] *adj.* （感情、天气等）多变的（changeable; capricious）

【例】The weather in this area is *fickle*, and you can never foretell.

*mercurial [mɜːrˈkjʊriəl] *adj.* （指人或情绪）善变的，喜怒无常的（changeable; fickle in temperament）；活泼的，机智的（animated; sprightly）

【记】来自mercury（*n.* 水银），水银流动性极强 → 活泼的

【反】constant（*adj.* 恒定的）

**mutability [ˌmjuːtəˈbɪləti] *n.* 易变性（changeableness）；性情不定

【例】Here, earlier in the work, his focus remains the *mutability* of artistic representation.

*protean [ˈproʊtiən] *adj.* 变化多端的，多变的（continually changing）

【反】static（*adj.* 静态的）

*volatile [ˈvɑːlətl] *adj.* （性情等）反复无常的，波动的（subject to rapid or unexpected change）；（液体等）挥发性的（readily vaporizable）

【记】volat(飞) + ile → 飞走的 → 挥发性的

【反】stable(*adj.* 稳定的)；constant(*adj.* 稳定的)

*alter [ˈɔːltər] *v.* 改变，更改（to change）

【派】alteration(*n.* 改变，变更)

*ameliorate [əˈmiːliəreɪt] *v.* 改善，改良（to improve）

【记】a + melior(=better 更好) + ate → 改善

【反】aggravate/deteriorate(*v.* 恶化)

【派】amelioration(*n.* 改善，改良)

**convert [kənˈvɜːrt] *vt.* 转换（to change; transform）

【记】con + vert(转) → 转换

【例】I *converted* the spare bedroom into a reading room.

*deform [dɪˈfɔːrm] *vt.* 使变形（to disfigure; distort）

【记】de(坏) + form(形状) → 使变形

【例】A constant wind *deformed* the tree.

**deteriorate [dɪˈtɪriəreɪt] *v.* （使）变坏，（使）恶化（to make inferior in quality or value）

【记】deterior(拉丁文，糟糕的) + ate → （使）恶化

*divert [daɪˈvɜːrt] *vt.* 使转向，使改道（to turn from one course to another）；使分心；娱乐（to entertain）

【记】di(偏离) + vert(转；偏离) → 使转向

diversion [daɪˈvɜːrʒn] *n.* 转移，转换（act of turning aside）；转移注意力；解闷，娱乐（pastime）

*enrich [ɪnˈrɪtʃ] *vt.* 丰富（to make rich; enhance）

【记】en + rich(富) → 丰富

【例】I *enriched* my coffee with cream and sugar.

garbled [ˈgɑːrbld] *adj.* 信息混乱的，引起误解的（misleading）；窜改的（falsifying）

*recant [rɪˈkænt] *v.* 改变，放弃（以前的信仰），撤回（原先的主张）(to withdraw or repudiate (a statement or belief))

【记】re(反) + cant(唱) → 唱反调 → 改变，放弃（以前的信仰）

【反】affirm(*v.* 断言，肯定)

*recast [ˌriːˈkæst] v. 重新铸造；彻底改造

【记】re(重新) + cast(铸造) → 重新铸造

【例】I just *recast* the parts of my car.

*reclaim [rɪˈkleɪm] vt. 纠正，使改过(to rescue from an undesirable state)；开垦(土地)

【记】re + claim(喊) → 喊回来 → 纠正

*rectify [ˈrektɪfaɪ] vt. 改正，调整 (to correct by removing errors; adjust)；提纯，精炼(to purify by repeated distillation)

【记】rect(直) + ify → 使⋯直 → 调整

【派】rectification(n. 改正，校正；提纯)

*refrigeration [rɪˌfrɪdʒəˈreɪʃn] n. 制冷，冷藏

【例】He has a *refrigeration* system of three different temperatures, and a whole host of proper glassware.

**sag [sæg] vi. (因负重或受压)向下凹或中间下陷(sink or curve down in the middle under weight or pressure)

【例】The tent began to *sag* as the canvas became wet.

shunt [ʃʌnt] v. 使 (火车) 转到另一轨道，转轨 (to switch a train from one track to another)

swerve [swɜːrv] v. (使) 突然改变方向，转弯 (to turn aside abruptly from a straight line or course; deviate)

【记】改变发球(serve)方向(swerve)

【反】maintain direction(保持方向)

*transform [trænsˈfɔːrm] v. (使)改变, (使)变换(to change; transmute)

【记】trans(变) + form(形) → 改变

【例】A fresh coat of paint can *transform* a room.

transmute [trænzˈmjuːt] vt. 使变形，使变化(to change or alter)

【记】trans(改变) + mute(变化) → 使变化

【例】He has failed to *transmute* this situation.

veer [vɪr] v. 调转船尾向上风; (使)改变方向(to turn; swerve)

【例】The car *veered* to the left toward ours and we were scared.

whim [wɪm] n. 奇想，怪念头(a sudden idea; fancy)

**alternate [ˈɔːltərnət] adj. 轮流的，交替的 (occurring or succeeding by turns)；供选择的 v. (使)轮流, (使)交替(to perform by turns or in succession) n. 候选人；替代性选择 (one that substitutes for or alternates with another)

*counterclockwise [ˌkaʊntər'klɑːkwaɪz] *adj./adv.* 逆时针方向的(地)
【记】counter(反) + clockwise(顺时针方向的) → 逆时针方向的
【例】For instance, scrolling down requires a *counterclockwise* turn of the wheel, instead of the expected clockwise direction.

*bifurcation [ˌbaɪfər'keɪʃn] *n.* 分歧;分叉(divergence)
【记】bi(二) + furca(=fork 叉子) + tion → 分叉
【例】If you keep your balance, such *bifurcation* can be useful.

*enrichment [ɪn'rɪtʃmənt] *n.* 丰富,富裕(abundance);添加肥料;增加食物营养
【例】Good books are an *enrichment* of life.

flux [flʌks] *n.* 不断的变动,动荡不定 (continual change; condition of not being settled);流出;涨潮
【记】flu(流动) + x → 不断的变动

transition [træn'zɪʃn] *n.* 转变,变迁;过渡(change; shift)
【记】trans(交换) + it(走) + ion → 转变
【例】Spring is a *transition* from winter into summer.

**upheaval [ʌp'hiːvl] *n.* 动乱,大变动(extreme agitation or disorder);举起;鼓起
【记】来自upheave(*v.* 举起;鼓起;(使)发生动乱)

*variability [ˌveriə'bɪləti] *n.* 可变性,变化性(adaptability)
【记】来自variable(*adj.* 易变的)
【例】There is a lot of *variability* in the appearance of skin tissue.

*vicissitude [vɪ'sɪsɪtjuːd] *n.* 变化,变迁;荣枯;盛衰 (natural change or mutation visible in nature or in human affairs)

扩 大

accrue [ə'kruː] *v.* (利息等)增加(to increase the interest on money);自然增多(to accumulate)
【记】ac + crue(增加) → 自然增多
【例】Some of this debt has *accrued* since the 1980s.

*amplify ['æmplɪfaɪ] *vt.* 放大,增强
【例】We need to *amplify* the electric current.

*bulge [bʌldʒ] *v.* (使)膨胀,(使)鼓起(to swell; protrude or project) *n.* 鼓起的部分;膨胀,鼓起;(短暂的)增加,上涨
【记】比较记忆:budge(*v.* 让步);bilge(*n.* 舱底);bugle(*n.* 军号)
【例】A green sensor light turned red when he touched the *bulge*.
【反】depressed region(凹陷的地方)

*enhance [ɪnˈhæns] *vt.* 增加，增强(to raise; improve; heighten)

【例】You can *enhance* your appearance with makeup.

*dilate [daɪˈleɪt] *v.* (使)膨胀，扩大(to expand; widen)

【记】di(分开) + late → 扩大

【例】I *dilated* the opening in the turkey and pushed the stuffing in.

*distend [dɪˈstend] *v.* (使)膨胀，扩大，扩张(to stretch out; become swollen; expand)

【记】dis(分开) + tend(拉) → 向四面拉 → 膨胀

【反】compress(*v.* 压缩)

*distension [dɪˈstenʃn] *n.* 膨胀，扩张(inflation; expansion)

【反】compression(*n.* 压缩)

*inflate [ɪnˈfleɪt] *v.* (使)(轮胎、气球等)充气，膨胀；使得意

【例】With a supply of compressed air the large balloon *inflated* in a matter of seconds.

**swell [swel] *v.* 肿胀，肿起(to become distended or puffed up)；(使)隆起；(使)增加

【例】My ankle began to *swell* when I injured it.

accretion [əˈkriːʃn] *n.* 自然的增加 (growth in size by accumulation)；增加物(addition)

【例】A chimney was blocked by an *accretion* of soot.

*escalate [ˈeskəleɪt] *v.* 乘自动升降梯；(使)(战争等)逐步升级 (to make a conflict more serious)；(使)扩大，(使)上升 (to grow or increase rapidly)

【记】来自escalator(*n.* 自动扶梯)

【反】diminish(*v.* 减少，减小)

*lengthen [ˈleŋθən] *v.* (使)延长，加长

*magnify [ˈmæɡnɪfaɪ] *v.* 放大(to enlarge)；赞美(to glorify; extol)

【记】magn(大) + ify → 放大

【派】magnification(*n.* 放大，扩大)

**supplement [ˈsʌplɪmənt] *vt./n.* 增补，补充 (sth that completes or makes an addition)

【记】supple(=supply 提供) + ment → 补充

*wax [wæks] *vi.* 增大，增强(to increase in phase or intensity)；月亮渐满

【反】decrease(*v.* 减少)

缩 减

abate [əˈbeɪt] *v.* 减轻，减少，减小，减弱(to lessen; diminish; dwindle; subside)
【例】It is reported that flu has been *abating* due to a warm winter.

*abbreviate [əˈbriːvieɪt] *vt.* 缩短 (to make shorter)；缩写 (to shorten a word or phrase)
【记】ab(加强) + brev(短) + iate → 缩短
【派】abbreviation(*n.* 缩短；缩写)

compress [kəmˈpres] *vt.* 压缩，浓缩(to press together; contract)
【记】com(全部) + press(压) → 全部压 → 压缩
【派】compression(*n.* 压缩)
【反】increase in volume(增大体积)

*constrict [kənˈstrɪkt] *v.* 收紧，束紧(to squeeze; make smaller or narrower)
【记】和strict(*adj.* 严格的)一起记
【例】The snake *constricted* its body around its prey and killed it.

*curtail [kɜːrˈteɪl] *vt.* 缩减；缩短，省略(to cut back; reduce)
【记】cur(看做cut，切) + tail(尾巴) → 切掉尾巴 → 减缩
【例】The discussions were *curtailed* when the fire alarm went off.

*diminish [dɪˈmɪnɪʃ] *v.* 减少，缩小(to decrease; dwindle)
【记】di(向下) + mini(小) + ish → 小下去 → 缩小
【例】Unexpected expenses *diminished* the size of my bank account.

**diminution [ˌdɪmɪˈnuːʃn] *n.* 减少，缩小
【记】di + minu(变小，减少) + tion → 减少，缩小

**dock [dɑːk] *vt.* 剪短(尾巴等)；扣除(工资、津贴的一部分)；使(船)进港
【记】把扣除的工资(docked wage)锁(lock)起来
【例】Bob's pay was *docked* for being late.

**dwindle [ˈdwɪndl] *v.* (使)减少，(使)缩小(to diminish; decrease)
【例】The stream will continue to *dwindle* if it doesn't rain.

*muffle [ˈmʌfl] *vt.* 使(声音)降低(to deaden the sound of)；裹住，蒙住(to envelop)

*reductive [rɪˈdʌktɪv] *adj.* 还原的；减少的
【记】来自reduce(*v.* 减少)

*retrench [rɪˈtrentʃ] v. 节省，紧缩(费用)(to economize; to cut down expenses)

【记】re + trench(切掉) → 把开支再切掉 → 节省

【反】enlarge(v. 增大)

retrenchment [rɪˈtrentʃmənt] n. 节省，削减 (reduction, especially a cutting of expenses)

【记】来自retrench(v. 节省)

*rundown [ˈrʌndaʊn] n. 裁减，减少；概要

**truncate [ˈtrʌŋkeɪt] vt. 将(树木等)截短，去尾(to shorten by cutting off)

【记】trunc(=trunk 树干) + ate → 截去树干的一部分 → 截短

【反】prolong(vt. 延长)

*whittle [ˈwɪtl] v. 削(木头)(to pare or cut off chips)；削减(to reduce; pare)

【记】wh(看做whet，磨刀) + ittle(看做little，小) → 磨刀把木头削小 → 削木头

*taper [ˈteɪpər] n. 细蜡烛(very thin candle) v. (长形物体的一头)逐渐变细(to become progressively smaller toward one end)；(使)逐渐减小或变弱

衰 弱

attenuate [əˈtenjueɪt] v. (使)变稀；(使)变细(to make slender)；(使)变弱(to lessen; weaken)

【记】at + ten(拉) + uate → 一再拉，力量用尽 → 变弱

【反】strengthen(vt. 加强)

【派】attenuation(n. 稀释；变细；减弱)

bate [beɪt] v. 减少，降低，衰落 (to let down; lessen the force of; moderate; restrain)

【例】The salesman won't *bate* a penny of it.

*debilitate [dɪˈbɪlɪteɪt] vt. 使衰弱，使虚弱 (to make weak or feeble; weaken)

【反】invigorate(vt. 使有活力)；fortify(vt. 加强)

*deplete [dɪˈpliːt] vt. 耗尽，用尽；使(精力等)衰竭(to exhaust)

【例】I always replenish my food supply before it is *depleted*.

*enervate [ˈenərveɪt] vt. 使失去活力，使衰弱(to enfeeble; weaken)

【例】The dullness of the lecture as well as the heat of the day *enervated* the students, who were all too tired.

languish [ˈlæŋgwɪʃ] *vi.* 变衰弱(to wither; fade)
【例】The prisoners have been *languishing* for years in the dungeon.

*unnerving [ˌʌnˈnɜːrvɪŋ] *adj.* 使人紧张不安的
【例】It's very *unnerving* but we can clearly see there are other priorities out the window.

*wane [weɪn] *vi.* 月亏，月缺；变小，变弱（to decrease in size, extent, or degree; dwindle）；衰败，衰落
【例】The moon *wanes* after it has become full.

attrition [əˈtrɪʃn] *n.* 消耗，消损（process of gradually weakening the strength and confidence by continuous harassment）
【例】a war of *attrition*

debauch [dɪˈbɔːtʃ] *v.* 使放荡，使堕落(to corrupt; make intemperate)
【记】de + bauch(看做beam，大梁) → 大梁倒塌 → 使堕落
【例】A vicious newspaper can *debauch* public ideals.

decadence [ˈdekədəns] *n.* 衰落，颓废
【记】de + cad(落下) + ence → 颓废
【例】The mayor criticized the teenagers for their *decadence*.

**decay [dɪˈkeɪ] *v.* (使)腐败(to rot; decompose)
【例】Sugar can cause tooth to *decay*.

degenerate [dɪˈdʒenərət] *adj.* 堕落的，衰退的 [dɪˈdʒenəreɪt] *vi.* 堕落，衰退(to degrade; deteriorate）
【记】de(坏) + gene(产生) + rate → 产生坏的行为 → 堕落的
【例】I was shocked by the lack of morals in this *degenerate* book.

*degrade [dɪˈgreɪd] *vt.* 使降级，使堕落(to degenerate; lower)
【记】de(向下) + grade(级) → 使降级
【例】He *degraded* himself by cheating and telling lies.

*depravity [dɪˈprævəti] *n.* 堕落，恶习
【记】de + prav (坏) + ity → 变坏 → 堕落；注意不要和deprivation (*n.* 剥夺)相混

*atrophy [ˈætrəfi] *n.* （身体或身体某部位因缺乏营养或不常使用而）萎缩（wasting away of the body or part of it through lack of nourishment or use）；衰退，萎缩
【例】The cultural life of the country will sink into *atrophy* unless more writers and artists emerge.

blighted [ˈblaɪtɪd] *adj.* 枯萎的(withered)
【反】flourishing(*adj.* 茂盛的)

*decomposition [ˌdiːkɑːmpəˈzɪʃn] *n.* 分解；腐烂

【记】来自decompose(*vt.* 分解；使腐烂)

*decrepit [dɪˈkrepɪt] *adj.* 衰老的；破旧的

【记】de + crepit(破裂声) → 破裂掉 → 破旧的

【反】sturdy(*adj.* 强健的)；vigorous(*adj.* 健壮的)

【派】decrepitude(*n.* 衰老，破旧)

gaunt [gɔːnt] *adj.* 面容憔悴的，瘦削的 (thin and bony; hollowed-eyed and haggard)

【记】因长期被嘲弄(taunt)，所以憔悴(gaunt)

*inanimate [ɪnˈænɪmət] *adj.* 无生命的(not animate; lifeless)

【记】in(无) + anim(生命) + ate → 无生命的

wither [ˈwɪðər] *vi.* 枯萎，凋零

【记】天气(weather)不好植物就会枯萎(wither)

【反】burgeon(*vi.* 发芽)；revive(*v.* 复活)

anguish [ˈæŋgwɪʃ] *n.* 极大痛苦(great suffering; distress)

【记】angu(折磨) + ish → 折磨使痛苦 → 极大痛苦

ashen [ˈæʃn] *adj.* 像灰的，灰白色的，苍白的(very pale)

【记】来自ash(*n.* 灰)

【例】a face *ashen* with grief // She listened to the tragic news *ashen*-faced.

*bedridden [ˈbedrɪdn] *adj.* 卧床不起的

【记】bed(床) + ridden → 卧床不起的

【例】With two sons *bedridden*, Mrs Smith was ill at ease.

emaciated [ɪˈmeɪʃieɪtɪd] *adj.* 瘦弱的，憔悴的(skinny; haggard)

【记】来自emaciate(*vt.* 使憔悴)

【例】A bus transported the *emaciated* refugees to the camp.

*fatigue [fəˈtiːg] *n.* 疲乏，劳累(physical or mental exhaustion; weariness)

【记】fat(胖的) + igue → 胖人容易劳累 → 疲乏，劳累

*frail [freɪl] *adj.* 身体虚弱的；脆弱的，不结实的(fragile; flimsy)

【例】My grandmother is *frail*, but she's still very alert.

infirmity [ɪnˈfɜːrməti] *n.* 虚弱，衰弱

【例】The little girl's *infirmity* was not the result of the local climate.

**malaise [məˈleɪz] *n.* 不适，不舒服(a feeling of illness)

【记】发音似"没累死" → 差点没累死 → 不适

*swoon [swuːn] *vi.* 昏厥，晕倒（to lose consciousness; faint）

【例】She *swooned* into his arms for joy.

**vulnerable ['vʌlnərəbl] *adj.* 易受伤害的，易受攻击的（capable of being physically wounded; assailable）

【记】vulner(受伤) + able → 易受伤的

【派】vulnerability(*n.* 易受攻击)

wispy ['wɪspi] *adj.* 纤细的，脆弱的

Why do you look at the speck of sawdust in your brother's eye and pay no attention to the plank in your own eye?

为什么看见你弟兄眼中有刺，却不想自己眼中有梁木呢。

——《圣经·新·太》7:3

填空题

abate	accrue	alter	ameliorate	bulge
capricious	compress	curtail	debilitate	deform
degrade	diminish	enrich	flux	garbled
lengthen	infirmity	muffle	swerve	unnerving

1. Romantic heroines are often _____.
2. The little girl's _____ was not the result of the local climate.
3. Property prices did not significantly _____ during 1999.
4. Steps have been taken to _____ the situation.
5. The disease had _____ his spine.
6. The study of science has _____ all our lives.
7. There was a _____ message from her on my answering machine.
8. The bus suddenly _____ into his path.
9. Our society is in a state of _____.
10. Interest will _____ if you keep your money in a savings account.
11. Her pockets were _____ with presents.
12. The afternoon shadows _____.
13. Steps are to be taken to _____ pollution.
14. As more snow fell, the bottom layer was _____ into ice.
15. The lecture was _____ by the fire alarm going off.
16. I don't wish to _____ the importance of their contribution.
17. He tried to _____ the alarm clock by putting it under his pillow.
18. The troops were severely _____ by hunger and disease.
19. She found the whole interview rather _____.
20. This poster is offensive and _____ women.

配对题

1. amorphous	自然的增加		11. distend	堕落，恶习
2. checkered	无定形的		12. accretion	(使)膨胀，胀大，扩张
3. mutability	放大，增强		13. constrict	易变性；性情不定
4. convert	变稀；变细		14. reductive	改变，放弃(以前的信仰)
5. recant	消耗，消损		15. retrench	改正，调整
6. rectify	枯萎的		16. attenuate	还原的；减少的
7. veer	(命运)盛衰无常的		17. attrition	节省，紧缩(费用)
8. whim	收紧，束紧		18. debauch	可变性，变化性
9. variability	转换		19. depravity	改变方向
10. amplify	使放荡，使堕落		20. blighted	奇想，怪念头

练习题答案

填空题答案

1. Romantic heroines are often <u>capricious</u>.
2. The little girl's <u>infirmity</u> was not the result of the local climate.
3. Property prices did not significantly <u>alter</u> during 1999.
4. Steps have been taken to <u>ameliorate</u> the situation.
5. The disease had <u>deformed</u> his spine.
6. The study of science has <u>enriched</u> all our lives.
7. There was a <u>garbled</u> message from her on my answering machine.
8. The bus suddenly <u>swerved</u> into his path.
9. Our society is in a state of <u>flux</u>.
10. Interest will <u>accrue</u> if you keep your money in a savings account.
11. Her pockets were <u>bulging</u> with presents.
12. The afternoon shadows <u>lengthened</u>.
13. Steps are to be taken to <u>abate</u> pollution.
14. As more snow fell, the bottom layer was <u>compressed</u> into ice.
15. The lecture was <u>curtailed</u> by the fire alarm going off.
16. I don't wish to <u>diminish</u> the importance of their contribution.
17. He tried to <u>muffle</u> the alarm clock by putting it under his pillow.
18. The troops were severely <u>debilitated</u> by hunger and disease.
19. She found the whole interview rather <u>unnerving</u>.
20. This poster is offensive and <u>degrades</u> women.

配对题答案

1. amorphous	无定形的	11. distend	（使）膨胀，胀大，扩张
2. checkered	（命运）盛衰无常的	12. accretion	自然的增加
3. mutability	易变性；性情不定	13. constrict	收紧，束紧
4. convert	转换	14. reductive	还原的；减少的
5. recant	改变，放弃(以前的信仰)	15. retrench	节省，紧缩（费用）
6. rectify	改正，调整	16. attenuate	变稀；变细
7. veer	改变方向	17. attrition	消耗，消损
8. whim	奇想，怪念头	18. debauch	使放荡，使堕落
9. variability	可变性，变化性	19. depravity	堕落，恶习
10. amplify	放大，增强	20. blighted	枯萎的

Word List 27
状态(二)

恢 复

irreparable [ɪ'repərəbl] *adj.*（指损失、伤害等）不可弥补的，无法修复的（of a loss, an injury, etc that cannot be put right, restored or repaired）
【记】来自 reparable（*adj.* 可弥补的，可恢复的）
【例】*irreparable* damage

*irretrievable [ˌɪrɪ'triːvəbl] *adj.* 不可挽回的，不能补救的（irreparable）
【例】The breakdown of their marriage was *irretrievable*.

*recyclable [ˌriː'saɪkləbl] *adj.* 可回收利用的，可再循环的
【例】Plastic pallets, relative newcomers, are *recyclable* and lighter, so less fuel is used in transport.

reparable [rɪ'perəbl] *adj.* 能弥补的，可恢复的（capable of being repaired）
【记】来自 repair（*v.* 修补）

*reproductive [ˌriːprə'dʌktɪv] *adj.* 生殖的；再生的，再现的；复制的
【例】The study does not provide any encouragement for dangerous human *reproductive* cloning attempts.

*resilient [rɪ'zɪliənt] *adj.* 有弹性的；能恢复活力的，适应力强的（tending to recover from or adjust easily to misfortune or change）

**reevaluation [ˌriːɪvæljuˈeɪʃn] *n.* 重新评价
【例】The official, however, appeared to agree that new intelligence has prompted a *reevaluation* of Israel's assessment on Iran.

**renewal [rɪ'nuːəl] *n.* 更新，恢复，复兴，重建
【例】But not all companies have their mark in commerce at the time of *renewal*.

**restoration [ˌrestə'reɪʃn] *n.* 恢复，复原；整修，重建（an act of restoring or the condition of being restored）

resumption [rɪ'zʌmpʃn] *n.*（停顿后的）重新开始，恢复
【记】来自 resume（*v.* 重新开始）
【例】no immediate *resumption* of building work

resurrection [ˌrezəˈrekʃn] *n.* 复活，复兴（recovery; retrieval）

【例】Walking deeper into the necropolis one discovers a *resurrection* of Catholic influences amid dizzily eclectic architecture.

*resuscitation [rɪˌsʌsɪˈteɪʃn] *n.* 复苏，复兴；复活

【记】来自 resuscitate(*v.* 复活；复兴)

【例】We must work out a practicable plan for the *resuscitation* of our country.

*reassure [ˌriːəˈʃʊr] *vt.* 使安心，安慰（to restore to confidence）

【例】Kate claps the man on the shoulder to *reassure* him.

recuperate [rɪˈkuːpəreɪt] *v.* 恢复（健康），复原（to recover health or strength）；挽回（损失）

【记】re(重新) + cuper(=gain 获得) + ate → 复原

【派】recuperative(*adj.* 有助于恢复健康的)

rejuvenate [rɪˈdʒuːvəneɪt] *vt.* 使年轻，使返老还童，使充满活力（to make young or youthful again）

【记】re + juven(年轻) + ate → 使年轻

【派】rejuvenation(*n.* 返老还童，恢复活力)

resurge [riˈsɜːrdʒ] *vi.* 复活，复苏（to rise again into life）

【派】resurgence(*n.* 复兴，再起)

revert [rɪˈvɜːrt] *v.* (使)恢复原状（to come back; return）

【例】After her divorce she *reverted* to using her maiden name.

*revitalize [ˌriːˈvaɪtəlaɪz] *vt.* 使重新充满活力（to give new life or vigor to; rejuvenate）

【记】re(重新) + vital(有活力的) + ize → 使重新充满活力

*revive [rɪˈvaɪv] *v.* (使)苏醒；(使)恢复精神；(使)复兴，(使)复苏

【记】re(重新) + vive(活) → 苏醒

【例】The fresh air soon *revived* him.

*energize [ˈenərdʒaɪz] *vt.* 供给…能量；使活跃

【记】来自 energy(*n.* 能量)

【例】I *energized* the motor when I turned on the electric switch.

*rebound [rɪˈbaʊnd] *v.* (使)弹回，(使)反弹（to spring; bounce）

【例】The ball *rebounded* from/off the wall into the pond.

*reconstitute [ˌriːˈkɑːnstətjuːt] *vt.* 再组成(to bring back into existence); (加水)使(脱水食物)复原(to restore by adding water)

【记】re(重新) + constitute(组成) → 再组成

【反】dehydrate(*vt.* 脱水)

*reenact [ˌriːɪˈnækt] *vt.* 重新制定(法律); 再扮演, 重演

【例】Nostalgia can make people do crazy things, like trying to *reenact* a 100-year-old social event.

*refresh [rɪˈfreʃ] *v.* 使清新; (使)恢复精神(to renew; revive)

【记】re(重新) + fresh(新鲜的) → 使清新

【例】I *refreshed* myself with a cup of coffee.

*refurbish [ˌriːˈfɜːrbɪʃ] *vt.* 刷新, 再擦亮(to brighten or freshen up; renovate)

【记】re(重新) + furbish(磨光, 磨亮) → 刷新

*regenerate [rɪˈdʒenəreɪt] *v.* 赋予…新的力量或生命, (使)恢复(to fresh; restore)

【例】The company soon *regenerated* under his leadership.

*regurgitate [rɪˈgɜːrdʒɪteɪt] *v.* (使)(咽下的食物)返回到口中, (使)反刍

**rehabilitate [ˌriːəˈbɪlɪteɪt] *vt.* 使恢复健康; 使恢复原状; 使恢复名誉(to restore)

【记】reh(重新) + abili(能力) + tate → 重新获得能力 → 使恢复原状

【例】After World War II, many factories were *rehabilitated* rather than bulldozed.

*reincorporate [ˌriːɪnˈkɔːrpəreɪt] *v.* (使)再合并, (使)再并入

**retract [rɪˈtrækt] *v.* 缩回 (爪、舌等); 收回, 撤回 (声明等)(to take back; withdraw)

【记】re(回) + tract(拉) → 拉回 → 收回

【例】The company *retracted* its offer of a free ham, because it ran out of hams.

**retrieve [rɪˈtriːv] *vt.* 重新找回(to recover; save)

【记】re(重新) + trieve(找到) → 重新找回

【例】Jane *retrieved* the lost document from the garbage can.

*revoke [rɪˈvoʊk] *vt.* 取消, 撤回, 废除(to cancel; repeal)

【记】re(反) + vok(喊) + e → 喊反话 → 取消

【例】The drunk driver had his driving licence *revoked*.

**unscramble [ˌʌnˈskræmbl] *vt.* 将(杂乱的信息)加以整理(以便理解)(to restore a scrambled message to a form that can be understood)

【例】This particular portion of your nest egg is going to be pretty tough to *unscramble*.

scramble: a disordered mess

缓 和

appease [əˈpiːz] *vt.* 使平静，安抚(to pacify or quiet)
【记】ap + pease(和平) → 使平静
【反】roil(*vt.* 煽动)；vex(*vt.* 烦恼)；rile(*vt.* 激怒)
【派】appeasement(*n.* 平息，缓和)

**console [kənˈsoʊl] *vt.* 安慰(to conciliate; comfort)
【例】The physician *consoled* the parents of the accident victim.

pacify [ˈpæsɪfaɪ] *vt.* 使镇定，抚慰(to appease; placate)
【记】pac(和平，平静) + ify(使) → 使镇定
【例】Even a written apology failed to *pacify* the indignant hostess.

propitiatory [prəˈpɪʃiətɔːri] *adj.* 安抚的，劝解的，讨好的(conciliatory)

**relent [rɪˈlent] *vi.* 动怜悯心，变宽容 (to become less severe or strict)；减弱 (to soften; mollify)
【记】re + lent(=bent 弯曲) → 弯曲下来 → 变宽容
【例】The wind blast has *relented*.

**solace [ˈsɑːləs] *n.* 安慰，慰藉(alleviation of grief or anxiety)
【记】sol(安慰) + ace → 安慰

*soothe [suːð] *v.* 安慰；缓和，减轻(to appease; relieve)；使平静
【例】Kind words can *soothe* when someone is upset.

allay [əˈleɪ] *vt.* 使平静；减轻，缓和(to relieve; reduce the intensity)
【反】aggravate(*vt.* 加重)；intensify(*vt.* 强化)

*alleviate [əˈliːvieɪt] *vt.* 使(痛苦等)减轻(to lighten or relieve)
【记】al + lev(轻) + iate → 使减轻
【反】exacerbate(*vt.* 使恶化)

*assuage [əˈsweɪdʒ] *vt.* 使(痛苦、饥渴等)缓和(to make pain, hunger, thirst, etc less intense)
【记】as + suage(甜) → 关系变甜蜜 → 使缓和
【例】I pray that our Heavenly Father may *assuage* the anguish of your bereavement.

**defuse [ˌdiːˈfjuːz] *vt.* 从(爆破装置)中卸除引信(to remove the fuse from a mine)；使(紧张状态或危急局面)缓和(to remove the tension from a potentially dangerous situation)
【记】de(表否定) + fuse(引信) → 从···中卸除引信
【反】foment(*vt.* 煽动)

**mitigate ['mɪtɪgeɪt] v. 缓和，减轻 (to alleviate; relieve)

【记】 miti(小) + gate(做) → 减轻

【例】 Nothing could *mitigate* the cruelty with which she had treated him.

**mitigator ['mɪtɪgeɪtər] n. 缓和者；缓解物，缓解剂

*mollify ['mɑːlɪfaɪ] vt. 安抚，使安静 (to calm in temper or feeling)

【记】 moll(软) + ify → 软化 → 缓和 → 安抚

【例】 He tries to find ways of *mollifying* her.

palliate ['pælieɪt] vt. 减轻(痛苦) (to reduce; abate)；掩饰(罪行)，为···辩解 (to extenuate)

【记】 pall(罩子) + iate → 盖上(罪行) → 掩饰(罪行)

【反】 exacerbate(vt. 使恶化)

【派】 palliation(n. 减轻，缓和)

*relieved [rɪ'liːvd] adj. 放心的，宽慰的；免除(职责)的 (exempted)

【派】 relief (n. 宽慰)

*release [rɪ'liːs] n. 释放；让渡，让与；豁免

slacken ['slækən] v. (使)松弛 (to loosen)；(使)迟缓 (to slow down)

【记】 来自slack(adj. 松弛的)

【例】 I *slackened* the line to let the fish swim.

temper ['tempər] vt. 缓和，调节 (to modify; modulate)

【例】 He *tempered* his doctrinaire logic with a little practical wisdom.

和 谐

*coexistence [ˌkoʊɪg'zɪstəns] n. 共存，和平共处

【例】 Languages are indeed essential to the identity of groups and individuals and to their peaceful *coexistence*.

*concord ['kɑːŋkɔːrd] n. 和睦 (friendly and peaceful relations)；公约 (agreement)

【记】 con + cord(心，一致) → 心在一起 → 和睦

【反】 dissonance(n. 不和谐); dissension(n. 分歧)

rapport [ræ'pɔːr] n. 关系和睦，意见一致 (relation marked by harmony, conformity)

【记】 和support(v. 支持)一起记

*solidarity [ˌsɑːlɪ'dærəti] n. 团结一致 (unity based on community of interests)

【记】 solid(坚固的) + arity → 团结一致

incongruous [ɪnˈkɑːŋɡruəs] *adj.* 不协调的(inconsistent)

【记】in(不) + congruous(协调的) → 不协调的

【例】It is *incongruous* to insert a dogfood ads into such a serious political report.

*incongruity [ˌɪnkɑːnˈɡruːəti] *n.* 不和谐(之物)

*mediate [ˈmiːdieɪt] *v.* 调停, 斡旋(to intercede; intervene)

【记】medi(中间) + ate → 在中间(走) → 调停

【例】The UN is reponsible for *mediating* between two countries which are at war.

安 静

sedate [sɪˈdeɪt] *adj.* 安静的, 沉着的(calm; composed)

【记】sed(=sid 坐) + ate → 安静地坐着 → 安静的

**tranquil [ˈtræŋkwɪl] *adj.* (生活)安静的, 安宁的(serene; quiet; peaceful)

【例】It is not easy to remain *tranquil* when events suddenly change your life.

**placid [ˈplæsɪd] *adj.* 安静的, 平静的(tranquil; serene)

【例】The baby looks so *placid* and content after she has been fed.

**quiescent [kwaɪˈesnt] *adj.* 不动的, 静止的(marked by inactivity or repose); 沉默的

【记】quie(=quiet 安静的) + scent(表状态) → 静止的

static [ˈstætɪk] *adj.* 静的, 静态的, 停滞的(changeless; stagnant)

【例】*Static* air pressure indicates that the weather will not change soon.

**unruffled [ʌnˈrʌfld] *adj.* 不受骚扰的, 平静的, 镇定的(not upset or agitated; imperturbable)

【例】She spoke with *unruffled* calm.

serenity [səˈrenəti] *n.* 安静, 从容(calmness; tranquility)

【记】来自 serence(*adj.* 平静的, 从容的)

still [stɪl] *adj.* 静止的(motionless; stationary; fixed)

quietude [ˈkwaɪətuːd] *n.* 安静(tranquility)

*reticent [ˈretɪsnt] *adj.* 沉默不语的(inclined to be silent; reserved)

【记】re + tic(=silent 安静) + ent → 沉默不语的

【反】loquacious(*adj.* 话多的); vociferous(*adj.* 大声叫喊的); voluble (*adj.* 爱说话的)

【派】reticence(*n.* 沉默寡言)

mute [mjuːt] *adj.* 沉默的(silent); 哑的 *vt.* 减弱(声音)(to muffle the sound of) *n.* 弱音器 (a device to soften or alter the tone of a musical instrument)

【反】amplify(*vt.* 放大(声音))

reserve [rɪˈzɜːrv] *n.* 储备(物), 储藏量; 缄默, 谨慎 *vt.* 保留, 储备 (to put aside or keep sth for a later occasion or special use)

equanimity [ˌekwəˈnɪməti] *n.* 镇定, 沉着(evenness of mind or temper)

【记】equ(平衡) + anim(精神, 生命) + ity → 精神平衡 → 沉着

【反】excitability(*n.* 激动); agitation(*n.* 煽动); perturbation(*n.* 慌乱)

冲 突

**ambivalent [æmˈbɪvələnt] *adj.* (对人或物)有矛盾看法的(having simultaneous and contradictory attitudes or feelings about)

【记】ambi(两者) + valent(强大) → 两种看法都强大 → 有矛盾看法的

【反】commitment(*n.* 一心一意; 许诺)

**discordant [dɪsˈkɔːrdənt] *adj.* 不一致的, 不调和的(inharmonious; conflicting)

【记】dis(不) + cord(心) + ant → 不一条心 → 不一致的

【例】She tried to unite the *discordant* factions.

**discrepancy [dɪsˈkrepənsi] *n.* 分歧, 矛盾

【记】dis(分开) + crep(破裂) + ancy → 裂开 → 矛盾

*dissonance [ˈdɪsənəns] *n.* 不和谐音; 不一致(lack of agreement, harmony)

【记】dis(不) + son(声音) + ance → 不和谐音

【反】concord (*n.* 和谐, 一致)

**divergent [daɪˈvɜːrdʒənt] *adj.* 分叉的; 分歧的(different)

【记】di(分开) + verg(弯曲, 转) + ent → 分叉的

【例】Thousands of divergent tree branches made a thick canopy overhead.

assail [əˈseɪl] *vt.* 猛击(to attack; assault); 决然面对

【记】as + sail(跳上去) → 跳上去打 → 猛击

【例】A police officer *assailed* the crook with a baton.

*dash [dæʃ] *v.* 猛冲; 猛然撞击(to hurl or thrust violently)

infight [ˈɪnfaɪt] *n.* 近距离击打；(团体内部长期的)暗斗

tantalize [ˈtæntəlaɪz] *vt.* 逗惹，使着急 (to provoke; tease)
【例】It's not her purpose to *tantalize* that guy.

*thump [θʌmp] *vt.* 重击，锤击 (to strike; pound)
【例】The salesman *thumped* the door knocker.

*wrestle [ˈresl] *v.* 与…摔跤；搏斗 (to force sb to the ground by wrestling)
【例】He *wrestled* his opponent to the floor/ground.

repel [rɪˈpel] *vt.* 拒绝，排斥 (to spurn)
【例】She *repelled* all offers of help.

*adverse [ædˈvɜːrs] *adj.* 敌对的 (hostile); 不利的 (unfavorable; negative)
【例】The *adverse* weather conditions made travel difficult.

**belligerent [bəˈlɪdʒərənt] *adj.* 好战的 (hostile; aggressive); 交战的
【例】It is unwise to take a *belligerent* attitude.

**hostile [ˈhɑːstl] *adj.* 敌对的，不友好的 (antagonistic; unfriendly)
【例】The *hostile* cat hissed whenever I came near.

**confrontational [ˌkɑːnfrʌnˈteɪʃnl] *adj.* 对抗的，对抗性的 (of or relating to confrontation)
【例】He was very cocky, *confrontational*, and he had the lead wrapped tightly around his right hand.

*vice versa [ˌvaɪs ˈvɜːrsə] *adv.* 反之亦然
【例】Stop being pissed about whether Apple is right to sue Psystar or *vice versa*.

*combative [kəmˈbætɪv] *adj.* 好战的，好事的 (aggressive)
【例】And there's no doubt that there's occasionally been a *combative* edge to the enterprise.

offensive [əˈfensɪv] *adj.* 无礼的；攻击性的 (aggressive)
【记】来自 offend (*v.* 冒犯)
【例】I would take it as an *offensive* action if you don't stop making those terrible noises.

repulsive [rɪˈpʌlsɪv] *adj.* 排斥的；使人反感的 (revolting; disgusting)

**fray [freɪ] *n.* 吵架，打斗 (a noisy quarrel or fight) *vi.* 磨破边缘 (to become worn, ragged or raveled by rubbing)
【记】比较记忆：flay (剥皮) 中的 l 像刀，可以剥皮；fray (ray *n.* 光线) 是衣服透光，打架打的，或是磨破的

melee [ˈmeɪleɪ] *n.* 混战，乱战（confused fight）

【例】The captain tried to ascertain the cause of the *melee* that had broken out among the crew members.

*friction [ˈfrɪkʃn] *n.* 摩擦

【例】The wheel has been expired due to *friction*.

*collision [kəˈlɪʒn] *n.* 碰撞，冲突（an act or instance of colliding）

【记】来自collide（*v.* 碰撞）

cordon [ˈkɔːrdn] *n.* 警戒线；防卫圈

*scuffle [ˈskʌfl] *n.* 扭打，混战（confused struggle between people who are close together）

【例】*Scuffles* broke out between police and demonstrators.

混 乱

*chaotic [keɪˈɑːtɪk] *adj.* 混乱的，无序的（in utter disorder）

【反】strictly structured（构造严谨的）; strictly featured（特征严谨的）

discursive [dɪsˈkɜːrsɪv] *adj.* 散漫的，无主题的（rambling wandering from topic to topic without order）

【记】dis + curs（跑）+ ive → 到处乱跑 → 散漫的

【反】keen on title（集中在主题上的）; succinct（*adj.* 简洁的）

*disheveled [dɪˈʃevəld] *adj.*（指头发或衣服）凌乱的（untidy of hair or clothing）

disjointed [dɪsˈdʒɔɪntɪd] *adj.* 脱节的，脱臼的；杂乱的（disconnected）

【记】dis（不）+ joint（关节）+ ed → 脱节的

【例】His remarks were so *disjointed* that we could not follow his reasoning.

**tumultuous [tuːˈmʌltʃuəs] *adj.* 吵闹的，骚乱的，狂暴的

【例】Not likely, but the early years of the Time Warner-Turner combination are sure to be *tumultuous*.

befuddle [biˈfʌdl] *vt.* 使混乱（to confuse）

【例】These fancy arguments *befuddled* us.

*bustle [ˈbʌsl] *v.*（使）奔忙（to move busily and energetically）

【例】She *bustled* the children off to school.

*jumble [ˈdʒʌmbl] *v.*（使）混杂（to muddle; mix）

【例】The papers in the office were all *jumbled* up.

**mingle ['mɪŋgl] *v.*混合（to bring or mix together）

*muddle ['mʌdl] *vt.*使混乱（to confuse; make into a mess）；使头脑糊涂

【记】mud（泥）+ dle → 混入泥 → 使混乱

【例】The lesson was not clear and it has *muddled* me.

alloy ['ælɔɪ] *n.*合金（mixture as of metals）*vt.*使成合金

【例】*Alloy* of gold are used more frequently than the pure metal.

【派】unalloyed（*adj.* 非合金的；纯粹的）

congestion [kən'dʒestʃən] *n.*拥挤，堵塞

*hodgepodge ['hɑːdʒpɑːdʒ] *n.* 混 杂 物 （a mixture of dissimilar ingredients; a jumble）；杂烩菜

【记】hodge（庄稼汉）+ podge（矮胖的人）→ 庄稼汉是又高又壮的人，与矮胖的人混在一起 → 混杂物

maelstrom ['meɪlstrɑːm] *n.*大漩涡 （violent whirlpool）；大混乱 （a violently agitated state of mind, emotion, etc）

【记】mael（=mal 坏）+ strom（水流，旋转）→ 大漩涡

medley ['medli] *n.* 混 合 曲 ，集 锦 ；混 杂 （heterogeneous assortment or collection）；各种团体（groups of different types mixed together）

【记】各种团体（medley）互相干涉（meddle）

【例】I usually sing a *medley* of old favourites when I'm in the shower.

*messiness ['mesɪnəs] *n.*乱糟糟，混乱

【例】Altman's movies spilled out beyond the edges of the frame, alive to the *messiness* of life.

*pandemonium [ˌpændə'mouniəm] *n.*地狱，极嘈杂的地方；喧嚣，大混乱 （a wild uproar; tumult）

【记】pan（全部）+ demon（魔鬼）+ ium → 全是魔鬼 → 地狱；来自弥尔顿所著《失乐园》中的地狱之都（Pandemonium）

pastiche [pæ'stiːʃ] *n.*混合拼凑的作品，混合曲 （a musical, literary, or artistic composition made up of selections from different works）

【记】pasti（看做paste，粘贴）+ che → 粘贴在一起的画 → 混合拼凑的作品

【反】original work（原作）

shambles ['ʃæmblz] *n.*凌乱景象，杂乱无章 （complete disorder or ruin; wreck; mess）

【记】sham（假货）+ bles（抱）→ 假货满地都是 → 凌乱景象

*turmoil ['tɜːrmɔɪl] *n.* 骚动，混乱 (disorder; chaos)

【记】tur + moil(喧闹) → 混乱

【例】The *turmoil* of exams made the students very irritable.

welter ['weltər] *n.* 混乱一堆，杂乱无章 (a disordered mixture)

【记】像一个大熔炉 (melter) 一片混乱 (welter)

【反】orderly arrangement (安排有序)

With the measure you use, it will be measured to you—and even more.

你们用什么量器量给人，也必用什么量器量给你们，并且要多给你们。

——《圣经·新·可》4:24

练 习 题

填空题

ambivalent	appease	console	defuse	equanimity
incongruous	irreparable	mediate	quiescent	rapport
reassure	refresh	rejuvenate	relent	relieved
resilient	resumption	solace	tranquil	wrestle

1. Her death is an _____ loss.
2. These plants are very _____ to rough handling.
3. We are hoping for an early _____ of peace talks.
4. The doctor _____ him that there was nothing seriously wrong.
5. His new job seemed to _____ him.
6. He _____ himself with a cool shower.
7. The move was widely seen as an attempt to _____ critics of the regime.
8. Nothing could _____ him when his wife died.
9. The police will not _____ in their fight against crime.
10. His grandchildren were a _____ in his old age.
11. Police closed the road while they _____ the bomb.
12. She understood the importance of establishing a close _____ with clients.
13. I'm just _____ that nobody was hurt.
14. Such traditional methods seem _____ in our technical age.
15. An independent body was brought in to _____ between staff and management.
16. She lead a _____ life in the country.
17. It is unlikely that such an extremist organization will remain _____ for long.
18. She accepted the prospect of her operation with _____ .
19. He has an _____ attitude towards her.
20. Armed guards _____ with the intruder.

配对题

1. irretrievable	共存，和平共处	11. palliate	安抚的，劝解的
2. recyclable	和睦	12. release	可回收利用的，可再循环的
3. renewal	不一致的，不调和的	13. coexistence	赋予…新的力量或生命
4. resurrection	供给…能量；使活跃	14. concord	释放；让渡
5. energize	不和谐(之物)	15. incongruity	更新，恢复；复兴，重建
6. regenerate	不可挽回的，不能补救的	16. sedate	拒绝，排斥
7. pacify	缓和者，缓解物	17. serenity	复活，复兴
8. propitiatory	沉默的	18. mute	安静的，沉着的
9. soothe	使镇定，抚慰	19. discordant	安静；从容
10. mitigator	减轻(痛苦)；掩饰(罪行)	20. repel	安慰；缓和，减轻

练习题答案

填空题答案

1. Her death is an <u>irreparable</u> loss.
2. These plants are very <u>resilient</u> to rough handling.
3. We are hoping for an early <u>resumption</u> of peace talks.
4. The doctor <u>reassured</u> him that there was nothing seriously wrong.
5. His new job seemed to <u>rejuvenate</u> him.
6. He <u>refreshed</u> himself with a cool shower.
7. The move was widely seen as an attempt to <u>appease</u> critics of the regime.
8. Nothing could <u>console</u> him when his wife died.
9. The police will not <u>relent</u> in their fight against crime.
10. His grandchildren were a <u>solace</u> in his old age.
11. Police closed the road while they <u>defused</u> the bomb.
12. She understood the importance of establishing a close <u>rapport</u> with clients.
13. I'm just <u>relieved</u> that nobody was hurt.
14. Such traditional methods seem <u>incongruous</u> in our technical age.
15. An independent body was brought in to <u>mediate</u> between staff and management.
16. She lead a <u>tranquil</u> life in the country.
17. It is unlikely that such an extremist organization will remain <u>quiescent</u> for long.
18. She accepted the prospect of her operation with <u>equanimity</u>.
19. He has an <u>ambivalent</u> attitude towards her.
20. Armed guards <u>wrestled</u> with the intruder.

配对题答案

1. irretrievable	不可挽回的, 不能补救的		11. palliate	减轻(痛苦); 掩饰(罪行)
2. recyclable	可回收利用的, 可再循环的		12. release	释放; 让渡
3. renewal	更新, 恢复; 复兴, 重建		13. coexistence	共存, 和平共处
4. resurrection	复活, 复兴		14. concord	和睦
5. energize	供给…能量; 使活跃		15. incongruity	不和谐(之物)
6. regenerate	赋予…新的力量或生命		16. sedate	安静的, 沉着的
7. pacify	使镇定, 抚慰		17. serenity	安静, 从容
8. propitiatory	安抚的, 劝解的		18. mute	沉默的
9. soothe	安慰; 缓和, 减轻		19. discordant	不一致的, 不调和的
10. mitigator	缓和者; 缓解物		20. repel	拒绝, 排斥

Word List 28
状态(三)

发 生

beget [bɪ'get] *vt.* 引起，产生 (to arise; bring)
【例】Hunger *begets* crime.

*engender [ɪn'dʒendər] *v.* 产生，引起 (to generate; produce)
【记】en(使) + gend(产生) + er → 产生
【例】John's kind acts *engendered* my friendship.

entail [ɪn'teɪl] *vt.* 使必要，牵涉 (to require; involve)
【例】The task *entailed* strict attention to procedure.

incidence ['ɪnsɪdəns] *n.* 事情发生 (an instance of happening)；发生率 (rate of occurrence or influence)
【记】和 coincidence(*n.* 同时发生)一起记

*occurrence [ə'kɜːrəns] *n.* 事件 (event; incident)；发生 (fact of occurring)
【记】来自 occur(*vi.* 发生)

spontaneity [ˌspɑːntə'neɪəti] *n.* 自然发生，自发性 (the quality or state of being spontaneous)
【记】来自 spontaneous(*adj.* 自然的，自发的)

开 始

*commencement [kə'mensmənt] *n.* 开始；(大学的)毕业典礼 (the ceremony at which degrees or diplomas are conferred at a school or college)
【反】cessation(*n.* 停止)；matriculation(*n.* 大学录取)

conception [kən'sepʃn] *n.* 概念，构思 (a general idea)；开始，创始 (beginning)
【记】concept(概念) + ion → 概念，构思

emanate ['eməneɪt] *v.* (气体等)散发，发出；发源 (to come out from a source)
【记】e(出) + man(人) + ate → 人类文明发源于人的智慧 → 发源
袁欢出(等你公领)

– 291 –

**inception [ɪnˈsepʃn] *n.* 开端，开始（an act, process, or instance of beginning）；取得学位（commencement）

【记】in(进入) + cept(拿) + ion → 拿进来 → 开始

inchoate [ɪnˈkoʊət] *adj.* 初期的，刚开始的（just begun; incipient）；未发展的（not yet completed or fully developed）

【记】inch(寸) + oat(燕麦) + e → 燕麦刚长一寸 → 初期的

【反】completely formed(完全形成的)；fully formed(完全形成的)

发 展

*ascent [əˈsent] *n.* 上升

【例】The rock climbers made their *ascent* slowly.

**befall [bɪˈfɔːl] *v.* (尤指不幸)降临(于)，发生(to happen to sb)

【例】We shall never leave you, whatever *befalls*.

*consequent [ˈkɑːnsəkwənt] *adj.* 由…引起的，随之发生的（following sth as a result or an effect）

【例】his resignation and the *consequent* public uproar

*dawn [dɔːn] *n.* 黎明；开始，开端（beginning; first signs of）

【例】the *dawn* of a new age

*foremost [ˈfɔːrmoʊst] *adj.* 最初的，最先的（prime）

【记】fore(前) + most(最) → 最初的，最先的

【例】He is one of the *foremost* atom scientists in China.

*pristine [ˈprɪstiːn] *adj.* 清新而纯净的（fresh and clean）

【例】The ground was covered in a *pristine* layer of snow.

*intensify [ɪnˈtensɪfaɪ] *vt.* 加强（to enhance; strengthen）

【例】The general *intensified* the defense of the northern border by sending more troops there.

*proceed [proʊˈsiːd] *vi.* 进行，开展（to carry on; go on）

【记】pro(向前) + ceed(走) → 进行

【例】Business *proceeded* as usual.

*uplift [ˈʌplɪft] *n./vt.* (在道德等方面)提高；(在精神或情绪方面)振奋，鼓舞

【例】Her encouragement gave me a great sense of *uplift*.

heyday [ˈheɪdeɪ] *n.* 全盛时期（the time of greatest health, vigor, or prosperity）

【记】hey(惊喜声) + day → 令人惊喜的日子 → 全盛时期

*highwater [ˌhaɪˈwɔːtər] *n.* 水位最高点

*mellow [ˈmeloʊ] v. (使)成熟，(使)芳醇；(使)老练，(使)圆润 adj. (水果) 成熟的，甘甜的(tender and sweet because ripeness)

【例】Age has *mellowed* his attitude to some things.

*thrive [θraɪv] vi. 茂盛生长；繁荣，旺盛(to flourish; do well on)

【例】The wild deer that *throve* here are no more visible due to deforestation.

*descending [dɪˈsendɪŋ] adj. 下降的，下行的

【例】Clinton recalled Winston Churchill's warning 60 years ago that an iron curtain was *descending* across Europe.

*exacerbate [ɪgˈzæsərbeɪt] vt. 加重，使恶化(to aggravate disease, pain, annoyance, etc)

【记】ex(出) + acerb(苦涩) + ate → 超出了苦涩 → 使恶化

【反】alleviate(vt. 减轻)；mitigate(vt. 减轻)

*phase [feɪz] n. 阶段，时期(stage; period)

【例】The child is going through a difficult *phase*.

结　束

*dusk [dʌsk] n. 黄昏，薄暮

ultimate [ˈʌltɪmət] adj. 最后的(final; eventual)

【例】*Ultimate* success can be only achieved by those who hang on.

*fruitless [ˈfruːtləs] adj. 无结果的，不成功的 (producing little or no result; unsuccessful)

【例】a *fruitless* attempt

*inconclusive [ˌɪnkənˈkluːsɪv] adj. 非决定性的，非结论性的，无结果的(not leading to a definite decision, conclusion or result)

【例】*inconclusive* arguments

*accomplishment [əˈkɑːmplɪʃmənt] n. 完成，成功(successful completion)

【例】celebrate the *accomplishment* of one's objectives

*culminate [ˈkʌlmɪneɪt] v. 终于获得(某种结局或结果)，以…结束(to have the specified final conclusion or result)；使结束

【例】a long struggle that *culminated* in success

fruition [fruˈɪʃn] n. 实现，完成(fulfillment of hopes, plans, etc)

【记】fruit(水果) + ion → 有果实，有成果 → 实现，完成

**moribund [ˈmɔːrɪbʌnd] *adj.* 即将结束的(coming to end)；垂死的(dying)

【记】mori(=mort 死) + bund(接近的) → 垂死的；谐音："末日伴的"

【反】increasingly vital（生机勃勃的）；nascent（*adj.* 新生的）；beginning(*adj.* 开始的)

*terminate [ˈtɜːrmeɪt] *vt.* 结束，终止(to end; finish; conclude; stop)

【记】termin(结束) + ate → 结束

【例】The author *terminated* his contract with the publisher.

decapitate [dɪˈkæpɪteɪt] *v.* 斩首(to behead)

【记】de(去掉) + capit(头) + ate → 去掉头 → 斩首

anticlimax [ˌænti'klaɪmæks] *n.* 令人扫兴的结局 (disappointing end to a series of events)

【记】anti(反) + climax(高潮，结局) → 与期望相反的结局 → 令人扫兴的结局

denouement [ˌdeɪnuːˈmɑːŋ] *n.* (小说、戏剧等的)结尾，结局(the outcome or solution of a plot in a drama or story)

【记】来自法语：de + noue (=knot 结) + ment → 解开结 → 结尾；注意不要和denouncement(*n.* 谴责)相混，在结尾的地方画蛇添足是要被谴责的

*sequel [ˈsiːkwəl] *n.* 继续，后续；(文艺作品的)续集，续编

【例】Do you have any questions regarding the *sequel* of your life?

upshot [ˈʌpʃɑːt] *n.* 结局，结果；(分析或论证的)结论，要点

【例】What was the *upshot* of it all? He resigned.

termination [ˌtɜːrmɪˈneɪʃn] *n.* 终点，结束(end in time or existence)

abeyance [əˈbeɪəns] *n.* 中止，搁置(temporary suspension of an activity)

【记】a(=at 在) + bey(=bay 港湾) + ance → 停驻在港湾，不开放 → 搁置

cessation [seˈseɪʃn] *n.* 中止，(短暂的)停止(a short pause or a stop)

【记】cess(拖延) + ation → 中止；和concession(*n.* 让步)一起记

【反】perseverance(*n.* 坚定不移)；commencement(*n.* 开始)

*intermission [ˌɪntərˈmɪʃn] *n.* 暂停，间歇(an interval of time)

【记】inter(在…之间) + mission(任务) → 在任务之间 → 间歇

*stagnant [ˈstæɡnənt] *adj.* 停滞的(not advancing or developing)

【记】stagn(＝stand 站住) + ant → 不动的 → 停滞的

【反】flowing(*adj.* 流动的)

valedictory [ˌvælɪˈdɪktəri] *adj.* 告别的，离别的(used in saying goodbye)

【记】vale(告别) + dict(说) + ory → 告别的

合 并

*affiliation [əˌfɪliˈeɪʃn] *n.* 联系，联合(link or connection made by affiliating)

**amalgamate [əˈmælgəmeɪt] *v.* (使公司等)合并(to unite; combine)；混合(to mix)

【例】I think it might be better to *amalgamate* both milk and flour.

【反】separate(*v./adj.* 分离(的))；isolate(*v.* 隔离)

coalesce [ˌkoʊəˈles] *vi.* (骨头)接合；联合，合并，聚集(to unite or merge into a single body; mix)

【记】co(一起)+ al(=ally 联盟)+ esce → 一起结成联盟 → 联合

【例】Andy's emotions *coalesced* and he started to cry.

【反】disaggregate(*v.* 分散)；bifurcate(*v.* 分叉)；fragment(*v.* 分裂)

**coalition [ˌkoʊəˈlɪʃn] *n.* 结合，联合，联盟(combination; union; alliance)

*incorporate [ɪnˈkɔːrpəreɪt] *v.* 合并，并入 (to combine or join with sth already formed; embody)

【记】in(进入)+ corpor(团体)+ ate → 进入团体 → 合并

splice [splaɪs] *vt.* 接合，衔接(to unite by interweaving the strands)

【记】注意不要和split(*v.* 分裂)相混

聚 集

*solidify [səˈlɪdɪfaɪ] *v.* 巩固；(使)凝固(to become solid, hard or firm)；(使)团结

【记】solid(坚固的)+ ify(使)→ 巩固

muster [ˈmʌstər] *v.* 召集，聚集(to gather or summon)

【记】a master(主人)has the power to muster(召集).

*glean [gliːn] *v.* 拾(落穗)；收集(信息等)(to collect; gather)

【例】The scientists were delighted at these information *gleaned* from the investigation.

**accumulate [əˈkjuːmjəleɪt] *v.* 积聚(to aggregate; amass; accrue)

【记】ac + cumul(堆积)+ ate → 积聚

【例】The television screen *accumulates* dust.

amass [əˈmæs] *v.* 堆积；积聚(to collect together; accumulate)

【记】a + mass(一团，一堆)→ 堆积

**converge [kənˈvɜːrdʒ] *v.* (使)会聚，(使)集中于一点(to come together at a point)

【记】con(共同)+ verge(转)→ 转到一起 → 会聚

*convene ［kən'viːn］ *vt.* 召集(会议)(to cause to come together formly)

【记】con(共同) + vene(走) → 走到一起 → 召集

【例】Party congresses at all levels are *convened* by Party committees at their respective levels.

*conjoin ［kən'dʒɔɪn］ *v.* (使)结合(to cause people or things to join together)

【记】con(共同) + join(结合，连接) → 使结合

*congregate ［'kɑːŋɡrɪɡeɪt］ *v.* (使)聚集(to assemble; gather)

【记】con(共同) + greg(集会) + ate → 聚集

【例】Each morning people at work *congregate* around the coffee pot.

*convergent ［kən'vɜːrdʒənt］ *adj.* 会聚的 (tending to move toward one point or to approach each other)

【反】moving apart(移开的); discrepant(*adj.* 有差异的)

*cumulative ［'kjuːmjəleɪtɪv］ *adj.* 累积的(growing by addition)

agglomeration ［əˌɡlɑːmə'reɪʃn］ *n.* 结块，凝聚(collection; heap)

*heap ［hiːp］ *n.* 堆

【例】a *heap* of books

increment ［'ɪŋkrəmənt］ *n.* 增值，增加(increase; gain; growth); 增加量

【记】in(进入) + cre(增加) + ment → 增加

分　离

asunder ［ə'sʌndər］ *adv.* 分离地(apart; separate); 化为碎片(into pieces)

【记】as + under → 好像在下面 → 分离地

deciduous ［dɪ'sɪdʒuəs］ *adj.* 非永久的，短暂的 (not lasting; ephemeral); 脱落的(falling off or out); 落叶的(shedding leaves annually)

【记】de + cid(落下) + uous → 脱落的

*dispersive ［dɪs'pɜːrsɪv］ *adj.* 分散的，弥散的

*estranged ［ɪ'streɪndʒd］ *adj.* 疏远的，分开的，分离的(alienated)

【记】e + strange(陌生的) + d → 变得陌生 → 疏远的，分离的

*inseparable ［ɪn'seprəbl］ *adj.* 不可分的，分不开的(that cannot be separated)

【例】Rights are *inseparable* from duties.

**alienate ［'eɪliəneɪt］ *v.* 疏远，离间 (to estrange; cause to become unfriendly or indifferent)

【记】alien(外国的) + ate → 把别人当外国人 → 疏远

【反】reunite(*vt.* 使再结合)

【派】alienated(*adj.* 疏远的，被隔开的); alienation(*n.* 疏远，

cleave [kliːv] *v.* 劈开 (to divide with an axe); 分裂 (to split; separate)

【记】c + leave(离开) → 让c离开 → 分裂

*discriminate [dɪˈskrɪmɪneɪt] *v.* 区分，辨别 (to make a clear distinction)

【记】dis + crimin(=crime 罪行) + ate → 区别对待有罪的人 → 区分

【反】confound(*v.* 混淆)

【派】discrimination(*n.* 鉴别力; 歧视)

disengage [ˌdɪsɪnˈɡeɪdʒ] *v.* 脱离，解开 (to release from sth engaged)

【反】mesh(*v.* 啮合)

maul [mɔːl] *vt.* 撕裂皮肉，伤害 (to injure by bearing bruise of; lacerate)

【例】The wolves *mauled* people and ate sheep.

*percolate [ˈpɜːrkəleɪt] *v.* 过滤出 (to cause to pass through a permeable substance); 渗透 (to penetrate; seep)

【记】per(贯穿) + col(1)ate(过滤) → 过滤过去 → 过滤出

polarize [ˈpoʊləraɪz] *v.* (使) 两极分化 (to divide into groups based on two completely opposite principles or political opinions)

【记】polar(两极的) + ize(…化) → (使)两极分化

ramify [ˈræmɪfaɪ] *vt.* 使分支，使分叉 (to split up into branches or constituents)

【记】ram(=ramus 分支) + ify(使) → 使分支

【派】ramification(*n.* 分支，分叉)

sever [ˈsevər] *v.* 分开，分离 (separate); 断绝(联系)

【例】The road was *severed* at several places.

smelt [smelt] *v.* (以熔炼法)提炼(金属)

【例】a copper-*smelting* works

stratify [ˈstrætɪfaɪ] *v.* (使)层化; (使)分层

【记】strat(层次) + ify → 层化

【反】homogenize(*vt.* 使一致，使均匀)

sunder [ˈsʌndər] *v.* 分裂，分离 (to separate by violence or by intervening time or space)

【记】发音似"散的" → 分离

【反】link (*v.* 连接); connect (*v.* 连接); combine(*v.* 结合); yoke(*v.* 束缚); bond (*v.* 结合)

【派】asunder(*adv.* 分离地)

*unhinge [ʌn'hɪndʒ] vt.取下…的铰链；使分开

【记】un(表否定) + hinge(铰链) → 取下…的铰链

unravel [ʌn'rævl] v.解开，拆散 (to resolve the complexity of)

【记】un(不) + ravel(纠缠) → 解开

**solitude ['sɑːlətjuːd] n.与外界隔绝，隐居 (isolation; loneliness)

sequester [sɪ'kwestər] v.(使)隐退 (to seclude; withdraw)；(使)隔离 (to set apart)

【记】注意不要和sequestrate(vt.扣押)相混

【反】mingle(v.混合)

partition [pɑːr'tɪʃn] n.隔开 (division)；分隔物，隔墙 (an interior dividing wall)

【记】part(部分) + ition → 分成部分 → 隔开

*isolation [ˌaɪsə'leɪʃn] n.隔离，脱离，孤立 (the state of isolating or being isolated)

【例】Looked at in isolation, these facts are not encouraging.

*isolate ['aɪsəleɪt] vt.使孤立；隔离；使绝缘

【例】Policies isolating Arab countries from one another through restrictions of visas and travel will be lifted.

*insulate ['ɪnsəleɪt] vt.使隔离；隔开(尤指热量、电流或声音)

【例】material which insulates well

hermitage ['hɜːrmɪtɪdʒ] n.隐士生活；隐士住处

**detachment [dɪ'tætʃmənt] n.分开，拆开；特遣部队，分遣队

**dissension [dɪ'senʃn] n.意见不合，纠纷，倾轧 (strong disagreement or discord)

【反】concord (n. 一致，和谐)

【派】dissent(vi. 不同意) → assent(vi. 赞成，同意)；consent(vi. 同意，赞成)

laceration [ˌlæsə'reɪʃn] n.撕裂；裂伤 (jagged tear or wound)

polarity [pə'lærəti] n.极端性，两极分化 (diametrical opposition)

【记】polar(两极的) + ity → 两极分化

schism ['skɪzəm] n.分裂 (division; separation)，不一致 (discord; disharmony)

【反】accord(n. 一致，调和)

【派】schismatic(adj. 分裂的)

secession [sɪ'seʃn] n.脱离，分离

【例】Separately, Sudan's vice-president has confirmed the north will accept the south's vote in favour of secession.

偏 离

*aberration [ˌæbəˈreɪʃn] *n.* 离开正路，脱离常轨

【记】ab + err(犯错误) + ation → 犯错误 → 离开正路

*career [kəˈriːn] *v.* (使船等) 倾斜 (进行维修) (to cause a ship to lean sideways)

【记】和career(*n.* 职业)一起记

【例】He *careened* his boat to repaint it.

*deflect [dɪˈflekt] *v.* (使)偏离 (to divert; deviate)

【记】de(偏离) + flect(弯曲) → 偏离

【例】The ball hit a wall and was *deflected* from its course.

deviate [ˈdiːvieɪt] *v.* (使)出轨 (to deflect; diverge); 离题

【记】de(偏离) + via(路) + te → 偏离正路 → 出轨

【例】I do not like to *deviate* from the set schedule.

*digress [daɪˈgres] *vi.* 离开本题 (to turn away from the main subject)

【记】di(偏离) + gress(走) → 走偏离 → 离来本题

【例】Mary *digressed* and forgot what she was originally talking about.

**digression [daɪˈgreʃn] *n.* 离题 (an act of turning aside from the main subject or talk about sth else); 题外话

For out of the overflow of his heart his mouth speaks.

心里所充满的，口里就说出来。

——《圣经·新·路》6:45

填空题

abeyance	affiliation	ascent	befall	beget
culminate	emanate	exacerbate	foremost	fruitless
inception	incorporate	intensify	mellow	occurrence
proceed	spontaneity	stagnant	terminate	thrive

1. War _____ misery and ruin.
2. The program counts the number of _____ of any word, or group of words, within the text.
3. There is a lack of _____ in her performance.
4. He _____ power and confidence.
5. The club has grown rapidly since its _____ in 1990.
6. The cart began its gradual _____ up the hill.
7. They were unaware of the fate that was to _____ them.
8. The Prime Minister was _____ among those who condemned the violence.
9. The opposition leader has _____ his attacks on the government.
10. We're not sure whether we still want to _____ with the sale.
11. She had _____ a great deal since their days at college.
12. New businesses _____ in this area.
13. The symptoms may be _____ by certain drugs.
14. Our efforts to persuade her proved _____.
15. Months of hard work _____ in success.
16. Your contract of employment _____ in December.
17. Legal proceedings are in _____, while further enquiries are made.
18. Major new investments are aimed at reviving the _____ economy.
19. He had been detained without trial because of his political _____.
20. The new car design _____ all the latest safety features.

配对题

1. engender	完成，成功	11. accomplishment	黄昏，薄暮
2. commencement	堆积；积聚	12. moribund	产生，引起
3. conception	令人扫兴的结局	13. anticlimax	收集(信息等)
4. inchoate	分离地	14. upshot	全盛时期
5. consequent	结合，联合	15. intermission	刚开始的
6. pristine	开始；(大学的)毕业典礼	16. coalition	暂停，间歇
7. uplift	概念；开始	17. glean	即将结束的
8. heyday	由…引起的，随之发生的	18. amass	清新而纯净的
9. descending	累积的	19. cumulative	提高；振奋，鼓舞
10. dusk	下降的，下行的	20. asunder	结局，结果

练习题答案

填空题答案

1. War <u>begets</u> misery and ruin.
2. The program counts the number of <u>occurrences</u> of any word, or group of words, within the text.
3. There is a lack of <u>spontaneity</u> in her performance.
4. He <u>emanates</u> power and confidence.
5. The club has grown rapidly since its <u>inception</u> in 1990.
6. The cart began its gradual <u>ascent</u> up the hill.
7. They were unaware of the fate that was to <u>befall</u> them.
8. The Prime Minister was <u>foremost</u> among those who condemned the violence.
9. The opposition leader has <u>intensified</u> his attacks on the government.
10. We're not sure whether we still want to <u>proceed</u> with the sale.
11. She had <u>mellowed</u> a great deal since their days at college.
12. New businesses <u>thrive</u> in this area.
13. The symptoms may be <u>exacerbated</u> by certain drugs.
14. Our efforts to persuade her proved <u>fruitless</u>.
15. Months of hard work <u>culminated</u> in success.
16. Your contract of employment <u>terminates</u> in December.
17. Legal proceedings are in <u>abeyance</u>, while further enquiries are made.
18. Major new investments are aimed at reviving the <u>stagnant</u> economy.
19. He had been detained without trial because of his political <u>affiliation</u>.
20. The new car design <u>incorporates</u> all the latest safety features.

配对题答案

1. engender	产生，引起	11. accomplishment	完成，成功
2. commencement	开始；(大学的)毕业典礼	12. moribund	即将结束的
3. conception	概念；开始	13. anticlimax	令人扫兴的结局
4. inchoate	刚开始的	14. upshot	结局，结果
5. consequent	由…引起的，随之发生的	15. intermission	暂停，间歇
6. pristine	清新而纯净的	16. coalition	结合，联合
7. uplift	提高；振奋，鼓舞	17. glean	收集(信息等)
8. heyday	全盛时期	18. amass	堆积；积聚
9. descending	下降的，下行的	19. cumulative	累积的
10. dusk	黄昏，薄暮	20. asunder	分离地

Word List 29
状态（四）

穿　透

embed ［ɪmˈbed］ *vt.* 牢牢插入，嵌于(to set or fix firmly in a surrounding mass; wedge)
【记】em(进入) + bed(床) → 深深进入内部 → 牢牢插入
【反】extract(*vt.* 拔出)

impale ［ɪmˈpeɪl］ *vt.* 刺穿，刺住(to pierce; penetrate)
【记】im(进入) + pale(尖木) → 刺穿
【例】She had the butterflies *impaled* on small pins.

infiltrate ［ˈɪnfɪltreɪt］ *v.* 渗透，渗入(to pass through)
【记】in(进入) + filtr(过滤) + ate → 过滤进去 → 渗透

***insert** ［ɪnˈsɜːrt］ *vt.* 插入(to put in)
【记】in(进入) + sert(插) → 插入
【例】He *inserted* the key in the lock but could not open the door.

****penetrate** ［ˈpenətreɪt］ *vt.* 刺穿，进入(to pierce)
【记】pen(全部) + etr(进入) + ate → 刺穿
【例】The knife *penetrated* her finger and made it bleed.

perforate ［ˈpɜːrfəreɪt］ *v.* 打洞(于)(to make a hole through)
【记】per(全部) + forate(=pierce 刺穿) → 全部刺穿 → 打洞
【派】perforation(*n.* 孔；穿孔，贯穿)

protrude ［proʊˈtruːd］ *v.* (使)突出(to project; stick out)
【记】pro(前) + trude(伸出) → 突出
【例】John's teeth *protrude* from his gums at an odd angle.

***puncture** ［ˈpʌŋktʃər］ *v.* 刺穿，刺破 (to pierce with a pointed instrument) *n.* 刺孔，穿孔
【记】punct(刺) + ure → 刺穿

sheathe ［ʃiːð］ *vt.* (将刀剑)入鞘；包，覆(to cover; encase)
【例】He *sheathes* his sword.

*spear [spɪr] *n.* 矛，鱼叉 *v.* 用矛（或鱼叉）刺戳（to thrust with a spear）

*stab [stæb] *v./n.* 刺，戳，刺伤（to jab; injure）

【例】 He *stabbed* the woman with a knife and she died.

*sting [stɪŋ] *v.* 蜇伤，刺伤（to prick or wound sb with or as if with a sting）*n.* 蜇针，刺毛

【例】 Not all nettles *sting*.

*wedge [wedʒ] *n.* 楔子，楔形物 *v.* 把…楔牢，用尖劈劈开（to fix sth firmly or force sth apart using a wedge）

【例】 The window doesn't stay closed unless you *wedge* it.

**impenetrable [ɪmˈpenɪtrəbl] *adj.* 不能穿透的（incapable of being penetrated）；不可理解的（unfathomable; inscrutable）

【记】 im(不) + penetrable(可刺穿的) → 不能穿透的

【反】 porous(*adj.* 多孔的)

*impervious [ɪmˈpɜːrviəs] *adj.* 不能渗透的（impenetrable; impermeable）

【记】 im(不) + pervious(渗透的) → 不能渗透的

【例】 Since my watch is *impervious* to water, I wear it while I swim.

*nonporous [nɑːnˈpɔːrəs] *adj.* 无孔的，不渗透的

【记】 non(不) + porous(多孔的) → 无孔的

*prick [prɪk] *n.* 小刺；刺，戳；刺痛（sharp feeling of remorse, regret, or sorrow）*v.* 刺伤(to prick sth)；截穿（to pierce with a sharp point）

移 动

*dangle [ˈdæŋgl] *v.* （使）悬摆（to suspend; hang）

【例】 The monkey loved to *dangle* from the branch and eat bananas.

migrant [ˈmaɪgrənt] *n.* 候鸟；移居者；随季节迁移的民工 *adj.* 移居的，流浪的

migratory [ˈmaɪgrətɔːri] *adj.* 迁移的，流浪的（having or of the habit of migrating）

【记】 migr(移动) + atory → 迁移的，流浪的

mobile [ˈmoʊbl] *adj.* 易于移动的（easy to move）

**rotate [ˈroʊteɪt] *v.* （使）旋转（to turn; alternate）；（使）轮换

【例】 The coach *rotates* her players frequently near the end of the game.

slither [ˈslɪðər] *v.* （蛇）滑动，扭动前进（to slop or slide like a snake）

【记】 slit(裂缝) + her(她) → 她像蛇一样滑进裂缝 → 滑动

吸　引

*captivating ［ˈkæptɪveɪtɪŋ］*adj.* 迷人的，有魅力的（attractive）

【例】Who could look away from Suzanne Somers's sad but *captivating* efforts to turn back time?

*conspicuous ［kənˈspɪkjuəs］*adj.* 明显的，引人注目的（noticeable; obvious）

【记】con（共同）+ spic（看）+ uous → 大家都看 → 引人注目的

【例】The crack in the ceiling was very *conspicuous*.

*fetching ［ˈfetʃɪŋ］*adj.* 动人的，吸引人的，迷人的

【例】a *fetching* new hairstyle

*glamorous ［ˈɡlæmərəs］*adj.* 富有魅力的（fascinating; charming）

【记】来自glamour（*n.* 魔力，魅力）

【例】The young president ceased to be *glamorous* when he announced a higher tax rate.

*inconspicuous ［ˌɪnkənˈspɪkjuəs］*adj.* 不引人注目的，不显眼的，不显著的（not conspicuous）

【例】The newcomer tried to make herself as *inconspicuous* as possible.

*seductive ［sɪˈdʌktɪv］*adj.* 诱人的；有魅力的，有吸引力的（attractive）

【例】This offer of a high salary and a free house is very *seductive*.

unprepossessing ［ˌʌnpriːpəˈzesɪŋ］*adj.* 不吸引人的，不讨人喜欢的（unattractive）

【记】un（不）+ prepossessing（讨人喜欢的）→ 不讨人喜欢的

【反】entrancing（*adj.* 使人入神的）；winsome（*adj.* 迷人的）

winsome ［ˈwɪnsəm］*adj.* 媚人的，可爱迷人的

【记】win（赢）+ some → 赢得别人的好感 → 可爱迷人的

【反】unprepossessing（*adj.* 不吸引人的）

addiction ［əˈdɪkʃn］*n.* 上瘾，沉溺

【例】The *addiction* would have to be reported to the relevant state or federal database.

*allure ［əˈlʊr］*v.* 引诱，诱惑（to entice; attract）*n.* 诱惑力

*bait ［beɪt］*n.* 饵；引诱物，诱饵，圈套（lure）

【例】Cheese is good *bait* for catfish.

**charisma ［kəˈrɪzmə］*n.* 魅力，感召力

【例】The performer's *charisma* kept our attention and caused us to listen to everything she said.

*entice [ɪnˈtaɪs] *vt.* 诱惑，引诱（to lure; tempt）

【例】I *enticed* Mary to dinner by offering to pay for her meal.

**fascination [ˌfæsɪˈneɪʃn] *n.* 魅力，魔力，入迷（charm; grace）

【例】For him, caves have the same peculiar *fascination* which high mountains have for the climber.

*induce [ɪnˈdjuːs] *vt.* 导致，引起（to cause; produce）; 引诱

【记】in(进入) + duce(引导) → 引诱

【例】The careless worker *induced* the fire with a cigarette butt.

*infatuation [ɪnˌfætʃuˈeɪʃn] *n.* 迷恋，着迷（infatuated love）

【记】来自infatuate(*vt.* 使着迷)

【反】odium(*n.* 厌恶)

**lure [lʊr] *vt.* 以诱饵吸引; 诱惑（to entice; tempt）

【记】和allure(*vt.* 引诱)一起记

【例】Many young Japanese engineers have been *lured* to the Middle East by the promise of high wages.

pall [pɔːl] *v.* 令人发腻，失去吸引力（to become boring）

【记】发音似"破儿" → 破了的东西 → 失去吸引力

【例】The jokes are *palling* gradually.

【反】interest(*vt.* 使感兴趣); intrigue(*vt.* 引起…的兴趣)

*rivet [ˈrɪvɪt] *n.* 铆钉 *vt.* 铆，铆接; 吸引(注意力)（to attract completely）

*temptation [tempˈteɪʃn] *n.* 诱惑，诱惑物（sth tempting）

【记】来自tempt(*vt.* 诱惑)

**engross [ɪnˈɡrəʊs] *vt.* 使全神贯注于，吸引（to absorb; preoccupy）

【例】The football game *engrossed* Tom completely.

**preoccupied [priˈɑːkjupaɪd] *adj.* 全神贯注的，入神的（concentrated）

【例】He might have something on his mind and be *preoccupied* but it didn't show.

rapt [ræpt] *adj.* 专心致志的，全神贯注的（engrossed; absorbed; enchanted）; 着迷的，痴迷的

【反】distracted(*adj.* 分心的)

cynosure [ˈsɪnəʃʊr] *n.* 注意的焦点（any person or thing that is a center of attention or interest）

【记】来自Cynosure(小熊星，北极星)，引申为人们注意的目标(the cynosure of all eyes)

*spark [spɑːrk] *n.* 火花，火星

粘　附

adhere ［əd ˈhɪr］ *vi.* 黏着（to stick; hold; cling）；坚持
【例】There is a piece of lettuce *adhering* to the side of your plate.

*adherent** ［əd ˈhɪrənt］ *adj.* 依附的（adhesive; sticky）*n.* 追随者，信徒
【例】The political party's loyal *adherents* contributed a lot of money.

align ［ə ˈlaɪn］ *vt.* 将…排列在一条直线上（to get or fall into line）；使结盟（to join as an ally）
【记】a + lign（木头）→（放）在（直的）木头上 → 将…排列在一条直线上
【反】irregular（*adj.* 不规则的）；curved（*adj.* 弯曲的）；askew（*adj.* 歪斜的）
【派】aligned（*adj.* 有序的）

cohere ［koʊ ˈhɪr］ *vi.* 附着，粘合，凝聚（to connect; fit）
【记】co（共同）+ here（粘）→ 共同粘 → 粘合
【例】The sushi rice grains *cohere*.

viscid ［ˈvɪsɪd］ *adj.* 粘性的（thick; adhesive）
【反】slick（*adj.* 光滑的）

viscous ［ˈvɪskəs］ *adj.* 粘的（glutinous）
【派】nonviscous（*adj.* 无粘性的）

缠　绕

embroil ［ɪm ˈbrɔɪl］ *vt.* 牵连，使卷入纠纷（to involve in conflict or difficulties）
【记】em（进入）+ broil（争吵）→ 进入争吵 → 牵连

encompass ［ɪn ˈkʌmpəs］ *vt.* 包围，环绕（to encircle; cover）；包含
【记】en（进入）+ compass（范围，界线）→ 使进入范围 → 包围
【例】A thick fog *encompassed* the village.

intertwine ［ˌɪntər ˈtwaɪn］ *v.* 纠缠，缠，绕（to twine together）
【记】inter（在中间）+ twine（编）→ 在中间编织 → 纠缠

ravel ［ˈrævl］ *vi.* 纠缠，纠结（to become twisted and knotted）；（线等）松开，散开（to unravel）
【反】knit（*v.* 编织）

*scroll** ［skroʊl］ *n.* 卷轴，纸卷，画卷

*wreathe [riːð] *v.* 盘绕（to coil about sth）；把…做成花环（to shape into a wreath）

【记】来自wreath（*n.* 花环）

prehensile [prɪˈhensl] *adj.* 能抓物的，能缠绕东西的（capable of grasping or holding）

【记】prehens(=prehend 抓住)+ ile(能…的) → 能抓物的

频 率

**consecutive [kənˈsekjətɪv] *adj.* 连续的（successive）

【例】In his speech the president said that agricultural exports went up for twelve *consecutive* years.

**incessant [ɪnˈsesnt] *adj.* 不断的（ceaseless; continual）

【记】in(不)+ cess(停止)+ ant → 不断的

perpetual [pərˈpetʃuəl] *adj.* 连续不断的（continuing endlessly; uninterrupted）；永久的（lasting forever）

【记】per + pet(追求)+ ual → 自始至终的追求 → 永久的

【反】evanescent（*adj.* 短暂易逝的）；intermittent（*adj.* 间歇的，间断的）；ephemeral（*adj.* 短暂的）

fitful [ˈfɪtfl] *adj.* 一阵阵的，断续的

【记】fit(一阵)+ ful → 一阵阵的

【例】Please sit. Your *fitful* pacing is bothering me.

*incoherent [ˌɪnkoʊˈhɪrənt] *adj.* 不连贯的（disconnected）

【记】in(不)+ coherent(连贯的) → 不连贯的

*periodic [ˌpɪriˈɑːdɪk] *adj.* 定期的，周期的（occurring or appearing at regular intervals）

【例】*periodic* attacks of dizziness

*repetitious [ˌrepəˈtɪʃəs] *adj.* 重复的，唠唠叨叨的

【例】For decades, the diagnosis was given only to kids with severe language and social impairments and unusual, *repetitious* behaviors.

*swift [swɪft] *adj.* 快速的（quick）

【例】The *swift* current carried the raft downstream.

tempo [ˈtempoʊ] *n.* （动作、生活的）步调，速度（rate of motion or activity）

稳定性

equable ['ekwəbl] *adj.* 稳定的，平静的（not varying or fluctuating; steady）；（脾气）温和的（tranquil; serene）

【记】equ（平等，均衡）+ able → 能够均衡的 → 稳定的

【反】intemperate（*adj.* 放纵的，无节制的）

immobility [ˌɪmə'bɪləti] *n.* 不动，固定（fixation）

【例】"Social *immobility*" can put the UK at a disadvantage against global competitors.

*immutable [ɪ'mjuːtəbl] *adj.* 永恒的，不可变的（not capable of or susceptible to change）

【记】im（不）+ mutable（易变的）→ 不可变的

【例】Human beings should obey the *immutable* law of nature.

【反】variable（*adj.* 多变的）

*inactive [ɪn'æktɪv] *adj.* 不活动的，不活跃的，懒散的（not active; idle）

【例】If you weren't so *inactive* you wouldn't be so fat!

**ingrained [ɪn'greɪnd] *adj.* 根深蒂固的（firmed, fixed or established）

【记】in（进入）+ grain（木头的纹理）+ ed → 进入纹理之内 → 根深蒂固的

【反】easily to change（容易改变的）

*instability [ˌɪnstə'bɪləti] *n.* 不稳定，不稳固（lack of stability）

【例】mental *instability*

ramshackle ['ræmʃækl] *adj.* 摇摇欲坠的（rickety）

【记】ram（羊）+ shackle（= shake摇动）→ 摇摇欲坠的

随 机

adventitious [ˌædven'tɪʃəs] *adj.* 偶然的（accidental; casual）

【记】advent（到来）+ itious →（突然）到来的 → 偶然的

**backfire [ˌbæk'faɪər] *n.* （引擎的）逆火 *vi.* 放出逆火；事与愿违，出现意外事件

episodic [ˌepɪ'sɑːdɪk] *adj.* 偶然发生的，分散性的（occurring irregularly）；（戏剧、小说等）情节多的

【记】来自episode（*n.* 片断）

*fortuitously [fɔːr'tuːɪtəsli] *adv.* 偶然地，意外地（accidentally; coincidentally）

【例】He is not a good swimmer; he just won the game *fortuitously*.

*haphazard ［hæp'hæzərd］*adj.* 偶然的，随便的（casual; random; ind

【记】hap + hazard（偶然，运气）→ 偶然的

【例】I didn't mean to meet my old friend at the airport ... *haphazard* meeting.

**obsolete ［ˌɑːbsə'liːt］*adj.* 过时的，废弃的（disused; outmoded）

【记】ob（不）+ solete（使用）→ 过时的

【例】This new computer rendered my old one *obsolete*.

*serendipitous ［ˌserən'dɪpətəs］*adj.* 偶然发现的

【例】Reading should be an adventure, a personal experience full of *serendipitous* surprises.

*potential ［pə'tenʃl］*adj.* 可能的，潜在的（possible; conceivable）

【例】The inventor determined *potential* markets for the new product.

promiscuous ［prə'mɪskjuəs］*adj.* 不加选择的，不加区别的，随便的 （not carefully chosen; indiscriminate or casual）

*random ［'rændəm］*adj.* 任意的，随意的（patternless; unplanned）

裂　缝

hiatus ［haɪ'eɪtəs］*n.* 空隙，裂缝（any gap or interruption）

【记】hi（音似：嘿）+ at + us → 对我们喊"嘿" → 隔着裂缝喊嘿 → 裂缝

【例】There's a *hiatus* between the theory and the practice of the party.

indentation ［ˌɪnden'teɪʃn］*n.* 压痕，刻痕

【记】来自indent（*vt.* 压印于）

serrated ［sə'reɪtɪd］*adj.* 呈锯齿状的（having marginal teeth）

【反】without notches（无刻痕的）; smooth（*adj.* 平滑的）

**slot ［slɑːt］*n.* 狭孔（a long straight narrow opening）

suture ［'suːtʃər］*n.*（伤口的）缝线（a strand or fiber used to sew parts of the living body）*vt.* 缝合（伤口）（to unite, close, or secure with sutures）

【记】和future（*n.* 将来）一起记

【反】incision（*n.* 切开）

练习题

填空题

adhere	align	captivating	charisma	consecutive
dangle	embed	embroil	impale	impervious
induce	insert	pall	perpetual	preoccupied
protrude	rotate	sting	swift	winsome

1. The bullet _____ itself in the wall.
2. She _____ a lump of meat on her fork.
3. They _____ a tube in his mouth to help him breathe.
4. He hung his coat on a nail _____ from the wall.
5. I was _____ on the arm by a wasp.
6. The Japanese economy is supposed to be _____ to market forces.
7. His legs _____ over the side of the boat.
8. Stay well away from the helicopter when its blades start to _____.
9. We spent a week relaxing on the _____ island of Capri.
10. She gave him a _____ smile.
11. The President has great personal _____.
12. Nothing would _____ me to take the job.
13. Even the impressive scenery began to _____ on me after a few hundred miles.
14. He was too _____ with his own thoughts to notice anything wrong.
15. There was oil _____ to the bird's feathers.
16. Make sure the shelf is _____ with the top of the cupboard.
17. I was reluctant to _____ myself in his problems.
18. She was absent for nine _____ days.
19. He was elected _____ president.
20. He rose to his feet in one _____ movement.

配对题

1. penetrate	依附的	11. spark	空隙，裂缝
2. impenetrable	引人注目的	12. adherent	候鸟；移居者
3. nonporous	包围，环绕	13. viscid	迁移的，流浪的
4. migrant	使全神贯注于，吸引	14. encompass	无孔的，不渗透的
5. conspicuous	诱惑，引诱	15. scroll	刺穿，进入
6. glamorous	一阵阵的，断续的	16. incessant	定期的，周期的
7. migratory	富有魅力的	17. fitful	卷轴，纸卷
8. hiatus	不能穿透的	18. incoherent	火花，火星
9. entice	不断的	19. periodic	步调，速度
10. engross	不连贯的	20. tempo	粘性的

练习题答案

填空题答案

1. The bullet <u>embedded</u> itself in the wall.
2. She <u>impaled</u> a lump of meat on her fork.
3. They <u>inserted</u> a tube in his mouth to help him breathe.
4. He hung his coat on a nail <u>protruding</u> from the wall.
5. I was <u>stung</u> on the arm by a wasp.
6. The Japanese economy is supposed to be <u>impervious</u> to market forces.
7. His legs <u>dangled</u> over the side of the boat.
8. Stay well away from the helicopter when its blades start to <u>rotate</u>.
9. We spent a week relaxing on the <u>captivating</u> island of Capri.
10. She gave him a <u>winsome</u> smile.
11. The President has great personal <u>charisma</u>.
12. Nothing would <u>induce</u> me to take the job.
13. Even the impressive scenery began to <u>pall</u> on me after a few hundred miles.
14. He was too <u>preoccupied</u> with his own thoughts to notice anything wrong.
15. There was oil <u>adhering</u> to the bird's feathers.
16. Make sure the shelf is <u>aligned</u> with the top of the cupboard.
17. I was reluctant to <u>embroil</u> myself in his problems.
18. She was absent for nine <u>consecutive</u> days.
19. He was elected <u>perpetual</u> president.
20. He rose to his feet in one <u>swift</u> movement.

配对题答案

1. penetrate	刺穿，进入		11. spark	火花，火星
2. impenetrable	不能穿透的		12. adherent	依附的
3. nonporous	无孔的，不渗透的		13. viscid	粘性的
4. migrant	候鸟；移居者		14. encompass	包围，环绕
5. conspicuous	引人注目的		15. scroll	卷轴，纸卷
6. glamorous	富有魅力的		16. incessant	不断的
7. migratory	迁移的，流浪的		17. fitful	一阵阵的，断续的
8. hiatus	空隙，裂缝		18. incoherent	不连贯的
9. entice	诱惑，引诱		19. periodic	定期的，周期的
10. engross	使全神贯注于，吸引		20. tempo	步调，速度

读者反馈表

尊敬的读者：

　　您好！非常感谢您对**新东方大愚图书**的信赖与支持，希望您抽出宝贵的时间填写这份反馈表，以便帮助我们改进工作，今后能为您提供更优秀的图书。谢谢！

　　为了答谢您对我们的支持，我们将对反馈的信息进行随机抽奖活动，当月将有20位幸运读者可获赠《**新东方英语**》期刊一份。我们将定期在新东方大愚图书网站www. dogwood. com. cn公布获奖者名单并及时寄出奖品，敬请关注。

来信请寄：

　　　　北京市海淀区海淀东三街 2 号欧美汇大厦 19 层

　　　　北京新东方大愚文化传播有限公司

　　　　　　　图书部收

　　　　邮编：100080　　　　　　E-mail：bj62605588@163. com

姓名：＿＿＿＿＿　年龄：＿＿＿＿＿　职业：＿＿＿＿＿　教育背景：＿＿＿＿＿

邮编：＿＿＿＿＿　通讯地址：＿＿＿＿＿＿＿＿＿＿＿＿＿＿＿＿＿＿＿＿＿＿

联系电话：＿＿＿＿＿＿＿＿＿　E-mail：＿＿＿＿＿＿＿＿＿＿＿＿＿

您所购买的书籍的名称是：＿＿＿＿＿＿＿＿＿＿＿＿＿＿＿＿＿＿＿＿

1. **您是通过何种渠道得知本书的（可多选）：**

　　□书店　□新东方网站　□大愚网站　□朋友推荐　□老师推荐

　　□@新东方大愚图书(http://weibo. com/dogwood)　□其他＿＿＿＿＿＿

2. **您是从何处购买到此书的？**

　　□书店　□新东方大愚淘宝网　□其他网上书店　□其他＿＿＿＿＿＿

3. 您购买此书的原因（可多选）：
   □封面设计　□书评广告　□正文内容　□图书价格　□新东方品牌
   □新东方名师　□其他＿＿＿＿＿＿＿＿＿＿＿

4. 您对本书的封面设计满意程度：
   □很满意　□比较满意　□一般　□不满意
   改进建议＿＿＿＿＿＿＿＿＿＿＿＿＿＿＿＿＿＿＿＿＿＿＿＿＿

5. 您认为本书的内文在哪些方面还需改进？
   □结构编排　□难易程度　□内容丰富性　□内文版式　□其他＿＿＿＿＿＿＿＿＿

6. 本书最令您满意的地方：□内文　□封面　□价格　□纸张

7. 您对本书的推荐率：□没有　□1人　□1—3人　□3—5人　□5人以上

8. 您更希望我们为您提供哪些方面的英语类图书？
   □四六级类　□考研类　□IELTS 类　□TOEFL 类　□GRE、GMAT 类
   □SAT、SSAT 类　□留学申请类　□BEC、TOEIC 类　□英语读物类
   □初高中英语类　□少儿英语类　□其他＿＿＿＿＿＿＿＿＿＿＿＿＿
   您目前最希望我们为您出版的图书是：＿＿＿＿＿＿＿＿＿＿＿＿＿

9. 您在学习英语过程中最需要哪些方面的帮助？（可多选）
   □词汇　□听力　□口语　□阅读　□写作　□翻译　□语法　□其他＿＿＿＿＿＿

10. 您最喜欢的英语图书品牌：＿＿＿＿＿＿＿＿＿＿＿＿＿＿＿＿＿
    理由是(可多选)：□版式漂亮　□内容实用　□难度适宜　□价格适中
    □对考试有帮助　□其他＿＿＿＿＿＿＿＿＿＿＿＿

11. 您对新东方图书品牌的评价：＿＿＿＿＿＿＿＿＿＿＿＿＿＿＿＿＿＿＿

12. 您对本书(或其他新东方图书)的意见和建议：＿＿＿＿＿＿＿＿＿＿＿＿＿
    ＿＿＿＿＿＿＿＿＿＿＿＿＿＿＿＿＿＿＿＿＿＿＿＿＿＿＿＿＿＿＿＿＿＿
    ＿＿＿＿＿＿＿＿＿＿＿＿＿＿＿＿＿＿＿＿＿＿＿＿＿＿＿＿＿＿＿＿＿＿
    ＿＿＿＿＿＿＿＿＿＿＿＿＿＿＿＿＿＿＿＿＿＿＿＿＿＿＿＿＿＿＿＿＿＿

13. 填表时间：＿＿＿＿＿年＿＿＿＿月＿＿日